Classical
SOUTHERN
Cooking

Classical SOUTHERN Cooking

DAMON LEE FOWLER

PHOTOGRAPHS BY JOHN ROBERT CARRINGTON III

GIBBS SMITH

TO ENRICH AND INSPIRE HUMANKIND

Salt Lake City | Charleston | Santa Fe | Santa Barbara

First Revised Edition
12 11 10 09 08   5 4 3 2 1

Published by
Gibbs Smith
P.O. Box 667
Layton, Utah 84041

Orders: 1.800.835.4993
www.gibbs-smith.com

Designed by Linda Herman
Printed and bound in Hong Kong

Library of Congress Cataloging-in-Publication Data
Fowler, Damon Lee.
  Classical southern cooking / Damon Lee Fowler ; photographs by
John Robert Carrington III. — 1st ed.
      p. cm.
  ISBN-13: 978-1-4236-0225-5
  ISBN-10: 1-4236-0225-0
  1. Cookery, American—Southern style. I. Title.
  TX715.2.S68F68 2008
  641.5975—dc22
                              2008007990

Four women have shaped the way that I think about food and its preparation. My grandmother, with her sense of playfulness in the kitchen, taught me not only the basics, but to think of cooking as adventurous fun. My mother, with her love of growing things, taught me to value the rhythms of the seasons and the rich flavors of freshly harvested fruits and vegetables. Karen Hess, with her passion both for history and good cooking, taught me to trust my own culinary instincts. And Marcella Hazan, with her love of the food of her own country and sense of magic and wonder at this alchemy we call cooking, taught me both the value of my own traditions and the joy of sharing them with others.

This book is for them.

Contents

Acknowledgments

During my years as a student of architecture, one of my design professors used to say that it was hard for him not to design a building like Le Corbusier, so taken was he by that gentleman's flair. What I find difficult is not writing about food as Marcella Hazan does. So lyrical, succinct, and captivating is her writing that every paragraph is a primer of what a cookbook ought to be. For years, those books have been constant companions and guides in my kitchen and, through them, she taught me to cook. Marcella Hazan's writing has not only instructed but also instilled in me a sense of the importance of my own culinary heritage and encouraged me to pursue it to its source. She and her husband Victor took me under their wings and pointed me in the right direction. They protest that they have done nothing, but without their example, guidance, and encouragement, I am not convinced that this book would ever have been finished.

With a book of this sort, where, in a real sense, nothing is "original" and everything has been resurrected from a sometimes very murky past, so many people make marked contributions that one almost needs a chapter for acknowledgments. I have credited sources for specific recipes in the text and bibliography, and to reiterate them here would double the size of this book.

But I would be remiss if I did not express my gratitude to my friend and teacher Karen Hess, whose work as a food historian is unparalleled in this country and, I suspect, everywhere else. Very early on, she became not only a trusted friend but my coach, teacher, mentor, and cheering section all in one. She kicked me in the seat of my pants when I got off track and buoyed me up with her irrepressible enthusiasm for history and good food when my own enthusiasm was lagging. And she never let our affection for one another stand in the way of a good lecture when I needed it. One of the great joys of my life has been those frequent phone calls, which Karen, roaring with laughter, would begin by telling me, "I am about to save you from an embarrassing mistake!" Her name appears in the dedication, but it really belongs on the title page.

John Martin Taylor, owner of Hoppin' John's bookstore and author of *Hoppin' John's Lowcountry Cooking*, and other fine books, was the first to take my research seriously and ensured that I would also take it seriously by introducing me to Mrs. Hess. I wrote John asking about facsimile reprints of certain sources, expecting to get a price list of those available. A few days later, a package arrived containing the books and an invoice. That kind of trust is rare nowadays, but that's the sort of person John is. He opened his personal library to my use, gave me access to rare Lowcountry books that I would otherwise not have seen, but most of all, gave me a friendship that I shall always treasure.

Every Southern cook, whether conscious of it or not, owes a debt of gratitude to the late Bill Neal, whose brief life was spent in championship of the cooking that was so near his heart. He leaves us, through his writing, a rich legacy.

Another important figure is Nathalie Dupree, who, with seemingly limitless energy, has brought the cooking of the South to a national audience and elevated its reputation above and beyond those myths of corn whiskey, granulated sugar, and vegetables swimming in hog fat. Though she came into my project late, she was always willing to drop whatever she was doing to offer her own insights and advice and has been ever generous.

Fellow Southern writers John Egerton, Ruth Bronz (who kept hollering her support from up North), June Baldree, Marie Rudisill, Martha Giddens Nesbit, and Margaret DeBolt have both directly and indirectly been helpful and generous in their support. Margaret in particular shared her own library—and rescued me more than once.

Stephen Bolin-Davis generously allowed me to use the Juliette Gordon Low collection and loaned me several books from his personal library. Porter Carswell, Jim Cox, Judy Mitchell, Laura Belle Macrae, Ann Otteson, Dean Owens, and Martha Pink all loaned me fragile family manuscripts and books. Dr. Willie Greer Todd helped me find Mrs. Hill's Georgia roots.

Many contributions had nothing to do with recipes per se. I am lucky to have the most generous parents in the country. They don't mince words telling me what they think, but then go right ahead and support whatever it is I'm doing anyway.

Without many patient friends this book might never have happened. Maryan Wilborn Harrell diligently sought out many old out-of-print books that were crucial to my research. She became not only a reliable source for information, but a trusted friend and ally through all sorts of adversity, and offers solace for the weary in the form of the best chocolate pound cake known to God or man. Maryan's mother, Mary Lizzie Kitchengs, has given freely of her many years experience in the kitchen, her advice about life in general, her sparkling sense of humor, and her lifesaving beach house at Alligator Point. Dean Owens, who has always been generous with his cooking, friendship, and sympathetic ear, helped to keep me sane and focused. Jim King, my best friend, ate and critiqued most of the test runs of the recipes—and mostly without complaining. He helped me remain objective. Jim's mother, Lillie King, was a vital link to Alabama. Two of my Yankee friends—Marion Pacquin, who gave freely of her experience as a cook and proofreader, and Peter Paar, my computer guru—saved my manuscript from literal disaster more than once. Peter would also trot down and get out his *OED* no matter what hour I called. Anita Raskin, a rare-book dealer, tracked down several treasures for me. Richard Galloway gave this poor Victorian free access to twentieth-century office equipment whenever I needed it. My friend and pastor, the Reverend William H. Ralston, has been a constant source of spiritual support and didn't tell me I had lost my mind when I quit my job to pursue food writing, even thought he thought so.

Friends Peter and Janie Brodhead, the proprietors of our local natural-food store, Brighter Day (Savannah's hippie grocers), have been a reliable source both of information and ingredients. And speaking of ingredients, the sure aim and generous nature of my friend Marcia Johnson's father, Mr. Ludean Falagan of Guyton, Georgia, and Todd Moss of Clover, South Carolina, kept me supplied with wonderful venison (and yes, those are real places).

My graduate professor, Dr. Cecilia Voelker, taught me to do scholarly research and kept my enthusiasm propped up with her own boundless energy. Cecilia protested that she had been of no value to me because she is a terrible cook. True. But I still have the scars on my shins from where she used to kick me and shout, "Where did you hear that? *Document* it!"

And yes, I really was an architect while I researched and developed the first draft of this book. I have moved on to other things, but that my boss, Paul Hansen, and my clients, especially Susan and Rick Sontag, put up with me at all is something I still find amazing.

Finally, many thanks to my agent, Elise Goodman, for believing in this book and finding it the right editor—Erica Marcus, who never let me lose sight of what we were trying to accomplish and, most important of all, never lost her sense of humor while dealing with the neurotic Southern boy. She made me laugh when I didn't feel like it, and made what might have been agony a lot of fun. Erica, enjoy them pork brains, honey.

Acknowledgments, Second Edition

So many dear friends have departed since this book was first published: my grandmother, Karen Hess, Marie Rudisill, Mary Lizzie Kitchengs, Edna Lewis, Mr. Falagan, Father Ralston, Anita Raskin, Dean Owens—all deeply missed.

To the long list of debts from the first edition of this book, I add Dale Reed, who tracked down Mrs. Bryan's history; Rick McDaniel, who led me to an earlier edition of *Housekeeping In Old Virginia* (1877) and earlier literary references to iced tea; the staff of the Jefferson Foundation, especially Beth Cheuk, Elizabeth Chew, Justin Sarafin, Leni Sorenson, Mary Scott-Fleming, and Gaye Wilson, who, with Mrs. Hess, helped me better understand the extraordinary food culture at Monticello and its deep connections to Mary Randolph; my colleagues at The Southern Foodways Alliance, particularly Toni Tipton-Martin, Jessica Harris, Ronni Lundy, Nathalie Dupree, John Egerton, Marcie Ferris, Elizabeth Sims, and the indomitable John T. Edge helped me keep going and believing that Southern cooking is a cuisine—and one worth saving; and Jill Conner Browne, who just made me laugh and remember to be grateful.

Preface

It was an improbable beginning for a cookbook. In the first place, I had been trained in (and spent the better part of two decades practicing) a profession completely removed from cooking. In the second place, the cooking that I had proposed to write about was out of fashion—so out of fashion that many did not believe it even existed. Most improbable of all, the idea for it was planted while I was living in a country whose cuisine had little to do with the cooking in question. Perhaps the only thing that seems probable to anyone who knows me is that the whole thing started because I was angry.

Nearly twenty years ago, the study of architecture took me away from my native American South (for the first time in my life) to Italy. There, it seems in retrospect, I was destined to learn about everything but architecture. From the first day, it was Italian cooking—and not buildings—that captivated me, awakening my consciousness not only to the patterns of a foreign kitchen, but to a completely different way of thinking about food. Steeped in thousands of years of tradition, the Italians were actually aware of, and secure in, their culinary heritage. It was something that this American had never seen before. With architecture all but forgotten, I immersed myself in Italian food, absorbing as much as possible without actually flunking out of school. While my friends were marveling over Michelangelo, I was happily tramping around the market, marveling over bread, vegetables, cheese, and Parma hams. While they were busily learning about design, I was in the kitchen with our cook, Ilda, learning about pasta. Needless to say, our professor was very annoyed.

After only a few months, I had to come home, but brought my new mistress with me; I discovered the writings of Marcella Hazan, whose cookbooks became my culinary bible. During my architectural apprenticeship, I lived in various places—North Carolina, south Florida, and, finally, Savannah—but my kitchen was, for all intents and purposes, an Italian one. In those days, Americans were just beginning to rediscover Italian cooking, as well as all sorts of cuisines from every corner of the globe. No country was too remote, no ingredient too costly and foreign. Though some of these cuisines were part of the culture of many Americans, many had little or nothing to do with us. At first, I found it exciting, and for a time even taught Italian cooking at a local cooking school.

But gradually all the clamor for the new, the exotic, began to disturb me. What about our own heritage? What about the security in one's own traditions that had made Italian cooking so distinctive and memorable? What about the quiet mastery of technique that made my grandmother's fried chicken consistent perfection? For a couple of years, discontent smoldered inside me, until one night, at a quiet little dinner party, I snapped.

Someone said something about Southern "cuisine." There was the predictable response: great guffaws. What Southern cuisine (ho, ho)—fried chicken? More guffaws. I exploded, pouring righteous indignation (and, if memory serves, a glass of wine) out onto the table. "Hell, yes, fried chicken! Every great cuisine in the world has it. What's the matter with it? And what's the matter with *us*? Why are we so fascinated with other cuisines and so insecure about our own? What's wrong with our own culinary heritage?"

Well, my friends found this little exhibition amusing if not downright ridiculous. When, in the ensuing months, I began tentatively to talk of writing a book on our culinary heritage, their amusement reached a new level of hilarity. After all, as they pointed out, this is the South, the land of grits, overcooked greens, and hog grease—what kind of heritage is that? And what did an architect-turned-food-writer hope to teach anyone about such things? In truth, I did not, at the time, know. The prospects for this book were not exactly heartening. But at the same time that my friends were having a field day at my expense, saying that Southern food was nothing worth remembering, there were others who painted a different, contradictory picture. Such writers as Nathalie Dupree, John Egerton, Camille Glenn, Bill Neal, and John Martin Taylor wrote with great charm of a culinary heritage that they seemed to believe was both valid and important, a heritage of which Southerners ought to be proud. I had no idea, at the time, what it was that had made Southerners so schizophrenic about our cooking, but I intended to find out, to uncover not only what had made the legends, but what had caused the legends to fall into disrepute. And, if possible, to do something about restoring their good name.

With hardly any idea where I was going, or what I was looking for, I started digging and asking questions. Old cookbooks began to turn up. Old friends, who grew up with Victorian parents, began to talk. Luckily, I made invaluable friends in my fellow historians John Taylor and Karen Hess. And, somewhere along the way, the old notions began to fall away, displaced by the reality of a cuisine that can only be described as magic, a cuisine of great subtlety and balance, redolent with herbs and spices, a cuisine so startlingly beautiful that it upset all preconceptions, including my own. But best of all, it was completely, and uniquely, ours.

This book tells its story.

—Damon Lee Fowler

INTRODUCTION

Understanding Southern Cooking

This is a story, told by way of recipes and a few ramblings, about a particular period in the history of a remarkable and uniquely American cuisine: the cooking of the South during the first half of the nineteenth century. I call it *Classical Southern Cooking* because this period was a kind of golden age for Southern cooking in much the same way that the fifth century BC (the original "classical" age) represented a pinnacle of artistic achievement in ancient Greece—and not because it has anything to do with music.

Most people talk of Southern cooking as if it's something that has neat, distinct boundaries, as if its story is obvious and easy to tell. I wish it were. You see, the trouble with talking about "Southern cooking" as such, is that there really isn't any single such thing, and those words can mean a million completely different things to as many people. To begin with, the South as a region is bigger than Europe (the state of Georgia is, by itself, almost half the size of France), and within its loose boundaries is a blending of as many different cultures as Europe has countries. What I grew up knowing as Southern cooking in the Carolina hills would be unrecognizable to a Louisiana-bayou Cajun, let alone to a Virginia-Tidewater aristocrat. There are similarities, but between the three there are endless differences in climate, terrain, and produce—not to mention attitude.

Complicating these regional differences is the mix of so many divergent peoples and cultures. Our mingling has not always been smooth or easy, and the South is far from being homogeneous. Take, for example, Charleston and Savannah—two old, important coastal cities with similar climates and economies. The distance between them is a matter of only a few miles—roughly the same as that between Genoa and Florence, Italy. Yet, like those two ancient Italian cities, they are so distinct from one another that they might as well be in different countries. Though each is frequently described as having Old World charm, Savannah, with its distinctly English plan, architecture, and sensibilities, has little of Charleston's West Indian flair. And while both cities lean heavily on rice and seafood as dietary staples, the way they treat these staples is very different. Charleston's cuisine is a subtle, elegant mix of English, French, West Indian, and West African cookery. The cooking of Savannah, on the other hand, despite a strong undercurrent of West African and French cooking, has strayed less from its essentially English roots, and has very little West Indian influence.

That isn't to say that there aren't many similarities—cultural undercurrents that are common to all. In fact, a closer look reveals many themes that are practically universal to all Southern cooking. That's because the complicated soup boils down to a union of two predominant elements: English cooking and African cooks. It was during the first half of the nineteenth century that the union of these two elements matured, and the cuisine loosely known as Southern cooking emerged. But in order to understand that union, and the resulting cuisine, we need to look further back, to the early days of the colonies.

Beginnings: Elements and Influences

First of all, it is useful to understand that English culture is the foundation upon which most of American culture is built. Though neither the first nor the only Europeans to make permanent settlements in North America, the English nevertheless came to dominate the continent north of Mexico (including what is now the American Southwest) and contributed the most lasting influence. Consequently, English culinary practice became the foundation for most of America's cooking—at least, east of the Great Plains.

Contrary to popular belief, it was a fine foundation on which to build. The seventeenth and early eighteenth centuries (the period of heaviest colonization) had been something of a golden age for English cooking. Such cookbooks as *The English Hus-wife* (1615), Hannah Glasse's *The Art of Cookery, Made Plain and Easy* (1747), or E(liza?) Smith's *The Compleat Housewife* (1727) record a cuisine that was lively, intelligent, gorgeously subtle, and rich with herbs, onions, garlic, and spices. Several of the dishes included in this book—trout steaks poached in a fragrant bath of wine, rosemary, and ginger; a classic fricassee, its sumptuous egg-thickened sauce piquant with lemon and herbs; a moist pound cake–based fruitcake, rich with plump fruit, spices, and almonds; subtle and elegant butter sauces—are lingering reminders of the richness and finesse of the cuisine. These English books were widely used in the early colonial period—at least, by the upper classes; *The Compleat Housewife* was particularly popular. Eventually reprinted in Williamsburg in 1742, it is thought to be the first cookbook printed in America. (Though some of these books were published in the first part of the eighteenth century, I should note here that they chronicle earlier practice. In fact, until recently, most recorded cooking practice followed its common use by at least a generation.)

Naturally, there were settlers besides the English—Scots, Irish, Germans, and Dutch—each group contributing its own culinary slant. Some established Americans, the Dutch in New York, and the Germans in Pennsylvania, for example, migrated to the South as the inland frontiers began to open up. Late in the seventeenth century and later, at the end of the eighteenth, the French Huguenots, first fleeing religious persecution in France and later, the slave revolts on West Indian sugar plantations, settled in the rice-growing regions of Carolina and Georgia.

There was also a smattering of French influence further north and west, in part because of early French colonization, and later, thanks to the acquisition of the Louisiana Territory. The Spanish, who had been in North America long before the English, held much of the Caribbean basin and South America throughout the eighteenth and early nineteenth centuries. Their close proximity to the South naturally led to some cross-cultural influence.

Rarer, though not insignificant, were the small groups of Asians who immigrated to the South during the nineteenth century. Along the coast, there were Jews, Greeks, and even a few Italians. All these peoples brought their own culinary traditions to the New World and had a limited influence on the cooking of the colonies and early Republic. In the main, however, their cooking tended to become Anglicized rather than the other way around. For example, in the first year of the colony, a large group of mostly Portuguese Sephardic Jews settled in Savannah. They have been a continuous and important presence, yet almost none of their early culinary traditions have survived. So as rich as these cultures may have been, they had no significant impact on the development and transformation of Southern food.

But there was one group of people who did, whose presence in the kitchen and whose flair for ingredients and skilled hands were to set Southern cooking apart. They were the Africans. Ironically, their arrival was barely noticed. In 1619, a Dutch ship landed at Jamestown and offered the colonists a handful of dark-skinned slaves that they simply called Negroes—a term derived from the romance language words *niger* or *negro*, meaning "black." It was a name they would carry for more than three centuries.

Since the South's economy was an agrarian one, based mainly on labor-intensive cash crops such as tobacco, rice, and, later, cotton, cheap labor was a necessity in those pre-machine days. The slave trade remained legal and flourished until the early part of the nineteenth century. Africans became so firmly entrenched in the South that, in some areas, they outnumbered whites by as much as ten to one. There is no way to explain away the ugly reality of slavery; its repercussions still echo through the entire nation more than a century after its ending. Yet, sometimes, from the ugliness of a great injustice, there can arise great beauty. Such can neither rectify the injustices nor justify the damage inflicted, but neither is its loveliness diminished.

So it is with Southern cooking.

For more than two hundred years, Africans were made to cook for all but the poorest white Southern households, whether they wanted to or not. Even in households where the white mistress was an accomplished cook in her own right, slaves still did the bulk of the work. And it was their hands that wrought the magic that made Southern cooking legendary, that put okra in the pot with the tomatoes, that continued to slip garlic into the kettle long after it was out of fashion in other parts of the country, that had the feel for the unique combinations of spices and herbs that gave the cooking its heady perfume.

Their contribution has unfortunately been little documented. As a black friend pointed out to me, African-American history and storytelling are verbal arts, and no one who might have provided a written record thought of it as important until it was almost too late. The plethora of "mammy" and "auntie" cookbooks from the early 1900s records a cooking that was rapidly deteriorating and already badly bowdlerized by the growing packaged-food industry. Nonetheless, the sure hand of African cooks can still be discerned. Most early cooking of other Anglo-American regions such as New England changed little from its English roots, whereas the South quickly went in its own direction. A good example of this is the difference between the Acadians of Maine and those of Louisiana: though both came from essentially the same group of immigrants, their cuisines are worlds apart. Even with climate, soil, produce, and economics taken into consideration, the only really significant difference lay in who was actually cooking. Who but an African cook would have had the experience to know that okra combined with tomatoes (a foundation of so many Southern dishes) was a natural? Who but an African could have introduced such distinctly African dishes as calas, gumbo, and bean pilau (the enigmatic Hoppin' John of the Lowcountry), or could have known how to use certain African ingredients like benne (sesame) seeds and okra? Such things are common in the South, but virtually unknown in other regions, except, significantly, in pockets where former slaves resettled. Only in the South do we find an enduring love for stewed leafy greens—a staple in so many African cuisines. And while such things as peanuts, eggplant, tomatoes, and sweet potatoes are not African in origin, it is clearly through Africa that these ingredients came into the South, and equally clear that Africans are the most likely reason that such things became common in the Southern diet long before they gained acceptance elsewhere in America. Even those Acadians (we know them as Cajun today), while mostly poor, were influenced by the cooking of the Africans they rubbed elbows with in the bayous of Louisiana.

The problem of documenting this influence is complicated by the fact that Africa didn't exist in a vacuum before slave trade with the west began. For millennia, this vast continent's many foodways had exerted a distinct influence on the entire Mediterranean basin, from Spain across Southern Europe to the Middle East. Who is to say whether the African touches that affect the Provençal-rooted cookery of the Lowcountry French Huguenots came directly from West Africa to the colonies, or was filtered through the cuisines of the West Indies or directly from Provence itself, whose cuisine had already been touched by Africa through the spread of the Turkish Empire or even Ancient Rome?

One significant and telling clue that points to the African influence is an aspect that is little influenced by it—the craft of baking. Southern baking strayed least from its Anglo roots; it was also the one over which African cooks had the least control. Baking remained a primary responsibility of the white mistress, often to the point that she actually did it herself; so while other aspects of the cookery changed—often radically—baking, especially sweets, remained solidly English, varying little from that of other regions of the country. The sweets and breads of such books as *The Improved Housewife*, by Mrs. A. L. Webster and the household notebook of Mrs. Abigail Townsend (both New England housewives) differ only in detail from contemporary Southern and English publications and household notebooks. On the other hand, all other aspects of the cuisine—soups, stews, pilaus, vegetables, and countless other savory dishes—brought into a new dimension with the use of cayenne, okra, sesame, peanuts, herbs, rice, and tomatoes—were transformed into something wholly new.

While we are on the subject of ingredients, there is one other factor in the history of this cooking that we have to consider. When the Europeans arrived, there were, of course, people already living in America. Up to this point, I've had little to say about their influence on Southern cooking. This is not without reason: their contribution is, unfortunately, one of the least documented and most difficult to assess. As was true of the Africans, Native Americans had no tradition of written history and have left behind them only a fragmented and incomplete record of how they lived in Pre-Colombian times. Today, it has become popular to credit native cooks with almost every Southern dish you can think of, but in truth, many such claims are difficult, if not impossible, to support. I once sat through a lecture given by a well-intentioned young man in which he credited Native Americans with the invention of everything from Virginia hams to French-fried potatoes and barbecue—all charming and politically correct, but unfortunately, untrue and riddled with misinformation and unsupported myth.

As for those hams, Indians didn't have swine or any kind of animal even approaching them (the lecturer did, at least, concede this much). It is true that they did use smoking as a means of preserving fish and small strips of meat, but as best we can tell, they didn't use salt in the process. On the other hand, Europeans had been dry salt curing and smoking pork hams at least since the Middle Ages. As for fried potatoes, well, white potatoes are native to South—and not North—America. Even if potatoes had been transplanted to North America before the Europeans got here (a subject of lively debate among botanists and historians), there is no solid evidence—such as the remains of a pot that could have withstood the intense heat of boiling fat—that North Americans fried potatoes or anything else. Yet those legends about bear grease persist. At any rate, they certainly didn't teach the Europeans about frying: ancient cooks from all around the Mediterranean basin were frying when Jesus was in diapers. As for that fabled barbecue, while we do know that natives used this cooking method, and the American name for it is believed to derive from a native word (Haitian-Taino *barbacoa*), it's pretty well a universal technique, perhaps the oldest form of cooking known in any civilization.

The truth is that, by the time Native cookery was recorded, it had already been heavily adulterated by the Europeans. The Pilgrims, on landing at Plymouth as early as 1620, were met by Native Americans who not only spoke English and French, but were cooking in European-made iron pots. No, we must accept that native North Americans contributed little in the way of actual cookery to the colonists. But that isn't to say that they didn't make significant and lasting contributions to Southern foods; they did. Most of these contributions, however, were in the form of raw materials.

The most significant was a native grain called maize. This hybrid grass had been a staple of the North American diet (except in the Caribbean Islands and a few other places) for centuries, if not millennia. The English dubbed it "Indian corn"—"corn" being the old English word for "grain"—later shortened to the generic "corn" by which it is generally known today. Maize was introduced to the Europeans early on, and was sometimes the only thing that kept the colonists from starving, so it quickly became a staple for Euro-Americans. Without it, much of what we recognize today as Southern cooking would be very different. A few of the myriad ways of using maize show a lingering native influence: hominy; a crude hearth or ash bread called "pone;" the roasting of whole, fresh ears in ashes; the mélange of corn and beans called succotash. Both "pone" and "succotash" in fact derive from Indian words. But, in the main, the Europeans adapted corn to the cooking they already knew—mush, fritters, yeasted bread, boiled and baked puddings, and chowders. Some people are misled by the fact that early recipes were sometimes named "Indian," but such was only a shortening of "Indian corn" or "Indian meal." Indian pound cake and Indian pudding are really old European dishes made with cornmeal or whole grain as opposed to European grains like wheat and rye.

Other important native contributions were squash, beans, and sweet potatoes. Though several edible gourds (which squash are) were already known in Europe (there are even Biblical references to them), as was the lone fava—or Windsor—bean, the squash and beans that are used today in Southern cooking are all descended from native plants, most of which were introduced to the settlers by the Indians. A few simple dishes, such as succotash, do have native roots, but most often the vegetables were adapted to European recipes. Even succotash was overhauled with such foreign additions as butter, cream, wheat flour, and sometimes tomatoes (which were not known north of Mexico until after European colonization). Sweet potatoes, another native vegetable, had been introduced to Europe by the Spanish in the sixteenth century (in England, for a time, they were even called Spanish potatoes). As early as Elizabethan days, they were well enough known in England for Shakespeare to make jokes in his plays about their reported qualities as an aphrodisiac. By the time the English colonists made permanent settlements in North America, sweet potatoes had already been adopted into their cuisine.

For the most part, then, European cooks adapted the new produce to old ways of cooking, and their kitchens were actually little affected by Indian cooking practice.

At the risk of over-generalizing, we can summarize Southern cooking by saying that it was founded on English (or Northern European) cooking, enriched and nourished by new, native (and African) ingredients, and transformed in the hands of African cooks. These elements were brought together during the colonial days and, fed by the rich, abundant produce of an agricultural economy, gradually solidified into the remarkable collection of cuisines that we now know today as Southern cooking.

In the first half of the nineteenth century, this cooking blossomed and entered its golden age, and Southern tables—at least, those of the upper classes, and even of some modest households—knew the likes of true spit-roasted (and rare) meat; delicate egg-thickened fricassees and rich, savory ragouts; crusty, satisfying loaves of yeast bread made from both wheat and corn; myriad vegetables, served simply as only very fresh and carefully cooked vegetables can be; real ice creams, moist, rich fruitcakes and delicate custards. Such cooking flourished as long as the agrarian economy and resulting society that nurtured it flourished, and as long as there were African cooks blending their own foodways with those that had been forced on them.

The Beginning of the End

But if this cooking was so wonderful, so highly developed, so delicious, then what happened to it? Where did it go—moreover, *why* did it go? How did it come to have the dubious reputation of recent times? This was what I wanted to know. Well, as I soon learned, there are no simple answers.

Several things happened, the most obvious of which was also the most critical: the War Between the States (or *The* War, as we call it down here). It not only wrecked the South's economy, it brought the fight over slavery to a head. With the passing of The Emancipation Proclamation, the legacy of the old black cooks began to fade. Though they stayed for a time in many kitchens, contemporary accounts of Reconstruction tell us that such cooks were always in short supply to the few who could still afford them, and beyond the means of most. The tables of both white and black Southerners would never again be the same, for white households lost the skill of the black cook, and black ones lost both the influence of European traditions and the access to many ingredients. Most critical of all, the old apprenticeship system, in which young slaves were trained by seasoned older cooks, vanished, never to return. When, at length, black cooks came back to white households as paid servants, the continuity was permanently broken. Both household and cook were a generation or so removed from the old cuisine.

The war changed Southern kitchens in ways other than who was doing the cooking. The South's male population was literally decimated, and many who survived were horribly maimed, either by enemy guns or by the crude medicine of army field hospitals. An entire generation of women was faced with carrying an additional burden of work that they had never done before. Probably they had little energy left over for any but the most necessary cooking.

Those bleak, lean years were also responsible for that notoriously ubiquitous salt pork and bacon grease. A little of this seasoning had long been common, though hardly universal, in Southern cookery. But with meat still scarce and poverty almost rampant, it became usual to supplement the meager diet of field peas, greens, sweet potatoes, and grits with cheap salt pork fat.

Another key factor in the demise of not only Southern but all American cooking was the revolution in kitchen technology. Until the second quarter of the nineteenth century, cooking practices had not changed significantly in hundreds of years. American kitchens differed little from the European ones on which they had been modeled. Then, mass-produced, relatively inexpensive iron ranges began to replace open hearths. Commercial canning came into prominence as a means of preservation and brought with it the beginnings of the modern packaged food industry. (Significantly, it was in part the need to safely provide field rations during the War Between the States that accelerated canning technology.) By the beginning of the twentieth century such new methods had eclipsed open-hearth cooking and the old preserving methods such as drying and smoking—especially in urban areas. Canned vegetables and milk products, commercially cured and packaged meats, bottled sauces, and other manufactured foods found their way into Southern kitchens, often changing the cooking beyond recognition. The food industry became "scientific," introducing chemically-engineered foods such as vegetable shortening. As commercial meatpackers took over the task of preserving meat, the old, lengthy curing processes were truncated and overhauled with shortcuts that boosted profits but adversely affected the quality of our hams, sausages, and bacon.

As printing became less expensive, there was an explosion in the cookbook market. A few authors attempted to preserve some of the quality and character of traditional cooking; others were wholly given over to the new technology. Manufacturers of packaged and engineered food products introduced books of recipes structured around their products, most of which were, unfortunately, as awful as they were popular.

The final blow came when Southern white women, of necessity, began to enter the workforce. Beginning with the hard years of Reconstruction, genteel white women baked, sewed, sold preserves, and taught school; poor ones went to work in the new factories as did some of the black women who had previously been domestics, forced by economic necessity into better paying factory jobs. The stream of homemakers leaving home for the workforce was at first a slow trickle, but the two world wars of the twentieth century turned it into a flood. By the end of World War II, the average Southern household was a two-income enterprise. Even farm wives had been forced to find jobs away from the farm. It is widely supposed that this was because of the women's liberation movement, but in the South, at least, it was really born of necessity. The consequence was that leisurely, labor-intensive cooking was banished to Sunday dinner and holidays. Even then, much of it was adulterated by shortcuts and convenience foods.

By mid-century, much of the old classical cooking had faded from the memories of almost all living Southerners, replaced by the bland, heavy, greasy institutional food that has given our cuisine such a bad reputation.

Well, its reputation needn't—and shouldn't—remain bad. As many Southerners know, not all our cookery sank to such dismal depths. Ours is a rich, elegant, and delicious heritage, and much of it has, fortunately, survived. In the recipes that follow, I have tried to supplement what does survive, to recapture some of the stirring grace and beauty, and restore to Southern cooking some of the reputation that it once justifiably possessed. It is a cuisine that transcends the harsh realities of our past, a cuisine of which all Southerners, but particularly (and especially) those of African descent, can be proud.

The Record

The question I am most frequently asked about this cooking is where I managed to find out about it. Fortunately, there are many written records and sources, from printed books to hundreds of handwritten manuscripts. The largest surviving record lies in the cookbooks of four remarkable women: *The Virginia House-wife* (1824), by Mary Randolph; *The Kentucky Housewife* (1839), by Lettice Bryan; *The Carolina Housewife* (1847), by Sarah Rutledge; and *Mrs. Hill's New Cook Book* (1867) by Annabella Hill. There are other American and English books that were widely used in Southern kitchens, but without these four women, our knowledge of the cuisine would be slim indeed.

The first and most interesting thing to note about these ladies is that they are from roughly succeeding generations. Mary Randolph, already an old woman when she published her book, was a product of the early days of the Republic—that is, the 1790s—when the South was just coming into its own; Annabella Hill lived through the South's last glory days and began her book as that world crumbled before her eyes.

But not only were these authors of different generations, they were also, significantly, of distinctly different regions and classes—from old aristocratic Virginia and Carolina, to frontier Kentucky and rough-and-ready western Georgia. Mary Randolph (1762–1828) and Sarah Rutledge (1782–1855) were from old and very aristocratic families whose bloodlines were, as historian Karen Hess put it, endlessly convoluted. Mrs. Randolph was Thomas Jefferson's cousin, and her brother was married to Jefferson's daughter, Martha. Mrs. Randolph was herself married to David Randolph, her first cousin. In short, a typical Southern family. Miss Rutledge's father signed the Declaration of Independence, and her blue-blooded Charleston family was a similarly tangled web of interconnected cousins. Lettice Bryan, born in 1805 to a family with large land holdings in eastern Kentucky, was married into the small but significant professional class (her husband, Edmund, was a physician). Her cookbook shows her to have been an educated, well-read woman, probably with a somewhat privileged upbringing, but with a more intimate knowledge of cookery than Miss Rutledge. Though removed from them by two generations, her family had roots in Virginia's Shenandoah Valley. It's significant to note that, unlike the other "Housewife" authors, she wrote her book while she and her family were fairly young. Annabella Hill (1810–1878), born and raised in rural central Georgia, was no aristocrat, but her family was well-to-do and had genteel Virginia roots. Like Mrs. Bryan, she, too, was married into the professional class (Edward Y. Hill was an attorney and, later, a superior court judge). Her world, while privileged by wealth and those genteel connections to Virginia, was that of rural, west-central Georgia, very different from the circles that Mrs. Randolph and Miss Rutledge knew.

In other words, these four women were of different generations, backgrounds, regions, and sensibilities, and each of their books bears the indelible imprint of these differences. Sarah Rutledge, for example, lived in the center of the rice-growing Lowcountry, and *The Carolina Housewife* includes dozens of recipes for rice breads, cakes, pilaus, and the like, while Mary Randolph, who lived where rice cultivation was little more than experimental and never widespread, gives rice little attention. Lettice Bryan's cookery shows subtle but distinct and suggestive traces of German influence, probably gleaned from German settlers migrating south through the Shenandoah Valley. Mrs. Hill's kitchen is typical of the blending found in north Georgia, but, in the main, is forthrightly, unapologetically rural. Yet for all their differences, these ladies record a cuisine with astonishing parallels and similarities. They were a considerable influence throughout the South—indeed, throughout the country. Their recipes appear verbatim in later cookbooks from New England to Texas. However, as significant as their influence might have been, their real importance lies in what they have to tell us about Southern cooking as they understood it.

Eventually, the cooking they recorded, centered around the ancient art of the open hearth, came to be thought of as old-fashioned. As they began to fade from active use, their influence also faded, yet their cooking remains lively, vital, and curiously timeless. Their books are the foundation upon which my research, and the cooking contained in this book, are based. For the better part of two decades, these women have been constant companions in my kitchen—coaching, upbraiding, at times spiritedly arguing with one another—and have turned it into a wonderful place that will never be the same again.

Well, in the end, the only way that you will be able to understand their cooking is to take these ladies' recipes into your own kitchen and let them show you what they know. Their history, interesting as it may well be, will not tell you the things that can only be understood by firsthand experience: the heady perfume of sage, nutmeg, and lemon peel simmering together in a ragout, the crunch of a crusty wedge of crackling bread, the moist richness of a homemade fruitcake, the silken texture of a properly executed butter sauce, the spring of a well-kneaded lump of dough. The best that a recipe can do is merely suggest those things. Yet, the recipes left by those four women are powerfully evocative of their particular magic for me. I can only hope that the recipes that follow succeed, in some small way, in passing that magic along to you.

Anyway, I've given it my best shot.

The Classical
Southern Kitchen

OF KITCHENS ANCIENT AND MODERN

ONE OF THE MOST ELUSIVE THINGS in understanding the cooking of a culture other than one's own is the kitchen in which that cooking is accomplished. Equipment, method, pantry stores, and routine flavorings vary from culture to culture; the very rhythms that mark the cook's patterns may be vastly different. When the kitchen is separated from us, not only by culture, but also by time, how much more elusive that understanding becomes!

This is particularly true of nineteenth-century Southern cookery, mainly because that century is split down the center by two revolutions, one social, the other technological. The War Between the States brought on a collapse of the social and economic structure of the South and, in ending slavery, precipitated a gradual exodus, at least for a time, of African women from white kitchens. Their leaving was to have serious implications for the quality of cooking in both white and black households. At roughly the same time, technological innovations were precipitating the most drastic change in cookery practice in a thousand years. In short, the difference between the cooking of the ante- and post-bellum South was marked both by who was cooking and how they cooked.

Until the mid-nineteenth century, the kitchens of the Southerners of European roots varied little in form, function, and basic equipment from the ones that they had known in Europe. Cooking continued to be centered on an open hearth, cast-iron Dutch oven, and (at least in well-to-do households) brick oven. But as the industrial revolution gathered momentum, the second half of the century saw a similar revolution in kitchen technology that changed the face of Southern—indeed, of American—cookery forever.

At the center of that revolution was the development of the mass-produced, cast-iron range. Cookstoves of a sort had been known before the nineteenth century, but only to the wealthiest households. As cast-iron technology evolved, factory-made iron ranges became a luxury that many could afford, and gradually they began to replace the open hearth in middle- and upper-class households. As the hearth gave way, certain ancient forms of cooking that had not changed for millennia were either lost or hopelessly confused with other methods. In order to understand much of antebellum Southern cooking (and post-bellum cooking of poorer households), it is therefore helpful to know a little of the structure of open-hearth cooking methods.

An open hearth is by no means crude, and allows far more control than we nowadays suppose, even on rudely equipped hearths of farmhouse and slave cabin. It also added subtle nuances to flavor and texture that cannot be accomplished with a cookstove. To be sure, it was backbreaking, dangerous work, and required of the cook a high level of skill and finesse, but there were tools that made the job somewhat easier. In wealthier households, the hearth boasted an impressive array of them. An adjustable spit was used for roasting—far more effective than our modern ranges, in whose closed chambers true roasting is not really possible. A series of cranes and pulleys made it possible to move pots closer to or further away from the heat, so that a stew pot could simmer lazily, while a water bath for vegetables could boil at a brisk clip over the same fire. There were pots of tin, brass, copper, and, especially, iron. There were spiders—iron skillets fitted with long legs that could be set among the coals; Dutch ovens, with legs and deep-rimmed lids so that coals could be piled both above and beneath for even heating; and numerous kettles and saucepans. And there was the chafing dish, a table-high tripod with a receptacle for coals, which was used for delicate cooking, such as the finishing of delicate fricassees and egg-thickened sauces. There were iron forks and tongs for toast, salamanders for delicate browning, long-handled waffle and wafer irons, and an array of trivets and gridirons for braising, frying, and grilling over fragrant hardwood coals.

Wealthy households often had a "stove"—not a range, but a masonry shelf fitted with a series of deep wells, each fitted with its own small fire chamber. Jefferson installed such a stove at Monticello in 1809. By the 1840s, the stove consisted of a single fire chamber topped with a cast-iron shelf. These "stoves" were used for slow simmers and for the delicate cooking previously done on the chafing dish.

For baking, the brick oven was—and still is—the most perfect chamber ever devised. Large ovens were usually either free-standing or housed in a separate out-building; in some communities, there was a single, communal oven for the use of all families, the firing of which was a once-a-week event in which all participated (even private ovens were rarely fired more often than once a week). In some households, a small oven might be built into the side of the kitchen hearth. But in any case, a private oven was always a sign of wealth and distinction.

The advantages of the brick oven were several. Clay has great heat-retentive qualities. The chamber was heated by building a wood fire on its floor. When the bricks of the floor and domed ceiling were extremely hot, the coals were swept out or in some cases pushed to one side and the bread was placed directly on the oven floor (in baker's parlance, it's called casting). The brick dome held the heat and cooled gradually, creating that phenomenon known as a "falling" oven that trapped and gradually dispersed the steam rising from the bread, aiding in the final, spectacular burst of growth before the yeast died. This also helped form the crisp, satisfyingly chewy crust that was once the mark of a well-made loaf. The oven was ideal for bread making, but pastries and other baked goods also benefited from the radiant heat of the brick floor, and baked meats—usually encased in pastry—achieved succulence that could be had in no other way.

The iron range was convenient, cooler, and (to a small degree) safer than the open fireplace, but in a way was more limiting than the hearth had been. For one thing, true roasting (spit roasting before a hot fire) cannot be done in a sealed oven chamber, to say nothing of ash-roasting in the banked coals of the fireplace. Though some early ranges had a brazier that held live coals for broiling, such attachments did not last, and the art of true broiling, over aromatic hardwood coals, eventually exited the kitchen.

The greatest loss, however, was the old brick oven. Iron and steel do not hold heat the way bricks do, and the oven chamber of the range had none of the subtleties of the falling-oven effect or the heat-retentive brick floor. It should be noted that the change to the iron range, and subsequently, to gas and electricity, occurred somewhat more slowly in the South than in the North. My grandmother, though she was raised in a house with an iron cookstove, set up house-keeping around 1930 in one that had only an open hearth.

Cooking equipment was not the only part of the Southern kitchen to change because of industrialization. There was also the development of the modern packaged-food industry. As canning became the standard means of preservation, factory bottled and tinned condiments, vegetables, and fish began to replace the labor-intensive conserves of earlier years. They saved labor, they made the endless toil of the housewife, perhaps, a little easier, but they lacked the subtlety that older ways of preserving had lent to food.

Well, all that said, we cannot, of course, go back to the kitchens of our past. Even if we could, none of us, I think, would stay. Cooking on an open hearth can in no way be described as romantic; it is grueling, backbreaking, dangerous, and sweltering work. The intense heat is blistering, the soot and ash omnipresent and inescapable, the constant stooping and lifting exhausting to back and shoulder and knee. But besides that, there is a level of skill required that the majority of us no longer possess. Few modern cooks—myself included—would willingly give up their range and laborsaving electric gadgets, the qualities that open-hearth cooking lends to food notwithstanding. The current fad for wood-fired pizza ovens, which, to be sure, make far better bread and pizza than the oven of a modern range, is a luxury naturally limited to those with plenty of space and money—not to mention time. If nothing else, the demand for fuel would soon strip the entire country of its green canopy.

So, you may well ask—how can we recapture some of the magic of this food without an open hearth, brick oven, a spit, a hardwood fire, and a gridiron? In many ways, of course, we can't. But our kitchens have their own advantages. Mary Randolph, the early-nineteenth-century cookbook author, would, I'm sure, have rejoiced to have a modern gas range. And with a very few simple tools, many of which are quite possibly already in your kitchen, we can get around some of the difficulties.

EQUIPPING THE MODERN CLASSICAL SOUTHERN KITCHEN

In presenting the recipes of this book, I have made every effort to offer them as they originally existed. I made no changes to the ingredients, seasonings, or intended final product, nor did I attempt to "modernize" them for contemporary tastes. However, in terms of equipment and, thus, method, there was no getting around the reality that a modern kitchen often differs substantially from the ones in which these recipes were originally formulated. In some cases, the translation to modern equipment was straightforward and actually made good results easier to accomplish. But at other times it was necessary to find ways to get around a modern kitchen in order to recapture some of the original character and intent, to give a suggestion of flavors and textures lent by those well-seasoned ancient iron pots, hardwood coals, brick ovens, and open roasting spits. Some pots and tools that had seen little use in my kitchen quickly became indispensable; some that were once used with great frequency are now gathering dust in the back of a drawer.

I'm not a gadget-oriented cook, and am little impressed by a lot of kitchen gadgets. Good cooking does not depend on a wide array of expensive pots, pans, and electric machines. Some of the best cooks I know turn out exceptional food in a kitchen the size of a closet without the aid of a food processor, microwave, or any of those other electric devices. All these things are convenient and nice to have, but in my own kitchen, there are only a few items that I find it difficult to do without:

Cast-iron pans: The most valued tool of any Southern cook is a well-seasoned iron skillet. An iron Dutch oven is a nice thing to have, but one can get along without it. An iron skillet, on the other hand, is a necessity without which most Southern cooks would be lost. It's the thing they are most likely to produce with pride when asked for their most treasured tool. If there were a fire, and I could save only one thing from my kitchen, it would be my grandmother's chicken-frying skillet.

Cast-iron pans are the original nonstick cookware. Once seasoned, they improve with age and use, unlike other nonstick pans, and are not expensive. New pans must be seasoned. To do this, preheat the oven to 200 degrees F. Wash the pan well with a mild detergent (this is the only time in the life of that pan that it should ever be touched by soap), rinse it well, and wipe it dry. Rub the inside of the pan well with lard or olive or peanut oil. Bake it for an hour. Turn off the oven, and let the pan sit, undisturbed, overnight. The next morning, wipe it out and repeat this process. After the second baking, wipe out the pan and rub the inside with a towel dipped in lard or oil.

To clean a cast-iron pan, wipe it out with a dry cloth, lightly rinse, and wipe it dry. A quick rinse with mild detergent won't hurt the seasoning, but don't let the pan soak in it, unless for some reason, you have to completely re-season it. If any food should stick to the pan, remove it by rubbing with salt or a non-abrasive plastic scrubber, wash it with a mild solution of detergent and warm water, rinse the pan well, and rub the inside surface well with a little lard or olive oil.

Romertopf (Roman clay pot): This is an unglazed terra-cotta baking dish based on the old clay pots of ancient cookery. Mine had been gathering dust on a hard-to-reach upper shelf in my kitchen for years, but after I began working with these recipes, it quickly became dark from frequent use and is now one pot I consider indispensable. It is ideal for roasting potatoes, especially sweet potatoes, and for slow-baking pork and venison.

Sharp knives: There are many home cooks who cut themselves more times than they care to discuss—and all because of dull knives. A cook that is prone to cutting herself does so because the knives she is working with are so dull that she ends up hacking or sawing away at things instead of cutting them. The best insurance against frequent cuts is to buy good, well-balanced knives and keep them sharp.

Food Mill: This is an inexpensive but ingenious gadget that grates and purées food. It consists of a bowl whose bottom is fitted with interchangeable perforated disks and a rotating blade attached to a hand crank, which catches the food and presses it through the perforations. It is ideal for puréeing soups and vegetables because it strains out the tough, stringy parts of the vegetables and the fine bones of fish as it grinds the pulp or flesh. It is also useful for grinding raw meat and some nuts if you don't have a meat grinder.

Wire strainers: I can get along without a wide array of kitchen tools, including the food mill, if I have several good wire-mesh strainers. They can be used in a pinch to sift flour, to dust the tops of cakes with sugar or casseroles with crumbs, even to drain pasta. A wide-mesh strainer, a wooden spoon, and a little elbow grease will do fine for puréeing soups and vegetables.

Mortar and pestle: Once widely used in all kitchens, the mortar and pestle have just about given way to the food processor and blender. Both machines will do the same job as the mortar, and with far less effort, but they will not pulverize spices nearly so well nor give as nice a texture to shrimp or ham paste.

Scale: Kitchen scales are not often seen as essential in American kitchens today, but they are an important baker's and confectioner's tool. Weighing is the most reliable way to measure ingredients for baking, preserving, and candy making. For years, like most American cooks, I limped along without one, but as soon as my mentor Karen Hess convinced me to get a scale and use it, there was a marked—and dramatic—improvement in my cooking. A good kitchen scale need not be expensive; just make sure it is balanced.

Charcoal grill: Unless you live in a city that does not permit charcoal fires within its limits, or in an apartment that has no place to put one, a small outdoor grill is something that is nice to have. You can, of course, use the oven broiler for almost all of the broiling recipes in this book, but only a good fire of aromatic hardwood coals will produce the fragrant results that nineteenth-century cooks accomplished on an open hearth.

Ice cream freezer: The hand-cranked machines seem to produce the best texture, but I have and use an electric-powered crank-type freezer. They are a blessing for arthritic shoulders and are widely available.

Miscellaneous gadgets that are useful though not essential include:

Meat grinder: This is the best tool for making sausage meat or for grinding nuts. My grandmother grated coconut through her meat grinder. However, a practiced hand and sharp knife will do every bit as good a job if you don't have one.

Pastry blender: This little gadget is excellent for cutting shortening into pastry and biscuit dough, but not indispensable: with a little practice, you can do the job as well with a wide-tined fork or two knives.

Wire whisk: The inventive person who devised wire whisks has my undying gratitude, but this, too, is not indispensable: two dinner forks held in one hand with the tines turned to face each other will do an excellent job of beating egg whites or whipping cream.

Biscuit cutter: Actually, you can use any sharp round that will let the air out of its top so that it won't compress the dough, or just use a sharp knife to cut the dough into squares or triangles.

Rolling pin: Convenient, but I've made fantastic piecrust, in front of twenty students, using a wine bottle, and in a pinch one can even roll out noodles with a broom handle.

Food processor, blender, and mixer: All of these are useful in their place and a blessing to those of us who have arthritis and like infirmities that make kitchen chores difficult, if not painful. I have all three machines and use them with joy, but again, there are other, simpler tools that will do the job when you are caught without them.

THE BUILDING BLOCKS
OF SOUTHERN FLAVOR:

Herbs, Spices, and Aromatics in the Classical Southern Pantry

The aromas and flavors of a Southern kitchen are diverse and have their foundations in many places. They are linked not only to the kitchens of the rest of America, but also to those of Europe, Africa, and eastern Asia. All the same, there are smells and tastes that have come to be almost peculiarly Southern, aromas that make Southerners close our eyes and smile, knowing that we are safe and at home. Here are some of the basic building blocks that are essential to good Southern cookery and the construction of distinctly Southern flavor.

A *Lexicon of Herbs Frequently Used in Southern Cookery*

It is popularly supposed that Southerners outside New Orleans have been largely ignorant of herbs, especially fresh ones, until recent times. But nothing could be further from the truth. In *The Virginia House-wife* (1824), Mary Randolph mentioned and used more than a dozen, including fennel, marjoram, sage, parsley, tarragon, thyme, and bay. The same profusion is recorded in most antebellum cookbooks and household notebooks. Some families' plants go back several generations, with each new household's plants transplanted and propagated from their parents' old beds.

Once, every Southern garden could be almost guaranteed to contain two things: a dusky bed of gray-green sage and a thick, almost wild growth of spearmint. Their fragrant leaves defined our seasons: brisk spearmint's cooling fragrance and bright, crisp flavor spoke of spring and summer, while sage's darker perfume was the very essence of autumn and winter. Other herbs and spices, of course, were known and used, but none of them has been so thoroughly woven into the fabric of our cooking as have these two. They are in many ways the alpha and omega of Southern herbal cookery, indigenous to every region and used by virtually every ethnic group.

If you don't grow your own herbs, fortunately both fresh and good-quality dried ones are available in most markets. One is not necessarily superior to the other. There are times when fresh herbs are preferred for their sweetness, and other times when dried ones are better because of their concentrated oils. Once you find a good source, buy herbs only in small quantities. Store dried ones in tightly lidded jars away from any kind of light or heat, since air, light, and heat all damage the volatile oils. Fresh herbs will keep fairly well for a few days in the refrigerator, provided they are well-sealed in plastic bags, but it is best to use them as soon as possible after they have been picked from the plant.

Bay leaf: Sweet bay laurel (*Laurus nobilis*), the noble herb of the ancient Greeks, grows easily in the temperate regions of the South and is widely used to flavor Southern soups, stews, and baked meats. It originated in the Mediterranean region and was transplanted to the South by the Spanish in the earliest days of the colonies. Along the Georgia coast, where the climate is mild enough for it to flourish, one frequently finds large, ancient bay trees that are a living legacy of those early colonists. Today, several varieties are grown, and the leaves can vary in shape from long, slender, and smooth to short and broad, with a slight curl to the edges.

If you live in a temperate climate, you can grow your own bay laurel in your garden; it makes a beautiful ornamental shrub and will eventually grow into a tree if it is never pruned back. However, it can also be grown in a pot indoors in any climate. If you are using commercial dried bay, look for imported leaves, preferably those that have been vacuum-sealed in the jar or a pouch to protect their flavor. Good dried bay leaves will still be bright green and have a pungent but agreeable odor.

Mint: When most Southerners say "mint," spearmint is the kind that they usually mean, the kind one finds wreathing the front porch of countless farm and plantation houses. It is the only one to use in making a mint julep and is the traditional one for flavoring mint sauce, new potatoes, or fresh green peas. Most of the recipes in this book call for fresh mint, but good-quality dried leaves can be used where indicated. When buying the dried variety, look for a nice green color and bright, intense fragrance.

Mint makes an excellent ground cover and thrives in warm, moist environments with lots of sunshine. It can be grown in your garden or in a pot on a sunny windowsill.

Parsley: Marcella Hazan reminds us of an old Italian proverb describing someone who is into everything, "he is like parsley—in every sauce," and how true it is. Few are the stews, baked meats, sauces, and vegetable dishes that do not contain this ubiquitous herb—not only in Italian cooking, but in that of Europe, Britain, and America. Its universality in Southern kitchens owes largely to the cookery of our European ancestors.

Parsley is one of the few herbs that should never be used dried. Whereas the flavor of other herbs becomes more concentrated when dried, parsley's flavor largely dissipates. It is easy to grow, and potted plants last up to two years. (Parsley is a biannual—that is, it flowers after two years and will usually die shortly thereafter.)

Fortunately, fresh parsley is widely available. When buying it, any variety will suffice, but Italian flat-leaf parsley has more flavor and is preferable if you can find it.

Sage: If I were asked to name any one herb that could be said to be the true flavor of the South, it would be sage. Even in urban households where there is no garden, a big box of dried sage is the one sure fixture of every pantry. I know of nowhere else in the world, except maybe Genoa with its basil, where any single herb is so thoroughly identified with a regional cuisine. Our European ancestors knew the happy affinity that sage has for game meats of all kinds, and the combination is still a common one in Southern kitchens. Here, the autumn air is inevitably fragrant with sage in many traditional game, poultry, and pork dishes of the season.

Sage can be grown in a pot, but is a little more temperamental than other herbs and requires more care. When buying it fresh, look for leaves that are still attached to the branches. When buying dried sage, whole leaves are preferred to powdered or "rubbed" sage, because the volatile oils are better preserved in whole leaves. Dried whole-leaf sage is available from Italian, Middle-eastern, and natural food grocers. You can also dry your own. Cut fresh branches, or buy them, tie them together, and hang them upside down until the leaves are dry and brittle. Pull them gently from the branch and store them in an airtight jar away from light and heat.

Thyme: I think of thyme as the herb of New Orleans. Without it, Creole food would be very different indeed. However, this herb was common in early English cookery, and it is found in all the Anglo kitchens of the South. Mary Randolph used it extensively in the stews, meat dishes, and herb-flavored vinegars of *The Virginia House-wife,* and it was frequently called for in all the other antebellum books as well. Today, thyme is not as widely used by other Southerners, but it is to Louisiana's kitchens what chilies and cilantro are to Southwestern ones: its pungent aroma is the essential flavoring of a good gumbo or seafood étouffée.

Thyme makes a beautiful, fragrant ground cover in the garden and also takes well to potting—or so I am told. Unhappily, I can't seem to keep a thyme plant alive. If you have no place to grow your own, or, like me, tend to kill it, fresh thyme is nowadays pretty widely available. For dried herbs, look for whole leaves and crumble them yourself.

Bouquet Garni

This classic French aromatic bundle of herbs was once widely used in seasoning soups, stews, and sauces. The traditional combination is parsley, bay leaf, and thyme, but often celery is included and another herb may be introduced, depending on the dish that it is meant to season. A real Bouquet Garni can only be made with fresh herbs, but you can make a fairly reasonable approximation of it using dried herbs tied up in cheesecloth, like a pre-industrial tea bag (or, for that matter, you can use a stainless-steel tea ball; see note). Allow a teaspoon of dried herbs for each sprig called for here. A sprig, in this case, should be about 3 inches long and full of healthy, unblemished leaves.

The Bouquet Garni should be used as soon as it is made, so don't put it together until you need it.

1 bay leaf, preferably fresh

2 sprigs thyme

1 sprig parsley

1 leafy celery rib top (optional)

Optional (use just one): 1 sprig marjoram, summer savory, chervil, rosemary, sage, or tarragon (if using tarragon, omit the thyme)

Gather everything into a bundle. If the bay leaf is dried, wrap it carefully so that it doesn't crumble. Tie it securely with kitchen twine, wrapping it crisscross (like the laces of a ballet slipper) around the herbs.

NOTES FOR USING DRIED THYME AND OTHER HERBS: *Gather the thyme and the optional herb (whole leaves are preferred) into a 3 inch square of cheesecloth. Tie securely then tie this packet to the bundle made from the fresh herbs. You may also just put everything—both dried and fresh herbs— into a large wire-mesh tea ball.*

A Few Southern Spices

Cayenne and other hot capsicum peppers: The inexpensive and easily grown seedpods of the family of Capsicum Frutescens, or chili peppers, have become more popular in Southern cookery than is good for them. Originally, they were used as a substitute for expensive imported black pepper, which is how they came by their name; they are actually not related to true pepper. In older times, capsicums were used with a judicious restraint that we would do well to relearn. When fiery cayenne is allowed to dominate to the point that heat is all one can distinguish, the subtlety of its distinctive flavor as a spice is lost. As Karen Hess puts it so well, capsicums should brighten, not inflame. In using them, keep in mind that discretion is the better part of valor.

There are literally dozens of variations of capsicum peppers available in the South from the family of chilies—from true cayenne and bird's-eye peppers to such exotic looking varieties as Scotch bonnets. Cayenne is the capsicum most traditional and the most frequently called for in this book—both in whole pod form and ground. Serrano peppers and other small red chilies are fine substitutes if you are not able to find true cayenne. Scotch bonnets, which are common in Caribbean cookery and often available in West Indian markets, are more fiery and assertive than cayenne. They can be substituted, but must be used with more care and restraint. Whole pods are preferable to the pre-ground powder, mainly because the flavoring oils are better preserved in whole pod form.

Pepper Vinegar

In Southern kitchens, hot peppers are pickled in vinegar, not only to use as a condiment in themselves, but to make a spicy aromatic vinegar used both at table and in the kitchen to flavor vegetables and stews. Pickled peppers are common in Southern markets (even supermarkets) and are sold in specialty West Indian markets in other regions. Keep in mind that they are not the same thing as hot sauce. When a recipe here calls for pepper vinegar, it means the liquid form of pickled peppers. If you can't find it, you can approximate it by mixing a few drops of bottled hot sauce with cider vinegar, or you can make your own.

6 ounces whole fresh red or green cayenne or   About 1 cup cider vinegar
  other hot peppers

1. Pack the peppers into a sterilized pint jar. Bring the vinegar to a boil and pour it over the peppers until the jar is filled to within 1/4 inch of the top and the peppers are completely submerged.

2. Seal the jar with a new canning lid and ring seal. Refrigerate and let stand for at least 2 weeks (a month is better) before using.

3. For more prolonged storage, or when you are making pepper vinegar in quantity, instead of refrigerating the jars, process them completely submerged in a boiling water bath for 10 minutes (see page 383), and then store them in a cool, dark cupboard. Makes 1 pint.

Curry: This East Indian blend of spices was introduced to England as English trade with the Orient expanded in the seventeenth and eighteenth centuries. By the middle of the eighteenth century, recipes for blending curry spices were appearing in English cookery books. It was a popular seasoning, both in England and its American colonies. Chicken Country Captain, a classic curried dish, can be found all along the East Coast—with each coastal city claiming that the dish originated in its community.

Most people with any cooking background at all can tell you that "curry" is not a particular spice blend but more of a culinary concept, and curry powder is completely unknown in Southeast Asia. Each cook makes her own blend, depending on her country and family traditions and on what she is seasoning. All the packaged blends were formulated for export to Western countries, especially England and America. Never mind that: in the nineteenth and for most of the twentieth century, "curry" for Southerners was a spice blend that was widely used as a seasoning.

You may, of course, use a commercial curry powder, but the end result will taste very different from that produced by nineteenth-century cooks; most curry blends today contain a higher proportion of cumin and usually include fenugreek, the spice that gives Indian curries much of their characteristic aroma. Fenugreek is rarely mentioned in nineteenth-century Southern recipes; Lettice Bryan used it, but she was the exception, not the rule. Modern blends also usually contain cinnamon and garlic powder, which old recipes do not mention.

The recipe that follows is Annabella Hill's blend from *Mrs. Hill's New Cook Book* (1867) and is close to the one given in *The Cook's Oracle* (1817) by Dr. William Kitchiner, a book that Mrs. Hill called her kitchen bible. There is a higher proportion of allspice and cumin, but otherwise her ingredients are the same as Dr. Kitchiner's.

Toasting curry powder before using it deepens and intensifies its flavor and makes for the slight nuttiness that one expects from a good curry, but once it has been toasted, the aromatic oils don't keep long. The ideal is to toast and grind the spices only as needed, as they do in India. Failing that, toast premixed curry powder as you use it.

Annabella Hill's Curry Powder

Mrs. Hill's formula made nearly a quart of curry powder. I have cut the original recipe by half. Use whole spices for this blend. For more of the classic modern curry powder flavor, add 1/4 ounce (1 tablespoon) of whole fenugreek seeds.

1-1/2 ounces (1/4 cup) each: whole coriander, turmeric, dried ginger, whole black peppercorns, whole mustard seeds, and whole allspice

1/4 ounce (1 tablespoon) each: whole cumin and cardamom seeds

1. Grind the spices with a mortar and pestle or electric spice mill to a fine powder (If you use an electric mill, make sure that you use it only for spices and never for coffee). You may grind the spices together or individually, whichever is easier for you.

2. Sift through a very fine wire mesh to get rid of any chaff, then pour the powder into a pint jar. Tightly seal and shake vigorously until the spices are well blended. Store the curry in a cool, dark cupboard. Before each use, shake the jar to redistribute the spices. Makes 1 pint.

Mustard: Everywhere else in the western world, "deviled," in culinary terms, means that pepper (and a lot of it) is present in a dish—literally, that it is "hot as the devil." In the South, however, it more often indicates the presence of mustard. Whether powdered and mixed with liquids and other spices to make a condiment, or used whole to flavor pickles, these peppery seeds are a common element in Southern cookery. Unfortunately, the quality of the mustard used is often overlooked.

In the recipes of this book, whole seeds or powdered mustard are called for more frequently than prepared mustard. Until the mid-nineteenth century, bottled prepared mustard was not available to most Southerners. When a recipe called for "mustard" it meant powdered mustard; "made mustard" was used when the prepared condiment was intended, and usually took for granted that it was homemade. Unless otherwise indicated, I've followed the original structure of the recipes, using dry, powdered mustard, and indicating the type of prepared condiment preferred when that was the original intention.

In keeping a Southern pantry, it is good to have a ready supply of both whole mustard seeds and dry powder blend (such as English mustard). The best prepared mustard condiment is that which is freshly made, for much the same reason that freshly ground herbs and spices are preferred to powder. But you can get good results from these recipes using a good-quality bottled English or French Dijon-style mustard. The preferred type is indicated with the recipe.

Where dry mustard powder or whole seeds are indicated, do not substitute prepared mustard, since it contains vinegar and often other spices which may not be compatible with the other flavors in the recipe.

Nutmeg (and mace): This aromatic nut was once so popular and common in England, that gentlemen carried a nut and a portable grater in their pockets wherever they went. It was universally popular among the English settlers of North America, but most particularly in the South. Mary Randolph and other early Southern cookery writers used it in almost prodigal quantities, in everything from soups and meats to vegetables and desserts. It is frequently called for in the recipes given in this book.

In order to take advantage of the full fragrance of this spice, it must be freshly grated as needed. As is true with most spices, the oils of nutmeg are quite volatile, and begin to evaporate as soon as they are exposed to the air. That's why their fine perfume is so heady. The nut itself will keep for a very long time, almost indefinitely, if stored in a sealed jar in a cool, dark place. But once the spice is grated, the oils evaporate rapidly, and much of the flavor and aroma is gone within a few hours. Kitchen stores frequently sell nutmeg mills, and they are convenient, but for small quantities, simply scrape the nut with the edge of a paring knife or microplane grater.

In their natural state, all nutmegs are covered with a delicate, orange-red lacy net-like membrane. This part of the spice is what we know as mace. The net is broken loose into individual slivers, called "blades," which can be crushed to a powder, or else used whole to more subtly flavor a soup or sauce. The flavor is similar to nutmeg, but more direct and intense. It was once extremely popular in England, and, in turn, the South.

For the best and fullest flavor, whole blade is preferable to pre-ground mace but, unfortunately, nutmegs are almost always sold without the mace netting attached, and whole blades are difficult to find. My local health-food store has to special-order them for me. Whole blades will keep indefinitely in a tightly sealed jar, but quickly lose their flavor once ground. Whole blade mace is called for throughout this book, but if you have trouble finding it, you can use a pinch or so of pre-ground mace (depending on its potency) for each blade, or else substitute freshly grated nutmeg.

Black Pepper: Black pepper is such a staple in most modern American kitchens that we fail to appreciate that it was once precious and expensive. Used as both flavoring and preservative, peppercorns are the dried berries of *piper nigrum*, of the genus *piperaceae*, a plant native to India. So prized were these berries that they were the vital center of the Eastern spice trade. Black and white pepper are both from the same plant; white pepper is merely the inner kernel of the berry from which the outer skin has been removed.

Unfortunately, most of the pepper used in American kitchens is as inferior as it is commonplace. Pre-ground pepper has lost most of its pungent oils and has only a ghost of its original flavor. Buy a mill for grinding pepper fresh, as needed, and fill it with the best peppercorns you can find. I keep two mills handy—one each for black and white pepper.

Vanilla: Vanilla is the dried bean of any of several varieties of orchid. It is popularly supposed to have been introduced to America by Thomas Jefferson, and while that's not true, Southerners love the idea that one of us may have been responsible. Regardless of how this spice came to be here, it has long been a universal flavoring in Southern desserts—almost too universal. While there are some flavors that do not fully develop until they are paired with the aromatic oils of the vanilla bean, there are others with which it is not at all compatible.

Homemade Vanilla Extract

This simple extract is so much more aromatic than commercial extract, that, once you become accustomed to using it, you will never be satisfied with less. The recipe is the classic one recorded by Bill Neal, but I have trimmed his restaurant-sized proportions, since a small bottle is sufficient for my needs and cramped kitchen cupboards. If you bake often and find you need a larger quantity, the recipe increases easily, allowing a whole vanilla bean for every 2 ounces (1/4 cup) of alcohol. I like a good bourbon with vanilla, but you may use brandy in its stead, if you prefer. Replenish the jar as you use the extract with an equal amount of whiskey, and it will last indefinitely. The batch I made for the first edition of this book lasted four years.

2 whole, imported vanilla beans	4 ounces (1/2 cup) bourbon or brandy

1. Using a sharp knife or single-edged razor blade, split the vanilla bean in half lengthwise, then cut the halves across into three equal pieces.
2. Put the vanilla bean and any stray seeds into a glass jar fitted with a tight lid. Pour the bourbon over it, tightly screw on the lid, and give it a good shake. Set it aside in a cool, dark cupboard that you will be going into frequently, and let stand for at least 2 weeks before using. During this steeping period, shake the jar whenever you go into the cupboard. Makes 4 ounces of extract.

ALCOHOL IN THE CLASSICAL SOUTHERN KITCHEN

Wine, whiskey, and other alcoholic beverages have long figured prominently in Southern kitchens—even Baptist ones. Annabella Hill (*Mrs. Hill's New Cook Book*), for example, was a staunch Baptist, yet she made great use of alcoholic preparations in her kitchen, and provided her readers with a number of recipes for cordials, wines, and beers.

In using alcohol in the kitchen, you needn't—in fact, shouldn't—spend a fortune on fine, well-aged vintages to get good results. I adhere to Elizabeth David's advice: the best cooking wine should be drinkable but not distinguished—not one you *can't* drink, only one you might not *care* to drink.

The following spirits and wines are frequently used in this book:

Spirits

Bourbon: Use a well-aged Kentucky corn whiskey from Bourbon County. My own favorite is W.L. Weller's.

Brandy: Any good French brandy or cognac will do, but truth to tell, when a recipe calls for brandy, I always use bourbon instead. It's smoother.

Rum: Once produced on the sugar plantations of the Caribbean, rum is distilled from sugar cane, and was widely available to Southern cooks. Any good rum will do, but for cooking, golden and dark rums give the most distinctive flavor.

Wines

A fortified wine is one that has alcohol or sugar added to it early in the fermentation process, making it impossible for the yeasts to consume all the sugar. The result is a sweeter wine with a higher alcohol content than conventionally fermented wine.

Claret: This is an old name, now mostly archaic (though in the last decade it has made a distinct come-back), for wine from the Bordeaux region of France. There are white Bordeaux, but generally "claret" refers to a rich, full-bodied red wine. Your wine merchant can direct you to a good Bordeaux for cooking.

Madeira: This fortified wine is produced on a small island of the same name off the coast of Morocco. It was an undistinguished wine until the producers discovered, quite by accident, that it was improved by heat and rough sea travel. Purveyors began shipping it around the Cape of Africa on purpose to mellow it (which is where the expression for describing fine Madeira "been around the Cape" originated). It was imported into Colonial and early Republican America in great quantities, and is reputed to have been George Washington's and Thomas Jefferson's favorite wine. It was very popular in Charleston and Savannah and was as widely used in the kitchen as it was at table. For cooking, choose a modestly-priced medium-dry (Sercial) or "Rainwater" Madeira.

Sherry: Sherry is another fortified wine from Spain. It can range from very sweet (as in cream sherry) to mouth-puckeringly dry. For most Southern kitchens, a medium-dry amontillado, or in English, "sack" (a corruption of "sec," meaning dry) was the most commonly used. Sherry and Madeira are often used interchangeably.

Port: The fortified wine of Portugal. It is invariably richer than either Madeira or sherry, and should not be used as a substitute for either of them. There are many varieties, varying both in sweetness and depth of color. For these recipes, use either a moderately priced ruby or tawny port.

Vinegar

Though cider vinegar is the most usual one in today's Southern pantries, and seems to evoke the most recognizably Southern taste, wine vinegar was once more widely used than it is today, and is frequently called for in this book. Use naturally-aged wine vinegar without herbs, garlic, or other flavorings, unless a recipe specifically calls for a flavored vinegar.

DRY-SALT CURED PORK AND ITS FAT

The foundation for so much that one recognizes as Southern in flavor is the distinctive taste of dry-salt cured pork, or salt pork. This is pork that is cured with dry salt (instead of a brine) and then air- or smoke-dried. The pork is first rubbed with salt and left lying for a several days. It is then wiped dry, rubbed with more salt and spices (and sometimes ashes), then hung to air dry, or smoked and then air-dried. Unfortunately, dry-salt cured pork is as misunderstood and unjustly maligned as it is essential. For most people outside the South or, for that matter, many within it, traditional Southern cookery invariably evokes the exclamation "but, all that pig fat!" Such prejudice is unfounded. Salt pork is an elemental and universal source of flavor in many of the world's cuisines. Whether it is the *petit salé* of Provence, Italy's *pancetta* and *prosciutto*, China's salt-dried and smoked hams and bacons, or England and America's bacon, salt pork is, along with anchovies, olives, and capers, an economical source of pure, concentrated flavor.

In Southern kitchens, salt pork is an integral part of the cooking, but is neither as all-pervasive nor saturating as is popularly believed. In the hands of traditional Southern cooks, it bolstered and enhanced flavor rather than cloaking it. The myth that all Southern cooking floats in a layer of hog grease is, fortunately, as false as it is popular. Salt pork is often used for an added earthy depth of flavor—to underpin a mild fruit or vegetable or to round out a roast or stew. And though it is used to flavor some Southern vegetables, we don't, and never have, used it in all of them—that would be tiresome and monotonous.

Often, salt pork is added directly to the pot, without a preliminary cooking, but it frequently turns up in what amounts to a classic soffritto (flavor base), with onion and parsley, the flavorful underpinning of Mediterranean and Caribbean cookery. Sometimes, only the salty flavor is wanted, in which case, it is fried to render all its fat, then carefully drained before it's used. The fat was never wasted: there were times when only it is needed—for example in a pilau, where it lends not only flavor, but essential viscosity.

Dry-salt cured pork is found in the Southern kitchen in four basic forms, each contributing its own distinct, and very different flavor. These flavors are very concentrated, and a little goes a long way, which is one of the reasons for its universal popularity. Just as pancetta and prosciutto are not used interchangeably in an Italian kitchen, neither are these various types. Each has its own voice and place.

Dry-Salt Cured Pork: Also known as streak-of-lean or simply as salt pork, this fat-streaked side meat is similar to breakfast bacon, but not smoked.

"Old" or Dry-Cured Ham: The country ham of legend, this is exactly the same cut and cure as prosciutto, though usually country ham is smoked, and most prosciutto isn't. In the old days, however, some families didn't smoke all their hams, so they were exactly like prosciutto and it,

in fact, makes an excellent substitute for country ham. In some places (even in the South), it may be easier to come by than country ham. Since dry-cured hams are actually subtler than a smoked brine-cured hams, the latter isn't an effective substitute, so if country ham isn't available where you live, mail order it or use a good-quality imported prosciutto. Like prosciutto, country ham is most often an end in itself, but it is occasionally used as a seasoning, especially the knuckle and scrap pieces, which are frequently used to season stews and vegetables.

Smoked Bacon (or side meat): This is identical to breakfast bacon. Use thick-sliced bacon.

Fat Back: Cheapest (and crudest) of all, this is a salted slab of pure back fat, hence the name. It is what was intended when an old recipe called for "white meat."

Substitutions: For various reasons, you may not want to or be able to cook with salt pork or pork fat. They have no real equivalents, but many of the recipes will stand up to substitutions even though the taste will in no way be the same. I've made parenthetical suggestions throughout the text only where the substitution still produces a recognizably Southern taste. Some cooks now-adays advocate factory-cured, smoke-flavored turkey meat as a substitute. For my taste, the smoked flavor of this product is overpowering and harsh, and its sodium content, for the most part, is nearly as high as the pork it purports to imitate. In no way does it make an acceptable substitute.

Exceptional, traditionally cured pork products are available from:
S. Wallace Edwards & Sons, Inc.
P.O. Box 25
Surrey, Virginia 23883
(800) 222-4267
www.virginiatraditions.com

COOKING FATS

Drippings and Lard

Frequently, fat rendered from dry-salt cured pork or smoked bacon, is used as shortening in bread or for sautéing. It plays not only an important role as fat, but as a distinctive flavoring on its own. Because it is rendered from cured meat and usually lightly browned in the process, it is very different from lard, both in flavor and in the way it performs in cooking.

Lard is rendered fresh pork fat, the finest of which comes from the hard, grainy fat found around the kidneys and saddle of the pig's belly, known as leaf fat (hence the name "leaf" lard). It has taken a lot of hard knocks in the last few years, and been given a worse reputation than it deserves. Lard was once extensively used in European cookery, and, hence, was a fixture in the larder of early colonists. It is unsurpassed for producing light, tender pastry and produces a crispness in the crust of fried foods that is not possible with any other fat.

Because lard is animal fat, it is high in saturated fat and all the allegedly terrible things that your doctor is trying to get you to give up. Naturally, you don't want to drown yourself in it, but pure lard (without emulsifiers and hardeners) used with common sense and discretion should do you no harm.

There are no real substitutes for lard or drippings. What they bring to the food, both in texture and flavor, cannot be imitated. But if you are not able to cook with them—whether for dietary, religious, or health reasons—butter makes perfectly good pastry on its own and can be substituted wherever lard is called for. John Martin Taylor also recommends goose and duck fat for pastries. For frying, I think peanut oil gives the next most satisfying results, and either peanut or olive oil (or butter) can be used for sautéing.

Unfortunately, most commercially made lard has been partially hydrogenated and treated with preservatives (we can't seem to leave well enough alone). Since it is sold in cardboard containers and stored at room temperature, the partial hydrogenation is used to hold its solid state at variable temperatures, and the preservatives are added to prolong shelf life. If you use commercial lard, try to find a brand that has been minimally processed, preferably without these treatments. Check the package carefully. If there is an expiration date, be sure it's still several months ahead of the day that you buy it. The package itself should be clean and dry. If it has brown, greasy splotches on it, the lard is old and has probably been stored at too high a temperature. Most of the packages aren't sealed; open the box and carefully examine the contents. It should be creamy and white, like shortening, and have a faintly oily, but not rancid smell.

The best insurance of quality and purity is to render your own lard. The process also assures you of a ready supply of excellent cracklings, those flavorful brown nuggets that give so much character to Southern cornbread. Most butchers that still get whole pigs will sell you pork fat, the finest of which is from the saddle of the belly. It's a good idea to ask the butcher ahead of time to reserve the fat for you, since they usually do not keep it on hand. You will get about a pound of lard for every 1-1/4 to 1-1/2 pounds of fat.

To Render Lard: Cut four pounds of fresh, uncured pork fat into half-inch cubes and wash it thoroughly in cold water. Press out the washing water and put the fat in a large, deep kettle with a heavy bottom—cast iron is ideal, but a soup kettle will work fine. Choose one with high sides to avoid hazardous splattering. Turn on the heat to medium and bring the fat to a good simmer. Let it cook until all the lingering traces of water have evaporated and the fat begins to melt from the solid tissues. Then reduce the heat to low and cook until the fat is completely rendered from the solids, checking the pot frequently. Do not leave the pot unattended once most of the fat is rendered, or it could overheat and burn. You will easily recognize when the lard is ready, as the solid tissue will sink to the bottom and start to brown. These little lumps are the cracklings. Reduce the heat to the barest simmer and cook the lard just long enough for the cracklings to turn a light brown and get crisp (if you are using back fat, the cracklings will not get crisp; stop when they turn brown). Remove the kettle from the heat and lift out the cracklings with a slotted spoon. Spread them to drain on butcher paper or paper towels. Let the melted fat cool enough to handle, but not so long that it starts to solidify. Carefully pour the fat into metal or heatproof glass containers and let it cool completely before sealing. Store the lard in a place that is consistently cool and dark (the refrigerator is best for most households). Properly sealed, this should keep for a couple of months and satisfy all your shortening needs. Lard does not take well to freezing since fat doesn't freeze at the temperatures of most home freezers.

Olive Oil

You didn't expect to find this one here, did you? To many people's surprise, this venerable staple was indeed known to Southern cooks and used to some degree during most of the eighteenth and nineteenth centuries. There were even attempts by the earliest settlers to grow olive trees on the Carolina and Georgia coasts; however the soil was too rich and the climate too severe. But port records in Savannah and Charleston indicate that olive oil was imported into Colonial Carolina and Georgia in surprisingly large quantities, and it was frequently advertised in early newspapers. Because this oil was entirely imported, it was, naturally, quite expensive. Yet it appeared frequently in nineteenth century cookbooks, and in many middle-class household notebooks, giving some indication that it was used all over the Southeast.

Because of its cost, olive oil was mainly reserved for salads and apothecary usage, and most families continued to depend exclusively on animal fats for cooking. Naturally, olive oil plays no part in the humbler food of tenant farm and slave cabin. When you see it in a modern Gullah or Cajun recipes, it is a sure sign that someone has been fooling around. Because olive oil spoils easily, when other vegetable oils made an appearance in the late nineteenth century, they for a time almost displaced olive oil in every Southern kitchen, but today it is more of a staple than salt pork.

I have used olive oil only when called for in a source recipe, and won't offend your intelligence by imposing my own taste on a recipe, saying that its use is "implied" by the method or by other ingredients. That would not only be cheating, it would give you an impression of the food that I would have no right to convey. However, if you are not able to use animal fat in your cooking, olive oil makes a very good substitute for sautéing and frying because it adds flavor. While not authentically Southern, it is more satisfying to use than a flavorless oil.

Use extra virgin olive oil for salads and for light sautéing or for basting a pork roast, as it has the purest and most distinctive flavor. Oils that are labeled "pure" or with no prefix at all are from later pressings and are mildly flavored—if they have any at all—but the point for our purposes is that they were unknown to nineteenth century cooks, and therefore have no place in these recipes.

Butter

Until the family finally persuaded her to give up the milk cow—about the time that I entered graduate school—my great-great Aunt Fanny Lou Hall made fresh butter weekly. It was the first real butter I ever tasted, and I would not taste its like again until I went to Italy. If you remember the taste of butter churned from rich, un-pasteurized cream, you know why I have such a cranky reputation where butter is concerned.

The recipes in this book were tested and formulated using unsalted butter. Salt covers up a multitude of evils, including the taste of inferior butter. But I use the unsalted variety not only because I believe it to be superior; it also makes seasoning easier to control. Salt was once a necessary preservative, but even in those days, cake recipes directed that it be washed from the butter before it was used. If you choose to continue using salted butter, please be judicious in your use of the saltshaker.

In any case, use the best that you can afford. Reasonably good French, Irish, and Danish butter is available in larger cities, though it is very expensive, and some small American dairies are beginning to make very good fresh butter again.

You will notice that I have not mentioned margarine. Neither should you.

OTHER DAIRY PRODUCTS

Buttermilk

True buttermilk is a by-product of butter making. Whole milk or cream is poured into a churn and agitated with a paddle until the fats separate and solidify into a lump. The leftover liquids are buttermilk, its lightly soured, tangy taste made by natural fermentation from enzymes that the milk contained. In the warm climate of the South, sweet (fresh) milk would sour quickly, but buttermilk would keep for days. Therefore, it became a staple in Southern kitchens, adding tenderness to the crumb of breads and cakes, and, when combined with soda, also providing leavening.

Unfortunately, real buttermilk is a rare commodity. The process of pasteurization not only kills the harmful bacteria, but also the good bacteria and enzymes that cause the natural fermentation. Commercial buttermilk is not actually a byproduct of butter making, but is skimmed milk soured using enzyme cultures. It is also salted, which makes it less desirable in recipes for sweets and for those who are restricting their sodium intake. True buttermilk is basically the same as yogurt, except that yogurt is thicker because it's usually made from milk that has been condensed slightly. All-natural low-fat yogurt (preferably biodynamic*), thinned to buttermilk consistency with water or milk, can be substituted if you find that the kind of buttermilk available to you isn't consistent. In fact, a good-quality yogurt often produces finer results than commercial buttermilk.

*Biodynamic is a specialized form of organic agriculture. In order to use the word on their label, these small, highly-specialized dairies must meet strict guidelines and the yogurt carrying this designation is therefore of a very high quality, and gives infinitely superior results. They are, unhappily, very difficult to find.

Cheese

The South has not, traditionally at least, been distinguished for its cheese making. Along coastal areas and in the deep South, the climate did not lend itself to curing cheese until refrigeration came into being. So while there are a growing number of excellent specialty cheese-makers in the South today, it isn't a long tradition. Nonetheless, cheese does figure prominently in traditional Southern cooking. On the coast, imported hard cheese was available such as English Cheddar and Cheshire, and Italian Parmesan (Parmigiano-Reggiano). In the country, there were simple homemade cottage and cream cheeses, and in cooler climates, possibly even homemade hard cheese; Mrs. Hill, who lived in West-central Georgia, left us a lucid recipe for classic cheddar as early as 1867.

Here are suggestions for the cheeses called for in this book:

Cheddar: If you can get imported English cheddar, it is ideal, but good, well-aged Vermont or Canadian cheddars are also acceptable.

Cream cheese: You can make your own from homemade *crème fraîche* (page 48) by hanging it in a double layer of cheesecloth overnight. Otherwise, use an all-natural cheese that does not contain gum thickeners.

Parmesan: Real Parmesan—Parmigiano-Reggiano—was available, at least in coastal cities, throughout the nineteenth century. Unfortunately, bottled pre-grated cheese became available early; recipes using it date as early as 1890. Bottled grated Parmesan is usually made from inferior cheese, and is not worth your notice. Use the best imported whole Parmesan you can find, preferably Parmigiano-Reggiano.

As an interesting side note, one cannot always be certain of the intent of a recipe that called for "Parmesan." In some places, at least for a time, Stilton cheese was known as English Parmesan.

Clabber

Clabber is the name Southerners used to use for a thick sour-milk product that hasn't been churned to remove the fat—essentially the same as whole milk yogurt. Use an all-natural, preferably biodynamic yogurt (see "Buttermilk" above).

Cream

Throughout traditional Southern cookery, and, therefore, this book, cream is used to enrich and naturally thicken sauces, stews, and delicate bisques, and to provide the necessary fat in baked goods and frozen desserts. Before refrigeration, lightly soured double cream (that with the highest fat content)—what is today fashionably called by its French name *crème fraîche*—was frequently used. Today, double cream and *crème fraîche* are difficult to come by, and, unfortunately, the ultra-pasteurized whipping cream available to most of us is not a good substitute.

Wherever this book calls for heavy cream, the recipe was tested with cream containing a minimum fat content of 36 percent. By law, "whipping" cream must be at least 30 percent milk fat, and it is seldom more than 34 percent. Often, it is too thin even to whip properly and will not thicken as readily in reductions, so don't rely on the name on the label. Look on the side panel to be sure that it contains at least 36 percent milk fat.

Commercial sour cream is usually no more than 24 percent and often as little as 16 percent milk fat. It will not answer for the "soured" cream of old recipes. If you can get true, double-cream crème fraîche, it will work fine, but it is rare these days. Heavy cream can be cultured to make a reasonable substitute using the following method. The result isn't by any means the same, but it is a plausible substitute.

Crème Fraîche

2 tablespoons all-natural yogurt, preferably biodynamic	2 cups 36% minimum milk fat heavy cream

1. Line a wire sieve with a double layer of cheesecloth and spoon the yogurt into it. Let it stand to drain away some of the whey (the watery liquid) for 30 minutes.

2. Pour the cream into a clean glass jar fitted with a tight lid that will hold it comfortably with room to spare. Add the drained yogurt, put on the lid, and screw it down tightly. Shake the jar until the yogurt is dissolved into the cream. Set it aside at room temperature until the cream is clotted and thick, about 4 to 6 hours if the weather is warm, or as long as 8 hours if it is fairly cool.

3. When the cream is thick, store it in the refrigerator. It should keep for about two weeks.
   Makes 1 pint.

Milk

Though buttermilk was the staple of old Southern pantries, fresh milk was used in much of our cooking. All the same, buttermilk was so ubiquitous that recipes differentiated fresh (that is, un-soured) milk by referring to it as "sweet." This practice lingers in many parts of the South, and one can even see it, from time to time, in supermarket advertisements. The ideal for all the recipes of this book would be certified raw milk, but it's sale is prohibited in many parts of the country. Use the freshest you can find, preferably not homogenized. Health or natural food grocers frequently sell certified raw milk where it is allowed, and non-homogenized pasteurized milk where it isn't.

In old cookery books, recipes frequently call for "rich milk." What they meant was true whole milk, that is, milk from which none (or very little) of the cream had been removed—very rich indeed. The closest we can come to approximating it is half-and-half. It isn't quite as rich, but it works fine. So wherever a recipe called for whole or rich milk, I have substituted half-and-half. If you can get true whole milk, it is preferable.

Eggs

Most of the recipes of this book specify "large" eggs, and were tested with fresh, large grade-A eggs locally produced from organically raised and fed hens. Almost all health food stores carry organically produced eggs, but commercial eggs will work if you are unable to get them. I prefer natural, organically raised eggs because they have more flavor and produce finer results in all instances. But also, since they are produced without hormones or antibiotics, they are less susceptible to contamination. Buying locally produced eggs gives you the added assurance that they are reasonably fresh.

FLOUR, MEAL, AND DRY GOODS

So critical is the proper flour and meal to Southern baking, that it seemed more prudent to discuss these ingredients in the pertinent section of the book. Only the briefest discussion and a few sources are given here. For detailed notes on Southern flour, see pages 307 to 308; for meal, see below; for grits, see page 284.

Wheat Flour: For the most part, Southern flours are milled from soft winter wheat. This wheat has a lower protein and gluten content, which makes it ideal for cakes, pastries, and quick breads. But the proteins and glutens that they do contain are of a very high quality, and I find that soft wheat flours also make excellent yeast bread, as well. In all cases, where recipes here call for plain, or all-purpose flour, unbleached, soft-winter wheat flour was used to formulate and test the recipe, but unbleached all-purpose flour gave acceptable results when tested in all the yeast bread recipes.

In other parts of the country, hard-summer wheat flour dominates. Its high protein and gluten content makes it difficult to work with in making good quick breads and pastries, because the glutens tend to toughen the dough. For quick breads and pastry, a reasonable substitute is unbleached pastry flour, or you can mail order soft wheat flour from some Southern mills:

White Lily Foods
P.O. Box 871
Knoxville, Tennessee 37901
(800) 663-6317
www.whitelily.com

The King Arthur Flour Company
Baker's Catalogue
P.O. Box 876
Norwich, Vermont 05055
(800) 827-6836
www.kingarthurflour.com
Ask for their unbleached, soft-wheat pastry flour

Corn Meal and Grits: For most Southerners, the preferred grain for meal and grits is white corn. But this isn't universal. My great-grandfather always had a little yellow meal ground for his family's use, though, admittedly, the miller thought he was strange. Nevertheless, Nathalie Dupree introduced me to at least one mill that produces both white and yellow meal, and it has regular Southern customers for both. Either type can be used in these recipes, though, for my taste, the most recognizably Southern flavor is provided by water-stone ground white meal and corn grits. It can be ordered by mail from a number of small Southern mills, among them:

The Old Mill of Guilford
1340 N.C. 68 North
Oak Ridge, North Carolina 27310
www.oldmillofguildford.com

The Kymulga Grist Mill (meal only)
Grist Mill Road
Childersburg, Alabama 35044

Hoppin' John's, John Martin Taylor's legendary cookbook store in Charleston, has closed since the first edition of this book was printed, but he still sells his excellent corn meal and whole corn grits, water-stone ground at a mill in Georgia, in his "online" store: on the web at www.hoppin-johns.com or call (800) 828-4412.

NUTS AND SEEDS

Almonds: These nuts were a frequently used ingredient in the pastry cookery of upper-class Southerners. For the recipes in this book, use whole, un-blanched almonds.

Benne Seeds (sesame seeds): Native to Africa, these flavorful little seeds have been an integral part of Southern cookery for more than two centuries, and almost always indicate the mind of an African cook. Look for raw sesame seeds. They are available in bulk from many health food stores and ethnic groceries, where they are usually fresher and less expensive than bottled seeds.

Peanuts: These are not actually a nut at all, but a legume that grows below ground. Though native to South America, peanuts were probably introduced into North America by way of Africa, where they had been taken by the Portuguese. They have been variously known in the South as groundnuts, groundpeas, goober peas, and goobers. They have myriad uses in the Southern kitchen. In the South, they are available whole (in shell), both green (freshly dug) and dried. They are also available shelled and blanched, both raw and toasted.

Pecans: Pecans are a native American nut closely related to walnuts. They were known to and enjoyed by Native Americans, who gave them the name by which they are still known, and introduced European settlers to their charms. They have long been used as a substitute for walnuts and almonds (they are also a wonderful substitute for pine nuts in pesto), but only since commercial cultivation have some of our more famous pecan recipes been developed. Pecan trees prefer a mild climate, and don't grow well much further north than Virginia (in fact, Jefferson had trouble growing them at Monticello), but they flourish in the milder climates of the Carolinas, Georgia, North Florida, Alabama, Mississippi, and Louisiana, where most of the commercial crops are cultivated. If you have trouble finding fresh pecans, excellent Georgia pecans can be ordered by mail from one of the sources given here.

Pearson Farms
1102 Highway 341
Fort Valley, Georgia 31030
(888) 423 4374
www.pearsonfarm.com

Ellis Brothers Pecans, Inc.
1315 Tippettville Road
Vienna, Georgia 31092
(912) 268-9041
www.werenuts.com

Sunnyland Farms, Inc.
Jane and Harry Wilson
Albany, Georgia 31706-8200
(800) 999-2488
www.sunnylandfarms.com

Pecans freeze well, and are best stored in the freezer if you must keep them for a prolonged period.

Walnuts: Black walnuts are also native to this continent and are widely used in Southern kitchens. Their flavor is richer, sharper, and more assertive than European (English) walnuts. Many Southern cooks today prefer black walnuts in their cooking and baking, but if they aren't available where you live, you may substitute English walnuts.

SALT

Salt, the universal mineral that has lately received so much adverse publicity (and without which we would die), has been used since the beginning of time by man to heal, to preserve, and to season. For most serious cooks, the only salt to use is pure kosher or sea salt, without additives. Both lend the best flavor and I find that I use far less when I cook with them than when using commercial table salt. Most stores carry kosher salt, and sea salt has become more common since the first edition of this book was published, but health food stores carry it in bulk, which is far more economical.

When buying packaged salt, look carefully to be sure that it is pure and free of additives, especially if you are using the salt for canning.

SUGAR AND CANE PRODUCTS

For the best and most authentically Southern flavor, use only pure cane sugar. White or refined sugar was once referred to as "loaf" sugar because it was packed in conical loaf shapes, but it was roughly the equivalent of our fine granulated sugar. Aside from that type, several varieties of cane products are called for in this book and are indispensable in a Southern pantry.

Demerara (or turbinado) sugar: This is a type of sugar that is sometimes marketed as "raw," but, actually, it has been partially processed. Since it is not completely refined, some of the natural molasses remains, lending a naturally blond, or light brown color. It is the original brown sugar. You should be able to find demerara in some health food stores and ethnic groceries. Turbinado sugar, which is similar, is more widely available and is even carried by some supermarkets. It can be substituted for demerara in any of these recipes. Commercial brown sugar is fully refined sugar into which molasses has been re-introduced. The flavor and texture is not as fine as demerara or turbinado sugar, but it can be substituted where either of these is called for in the recipes.

Molasses: Molasses is syrup produced by slow-cooking the juice of sugar cane. There are varying grades, seldom available outside the South. Look for pure, unsulphured molasses.

Sorghum syrup: Sorghum is an African grass related to sugar cane. The syrup produced from it has a distinctive taste all its own. It had long been used in the South, but during the War Between the States, it became particularly popular as a substitute for sugar and molasses, and has been common in the South ever since, so much so that to this day it is often simply referred to as "sorghum." It can be used interchangeably with molasses.

MISCELLANEOUS PANTRY STORES

Anchovies: Whole salt-packed anchovies from Spain were once imported into America by the barrelful. They were used not only as a flavoring agent on their own, but also as an ingredient in savory sauces, particularly a ketchup resembling the Southeast Asian fish sauce from which the name "ketchup" derives. Whole salt-packed anchovies, available in larger cities at some Italian grocers, are the highest quality and are preferable, but a good second choice is oil-packed fillets in clear glass jars (that way you can be sure of their quality). A distant third choice is canned fillets. I do not recommend anchovy paste.

Capers: Capers are the unopened flower buds of a plant native to the Mediterranean region. Salt-pickled capers have been used by cooks for thousands of years as a source of pure, concentrated flavor. Capers available to early Americans were, of course, imported and expensive—but they were available. Though advertised in newspapers as early as the late Colonial period, and frequently mentioned in cookbooks, that pickled nasturtium buds are a commonly suggested substitution for capers hints the real thing wasn't always available. The first choice is salt-packed capers, but if you can't get them, those packed in brine are perfectly acceptable. Salt-packed capers must be well washed before using.

Olives: The trustees of Colonial Savannah tried growing olives in their experimental garden on the east side of the settlement. Though the experiment was a failure, period newspapers advertised imported olives for sale, telling us that even the youngest and least developed of the thirteen colonies had such delicacies available to them. Whether the recipe calls for green or black (ripe) olives, for the flavor that old cooks would have known, use only imported Greek, French, or Italian brine-cured olives. So-called "ripe" canned domestic olives are often cured in ways you don't want to know about, and at any rate, will not bring the right flavor to the pot.

Beverages

NO OTHER PLACE IN THE WORLD is fonder of iced drinks than the South. That infamous Southern heat makes us turn early in the year to tall, cool glasses and linger over them well into autumn. Indeed, some of us never give them up at all. The origins of the peculiar ice habit that Europeans find so amusing in Americans can be blamed mainly on Southerners. In the eighteenth century, planters harvested ice from nearby lakes and rivers and kept it through the summer in half-buried, earth-covered icehouses. Harvested ice was also packed in straw and sawdust and shipped into the Deep South where cold weather was not prolonged enough to produce ice thick enough to be harvested. It was chipped or crushed to fill silver, copper, brass, or lead-lined mahogany wine coolers, where bottled beverages were embedded to chill. Needless to say, it was very expensive and only the wealthy could afford such a hot weather luxury. We didn't put ice directly in our glasses until the middle of the nineteenth century, when ice could be made without impurities inherent in the surface of a frozen lake, pond, or river.

Ordinary folk didn't use much ice in the summer until after manufactured ice made it widely accessible and affordable. It was then that our most famous iced beverages developed. Many have become so popular that they nearly eclipsed their parent preparations that were served either hot or at room temperature. For example, many Southerners still drink hot tea, but visitors to the South who want their tea hot had better say so; we Southerners take the ice for granted.

ICED TEA

There is an oft-repeated story that iced tea was invented at the 1904 St. Louis World's Fair by an English tea vendor to adapt his beleaguered business to the wilting heat of a Missouri summer. It's a good story; even some historians have fallen for it (at least two histories of tea have included it); and it appears regularly even in Southern newspapers and magazines, but it isn't true. By 1904, iced tea had been enjoyed in the South for at least thirty years and probably longer. The oldest printed recipe we know of is in Marion Cabell Tyree's *Housekeeping in Old Virginia* (1879); I have heard of (but not seen) an earlier, 1877, edition, and even earlier fictional references to iced tea. It is almost axiomatic that historical recipes predate their publication by at least a generation. Cold green tea punch was enjoyed in England at least by the late eighteenth century, and appeared in printed Southern books as early as Lettice Bryan's *The Kentucky Housewife* (1839). Except for being enlivened with alcohol, these punches weren't fundamentally different from the earliest recipes for iced tea—indeed, some early iced teas were laced with sherry, and most were made with green tea. When Indian black tea began flooding the market in the late nineteenth century, it eventually replaced green tea as the preferred leaf for an iced brew, though for a time, a few housewives continued to use a blend of both green and black tea.

Well. History is history: what's to the point today is that no beverage is as much loved as iced tea is in the South, and yet nothing is as often so poorly or indifferently prepared. In pursuit of the perfect brew, modern recipes use a dozen different and often contradictory methods to extract the liquor from tea leaves—the sun, a dark refrigerator, warm tap water, cold tap water, microwaves, drip coffeemakers—you name it, we've thought of it. But none work as well in practice as the time-honored method of steeping the leaves in water that is, as the English put it, just off the boil. You can make iced tea in cold water or with the warmth of the sun, and, while neither method produces as nicely developed a flavor, handled with care, they make fairly good iced tea.

There are recipes around that use hot tap water, but I must strongly admonish you never to use this method. Water heaters contain trace chemicals intended to keep the pipes from corroding. They weren't intended to produce drinking water and shouldn't be used for anything that you will eat or drink.

A few words of caution to ensure a clear, perfect brew: tea often clouds when refrigerated. This means the cook has made one of several mistakes: the brew has been allowed to boil, or was steeped for too long (and is therefore too strong), or was made with hard water (most city water is hard; use filtered water or a reliable bottled water instead). Finally, loose leaves are preferable to tea bags (with exceptions—see the notes with the recipe); the leaves are messy, but then you know you are not getting the crumbled dregs from the bottom of the crate.

2 quarts bottled or filtered water	Sliced lemon
1/4 cup loose black tea	Mint sprigs
Sugar to taste	

1. Bring 1 quart water to a boil in a clean kettle. Put the tea in a deep, heatproof bowl or large teapot. Just as the water begins to roll, pour it over the tea, give it a stir, and let stand 5 minutes.

2. Strain the tea through a coffee filter or fine wire-mesh sieve into a pitcher. Add the remaining quart of water and stir. Allow it to cool completely and serve it over ice with sugar, lemon and mint passed separately. Makes 2 quarts, serving 8 to 10.

NOTES ON VARIETIES: *Both Chinese green and Indian black teas were used in old recipes, but by the early twentieth century, the widespread importation of inexpensive Indian black tea took firm hold of the market and became the preferred variety for iced tea in most markets. America's first and only domestic tea plantation, near Charleston, South Carolina, (now owned by Bigelow) produces American Classic Tea. They don't sell loose tea, but the bags are made with whole leaves specially blended for iced tea. You may also check their website, www.charlestonteaplantation.com.*

House Wine of the South: Pre-sweetened tea, affectionately known as the "house wine" of the South, began to appear as early as 1880 but did not become commonplace until the 1930s, so I have given only the unsweetened version above. To make sweet tea, dissolve sugar in the strained but still warm infusion before cutting it with cold water, making it twice as sweet as you intend to serve it. I can't give you quantities; only your taste buds can guide you there; begin with about half a cup for the amount given above and adjust it to suit your taste. The advantage of sweetening the tea at the brew is that the sugar dissolves more easily and completely. The disadvantage is that once sweetened, it is far more perishable, so refrigerate leftovers promptly and use them within 2 days.

Alternative Method I—Sun Tea: This tea will not have as nicely developed a flavor as the previous method, but is still pretty good and completely foolproof. For this method, the water should be at room temperature. Put the tea into a 3-quart jar and pour all the water over it. Cover and put it out in full sunlight and let it steep until the tea reaches the strength you like. How long will depend on the ambient temperature, time of day, and intensity of the sunlight. At midday in the dog days of summer, I make tea by this method in as little as half an hour. In the winter, it may take 3 hours or more. Strain the tea through a coffee filter or wire-mesh strainer into a clean pitcher before serving.

Alternative Method II—Countertop Tea: Your apartment has no windows in the kitchen, and the living room faces north and hasn't got a balcony. First, you have my sympathy. You can still make creditable tea without boiling water. This method has the least developed flavor, but works when you don't want to heat up the kitchen and the tea will never cloud or be bitter. Put the tea in a 3-quart jar, add the water (all cold), cover, and let it stand for at least 4 hours or overnight. Strain it into a pitcher before serving. A similar method has become popular in recent years in which the tea steeps in the refrigerator. I always think tea made that way has an off taste, though that may just be my imagination.

Storing Iced Tea: Regardless of the method you use to make iced tea, refrigerate it when the weather turns warm, or it will ferment and taste sour. Keep it in a glass or glazed ceramic container that seals tightly. Plastic picks up, transfers, and holds odors that can be transferred to the tea, and metal can often give it an off, metallic taste.

COFFEE

"To have it in perfection, it should be toasted but a short time before it is made, and ground while it is yet warm: if it lies only twenty four hours after it has toasted, part of the flavor will be lost."

—Lettice Bryan, *The Kentucky Housewife*, 1839

"If you are particular about the flavor of your coffee, buy the best and roast it at home. To have it in perfection, coffee should be roasted, ground, and made in immediate succession . . . the quicker the roasting without scorching, the better."

—Theresa C. Brown, *Theresa C. Brown's Modern Domestic Cookery*, 1871

"Take equal quantities of Mocha, Java, Laguayra, and Rio. Have the coffee roasted a chestnut brown."

—Mrs. Mary C. Campbell, contributor to *Housekeeping in Old Virginia*, 1877

"Buy Java and Laguayra mixed, two-thirds Java and one-third Laguayra, which will give a delightful aroma to the Java."

—Mrs. J.P., contributor to *Housekeeping in Old Virginia*, 1877

Sadly, these careful instructions have virtually disappeared from American books, and the knowledge of them from our kitchens, even in the aftermath of the recent coffeehouse craze that swept our country in the nineties. But once, the blending and roasting of coffee in America was an accomplished domestic art; the quoted passages are only a sampling, and only from Southern writers, but the wisdom was not limited to Southerners. Eliza Leslie, one of America's foremost antebellum cookbook authors, wrote much the same words as Lettice Bryan in *Directions for Cookery in its Various Branches* (1837). Such instructions continued to be included in American books well into the twentieth century.

To some, coffee may seem out of place here, since iced tea has become the stereotypically Southern beverage of choice. However, coffee was so commonplace and important in antebellum Southern households, that when supplies were virtually cut off during the War Between the States, it was one of the most missed and lamented commodities. Many households had a store of green coffee laid by when the war began, and small amounts managed to filter into the Confederacy by way of blockade-runners, but by 1863, real coffee beans were so rare and expensive that there was a rumor in Atlanta that jewelers had bought them up and were using them as gemstones. Newspapers were filled with advertisements for imitation coffee, and housewives prided themselves on their own unique blends of almost everything imaginable, from parched acorns and okra seeds to pumpkins and sweet potatoes. The most common and, apparently, satisfactory of these substitutes was rye. Chicory, another common substitute, became so well liked that to this day it is still mixed with coffee in Creole New Orleans.

Modern Americans drink more coffee per person than ever before in our history—even more than when this book was first published a decade ago, and most households fortunately have better coffee choices. Yet despite that, most home-brewed coffee is not significantly better. Instant still claims a major share of the market, and much of the fresh brewed coffee is made from badly roasted beans and is so weak that it resembles nothing more than stump water. We look back on the coffee ads I cited a decade ago—in which a so-called gourmet restaurant duped its customers with an instant brew or pushed its brand with a serial romance between two supposed coffee connoisseurs who cannot live without their brand of instant—and think them naïve and dated, but our real appreciation for well-roasted and brewed coffee at home has not really improved with time.

Even with better choices in shop-roasted beans, it's still worth a coffee lover's time to learn to roast coffee beans for himself, if nothing else than to gain a better understanding of this fine art and of its importance in good American housekeeping during the first two hundred years of our history.

Green (un-roasted) coffee beans keep for a very long time, almost indefinitely, and there are aficionados who insist that aging improves them. Roasting causes the bean to expand and brings the oils with their heady fragrance to the surface. These volatile oils immediately begin to evaporate, and within a day, much of the flavor is gone forever. Once the beans are ground, even more surface is exposed to air, and evaporation is rapid indeed. All this is why, as Karen and John Hess have written in *The Taste of America* (1989), coffee shops smell so good, and yet the coffee never seems to match that aroma once you get it home. Vacuum-sealed containers prolong the shelf life, but once they're opened, the deterioration is immediate and rapid. Even though I immediately put shop-roasted beans in a sealed container, I begin to notice a difference within two days.

If you buy shop-roasted coffee (and most of us do), buy whole beans when they have just been roasted, or else have been sealed in a vacuum-pack, and in small quantities, certainly no more than you will use in a week. Keep the beans in a sealed canister in a cool place. Some recommend the refrigerator, but I think the cold damages the flavor, though this may be idiosyncratic on my part. Freezing is sometimes recommended, but it really does do irreparable damage to the oils. Always keep the beans whole and grind them just before brewing.

Stove-Top Pan-Roasted Coffee Beans

There are several ways of roasting beans at home. The first (and easiest) is in a roaster designed for home use, which are available from many online resources (see notes). Follow the manufacturer's instructions. However, you need not have a special appliance. They can also be roasted in your oven or on top of the stove. I haven't had very good luck with the oven method, but the stovetop method works very well.

1. Select a deep, heavy-bottomed, lidded pan (a long-handled one of coated aluminum is easiest to handle) that will hold all the amount of coffee you plan to roast in one layer. Heat it over medium heat. When it's quite hot, add the coffee beans, allowing at least a level tablespoon for each cup of coffee you plan to brew (or more if you like it stronger), and shake the pan to spread them evenly. They must lie in a single layer.

2. Immediately begin shaking the pan in a back-and-forth motion. If it begins to smell overheated and slightly scorched, raise the pan a little above the heat.

3. As the beans begin to color they will at first be uneven. Don't worry; they will even out as they roast. Cover and continue shaking and tossing until they begin to pop. They won't explode like popcorn, but they do swell considerably and make a distinct popping noise.

4. When the popping sounds begin to subside, remove the lid and keep shaking until the beans are a rich brown—about 15 to 20 seconds more. For French or Italian roast, toss them for another half minute or so, but don't let them scorch, and never stop shaking the pan. Remember, "dark roasted" does not mean burned. If the beans begin to smell like burned coffee, immediately pour them into a cold metal pan and spread them to cool.

5. When the beans are toasted, pour them into a cold metal pan and toss them for a minute or two more to let them cool and develop their aroma. They are ready to grind when they are almost cool, and they are best used within the hour. If possible, grind the beans and brew the coffee right away. If that isn't possible, let them cool completely and store them in a tightly sealed canister. In no case let the beans sit out for more than an hour.

NOTES: *Don't expect perfection from your first batch; it will take several tries to perfect your technique. As to the kind of coffee beans, I have experimented with Colombian, Kenyan, and Java beans. Java by itself is rather on the bland side for my taste. Colombian beans have a nice aroma and are good for everyday coffee; they are the flavor most Americans have grown accustomed to. Kenyan beans have a marvelously rich aroma and flavor. They cost more than Colombian beans, but are certainly worth it. Historically, a blend of Mocha and Java beans was highly prized.*

Despite (or, perhaps, because of) the popularity of gourmet coffee houses, home coffee roasting has grown in popularity since the first edition of this book was published. Just type "green coffee" into the search engine of your computer: you'll bring up dozens of companies specializing in home coffee roasters and green coffee beans. If you don't want to deal with online ordering, some specialty coffee-roasting shops will still sell you green beans, though often their selection may be limited. Ask your local shop. You can also still order green coffee from Epicurean Foods, 43 East Tennessee Avenue, Oak Ridge, TN 37830. Call (865) 483-1541 to check for current stock and prices.

BOURBON DRINKS

Juleps, possibly the most famous of Southern drinks after iced tea, are popularly supposed to have originated in Kentucky, where true bourbon is made—allegedly to take the edge of poorly made whiskey. Possibly, but both the name "julep" and the idea are very old, having Medieval French origins in a drink of sweetened water flavored with the fragrant oils of herbs and flowers. The modern julep of sweetened whiskey, mint, and shaved ice dates back to the second half of the nineteenth century. Early recipes contained no ice and were not necessarily flavored with mint. Mrs. Bryan's recipe, in *The Kentucky Housewife* (1839), which may be the oldest one in print, wasn't even called a julep. In a footnote to the recipe for rum toddy (sweetened rum cut with chilled water and flavored with nutmeg), she noted that the same drink could be made with brandy or whiskey and flavored with mint, anise, clove, lemon, or cinnamon. It's hard to imagine a cinnamon julep, but one flavored with strawberries is included here.

Recipes have evolved over the years, and many Southerners today use a pre-made simple syrup. Some even go so far as to boil the mint in this syrup, or even steep it in the refrigerator for a couple of days. No, no: there I draw the line. Absolutely, positively, do not use such an awful concoction. It makes the julep taste like mouthwash, and loses altogether the delicate flavor of freshly picked mint—which is, after all, the whole point.

Two Classic Juleps

Of the two recipes given here, the Corinthian julep is the traditional mint drink that most people have grown accustomed to. Both drinks are best made in silver julep cups, not only because they frost up better, but also because they keep the drink cold longer. You may, of course, use a glass tumbler. I am fondest of the Corinthian Julep both for its picturesque name and for the extra kick provided by hope and charity.

Have the cups ready on a tray so they can be served without your touching the frosty outer surface. There's nothing quite like taking hold of a frosty julep on a hot summer day. But go easy: there's also nothing like a frosty julep taking hold of you, either.

Corinthian Julep

"Corinthian," in this case, is a reference to St. Paul's famous poem to charity in his first epistle to the Corinthians, chapter 13, and refers to a julep made with 3 jiggers of whiskey (one each for faith, hope, and charity). It comes from Virginia Hudson's childhood essays *Oh Ye Jigs and Juleps*, written around 1900, and was coined by young Virginia's adult friend Mrs. Ada Harris, who, apparently, was never at a loss for words.

2 large, leafy sprigs mint, at least 2 inches long   3 jiggers (about 1/2 cup) bourbon

1 teaspoon sugar (or more, to taste)

1. Strip the leaves from 1 sprig of mint and drop them into the bottom of a julep cup or tumbler with the sugar. Muddle the mint and sugar until the mint is crushed. Add just enough bourbon to melt the sugar and muddle to combine.

2. Fill half the cup or tumbler with shaved ice and pour in the remaining bourbon. Without touching the cup or tumbler, stir until the outside of the cup begins to frost over.

3. Pack in the ice to the rim, insert a straw, and stir with the straw, again, never touching the sides of the cup, until the entire outside is frosty. Garnish with the reserved mint, pull out the straw (it isn't properly used for drinking), and serve at once. Serves 1.

Strawberry Julep

Before the howl of protest starts over this recipe's being neither Southern nor traditional, let me give you its pedigree. It was published more than half a century ago by Marion Flexner in *Dixie Dishes*. Mrs. Flexner's source was the household notebook of a famous antebellum Kentucky hostess, Mrs. Henry Humphries, a book that was then at least a hundred years old.

2 large, ripe strawberries   1-1/2 jiggers (about 1/4 cup) bourbon

1 teaspoon sugar   1 sprig mint

1. Have the julep cup or glass ready on a serving tray. Crush 1 strawberry well in the cup. Add the sugar and just enough bourbon to melt it, and stir until the sugar dissolves. Pack half the cup with shaved ice and add the remaining bourbon. Stir without touching the cup with your hands until the outside of the cup begins to frost over.

2. Pack the cup with ice to the rim and add a straw to one side. Stir with the straw until the cup frosts, never touching it with your hands. Remove the straw, garnish with the mint and remaining strawberry, and serve at once. Serves 1.

NOTES: *Since I did not have access to the original recipe, I do not know if the mint garnish and ice are original. I am inclined to doubt it, but have followed Mrs. Flexner on faith.*

Eggnog Kentuckian

Although eggnog is not an exclusively Southern holiday treat and can be made with virtually any spirit (except, God forbid, gin), and was originally made with French brandy, the version I prefer is this one from Kentucky, made with a well-aged bourbon. The eggs should be very fresh and the cream not ultra-pasteurized—if you can get it.

An interesting footnote to nineteenth century medicine is that eggnog sometimes turned up in household notebooks and cookbooks in the section for "invalid cookery." Well, one way or the other, you certainly wouldn't be sick long.

12 large eggs	1 quart half-and-half
1 cup sugar	1 quart heavy cream (minimum 36% milk fat)
1 fifth good, well-aged bourbon	Whole nutmeg in a grater

1. Separate the eggs into glass or stainless steel bowls; cover and refrigerate the whites. Beat together the yolks and sugar until they are light, lemon colored, and fall in ribbons from the spoon. Stir in the bourbon, cover, and refrigerate at least 8 hours.

2. Just before serving, beat the whiskey-yolk base until smooth again. Pour it into a punch bowl and stir in the half-and-half.

3. In separate bowls, whip the egg whites and heavy cream until they form soft peaks. Carefully, but thoroughly, fold each into the base—first the egg whites and then the cream. Dust the top of the eggnog with the grated nutmeg and serve it promptly with a shaker of grated nutmeg on the side for the individual servings. Serves about 30.

NOTES: *Pasteurized eggs are now widely available and remove most doubts about safely using raw eggs, but if these are not available to you and you have doubts about the safety of your eggs, or if you have health reasons for avoiding raw ones, you can make a very good eggnog with Boiled Custard (see page 377). Make a custard using the egg yolks, sugar, and half-and-half as directed in that recipe. Chill thoroughly, then mix in the bourbon. Omit the egg whites, but save and freeze them for another use.*

RUM

For centuries, rum from the Caribbean sugar plantations has been imported into the South, and it is one of the most widely used spirits in Southern kitchens. In colonial and early Republican America it was not supposed to have been considered suitable for "straight" consumption by anyone but sailors and was combined with fruit juice, tea, milk, and sugar before it came to the lips of a gentleman. It was never supposed to come into contact with those of a lady, except in cooking or a holiday eggnog. Though bourbon has, perhaps, replaced it as our national spirit of choice, rum remains an essential part of the Southern kitchen and is found in many venerable family recipes. Rum-and-fruit drinks (sometimes called planter's punch), descended from those cold tea and rum punches of the late-eighteenth and early-nineteenth centuries, remain popular here in the South. One particularly jolting version is Savannah's own Chatham Artillery Punch.

Chatham Artillery Punch

There's an old anecdote about the Georgia-Carolina tidewater saying that the question asked by three key cities when sizing up a newcomer actually reveals more of the character of each city's inhabitants than they may want you to know. In Charleston, they want to know who your "people" are; in Augusta, what your church is; and in Savannah, what your drink is. Nothing better confirms Savannah's reputation as a town that loves its spirits than its infamous Chatham Artillery Punch. This powerful concoction, like the advice of the old mountaineer to his son, speaks softly and carries a big stick. Though it is made with the most civilized of spirits, champagne, it can in no way be described as genteel. Try it only if you must, and don't bother to use a good champagne; though I am as devoted a Savannahian as they come, I think this is a hell of a thing to do to good wine and good friends.

The original recipe was supposedly devised just before the War Between the States by the Chatham Artillery to "honor" a rival military group, the Republican Blues, but another story, including a tale of its being served to President Monroe in 1819, and claims a Colonial origin—as unlikely as it is entertaining. More suggestive is its more than passing resemblance to Regent's Punch, a potent concoction from the table of England's Prince Regent, George IV, which was popular all along America's eastern seaboard. In the original recipe, brandy, whiskey, and rum in equal parts were mixed with sugar and thinly sliced lemons and left to steep for several days while the punch "matured." As a testament to its durability, it was mixed in horse-watering buckets. The tubs were filled with ice, over which large quantities of champagne were poured.

You'll need to start making this about a week before you plan to serve it. You've been warned.

1/2 pound green tea leaves
1 gallon cold water
14 large lemons
2 pounds turbinado or light brown sugar
1 gallon dark rum

1 gallon brandy
1 gallon rye or bourbon whiskey (it won't matter which)
1 case (12 bottles) champagne (are you sure you want to do this?)

1. In a large container, soak the tea leaves in the cold water overnight. Strain them into a large tub that will hold all the spirits. Juice 12 lemons and add the juice and sugar to the tea, stirring until the sugar dissolves.

2. Add the rum, brandy, and whiskey, stir, and cover. Let this stand at room temperature for several days, undisturbed. Trust me: nothing could hurt it at this point.

3. When ready to serve, thinly slice the remaining lemons. Pour the brew over a large cake of ice in a tub big enough to hold all the ingredients. Gently swirl in the champagne to disturb as little of the effervescence as possible, and garnish with the sliced lemons.

4. Put away anything breakable and serve. Makes 100 servings (that's 50 friends or 25 enemies).

NOTES: *The oldest recipes do not mention green tea or candied cherries, both of which are common today. Gin is often included in modern recipes, but that really seems like pushing an already pushy thing rather too far. This recipe includes tea, which has been traditional for a century and does have some historical precedence, but omits the questionable candied fruit and—God forbid—gin.*

Sherry Cobbler

The origin of the name for this old summer drink is lost in folklore, but it goes back at least to the early nineteenth century and is probably much older. The usual explanation is that the word "cobble" in old English meant "to patch up," which is presumably what it does for those who imbibe it. Regardless of its pedigree or meaning, cobbler is light, refreshing, and wonderfully cooling, with just enough kick to get you through a wilting August afternoon. Think of it as lemonade for adults.

12 to 14 large lemons	1 pint dry sherry, or more, to taste
1 cup sugar, or more, to taste	Mint sprigs, for garnish
5 quarts cold water	

1. Roll 10 to 12 lemons well, then halve and juice them through a strainer into a large punch bowl until you have 1-1/2 cups of juice. Dissolve the sugar in it. Slice the remaining 2 lemons as thinly as possible and add them to the bowl. Cover and let sit for at least 1 hour—2 is better.

2. When ready to serve the cobbler, add the water and sherry and stir until well mixed. Taste and adjust the sugar and sherry to suit, and add enough ice to chill it thoroughly.

3. Serve in tall glasses over plenty of ice, garnishing each serving with mint. Makes about 1-1/2 gallons, serving about 30.

Dishes for Teas, Receptions, and In-Betweens

AN APPETIZER IS A RECENT PHENOMENON that few nineteenth-century Southerners would recognize. Traditional Southern meals, except for the formal dinners of the gentry, have seldom been served in courses—at least, not in courses as we know them today. The elements of a multi-course meal may be on the table, but they are usually there all at once. Whenever I serve my family and Southern friends an Italian meal, with its graceful progression of antipasto, pasta, meat, vegetable, salad, and fruit, it is usually met with resistance, if not downright hostility. They do not want their food, as they put it, "dribbled at them."

During the nineteenth century, there was, thankfully, no such thing as a cocktail party with its array of "interesting" finger food, so this section does not contain the usual appetizers and cocktail tidbits that turn up so often in modern Southern cookbooks.

Southerners have not, historically, been snackers or grazers. Meals are ample and filling, leaving little room or desire for what is nowadays so aptly termed "junk food." Nonetheless, there have always been treats in the Southern pantry, ready to be offered with a morning cup of coffee, an afternoon glass of iced tea, or a reception cup of punch or champagne.

The reason is simple. For a Southerner, "hospitality" means just one thing: food. We may offer shelter to the storm-battered, a warm bed to the travel-weary, a strong shoulder for the bereaved, or a sympathetic ear to the heartsick. But it isn't hospitality to us unless something to eat and drink is offered with it. The horror of every Southern host is to be unable to offer unexpected company anything. In fact, a visitor, upon returning home, is inevitably asked, "Well, what did they give you to eat?" If it is nothing more than a bowl of toasted nuts and a glass of tea, we take for granted that we must offer *something*. So whether it's an elaborate wedding buffet or only a bowl of potato salad silently offered to a bereaved household, food is inevitably nearby whenever Southerners open their homes or hearts to you.

Except for one recipe, the contents of this section are a sampling of some of those traditional in-between foods. Some of them might have been served at the most elaborate reception or tea, a few would only be found in the humblest of households. But all of them have a lot to offer a modern reception or, if you really must, a cocktail party.

A PAIR OF CLASSIC SANDWICH PASTES

In the days before refrigeration, one way of preserving cooked meat was to spice it up, mix it with butter or some other fat, and pound it to a paste with a mortar and pestle. The paste was stored in a crock—or pot—and sealed with a coating of purified fat such as clarified butter or filtered lard. Hence the name "potted" meat. Now you know how those dismal commercial tins of ground up meat scraps called "potted meat" originated. Here are two classics that may change your mind about the whole idea.

Shrimp Paste

Modern recipes for this venerable Lowcountry dish can be complicated by up to a dozen ingredients. But the traditional ones, which have withstood the test of time and the canned-soup craze, are simple almost to the point of austerity, containing little more than butter and shrimp. To my way of thinking, those are the best, for their apparent simplicity is deceptive; rich, creamy butter is the perfect background for the delicate taste of the tiny inlet shrimp that inhabit our coast. One needs only the barest trace of onion or pepper to point up and enliven the taste; too much of either throws the entire dish out of balance.

Traditionally, shrimp paste appeared mostly on tea tables, supper-party buffets, and at breakfast, where it might be served sliced and lightly fried. Its richness withstands most cocktails, so it translates nicely to a modern cocktail hour, and makes a handsome first course for a summer luncheon. Still, there is nothing to equal a shrimp paste sandwich cut thin and served with a cup of good, hot tea.

1-1/2 pounds cooked shrimp, peeled	Salt and whole white pepper in a peppermill
1/4 pound (1 stick) unsalted butter, softened	Ground cayenne pepper
2 tablespoons grated shallots or yellow onion	Beaten Biscuits (page 320), crisp toast points, or Melba toasts

Modern food-processor method: The traditional methods for making this paste are given on the following page, and their texture is perhaps more interesting than the smooth paste made by the processor, but the machine makes such short work of it and produces a paste that is so much easier to mold and spread that, just this once, even I will admit to preferring it.

1. Fit the bowl of the processor with a steel blade and put in the shrimp. Cover and pulse until coarsely ground.

2. Add the butter and shallots and process until the mixture forms a paste. Don't over-process it to a mousse consistency: there should still be some texture. Season to taste with salt, a liberal grinding of white pepper, and a pinch or so of cayenne. Pulse a few times to mix the seasonings. Taste and adjust the seasoning and pulse until mixed.

3. Lightly butter a 3-cup metal mold, or two smaller molds, or a small loaf pan. Press the paste firmly into it, making sure there are no pockets of trapped air. Cover with a plate or plastic wrap and chill for several hours until firm.

4. To unmold, stand the mold in a basin of hot water for 1 minute. Loosen the edges with a knife, and invert the mold over a serving plate—the paste should come out with a couple of firm taps on the top of the mold. Smooth any gaps with a spatula and let it stand until it's soft enough to spread. Serve with Beaten Biscuits, toast points, or Melba toasts. Serves 6 as a first course, or 20 for cocktails or tea.

The Traditional Methods

If you want a taste of deep tradition, here are the two older methods for making shrimp paste:

With a mortar and pestle: This method was, of course, the original way of grinding the shrimp or meat to a paste. It is time-consuming, hard work, but nothing else will come close to the texture and flavor achieved by gradual pounding.

1. Coarsely chop the shrimp and put them, a few at a time, into a mortar with the shallots, pounding it gradually to a paste with the pestle. This will take a while and do weird things to your shoulder sockets, but it's a great arm workout.
2. Work the butter gradually into the paste with the pestle until it is smooth. Taste the paste and season it lightly with salt, white pepper, and the cayenne or hot sauce. Mix in the seasonings, then mold, chill, and finish the paste as directed in steps 3 and 4, above.

With a meat grinder: Later in the nineteenth century, cooks employed a meat grinder to make the paste. The end product was not nearly the same, but the shrimp did not completely surrender their original texture as they do with modern equipment.

1. Put the shrimp through the finest holes of a meat grinder. Mix them thoroughly with the shallots and put them through the grinder a second time.
2. Mix the shrimp with the softened butter. Taste and season the paste with salt, white pepper, and the cayenne or hot sauce. Mix in the seasonings, mold, and chill the paste as directed in steps 3 and 4, above.

Potted Ham Paste

Once, there was always a cooked ham in the pantry of large Southern households, even those of modest means. Most everyone raised pigs and cured their own hams, so there was always plenty. In some households, there was seldom any left over to put in the pantry. Martha Washington is reported to have ordered a ham from Mount Vernon's kitchen every day (that's nearly two hundred pigs a year). A cooked dry-cured ham kept for weeks if the cut end was covered with paraffin, and made an ideal supplement for a meager menu when unexpected company stayed to supper. Mrs. Washington, you understand, had a *lot* of unexpected company.

   This simple paste came out of those days when there was always cooked ham on hand to shave a few thin slices from (or salvage the last morsels from the bones) and beat them to a paste with softened butter. The paste was stored in a crock covered with a seal of clarified butter—true potted ham. Some cooks today mix in about 1/2 cup of chutney just before serving. Few of us can nowadays afford to keep a baked ham in the back of the refrigerator, but if you have more Christmas or Easter ham left over than you know what to do with, this rich, but simple spread is a fine alternative to sandwiches or bean casserole. Since the first edition of this book came out, many supermarkets and delis have started selling fully-cooked country ham, and it is also available online from vendors such as S. Wallace Edwards (see page 43).

Like Shrimp Paste, this was originally made with a mortar and pestle and, later, the meat grinder, but in this case, the food processor does an equally good job.

1 cup roughly chopped cooked country ham (see Country Ham in Champagne, page 200)	Ground cayenne
	Whole nutmeg in a grater
1 to 2 tablespoons bourbon	Beaten Biscuits (page 320), crisp toast points,
1/4 pound unsalted butter, softened	Melba toasts, or crackers
Whole black pepper in a peppermill	

1. Put the ham in the bowl of the food processor fitted with the steel blade. Pulse the machine until it is ground fine. Add a tablespoon of bourbon and the butter and pulse until it is a smooth paste. Add a few grindings of pepper and cayenne and nutmeg to taste. Pulse to mix, taste, and adjust the bourbon and other flavorings accordingly.

2. Press the paste into a crock and refrigerate until needed. If you like, for authenticity's sake you may cover it with clarified butter, a nice touch if you are serving it directly from the crock. Always let it soften to room temperature before serving, or spreading it will be next to impossible. Traditional accompaniments are Beaten Biscuits, but you may serve it with crisp toast points, Melba toasts, or crackers. Makes 1-1/2 cups of spread, serving about 20 (the recipe may be doubled).

A QUARTET OF CLASSIC TEA SANDWICHES

Small sandwiches were especially popular when tea parties became fashionable in the latter part of the nineteenth century. We find such sandwiches in Southern cookbooks as early as *Mrs. Hill's New Cook Book* (1867), and they have only grown more popular with time. Here are four that are timeless classics:

Cucumber Sandwiches

The essential tea sandwich, cucumber sandwiches also make a cooling quick lunch in the dead heat of summer. As an afternoon reception refreshment, they are predictable and maybe even a little hokey, but they are almost de rigueur for wedding receptions here in Savannah, and I never knew anyone who tired of them.

1 large (or two medium-sized) fresh cucumber	4 tablespoons unsalted butter, softened
Salt	Whole white pepper in a peppermill
6 slices firm, homemade sandwich bread	Fresh dill (optional)

1. If the cucumbers have been waxed, lightly peel them (I like to leave a blush of darker green) and slice them thinly with a mandolin, food processor, or sharp knife. Spread them on a platter in one layer, lightly sprinkle with salt, and set aside for about half an hour.
2. Trim the crusts from the bread and cut each slice into four equal squares. Lightly spread one side of each piece with butter.
3. Pat the cucumbers dry with a tea towel or absorbent paper. They will have thrown off a lot of liquid. Cover the buttered side of half the bread with them, slightly overlapping. Sprinkle with a few grindings of white pepper, and, if you like, a little chopped fresh dill. Top with the remaining bread, buttered side down. These are best eaten right away, but you may make them up to an hour ahead and cover them with a damp towel until ready to be served. Makes 12 tea sandwiches.

Radish Sandwiches

No taste is as evocative of spring as that of a crisp, spicy radish, and nowhere is that taste better showcased than in this light, but full-flavored sandwich. It is no mere variation of the previous recipe, even though, except for the vegetables, the ingredients are otherwise identical. Radishes lend a peppery bite that is miles away from the soothing coolness of cucumber.

These sandwiches translate well to cocktail hour, since radishes hold their own quite well against strong drinks. For a cocktail canapé, break with tradition (you're doing that anyway with the martinis), double the amount of radishes, covering all 24 pieces of bread (or even crisp toast points or crackers), and serve them open-faced.

6 to 8 red radishes, well scrubbed	About 4 tablespoons unsalted butter, softened
6 slices firm homemade white bread	Salt and whole white pepper in a peppermill

1. Slice the radishes cross-wise into paper-thin circles.

2. Trim, cut, and butter the bread, and assemble them exactly as you would the Cucumber Sandwiches (previous page), or double the amount of radish and leave them open-faced. Makes 12 tea sandwiches.

Tomato Sandwiches

The essence of summer in the South is a tomato sandwich—spread thickly with homemade mayonnaise and stuffed with beefy slices of juicy fresh tomato. They're by nature informal, easiest to eat over the sink while wearing an old T-shirt, because the juice inevitably runs down your arms and squirts all over your shirtfront. These, however, are safe even for formal occasions. I can (almost) guarantee that you can eat them without disaster. The secret is to salt the sliced tomatoes, press them flat, and let them shed the lubricating juice that otherwise sends the filling flying into your lap with your first bite.

2 large (or 3 medium-sized) fresh tomatoes	Whole black or white pepper in a peppermill
Salt	About 2 tablespoons freshly minced basil or
6 slices firm homemade white bread	mint (optional)
About 2 tablespoons Mayonnaise (page 117), or unsalted butter, softened	

1. Peel the tomatoes with a vegetable peeler and cut them in half crosswise (or lengthwise, if they are plum tomatoes). Gently squeeze out the seeds and juice. Slice them as thinly as you can (about $3/16$ inch thick), and lay them on a platter in one layer. Lightly sprinkle them with salt, tip one end of the platter to allow the excess juice to run off, and let them stand for half an hour.

2. Pat the tomatoes dry with absorbent paper or tea towels and assemble the sandwiches exactly as for Cucumber Sandwiches (previous page), spreading the bread with either mayonnaise or butter and using either white or black pepper as seasoning, to taste. If you like, you may chop a few fresh basil or mint leaves and sprinkle them over the tomatoes before covering them. Serve at once, or they will get soggy. Makes 12 tea sandwiches.

Strawberry Sandwiches

Really a variation on strawberry shortcake, these sweet sandwiches are a nice thing for wedding receptions or to pass with coffee at brunch in spring or early summer, when the strawberries are at their peak. For some Southerners, they were also a favorite childhood breakfast and supper. Don't make them ahead, as the sugar draws out the juice of the berries and make them soggy. You can have everything ready up through step 2, cover the biscuits and strawberries, and assemble them at the last minute.

12 Soda Biscuits (page 319)
1 pint ripe strawberries

1/2 cup Lettice Bryan's Cold Cream Sauce
  (page 378)
Sugar

1. Split the biscuits crosswise. Wash, stem, core, and slice the strawberries.
2. Spread a scant teaspoon of cream sauce over the bottom of each biscuit and top it with an overlapping layer of strawberries. Sprinkle the berries lightly with sugar, put on a small dollop of the cream sauce, and cover with the top half of the biscuit. Serve at once. Makes 12 sandwiches.

A PAIR OF PEANUT RECIPES

Peas, peas, peas, peas, eatin' goober peas!
Goodness, how delicious, eatin' goober peas!
—Civil War Era Confederate Soldier's Ballad

Groundnuts, groundpeas, peanuts, goober peas, or just plain goobers—whatever they've called them over the years, Southerners have long thrived on them. Margaret Mitchell didn't make it up; many men in gray stayed alive on a diet of corndodgers and parched or boiled peanuts. In some cases, goobers were the only rations the troops had, and, in the lean years of Reconstruction, they became a staple for civilians as well. You would think that Southerners would have had enough of them, and yet their popularity endures. Whether they are parched or boiled, most of us can eat them by the gallon.

Peanuts have an interesting history. Originating in South America, where remains have been found dating back thousands of years, they were introduced to Africa by the Portuguese, and so quickly assimilated into the food culture of that continent that, for a time, botanists believed them to be indigenous. Their early popularity in the South is surely due to African slaves, and some historians speculate that peanuts may have been introduced as a food crop for   slaves.

Parched (Toasted) Peanuts

Nothing more readily evokes thoughts of my father and grandfather for me as a pan of parched peanuts. As soon as the peanut harvest had cured and the weather turned crisp, one of them was always firing up the oven for a batch. I know of no snack that is simpler to prepare or more satisfying to eat. One pound of raw peanuts (in the shell) will last two polite people through about half an average football game, but it wouldn't last my father through the first quarter.

1 pound raw, whole peanuts (in shell)

1. Position a rack in the center of the oven, and preheat it to 275 degrees F. Wash and thoroughly dry the peanuts. Spread them on a rimmed baking sheet or sheet cake pan.

2. Toast in the center of the oven until the shells are dry and the nuts are crisp and colored a light, tawny gold. Begin testing them after about 45 minutes: take one out, let it cool enough to handle, and crack it. When done, the papery skin coating each nut will be flaky and dry and the flesh will be snapping crisp and lightly colored. If they're not ready, continue roasting, testing them every 10 minutes. They may take as long as 1-1/2 hours. Makes 1 pound, serving 2 to 4.

Boiled Peanuts

Here, peanuts cook in a way that reflects their true nature as legumes. They're supposed to be an acquired taste, but I've met few people worth knowing who didn't (eventually) love them. This is a regional specialty, since green peanuts must be freshly dug and don't take kindly to being shipped, so they aren't available outside their growing areas. In South Georgia, where former President Carter was raised, peanut farmers used to celebrate the harvest with "peanut boilings"—large outdoor parties where the peanuts were boiled in iron wash pots. A good boiling could draw several hundred people.

I can't give you quantities for a serving. If you love boiled peanuts, you won't be able to stop eating them; if you hate them, you won't eat more than it takes to find out. There isn't anybody in the country in between.

1 pound unshelled green peanuts　　　　　　　　Salt

1. Wash the peanuts in cold water to cover and drain well. Put them whole into a large pot in which the water can comfortably cover them by about an inch. Add cold water in quart batches until it covers them by at least an inch: the nuts will float, so test the depth of the

water by pressing them down. Sprinkle in a rounded tablespoon of salt for each quart of water and stir until it dissolves.

2. Turn on the heat to medium and bring to a boil. Reduce the heat to a simmer and cook until the peanuts are tender, at least an hour. Start tasting them after the hour and continue simmering until done to your taste. This could take as long as 2 hours; a lot will depend on the freshness and youth of the peanuts and how soft you like them.

3. Turn off the heat and let the peanuts stand in the brine until they are salty enough to suit you. Again, this varies from person to person, so let your own taste be your guide. They may be salty enough without any additional soaking, or they may need to soak for as much as half an hour. When they reach the right stage of saltiness, drain off and discard the brine. Serve the peanuts either warm or cold, but store the leftovers in the refrigerator—that is, if you have any. Makes 1 pound, serving 3 to 4 boiled peanut lovers (multiplies easily).

A PAIR OF PECAN RECIPES

Though pecans have long been used in Southern cooking, they've only been commonplace in the last century, when they became a commercial crop across the Deep South. In the last fifty years, toasted pecans have become standard at Southern receptions and cocktail parties. When I was growing up, there was a bowl of them in nearly every living room all through Christmas. Today, people expect them at my house whether the occasion is a quick drink after work, a glass of tea on a lazy Sunday afternoon, or a formal dinner. Pecan meats form in two distinct lobes in the shell, which are broken apart when the nuts are shelled. "Whole" here means one unbroken lobe.

Toasted Pecans

Pecans are usually roasted at a higher temperature, cooking in half the time given here. But I'm so absentminded that I was always forgetting them, ending up with more burned nuts than I care to admit. But since Martha Nesbit, a local food writer, taught me this slow-roasting method, my toasted pecans are always perfect. Don't feel confined to pecans. If you live where they're scarce and expensive, almost any fresh raw nuts are fine for roasting this way—almonds, cashews, filberts, shelled peanuts, or even walnuts.

A pound of toasted nuts will last comfortably through two drinks for 4 people, or 6, if you are serving other things and they are unbelievably polite. The quantities given here are for one pound. You may toast up to 4 pounds at a time, but don't try to roast more than that at once. Use a large, rimmed baking sheet for more than 2 pounds.

1 pound shelled whole pecans   Salt
2 tablespoons unsalted butter

1. Position a rack in the center of the oven, and preheat it to 250 degrees F. Spread the pecans on a sheet cake pan or rimmed baking sheet and place them on the center rack. Roast, stirring once, until they are hot, about 10 minutes. Cut the butter in bits, take the pecans from the oven, and scatter the butter over them. Stir until it has just melted and the pecans are coated.

2. Return the pan to the oven and roast, stirring occasionally until they begin to color, about 45 minutes. Don't let them turn dark; the nuts will darken and crisp as they cool, so don't over-roast them.

3. Salt the pecans to taste while they are still hot, tossing until uniformly coated, and let them cool before serving. In the winter, they make a welcome snack when they are still toasty-warm. Store them in a tightly sealed container, such as a glass jar or tin box.

Marcella's Pecans and Camembert

It was a golden moment: my mentor, Marcella Hazan, was sitting in my living room, enjoying Toasted Pecans for the first time in her life. Her husband, Victor, was pouring wine and passing crackers spread with Camembert. Suddenly, Marcella got the thoughtful look that all her students recognize, and, taking a couple of pecans, she pressed them into the soft cheese on the cracker she'd just been served. "I think this will be good," she said, and tasted. Naturally, it was. Turning to me, she laughed, "There, Damon, you can put that in your book and say that Marcella Hazan invented it for you in your living room."

As we talked about the different ways to serve the combination, I learned an important lesson about a master cook. She asked whether Southerners sometimes did things with pecans and cheese, and right away we thought of several. After all, cheese and nuts is a combination as old as civilization. Instead of being proprietary about her idea, however, Marcella was reassured. "There, you see?" she smiled, "It's a good idea."

Well, this is my book, and here is her recipe, invented for me in my living room. It is neither old, nor Southern, having come from the mind of an Italian cook, albeit one who loves good bourbon, and who thought of it while on Southern soil. So sue me.

1/2 pound Camembert cheese, in a single   1 dozen Beaten Biscuits (see page 320), or 24
   wedge, chilled   unsalted crackers
1 cup Toasted Pecans (see previous page)

1. Chill the cheese thoroughly. Meanwhile, set aside enough of the whole pecans to cover the top of the cheese. Coarsely chop the remaining nuts and spread them on a plate.

2. Remove the cheese from the refrigerator, trim off all the rind, and let it soften at room temperature until the surface is a little sticky. Place it on top of the chopped pecans. Gently press them into the sides of the cheese until they are covered.

3. Take the whole pecans and arrange them in rows on the top of the cheese, pressing lightly to make them adhere. Turn it and press chopped nuts into the bottom, carefully filling in any gaps. Turn it top-side-up onto a serving plate, let it soften to room temperature, then surround it with biscuits or crackers and serve. Serves 6 to 8.

NOTES: *Don't make this more than 2 hours ahead, or refrigerate it after applying the nut crust.*

Soups

SOUP, ON HOME TABLES IN THE SOUTH, tends to be a casual affair. Often, it is served right along with the main course, even, in some families, when the meal is formal, following the old style prevalent in England during the colonial period. When it stands alone as the main course, the atmosphere is always relaxed and easy. Likewise, soup making is a relaxed undertaking, especially when the cauldron is full of gumbo or catfish stew. Relaxed and casual does not, however, mean careless; good soup is easier to make than bad, but it still requires attention and care. It cannot be made to surpass what you put into it, and deserves the best that you can offer.

BROTH

A good broth is the foundation of so much good cooking, but especially of soups. It was once so important in the South that traditional recipes often began with instructions for making the broth. Many modern cooks who would not otherwise use canned goods are loose with canned broth in the soup kettle. Some even resort to using one or even several canned cream soups as a base. The only possible explanation for this slap-dash approach is that these cooks are so far removed from the original article that they have forgotten how a good soup is supposed to taste. Canned broth is convenient, but the penalty you pay in flavor is a stiff one. Once something from a can goes into the soup kettle, the taste can never be totally eradicated.

Traditional Southern cooks once used three kinds of broth: beef when they wanted deep color and robust flavor; veal when they were after subtlety; and chicken for a rich, but delicate flavor. Once, chicken was the most prized of all stocks and the most expensive, because it was made with a whole bird (whence came that old politician's promise of a chicken in every pot). Both fish stock and veal broth were used in fish soups and stews.

Broth takes a long time to cook, but requires little of the cook's attention, and now that we have freezers, keeping homemade broth on hand ought never to be a problem. The recipe following is for a moderate quantity. You can make more or less, allowing a quart of water for each pound of meat and bones.

Basic Meat Broth

This is a kind of master recipe, since the kind of bones determines the broth. The most usual were beef and veal, though pork was occasionally mentioned. For the best color and flavor, don't mix veal and beef bones.

For a broth of more intense color, the bones can be browned first in the oven. Toss them with just enough oil to coat them and bake them in a 400-degree F oven until well browned, about half an hour. Be careful not to scorch them, or they'll give the broth an unpleasantly acrid taste. Veal bones are never browned, since part of the appeal of veal broth is its pale, delicate color.

Careful skimming is critical to insure a broth of clarity and delicacy. If it is skimmed diligently and the simmer is kept imperceptible, the broth will be crystal clear without clarifying.

6 pounds meaty bones, shank, neck, tail, knuckles, or feet

6 quarts cold water

2 medium onions, 1 peeled but left whole and 1 peeled and thinly sliced

3 whole cloves

1 ripe tomato (optional, for beef broth)

1 carrot, peeled and thinly sliced

1 rib celery with leaves attached, thinly sliced, but with leafy top left whole

2 or 3 sprigs each parsley and thyme

2 bay leaves

1 teaspoon peppercorns

1 quarter-size slice fresh ginger

Salt

1. Warm the bones and water in a heavy-bottomed 10- to 12-quart pot over very low heat until the scum begins rising to the top, about 45 minutes. As soon as scum begins to form, carefully skim it off, and continue to do so as more forms. Do not stir the broth, now or hereafter.

2. When the scum no longer forms, let it simmer for half an hour. Meanwhile, stick the whole onion with the cloves. Raise the heat to medium and add both onions, the optional tomato, carrot, celery, parsley and thyme, bay leaves, peppercorns, and ginger. Add a large pinch of salt and let it return to a simmer, again carefully skimming off the scum as it rises to the surface.

3. When it returns to a simmer, reduce the heat as low as you can get it and gently simmer, uncovered, for at least 3 hours, checking periodically to make sure it never boils, but simmers very slowly, the steam bubbles not quite breaking the surface. Turn off the heat and let it cool.

4. Carefully strain the broth into lidded stainless steel, enameled metal, ceramic, or glass containers, discarding the solids. Let it cool uncovered, then cover tightly and refrigerate. It will keep like this for 4 or 5 days. To store it longer, chill it, skim off the fat, spoon it into freezable containers, seal, and freeze. It will keep for at least 3 months. Makes about 5 quarts.

Chicken Broth

Stewing hens or scrap parts make excellent broth, and they are inexpensive. Alas, rare is the butcher who can give you the feet nowadays; they make the finest consommé. For a broth of almost unimaginable body and flavor, splurge on a fat capon. When I make chicken drummettes, I'll save and freeze the wing tips to use in the broth pot: they add wonderful body.

1 whole stewing hen, about 6 pounds, or the same weight in necks, backs, wings, and feet

6 quarts water

2 medium onions, 1 peeled but left whole and 1 peeled and thinly sliced

2 to 3 whole cloves

2 medium carrots, peeled and thinly sliced

1 rib celery, with leaves attached, thinly sliced but with the leafy top left whole

2 to 3 sprigs each parsley, sage, and thyme

2 bay leaves

1 teaspoon whole peppercorns

2 quarter-sized slices ginger

Salt

1. Using the above ingredients, make and store the broth in exactly the same way as Basic Meat Broth (page 80), cooling and refrigerating it as soon as possible. Makes about 5 quarts.

> NOTES: *If you have used a whole chicken, it can be retained and served as a main course, cold, with Mayonnaise (page 117), or in Theresa Brown's Chicken Salad (page 279), or warm, with Oyster Sauce (page 120).*

A FEW SOUP ESSENTIALS

While making good soup is not complicated, it is not as simplistic as many people seem to think. Cooks who should know better dump everything in a pot and boil until it is tender, pasting it up with flour if there's company, entombing it in the refrigerator if the weather is hot. For them, soup is an afterthought, something to dress up a company dinner at the last minute or feed an invalid who doesn't much care what his food is like. It's no wonder such cooks seldom bother. Contrary to this indifference, good soup does require more attention and care than it is usually given. A few words, then, on basic technique:

- Meat, fish, shellfish, and poultry, regardless of whether they're only for flavor or will turn up in the soup later on, must poach gently at a barely perceptible simmer, the surface of the liquid merely shimmering, with the air bubbles not quite breaking the surface. When it is used only to flavor broth, the meat is added to cold water, to extract all its flavor; but when it is an integral part of the soup, it is added when the liquid (usually an already flavorful broth) is not quite boiling, to help preserve its texture and flavor.

* Vegetables, especially green ones, are added to liquid that is fully boiling and are cooked quickly to preserve their color and texture. There are exceptions, of course, when the vegetables are meant to surrender their flavor and texture to a mellow blending with the other ingredients.

* Most soups should not be held over heat after they are ready. They can in many cases be made ahead, which, of course, is one of their charms, but most of the time should not be reheated and finished until just before serving. Though some soups benefit from an indeterminate simmer, for others such treatment is fatal. A soup that has been thickened, for example, may separate and curdle if it cooks any further.

Thickeners

The free hand that modern cooks have with flour in soup is probably one reason that they turn to cans of cream soup with such frequency. Really old recipes did not use flour as a thickener; traditional Southern ones use it sparingly. The true art of thickening soup is the art of reduction, of egg liaisons, and of suspended purées.

Reduction: When the water content of broth or cream is evaporated, the solids and fats are concentrated and suspended, naturally thickening the liquid that remains. It is a simple process, requiring of the cook only a modest heat and enough patience to watch, stir, and wait while the soup does all the work. Reduction is most often used in soups where cream is present, but it can also benefit certain broth-based preparations. Using reduction, one can also transform a broth or pot liquor into a sauce of great delicacy and character. The only trick is to pay attention. Frequent stirring prevents the solids from abandoning the liquid and sticking to the pan.

Egg liaisons: Chicken eggs, whether raw or previously hard-boiled, are the most usual egg thickeners for soup, but sometimes, as with turtles and crabs, the animal comes with its own eggs, and a good Southern cook will press them into service (where conservation laws allow it).

Whether they are raw or already cooked, eggs should only be added to the soup when you are ready to serve it. An egg liaison is a delicate thing and cannot be reheated. The secrets to success are several: a careful tempering of the yolks, a soup that is simmering, but not boiling, and a constant, vigorous hand at stirring. Using a wire whip to stir an egg liaison will help hold it in suspension and lessen the risk of the egg curdling.

Puréeing: The most artless of thickeners, but often the most delicious and satisfying, are purées of part of the solids that have gone into the making of the soup. With the advent of electric blenders and food processors, this old art is coming back, but, unfortunately, the machines do their job too well, and the purées that are popular today do not have as nice a texture. The problem is that machines are so effective at pulverizing the vegetables that their texture is eliminated altogether. Nothing is more boring than a soup that is smooth through and through.

Purées were traditionally accomplished by forcing the solids through a sieve or by pounding them in a mortar. Neither process totally breaks down the food, and leaves some texture to give the soup character. The best way to approximate the texture of these methods is to use a food mill. In some instances, it is superior to a food processor because it strains out strings, bones, and bits of peeling that the machine cannot. You can, however, come close to the original intent with a stick blender, or with the food processor if you pulse it so that some of the solids are tossed away from the blades and remain partially intact, or purée only enough of the solids to thicken the soup, leaving the remainder intact for additional texture and interest.

Flour: Wheat flour is the simplest and most foolproof thickener, but also the one with the least character and finesse. Old cooks used a handful of soft breadcrumbs, a far better choice. When flour finally appeared in the soup kettle, it was used sparingly in a buerre manié, lumps of butter rolled or kneaded with a little flour. These were swirled into the soup at the end of the cooking, delicately suspending the butter and flour in the broth. As the nineteenth century progressed, the amount of flour in recipes increased; the subtlety of delicately suspended butter was lost. Our century has done no better; soups that began with a teaspoon of flour for three cups of liquid have ended up with as many as three tablespoons for the same amount. That's not soup; it's gravy, and not even a very good one.

Soft breadcrumbs: Made from the tender, inside part of the loaf, these make a delicate, almost gossamer liaison for soups and sauces, providing body without the pasty quality that raw flour sometimes lends. In most cases they make a superior thickener; they simply simmer in the broth until they have disintegrated into a delicate suspension. But when you don't have them, flour can be used successfully. Just remember that subtlety is the aim; a little goes a long way. Suspend the flour first in fat or cold water, or it will stick to itself and coagulate into hard lumps. Be sure that it cooks, either before it goes into the soup (as in browned flour), or after it is added, to keep it from tasting pasty and raw.

Garnishes

Old Southern soups were often served with some kind of embellishment: a few crisp croutons, a bit of sliced egg or lemon, a sprinkling of herbs, a dollop of cream. On the surface, they appear to be mere window dressing, but they are actually an integral part of the soup, the final touch that transforms it from broth and meat to magic. A proper garnish is never an afterthought, but a careful pairing of flavor and texture.

Croutons: Bits of crisply toasted bread are an ancient garnish for all kinds of soups. They complement fish stews, give contrasting texture to creamy purées, and lend substance to clear consommés. In the South, the fat is usually butter, and the bread a good, crusty loaf of wheat bread, but some have made them with cornbread. Making them is simple.

Buttered Croutons

Cut 1/2-inch-thick slices of a good but day-old homemade bread into small, bite-sized cubes. For every cup of cubed bread, allow 2 tablespoons of butter. Melt the butter over medium heat in a heavy skillet that will comfortably hold all the bread. Add the bread cubes and quickly toss them until they are coated. Sauté, tossing frequently, until they are golden brown and crisp.

For another way requiring less attention, preheat the oven to 300 degrees F. Put the butter in a shallow baking pan that will hold all the bread cubes in a single layer, and melt it in the oven. Add the bread and toss until it is well coated. Return the pan to the oven and bake, stirring from time to time, until they are lightly browned and crisp, about half an hour.

Dumplings and quenelles: Whether they poach delicately in a clear consommé, enrich a cream soup, or are encased in leaves (such as in Green Frog, or Stuffed Spinach Soup, page 94), or in shells such as crawfish or shrimp heads, delectable dumplings often appear in Southern soups. Recipes for each are contained in the ones for the soups where they appear, but a few words on techniques for using them are in order.

- Dumplings should be kept light and delicate. Use only enough egg to bind them together, and take care not to make them heavy with too much egg, flour, or crumbs. Keep the seasonings lively, especially in quenelles or stuffed casings, as some of their flavor will be lost to the broth.

- Dumplings must never be indifferently dropped into boiling broth or soup or they will fall apart, even if they are encased in something. Carefully slip them into simmering liquid, using a slotted spoon.

Eggs: Sometimes, egg is not used as a thickener, but as an enrichment for an already thick soup. When this is the case, whether they are poultry eggs or fish roe, they are almost never added to the soup until after it has been taken from the heat. Once they are added, the soup is disturbed as little as possible, to keep them from breaking up and dissolving into the liquid. They are not an optional extra; the texture and flavor that they bring to a soup is an integral part of it.

Lemons: Sometimes, lemon juice or rind is added to a soup as a seasoning, but, more often, lemons appear in Southern soups in paper-thin slices floating on the top of an individual serving. As each person eats, the lemon is gently pressed with the back of the spoon, gradually releasing fresh lemon juice into his portion. The flavor is not blunted by cooking, nor totally dispersed, and meets the taste buds in unexpected, fragrant bits.

Cream: When uncooked cream is dolloped into the center of a portion of soup, it does much more than make an attractive spot of white in the center. Wonderful things happen to the texture and flavor. As one dips into the soup, the cream disperses gradually, adding dimension to the texture and flavor. In combination with hot soup, it adds interest, and enriches a cold one without the graininess of coagulated cooked fat.

TOMATOES IN SOUP

Tomatoes are so important to Southern soups that I end here with a few words about them. One is always learning from unexpected sources. I know I will learn whenever I talk to cooks like Karen Hess or Marcella Hazan, but one of my most important lessons with tomatoes came from my older brother, who is not a cook at all. While were talking one day, he remarked on the difference in fragrance between fresh and canned tomatoes. "That's what made MaMa's soup so good: The smell of those fresh tomatoes cooking. Most of the cooks that I know use canned tomatoes in their vegetable soup, even if everything else they put in it is fresh, and it doesn't smell right." How right he is; it doesn't taste right, either. I still sometimes use canned tomatoes, but no longer happily ignore the sharp bite they sometimes bring to my cooking, and have learned not to use them in some soups, such as the Tomato Bisque found on page 97.

In an ideal world, these recipes would only be made with fresh, truly vine-ripened tomatoes. But, our world, alas, is far from ideal. When you must, reasonable results can be gotten with good-quality canned Italian *San Marzano* tomatoes. Be careful: *tipo italiano* on the label does not necessarily mean that they came from Italy or are a true Italian variety. The one soup in this book that absolutely cannot be made with canned tomatoes is the Tomato Bisque mentioned above; only fresh ones will bring to it the lovely flavor that sets it apart.

I am told that frozen tomatoes are beginning to appear in some markets, though I haven't seen them. Freezing irreparably damages the texture, but where texture is not critical to a recipe, they work well in soups, sauces, gumbos, and in scalloped or stewed tomato dishes. Though cold does affect their flavor, it does not do so nearly as severely as does canning. If you have a nice, roomy freezer, try freezing them yourself. My mother blanches, peels, seeds, and crushes the tomatoes before freezing them, but all you have to do is wash, pat dry, and freeze them whole—without blanching or peeling them—in tightly sealed freezer bags. The peeling helps to protect the flesh from freezer damage, and it slips right off when the fruit is thawed.

VEGETABLE SOUPS

Paradoxically, my grandmother made her best soup in the summer, when vegetables were their freshest and the last thing anybody wanted was hot soup. But hot soup today meant cold vegetable soup tomorrow, when the flavors had melded and the soothing coolness went a long way to make one forget, for the moment, a searing August day.

Southern Vegetable Soup

If you are familiar with Italian Minestrone, you will be struck by the similarities this recipe bears to the basic method. The big difference here is that the vegetables are added directly to the boiling broth instead of simmering butter, but the progression of additions is virtually the same. This similarity really shouldn't surprise; both are stout country soups making do with whatever happens to be on hand.

It was characteristic of my grandmother to advise that her soup was all guesswork. "I never measured anything for soup, so just guess." Of course, she measured—with the eyes and nose and taste buds of an experienced cook. She also drew on the experience of generations of family cooks, all of whom had learned to cook not by reading, but rather with their senses by watching, feeling, tasting, and smelling. Her "recipe" evolved from years of doing the same. When she tried to write it down for me, it was a hopeless, unintelligible mess. I have basically constructed this recipe from years of watching her cook. While I can't give you her measuring tools, I've tried to compensate by giving you some of her spirit.

Everyone must have a secret favorite dish that does as much to feed the soul as it does the body with its memory-packed flavors and smells. This one is mine. In it are all the best memories of my childhood: a sunny, yellow kitchen, a laughing, teasing grandfather, and a loving grandmother who was a peculiar little boy's best friend.

1/4 pound lean salt-cured pork side meat, rinsed and patted dry

1 pound leftover pot roast (with broth), or stewing beef such as chuck

10 to 12 medium tomatoes, scalded, peeled, and seeded as directed on page 262, with their juices reserved, chopped

1 cup butter beans or butter peas (see notes)

1 cup speckled butter beans (see notes)

1 cup mature pole beans, shelled (see notes)

1 cup pole beans, strung and cut up

2 large white or yellow onions, trimmed, split lengthwise, peeled, and chopped

2 ribs celery, strung and chopped

3 carrots, peeled and sliced about 1/4-inch thick

2 cups shredded fresh cabbage

1 teaspoon or so of sugar

Salt and whole black pepper in a peppermill

3 medium yellow crookneck squash or zucchini or both, mixed quartered and sliced

1 cup fresh, thinly sliced okra

1 cup green peas (see notes)

1 cup corn kernels, freshly cut from the cob

1. In a 6-quart kettle, sauté the salt pork over medium heat until the fat is rendered out of it and the fatty tissues are golden brown. Drain off all but a spoonful of the fat.

2. If you are using pot roast, add its broth to the pot with enough water to make three quarts of liquid. Cut the meat into 1-inch cubes and add it after the broth begins to boil. Skip to step 3. If, you are using fresh beef, put it in the kettle and brown it first in the fat rendered from the salt pork over medium-high heat, then add 3 quarts water. Let this simmer for at least 1 hour before any vegetables are added to the pot.

3. Add the tomatoes and return the soup to a boil. Add the butter beans or peas, speckled butter beans, and shelled pole beans. Return to a boil, reduce the heat to low and cook at a simmer, loosely covered, for half an hour.

4. Stir in the chopped onions and celery, then the sliced carrots. Cover again and simmer for another half hour, and add the cabbage. Taste the broth and season it with the sugar, and salt and pepper to taste at this point, then cover it and let it simmer for another half hour, or until the cabbage is tender. By now the beans should be very tender, but not mushy.

5. Add the squash and okra to the pot. Simmer 20 minutes more and then add the peas and corn. Now cook the soup only until the corn and peas are cooked through—no more than 15 to 20 minutes more. The heat in the soup will continue to cook the vegetables for a while after you have actually turned off the heat. If you plan to serve the soup cold, turn off the heat immediately after adding the corn and peas and let it sit, tightly covered, for about 10 minutes. Then remove the lid and set the pot in a cool place until it is cool enough to refrigerate. If the weather is especially warm, and it is likely to be so when you make this soup, cool the soup in a large bowl set in an ice water bath to hasten the cooling. Refrigerate as soon as possible. Serves 16 to 20 as a first course, or 8 to 10 as a one dish meal.

To serve vegetable soup cold, refrigerate it overnight (24 hours is even better) to allow the flavors to meld. The next day, take it from the refrigerator an hour before serving, skim off any fat that has congealed on the top, and allow it to return almost to room temperature. Add a little cold water if it's too thick, but don't dilute it too much, as it should be thick and rich.

> NOTES: *My grandmother was a native of North Georgia, and it was reassuring to find that her way of doing vegetable soup is very much like Annabella Hill's.* Mrs. Hill's New Cook Book *also included a vegetable soup au maigre that was virtually identical to Minestrone alla Romagna, with the vegetables added one at a time to simmering butter. In New Orleans, vegetable soup au maigre was puréed and enriched with cream—so much for meager: au maigre in old French Creole cookery just meant that there was no meat in the pot.*

- If you have a good, rich meat broth on hand, you may omit the beef and skip steps 2 and 3, and make the soup with the broth instead. If you use canned broth, don't tell me about it, and dilute it with 2 parts water to 1 part broth.

- Unfortunately, this soup will be very different made outside the South. Many ingredients that my grandmother routinely used will not be in season at the same time in cooler climates, and some of the beans given here are difficult to find in other regions.

- Butter beans are related to limas, but are smaller and have a buttery taste, hence the name. Butter peas are in the same family, but smaller, about the size of a navy bean. You may substitute fresh small limas such as Ford Hooks for these, or use good-quality frozen ones.

- Speckled butter beans are brightly colored when mature, like cranberry beans, but turn brown when cooked. They have a distinctive flavor of their own for which there is no equivalent. You could try substituting fresh fava or cranberry beans.

- "Pole bean" is a generic Southern term for any green bean that grows on climbing vines. As a rule, they have a more distinctive flavor than supermarket green beans. They produce lovely legumes when mature (in the deep South, mature ones are called, "shelly beans" because the pod is too tough to eat). They're essentially the same as French flageolets. If you can't get them, substitute pinto, Great Northern, or cranberry beans—either fresh or reconstituted and parboiled dried ones. For pole beans, use the broad, flat green beans, sometimes labeled "Italian" beans. It was pointed out to me by Northern friends that there was no way that English peas would be in season at the same time as most corn and tomatoes. Actually, my grandmother used them only when she could get late peas that occasionally overlap the early corn and tomatoes down here. In some seasons this happened, in some it didn't. If memory serves, she left them out more often than not, and sometimes even opened a can. I do like peas in it, however, even if they are frozen.

Asparagus Soup

Few modern Southern cookbooks have any good recipes for asparagus soup (why, I do not know), but it was so universal with nineteenth century books that I found myself using each recipe as a standard by which the rest of the book was judged. How each author dealt with asparagus told me what kind of cook she really was. This fragile and precious vegetable must be treated with finesse and respect, never indifferently, and certainly not with overblown vulgarity. It is so exquisitely simple that it can be ruined in a heartbeat. The only thing easier to cook and even easier to ruin is an omelet.

The best recipe for asparagus soup was Lettice Bryan's in *The Kentucky Housewife*. Mrs. Bryan's reputation as a cook could stand on her recipes for asparagus alone. After studying her book, I decided that sitting down at her table would have been more than a privilege; it would have been a religious experience. Trying to improve on Mrs. Bryan would be like trying to rewrite one of Beethoven's sonatas. This recipe is hers.

1 quart Chicken Broth (page 82) or Basic Meat Broth made with veal bones (page 80)
1-1/2 pounds young asparagus
1 tablespoon butter
Salt and whole black pepper in a peppermill
1 cup heavy cream at room temperature
1 cup Buttered Croutons (page 85)

1. Bring the broth to a boil in a large pot set over medium heat. Meanwhile, peel the asparagus and drop it briefly into a basin of cold water.

2. When the broth begins to boil, take up the asparagus, cut off the pointed tips, and cut the stems crosswise into 1-inch-long pieces. Set aside a dozen or so of the tips.

3. Drop the remaining asparagus and the butter into the boiling broth. Let it return to a boil, then cover and lower the heat. Cook at a good simmer until the asparagus is tender, about 5—and no more than 10—minutes. Season it to taste with the salt and pepper. While the soup is simmering, coarsely chop the reserved tips and set them aside.

4. With a slotted spoon, take out about a cup and a half of the greenest stems and tips and put them to the side in a covered bowl. Purée the remaining solids with the broth by forcing them through a sieve as Mrs. Bryan originally directed, or through a food mill. If you are not that energetic, a stick blender or food processor does this job nearly as well.

5. Return the soup to the pot and heat it through over medium heat. Stir in the reserved cooked asparagus and cream. Simmer until just heated through, stirring well, and turn off the heat.

6. Ladle out the soup into individual heated soup plates and garnish with croutons and a sprinkling of the chopped raw tips. Serves 6.

Black (or Turtle) Bean Soup

This is one of only a few dried bean soups to be found in nineteenth century household note-books, and was considered elegant enough for company. In Savannah, it ranked in elegance just below turtle soup—a very high ranking indeed. In Florida, where black beans and rice are a staple of the bourgeoning Cuban population, it is widely assumed there that this soup was intro-duced to the peninsula by the wave of political émigrés, but it wasn't. It was almost universal in America, turning up with only minor variations from Boston to Charleston, Savannah and New Orleans. In that latter city, virtually the same treatment is given to red beans, but instead of lemon, raw egg is beaten into the soup after it has been taken off the heat.

Some notes on the ingredients: Garlic is listed as optional because not all recipes contained it, (though some did, and it is nowadays usual in Savannah). The slices of lemon are not an option; they are not merely garnish, but an important part of the seasoning that each diner infuses into his portion by pressing the slice with the back of his spoon.

1 pound dried black beans	2 fresh ripe tomatoes, scalded, peeled, and seeded as directed on page 262, and chopped
1/2 pound lean salt-cured pork	
1 quart Basic Meat Broth (page 80)	1 bay leaf
2 large white onions, trimmed, split length-wise, peeled, and chopped	2 or 3 sprigs parsley
	6 whole cloves
1 large clove garlic (optional), lightly crushed, peeled, and minced	Salt and whole black pepper in a peppermill
	2 large hard-boiled eggs, peeled (optional)
1 large carrot, trimmed, peeled, and chopped	6 to 8 tablespoons sherry (1 tablespoon per serving)
1 small turnip, trimmed, peeled, and chopped	
2 ribs celery, strung and chopped	1 or 2 lemons, sliced thin

1. Wash the beans thoroughly, drain well, and put them in a pot that will hold all the ingred-ients. Add enough water to cover by 2 inches and soak them for at least 6 hours or overnight.

2. Pour off any remaining soaking liquid and measure it. Put it back in the pot with enough water to make 2 quarts. (If you live in an area with especially hard water, you might use distilled water or add a pinch of soda.) Bring it slowly to a boil over medium heat, skim-ming off any scum that rises to the top. When it begins boiling, reduce the heat to a bare simmer and cook, uncovered, until the beans are tender, about 45 minutes.

3. Add the salt pork and meat broth, raise the heat again to medium, and bring the soup back to a boil. Add the onions, garlic, carrot, turnip, celery, and tomatoes. Let it return to

a boil and skim off any scum that rises. Add the bay leaf and parsley. Pound the cloves to a powder with a mortar and pestle or spice mill, and add them with a healthy pinch of salt and a liberal grinding of black pepper. Go easy on the salt at first; the pork and broth will both contribute some salt and you can adjust the seasonings later. Reduce the heat to a slow simmer, cover, and cook until the beans are very tender, about 2 hours.

4. Take out a cup of the beans and purée them through a food mill or force them through a wire sieve. This step can also be done in a food processor. Usually the old recipes directed that all the beans be puréed, and while that does make the soup more elegant, it is also less interesting. (If you choose to purée all the beans, you may need to thin the soup some with additional water or stock.) Stir the puréed beans back into the broth to thicken the soup, and let it heat through. If it isn't thick enough, purée a few more spoonfuls of beans until it is thick enough to suit you.

5. Scald a tureen with boiling water and wipe it dry, or warm individual soup plates. Some old recipes enriched the soup with eggs. I often omit them, as did many old Savannah cooks, but they are good. If you are using them, slice the eggs and put them in the bottom of the tureen, or put a slice or two into each heated soup plate. Add the sherry (a tablespoon for each serving) and ladle the soup over them. Float a slice of lemon on top of each serving. Serves 8 as a first course, or 6 as a main course.

Mrs. S. C. Manning's Celery and Oyster Bisque

This handsome soup is from New Orleans, but there's not much of Creole cookery discernable in the recipe; Mrs. Manning's seasonings are restrained and delicate. But if the flavor lacks the robust exuberance of the old French Quarter, the oysters let us know that we are, nevertheless, not far from the Gulf. The only change I've made to Mrs. Manning's recipe is to cut it in half. Her quantities were enough for a dinner party of twelve. If you have that kind of stamina, you may double the recipe without damage, but only increase the butter by half.

For good celery soup without oysters, Mrs. Manning would add 2 tablespoons of minced onion to the celery in step 2, and garnished it with a little minced parsley and hard-boiled egg.

1 head celery, with leaves	1 pint half-and-half
1 pint water	Salt and whole black pepper in a peppermill
4 tablespoons butter	1 pint oysters, well-drained
1 tablespoon all-purpose flour	Buttered Croutons (page 85)

1. Cut off the root of the celery and break apart the ribs. Wash them thoroughly and string them as follows: Snap the top of the head without breaking the strings, then carefully pull it down the stalk, pulling the strings off with it. Don't worry if you can't get all the strings; the cooking will soften it and the sieve will catch any tough bits that are left. Chop the ribs and leaves, reserving 2 tablespoons of the leaves for garnish.

2. Bring the celery and water to a boil in a 4-quart pot with the water over medium heat. Lower the heat to a bare simmer and cook, covered, until the celery is tender and the water is infused with its flavor, about half an hour.

3. In a separate saucepan, melt the butter over medium heat and stir in flour until it forms a smooth paste. Gradually whisk in the half-and-half and simmer, stirring constantly, until it is thick. Turn off the heat.

4. Strain the celery and broth through a sieve, forcing the solids through with the back of a wooden spoon (or purée it through a food mill) and return it to the pot. Discard any string left in the sieve or mill. Bring it back to a boil and reduce the heat to medium-low. Gradually whisk in the thickened half-and-half and season to taste with the salt and pepper. Simmer until thickened. You may make the soup several hours ahead up to this point.

5. Just before serving, bring the soup back to a simmer, add the drained oysters, and cook until they are just plumped up;. Don't try to hold and reheat the soup after the oysters have been added; serve it immediately with buttered croutons and a garnish of the reserved chopped leaves. Serves 6.

Green Frog, or Stuffed Spinach Soup

There's no need to be put off by the picturesque name of this delightful soup. There are no frogs; only stuffed spinach leaves, whose roughly triangular shapes resemble little green amphibians floating around in the bottom of the bowl.

This recipe is from *The Carolina Housewife* and probably came out of Miss Rutledge's years in Europe. While she identified it as a German recipe, it bears close resemblance to the stuffed leaf soups of the Mediterranean. The whole secret is a good, rich homemade broth, preferably one from a mature hen or capon. Don't try it with canned broth—there is nothing to cover up its tinny, over-salted taste.

18 large raw spinach leaves

1 large egg

1 cup breadcrumbs

1 tablespoon minced white onion

2 tablespoons butter, softened

1/4 cup cooked green peas, mashed to a purée with a fork

Salt and whole black pepper in a peppermill

Whole nutmeg in a grater

2 quarts rich, but clear Chicken Broth (page 82)

1/2 cup freshly grated Parmigiano-Reggiano cheese (optional)

1. Bring a pot of water to a boil and plunge the spinach leaves into it until they wilt, no more than 2 minutes. Immediately drain and drop the leaves in ice water to prevent further cooking. Drain them well and spread them carefully on a flat work surface.

2. In a bowl large enough to hold all the crumbs and peas, beat the egg until light. Stir in the crumbs, onion, butter and pea purée. Season to taste with salt, pepper, and nutmeg, and mix well.

3. Divide the stuffing among the spinach leaves, placing a spoonful toward one end of each. Beginning at the stuffing end, fold and roll the leaves around the stuffing as you would fold a flag, into a neat, triangular package—like a frog. You may make them several hours ahead; cover and refrigerate them, but take them out at least half an hour before cooking them.

4. Place the broth in a 4-quart pot and bring it to a simmer over medium heat. Carefully lower the stuffed leaves into the broth with a slotted spoon, one at a time. Lower the heat to a bare simmer—do not let them boil—and cook gently 15 minutes.

5. Rinse a tureen with boiling water, or warm six soup plates. With a slotted spoon, transfer the leaf dumplings to the tureen or divide them among the soup plates, and ladle the broth over them. You may pass grated Parmigiano cheese separately with Miss Rutledge's full approval. Serves 6.

Ground Nut (Peanut) and Oyster Soup

Ground nut and ground pea are just two of a number of old names for what we now know as peanuts. As the names suggest, they are legumes that literally develop underground on the roots of the plant. Though neither really a nut nor pea, nineteenth-century Southerners, especially during the lean years of Reconstruction, treated them as both. It was not unusual to have peanuts cooked like peas one day, and another day parched in their shells as a snack. Nowadays, people seem inclined to treat peanut soup (or, for that matter, peanuts cooked any way but toasted) as a novelty, something Reconstruction era Southerners would have found amusing. They would have found this soup about as novel as boiled grits.

George Washington Carver, the eminent black scientist whose study of peanuts is so widely known and justly respected, is credited with the modern popularity of peanut soup, and there are even places where it is called Tuskegee Soup (after the Tuskegee Institute) in his honor. But Dr. Carver didn't invent it, as a glance at many cookbooks predating him will reveal. All the same, peanuts, though they originated in South America, came to us by way of Africa, and always suggest the hand of a black cook.

The oldest recipes are little more than peanuts, oysters, and hot pepper, but don't let that seeming simplicity fool you. Peanuts need few seasonings to enhance their distinctive flavor. Once that is understood, one recognizes that this soup is not simplistic, but an exercise in judicious restraint from a striking imagination. Most early recipes included oysters; but twentieth-century versions rarely did. You may omit them, and add a cup of cream during the final simmer.

1 cup shelled peanuts (raw or toasted, see notes)	1 pod hot red pepper, left whole, or a pinch of cayenne
2 tablespoons grated white onion	Salt and whole black pepper in a peppermill
1 tablespoon butter	1 pint shucked oysters, well drained (but with liquor reserved; see above)
3 cups light broth, or water and oyster liquor, mixed	1/3 cup toasted peanuts, chopped (optional)

1. Grind the peanuts to a paste either with a mortar and pestle, blender, or food processor.

2. Sauté the onion and butter in a heavy-bottomed pot over medium heat until soft and colored pale gold. Mix in the peanut paste. Slowly add the broth (or water and liquor) and pepper pod. Bring to a simmer, reduce the heat to low, and simmer until thick and the nuts are tender, about half an hour. Remove and discard the pepper pod, taste, and season with salt and pepper. The soup may be made ahead to this point; cover and refrigerate if made more than 3 hours ahead.

3. When you're ready to serve the soup, bring it back to a simmer over medium-low heat. Stir in the oysters and simmer until they plump and their edges curl. Immediately take the soup from the heat, and, if it's too thick, thin it with a little broth. Taste and correct the seasonings.

4. Ladle the soup into a warm tureen or soup plates and serve at once. Though not historical, today a tablespoon of chopped toasted nuts is often sprinkled over each serving as a garnish. Serves 6.

NOTES: *Did Miss Rutledge and the other early cooks use toasted peanuts? Alas, that lady didn't say. But as she was elsewhere specific about toasted nuts, I am inclined to believe her intention was raw nuts. By the turn of the century, toasted nuts were the norm. The difference is distinct, but both ways are delicious. If you are not able to grind the nuts yourself and are using toasted peanuts, use an all-natural peanut butter, preferably freshly ground at a health food store. Don't use commercial peanut butter; it's full of sugar, preservatives, and fats other than peanut.*

Okra Soup

The pairing of African okra with American tomatoes is one of those inspired and happy marriages of texture and flavor that could only have come from the mind of an African cook. It's a fundamental combination on which much of Southern cooking is built—the granddaddy of Creole gumbos and the heart of a good Southern vegetable soup. Recipes for this soup vary little: some contained onions, others were a simple triad of broth, tomato, and okra. The simplest—and clearest—recipe I found had pared the directions down to two short sentences. (Remember that dinner in a Southern household of the nineteenth century was at two o'clock in the afternoon.) For a yield of *four gallons* of soup, it listed the ingredients and simply said: "Put the soup on early in the morning. Add the tomatoes at twelve o'clock."

1/2 cup minced white onion (optional)

1 tablespoon lard, butter, or rendered bacon fat (only if using onion)

1 quart Basic Meat Broth (page 80, made with beef)

6 large, ripe tomatoes

1/2 pound okra

Salt and whole black pepper in a peppermill

1 tablespoon butter

1. If using the onions, heat them with the fat in a large, heavy-bottomed pot over medium heat. Sauté until golden. Add the broth, cover, and bring it to a boil over medium heat. Meanwhile, scald, peel and chop the tomatoes as directed in step one of Stewed Tomatoes, page 262. Wash and trim the okra, and thinly slice it crosswise.

2. When the broth is boiling, stir in the okra and tomatoes, and let it come back to a simmer. Lower the heat, loosely cover, and simmer for about 20 minutes.

3. Uncover and season it to taste with salt and a liberal grinding of pepper. Simmer, uncovered, for about 40 minutes longer, or until the vegetables are very tender and the soup is quite thick. Turn off the heat, swirl in the butter, and ladle it into a heated tureen or individual soup plates. Serves 6.

Tomato Bisque

Just how Southern this lovely late Victorian soup really is I cannot honestly say, though it has been enjoyed in the Lowcountry for most of this century. Equally good hot or cold, it will complement virtually any meat course that does not contain tomato, though I like it best chilled as a summer first course for grilled beef. It's an ideal first course for a large dinner party because it can be made entirely in advance.

The flavor of fresh tomatoes is the whole point of this recipe; canned tomatoes will not work. While most old recipes call for meat broth, I prefer to let the tomato flavor shine through on its own. Vidalia onion is not authentic, but sweet onions were usually preferred, and Vidalias are such an improvement that I have substituted them with a clear conscience. If you like, fresh basil, never mentioned in the old recipes, also makes a delicious garnish instead of the chives.

8 medium, ripe tomatoes (do not use canned tomatoes)

1/2 cup minced Vidalia Sweet, Texas 1015, Wadmalaw Sweet, or Bermuda onions

2 tablespoons unsalted butter

1-1/2 cups water or broth (see headnotes)

Salt and whole white pepper in a peppermill

1-1/2 to 2 cups half-and-half

Freshly snipped chives

About 6 tablespoons heavy cream (minimum 36% milk fat)

1. Scald, peel, quarter, and seed the tomatoes as directed on page 262.

2. Sauté the onion in the butter in a large heavy-bottomed pot over medium heat, until softened, but not colored, about 4 minutes. Add the tomatoes and cook until heated through, about 2 minutes.

3. Add the water or broth and turn up the heat to medium-high. Let it come to a boil, reduce the heat to a bare simmer, cover, and simmer, stirring occasionally, until the tomatoes are softened, about 15 minutes. Season to taste with salt and a few grindings of pepper.

4. Purée the soup through a food mill or sieve, or with a stick blender or food processor. The

advantage of the food mill and sieve is that they catch any seeds that you may have missed.

5. Return the soup to the pot and stir in the half-and-half. Add a little more if it seems too thick, but don't make it too milky or it will lose its light, fresh taste. If you are serving it warm, simmer until it is just heated through. If serving it cold, allow it to cool to room temperature, uncovered, and then cover and chill it in the refrigerator or in a bowl set in an ice bath.

6. Hot or cold, garnish with chopped chives, white pepper, and a spoonful of cream. It's a nice added touch to whip the cream if you're serving the soup cold. Serves 6.

Great Grandmother Lillie's Turnip Soup

This sturdy country soup is exemplary of the simple grace that was the hallmark of my great-grandmother's kitchen. Its ingredients are few, its preparation virtually artless, but, oh, how satisfying and good it is to eat! Like most simple dishes, its strength lies in the quality of its ingredients. It's at its best made with the first fall turnips, when they are so crisp and fragrant that eating them any way other than raw seems almost a sacrilege.

Few country cooks served meals in courses, and my Great Grandmother usually put this soup on the table along with the meat. But occasionally it sufficed as supper all on its own, accompanied by cornbread made with the season's first cracklings.

1 pound young white turnips	Salt and whole black pepper in a peppermill
1/2 pound lean salt pork	3 tablespoons white cornmeal or polenta (see notes)
1 quart water	1/4 cup heavy cream (optional)

1. Gently but thoroughly scrub the turnips under cold running water. Trim off the root tendrils and green tops. They should be young and fresh enough not to need peeling, but if they are suspect, go ahead and peel them. Slice them a little thicker than a quarter of an inch.

2. Rinse the salt pork and put it in a heavy-bottomed 3-quart pot. Add the water and bring it slowly to the boiling point over medium-low heat, carefully skimming the scum as it rises. Lower the heat to a bare simmer and cook gently for about 1 hour.

3. Raise the heat to medium-high and add the turnips. Let it come back to a boil, skim it again, and then reduce the heat to low. Simmer until the turnips are tender, about 20 to 30 minutes. Discard the pork and skim off any excess fat floating on top of the soup.

4. Take up a cup of the turnips with a slotted spoon and cut them into cubes. Purée the remainder of the soup through a colander or a food mill (or with a stick blender). Add the

diced turnips back to the soup and let it return to a simmer. Taste and correct the salt, and add a liberal grinding of black pepper.

5. Take the meal up in your hand and, stirring constantly, let it fall between your fingers into the soup in a thin stream. Never stop stirring or the meal will lump up. Simmer, stirring constantly, until thick, about 5 minutes. Let it simmer about 5 minutes longer. Then, if you like, stir in the cream. Let it heat through, about 2 minutes more, and serve at once. Serves 4.

NOTES: *Water-stone ground white meal is the first and best choice for making this soup, both because of its color and flavor. But if you cannot get good stone-ground meal, polenta, while not as pristine, is preferable to commercially milled meal.*

SOUPS OF FISH AND SHELLFISH

Except for the catfish stew included here, the fish based soups that follow all come from the coastal regions of Georgia, Carolina, Virginia and the Gulf states where, of course, the essential ingredients were readily available. Even with modern refrigerated transportation, upcountry visitors to the coast still look forward to dining largely on fresh fish from the sea. Seafood perhaps unfairly overshadows many a delicious traditional dish of game and local vegetables on the coast, but the region's cooks have done so much with the fruits of the sea that it's easy to understand why the most famous dishes all feature fish and shellfish in some form.

In all but a rare few Southern fish and shellfish soups, milk and cream play a prominent role. Early cooks understood very well how kind cream and butter are to the delicate, sweet taste of shellfish. Seasonings were spare, limited mostly to salt and pepper, but those who could afford it made great use of mace and applied liberal doses of sherry.

An especially popular and luxurious soup in the nineteenth century was turtle (or terrapin) soup. Mrs. Leila Habersham, a Savannah aristocrat who operated what may have been the first cooking school in Georgia, was famous for her terrapin soup, and one frequently finds recipes reputing to be her secret formula in old Savannah cookbooks and household notebooks, but seldom do they agree with one another. Though Turtle Soup is still popular in places, many once-common species of turtle are today endangered, and the main ingredient is increasingly hard to come by, so I have not included any of those old recipes here.

She-Crab Soup

This classic Charleston soup today defines the city. Attributed in *Two Hundred Years of Charleston Cooking* to William Deas, the butler (and gifted cook) for Governor and Mrs. Goodwyn Rhett, it is reputed to have been created when Deas was asked to dress up his already celebrated crab soup for a Presidential dinner. Without doubt, it is the queen of Southern shellfish cookery, and appears in nearly every modern anthology of American food, but seldom is its author mentioned and rarely is his recipe followed faithfully. To understand its popularity, one has only to taste it. Cream has a natural affinity for shellfish, but it is particularly kind to crab. Here, it enrobes the meat with its silken richness while naturally taking on the sweetness of the crab and its roe.

But there is much more going on here than the magic of shellfish and cream. The name is not merely picturesque; crab roe is essential to round out the flavor and give this soup its lovely color and texture. Modern recipes badly abuse this soup by gooping it up with as many as 3 table-spoons of flour and suggesting that hard-cooked chicken egg yolks can be substituted for the roe, a truly strange idea. Chicken eggs and crab roe are not remotely alike, either in flavor or in the way they react to cooking. You absolutely cannot make she-crab soup without crab roe. What would be the point? It will not have even a ghost of the flavor, let alone the texture and color. Better to try the crab stew that follows and save this for the special day when you find female blue crabs that are fat with coral colored roe. Please see page 129 about blue crabs for how to determine gender.

2 tablespoons butter
2 tablespoons grated yellow onion
1 rounded teaspoon all-purpose flour
2 cups whole milk
1 cup heavy cream (minimum 36% milk fat)

8 medium-sized female blue crabs, cooked and cleaned as directed on page 129, with the roe reserved separately
Salt and whole white pepper in a peppermill
4 tablespoons dry sherry
4 very thin slices lemon

1. Have ready a large double-boiler bottom with water simmering over medium heat. In the top boiler, over direct but low heat, melt the butter and stir in the onion. Sauté until it is soft, but not colored. Sprinkle in the flour and stir until smooth. Gradually whisk in the milk and cream. Heat, stirring constantly, until lightly thickened.

2. Put the pan over, but not touching, the simmering water and add the crabmeat. Heat through, stirring constantly. Stir in the roe, and simmer until the soup is just heated through and lightly thickened. Taste it and season with salt and a few grindings of white pepper and remove it from the heat.

3. Put a tablespoon of sherry into the bottom of each heated soup plate, ladle in the soup, and float a slice of lemon on top. Serve immediately. Serves 4.

White Crab Stew

If food, like the formality of social occasions, could be described in terms of clothing, then she-crab soup would be black tie and patent leather pumps and this simple, earthy stew would be old tweeds and brogues—easy, warming, and comfortable. Like many of our traditional seafood stews, its base is rich milk and it contains little more than salt and pepper as seasoning. Stews like this go back to the earliest English settlements, and this one probably is the evolutionary grand-parent of Mr. Deas' celebrated she-crab soup, but in no way does its simplicity diminish its fine, comforting flavor.

10 to 12 large blue crabs, cooked and picked as directed on page 129, or 1 pound commercially packed fresh blue crab meat

1 quart half-and-half

1 blade mace, powdered, or a pinch powdered mace

1 tablespoon grated onion

Salt and whole black pepper in a peppermill

Ground cayenne pepper

1. Carefully pick over the crabmeat to be sure there are no lingering pieces of shell.
2. Warm the half-and-half in a heavy-bottomed 3- to 4-quart pot over medium heat. Stir in the pounded mace and onion and bring the soup slowly to a boil, stirring it constantly to keep the milk from scorching and sticking. When the soup begins to bubble, add the crabmeat and let it come back to the boiling point. Season the stew to taste with a pinch or so of salt, a few grindings of black pepper, and a small pinch of cayenne.
3. Reduce the heat and cook, uncovered, at a bare simmer for about 10 minutes, stirring often. This will be long enough for the flavor of the crab to be infused into the milk with-out overcooking it. Remove it from the heat and serve at once with lots of crusty bread. Serves 4.

NOTES: *You may thicken the stew, if you like, with about 1/2 cup soft, fine white breadcrumbs. Add them with the crabmeat in step 2 and stir frequently. They will completely dissolve and give the soup a lovely texture. An old Georgia recipe, from the household notebook of Nellie Kenzie Gordon (mother of Girl Scout founder Juliette Gordon Low), was both thickened and seasoned with a paste made from the yolks of two large hard-cooked eggs, as follows: separate the yolks and whites of the eggs, and chop the whites roughly. Make a paste of the yolks with 1 tablespoon butter, 1 teaspoon flour, 1 teaspoon dry mustard, and a pinch of salt. Add this to the milk before adding the crab and let it thicken lightly. Then stir in the crab and chopped whites. Serve it with thinly sliced lemons as for She-Crab Soup.*

Crab Stew with Tomatoes

This recipe is taken from two sources: *Housekeeping in Old Virginia* (1879), and Nellie Gordon's household notebook. It departs from the previous stews in that it contains very little butter and no cream. Instead, the crab simmers gently in a rich, herb-scented bath of tomatoes. Though the two recipes vary only in detail, I have deviated from the Virginia recipe by cutting the cooking time prescribed after the addition of the crabmeat. In order to preserve the flavor of the soup without reducing the crabmeat to tasteless string, a stock made from the shells, which old recipes often recommend, is used. If you are using packaged crabmeat, omit the first two steps and use a stock made from shrimp or crawfish shells.

1 dozen medium blue crabs

1 dozen crawfish or shrimp heads

6 medium ripe tomatoes

1 large onion, split lengthwise, trimmed, peeled, and chopped

2 tablespoons butter

1 large clove garlic, lightly crushed, peeled, and minced

1 large sprig each parsley, marjoram, and thyme or mint

Salt, cayenne pepper, and whole black pepper in a peppermill

2 lemons

2 tablespoons finely powdered cracker crumbs, preferably unsalted

1. Cook and pick the crab as directed on page 129, using no spices or salt, reserving both the cooking water and all the shells. Cover and refrigerate the crabmeat until needed.

2. Put the shells in the pot with the broth and crawfish or shrimp heads. Bring it to a boil, carefully skimming it, reduce the heat to low, loosely cover, and simmer for 1 hour. Uncover and raise the heat to medium-high. Let it boil until it is reduced to about 4 cups. Strain it through a fine wire sieve, discarding the shells, and put it back into the pot. Meanwhile, scald, peel, seed and chop the tomatoes as directed in step 1 of Stewed Tomatoes (page 262).

3. Sauté the onion in the butter in a large sauté pan over medium heat until softened, but not colored, about 5 minutes. Add the garlic and sauté until fragrant, about half a minute, then put in the tomatoes and their juice, bring to a simmer, and let simmer about 5 minutes.

4. Meanwhile, reheat the broth over medium heat. When it is simmering, add the tomato, onion,

and garlic, let it return to a simmer and reduce the heat to medium-low. Add the herbs, and season with salt, a stingy pinch of cayenne and a grinding of pepper. Remember that crab is delicate and ought never to be drowned in hot pepper as current fashion dictates.

5. Cut the zest from 1 lemon (in one piece, if possible), then cut the lemon in half and squeeze the juice from one half into the soup. Add the zest, cover, reduce the heat to low, and simmer about half and hour, stirring occasionally. Remove and discard the lemon zest. The soup can be made ahead to this point; cool, cover, and refrigerate it if making it more than a couple of hours ahead.

6. When you are ready serve it, let the crabmeat come to room temperature and reheat the soup over medium heat. Stir in the crumbs, cover, and simmer another 15 minutes. Add the crabmeat and let it simmer for no more than 10 minutes—just enough to let the meat absorb some of the seasonings. Meanwhile, thinly slice the remaining lemon. Ladle the soup into a heated tureen or individual soup plates and float a single slice of lemon on each serving. Serves 6 as a first course, or 4 as a main course.

Oyster and Benne Seed Soup

Benne are sesame seeds, introduced to Carolina by way of the African trade. Just how they got here nobody knows. There is a romantic myth that perhaps the slaves had secreted the precious tokens of their homeland into their pockets as they were led away in chains—a picturesque story, but one that cannot possibly be true. Africans sold into slavery didn't wear European trousers with pockets until after they got to North America (indeed, many of them were carried away literally naked). Equally unlikely are the stories that the seeds were shoved into their ears or hair. There was a lively trade with Africa for products other than slaves and it seems more likely that benne arrived by that route. Still, as anyone forced from their homeland knows, where there's a will, there's a way, and it is easy to imagine the early slaves secreting a tiny piece of a home they were never to see again.

Since their uncertain arrival, benne have become a Lowcountry specialty, their presence in a dish almost always signaling the hand of an African cook. There are as many variations of this soup as there are old Charleston families. Some are little more than oysters, benne seeds, and flour, while other contain onions, bacon, hot pepper, and a flavoring ketchup made from walnuts, mushrooms, or anchovies. This recipe follows Sarah Rutledge's *The Carolina Housewife*.

1 cup benne (sesame) seeds

3 tablespoons unsalted butter

1 small white onion, minced

1 rounded teaspoon flour

2 cups oyster liquor

Salt and whole black pepper in a peppermill

1 whole hot pepper pod

2 cups shucked oysters

1. Toast the benne in a small skillet over medium heat until golden brown, but not scorched. They should not be allowed to get too brown or they will give the soup a sharp, bitter taste. Immediately take them up into a shallow plate and spread them out to cool.

2. When the seeds are completely cool, grind them to a powder like coarse whole wheat flour with a mortar and pestle or blender (or see the notes, below).

3. Melt the butter in a heavy-bottomed 3- to 4-quart pot over medium heat. Add the onion and sauté until golden, but not browned, about 5 minutes. Sprinkle in the flour and, stirring constantly, cook until it is light brown, but not scorched. Stir in the ground benne. Remove the pot from the heat and gradually beat in the oyster liquor until it is well blended and smooth.

4. Return it to the heat and gradually bring it to a boil, stirring constantly, then simmer until the liquid is thickened, about 5 minutes. Gradually stir in 2 cups hot water, taste, and season with a small pinch of salt and a few liberal grindings of pepper. Add the whole pepper pod, stir, and simmer, stirring frequently, until thickened, about 5 minutes.

5. Add the oysters and simmer until they curl at their gills. Immediately remove the pot from the heat, take out the hot pepper, and ladle the soup into a warm tureen or individual soup plates. Serve at once. Serves 4.

NOTES: *If you have neither a mortar and pestle nor the stamina to grind the seeds by hand, omit step 2 and proceed with the soup through the end of step 3, putting the toasted seeds in whole. Before proceeding with step 4, purée the soup in a blender until the seeds are ground and smooth, then return it to a simmer and finish as directed in steps 4 and 5.*

Oyster Bisque

This is a good, rich old standby that has graced Southern tables for two centuries. All the old cookbooks from the eastern seaboard contained at least one variation of what they called "oyster soup." Since they are almost all thickened with eggs and cream, they more closely resemble what we nowadays call bisque and I have named the recipe accordingly. This calls for more liquor than you are likely to get if you buy your oysters already shucked and cartoned. Fish markets that sell shucked oysters in bulk will often give you an extra pint of liquor if you ask, since most of them pour it down the drain anyway. Failing that, you may substitute fish stock, or, as I often do, you may freeze excess oyster liquor to use in recipes like this one.

1 pint well-drained, shucked oysters	1 pint light cream
1 pint oyster liquor	Whole black pepper in a peppermill
2 tablespoons butter	3 egg yolks
1 tablespoon minced shallot or onion	Salt
1 blade of mace	1 cup Buttered Croutons (page 85)

1. Pick over the oysters for bits of shell, and put them in a sieve set over a bowl to catch any liquor that drains from them.

2. Put the butter and shallots in a 3-quart heavy-bottomed pot, turn on the heat to medium, and sauté until softened, about 4 minutes. Add the oyster liquor, and bring to a boil. Skim it well, add the mace and a few grindings of pepper, reduce the heat to a low, and simmer 20 minutes.

3. Stir in the cream, and bring it to a simmer, stirring constantly. Add the oysters and cook only long enough for the gills to curl, about 2 minutes.

4. While the oysters are poaching, beat the egg yolks in a separate bowl and beat in a ladleful of the hot soup to temper them and keep them from curdling. Gradually stir the yolk mixture into the soup and simmer, stirring constantly, until thickened, about 1 minute. Immediately remove it from the heat, taste, season well with salt, and adjust the pepper. The amount will vary depending on the saltiness of the oysters. Serve at once in heated soup plates with croutons passed separately. Serves 4.

Shrimp Bisque

This is a first cousin to creamy She-Crab Soup and makes an elegant and appropriate first course to precede virtually any meat. It has survived into this century, but you will not find it on restaurant menus, or anywhere outside the Lowcountry of Carolina and Georgia. It is rare even to find a recipe for it in household notebooks, but fortunately, a few do survive.

2-1/2 pounds whole (heads-on) shrimp	Salt, cayenne, and whole black pepper in a peppermill
3 tablespoons unsalted butter	1 blade mace, or a pinch of powdered mace
2 tablespoons grated onion	3 egg yolks
1 teaspoon all-purpose flour	6 tablespoons sherry
1 cup heavy cream	6 very thin slices lemon

1. Bring 3 quarts water to a boil in a heavy-bottomed 5-quart pot. Drop in the shrimp, cover, and count 2 minutes. Immediately take the pot from the heat and lift out the shrimp, reserving the liquid. Quickly rinse the shrimp with cold water to arrest the cooking.

2. Head and peel the shrimp, saving the shells and heads. Put the shrimp through a food mill or chop them in a food processor. If you use the machine, don't grind them too fine. Put them in a covered bowl and refrigerate until needed. You may prepare the shrimp several hours ahead.

3. Put the shells back in the pot with their cooking liquid. Bring it to a boil over medium heat, watching the pot carefully; it boils over easily. Reduce the heat to low and simmer, uncovered, until the liquid is reduced to 3 cups. Strain the broth, discarding the shells.

4. Prepare a large double boiler bottom with an inch of simmering water. Over direct heat, sauté the butter and onion over low heat in the top half of the double boiler until the onion is softened, but not in the least colored. Sprinkle the flour over the onion and stir until smooth.

5. Put the top over, but not touching, the simmering water. Gradually whisk in the broth and cream and cook, whisking or stirring, until the soup is lightly thickened. It will still be somewhat thin. Add the shrimp, a pinch of salt, a tiny pinch of cayenne, a few grindings of white pepper, and the mace and simmer the soup, stirring constantly, until heated through, about 2 minutes.

6. Beat the egg yolks until smooth, then slowly beat in 1 cup of the hot soup to temper them. Gradually stir this into the soup and heat, stirring constantly, until thickened. Remove it from the heat, taste, and adjust the seasoning. Put a tablespoon of sherry in the bottom of each heated soup plate, ladle in the soup, float a thin slice of lemon on top and serve immediately. Serves 6.

Catfish Stew

This is an upcountry, or inland chowder that is made with freshwater catfish, blue catfish being the most preferred. But it is also a fine recipe for whole grouper, bass, or trout. It's a masculine dish, originally cooked outdoors over an open campfire, where men have traditionally been the cooks, and reflects the forthright simplicity that characterizes most outdoor cooking. Paring the recipe down to size for the kitchen is tricky—not that the ingredients must be in exact amounts, but there must be plenty of fish and onions to infuse the soup with flavor.

8 medium whole catfish (about 4 pounds), skinned, gutted and cleaned, or other firm-fleshed fish (see notes)

3 large white onions, peeled and chopped fine

Salt, cayenne, and whole black pepper in a peppermill

1 quart half-and-half

3 tablespoons butter, rolled in 1 tablespoon flour

1/2 cup soft breadcrumbs or finely crushed cracker crumbs (do not use packaged cracker crumbs)

3 tablespoons chopped parsley

1. Put on a quart of water to boil. Put the fish into a 5- to 6-quart pot. Spread the onions over them and season liberally with salt, cayenne, and a few liberal grindings of pepper. When the water is boiling, pour it over the fish and turn on the heat to medium-low. Cover, bring it to a simmer, and cook until the fish are tender and flake easily, about 20 minutes. Turn off the heat.

2. Lift out the catfish, leaving their broth and the onions in the pot, and let them cool enough to handle. Bone the fish, being careful and diligent; in small catfish, there are bones as fine as hairs. Discard the bones.

3. Turn on the heat to medium and bring the broth back to a simmer. Gradually add the half-and-half, stirring constantly, and heat through. Add the fish and season with salt and the two peppers to taste. Add the butter rolled in flour and the crumbs. Simmer until the fish is heated through and the crumbs dissolve and thicken the stew, about 10 minutes. Ladle into heated bowls and sprinkle with parsley. Serve immediately. Serves 8.

NOTES: *Use only freshwater catfish; saltwater catfish are not satisfactory. But you needn't feel bound to catfish; the recipe is delicious with any firm-fleshed fresh or saltwater fish, especially whole grouper. Leave the head on—the sweetest meat is located in the cheeks and throat. The onions are included in the earliest versions of this stew. Sometimes, they were given a preliminary frying with the salt pork, but more often, not. In modern recipes, white potatoes are often added. Allow about 2 pounds of potatoes for the quantity given here. Peel, dice, and add them to the stew after step 3. Simmer them while you bone the fish. And speaking of which, the old recipes are specific: The fish was meant to be sent to the table whole. But this practice has disappeared, and nowadays all the bones are carefully removed, but only after they have surrendered their flavor to the broth.*

Savory Sauces

"Upon many tables the only gravy which makes its appearance is the grease or drippings from the meat, thickened with a paste of water and flour, or the pure unadulterated grease minus the thickening. I earnestly advise all housewives to make themselves familiar with the art of preparing different kinds of sauces. I have seen the character of poor *steak, joints, and puddings in part redeemed by a well selected, well prepared sauce."*

—Annabella Hill, *Mrs. Hill's New Cook Book,* (1867)

IN MANY A TRADITIONAL SOUTHERN COOK'S KITCHEN, Mrs. Hill's words ring painfully true. Pan gravy can be, and often is, the best possible sauce, based as it is on the rich, flavorful residue of juices and fats that are left in the pan. Yet seldom is it well-prepared, and, all too often, the only other sauce in the cook's repertory is an equally bad white sauce made from a thick paste of flour and milk, or worse, a can of soup? It has not always been that way. Mrs. Hill and all the other antebellum Southern cookery writers record dozens of lovely sauces—gossamer melted butters, silky cream reductions, savory anchovy, caper, herb, lemon, mushroom, and onion sauces, richly flavored with shallots, garlic, and homemade ketchups. These lovely things survived even into some of the early books of the twentieth century, then quietly, sadly, began to disappear.

Several important elements of sauces are discussed elsewhere in this book—flavoring agents such as curry powder, ketchups, and the bouquet garni, and bases such as broth and cream. Another critical element is browning.

Southern Browning

Southern browning is nothing more than plain flour toasted over low heat in a dry pan until it is colored. Old cooks made this in quantity and put it away in corked bottles so that the flour did not have to be browned at the last minute. Sometimes, it was mixed with water after it had cooled, but it is more versatile and keeps better if left dry. You can actually make any quantity that you like, but I have found that a cup of flour is about the outside limit that I can handle in my skillet.

To use browning, measure out as much as you need and follow the instructions of the individual recipe. If you are using it instead of plain flour, keep in mind that the toasting affects its ability to thicken; you'll need roughly twice as much.

1. Put the quantity of flour you want to brown in a well-seasoned iron, enameled iron, or non-stick skillet. Turn on the heat to medium-low and cook, stirring constantly, until it is a rich medium brown, about 5 to 10 minutes, and turn off the heat. There shouldn't be even a hint of burned flavor, so be careful not to let it scorch, and keep stirring until the flour has cooled, about 5 minutes more.

2. Pour it into a glass jar, seal it with a tight lid, and store it away from heat and light.

THREE CLASSIC PAN GRAVIES

Rich with the browned essence of the roast or bits of crust from pan-frying, lightly seasoned to bring up the flavor of the meat without masking it, pan gravy is the best possible sauce. But it is often ruined, either through indifferent handling or, as Mrs. Hill observed, by pasting it up with too much flour. Worcestershire sauce, one of the earliest commercial condiments, was introduced in the second quarter of the nineteenth century, shortly followed by commercial ketchups. Home-made ketchups gradually disappeared, and a free a hand with this growing array of bottled condiments began to erode the quality of our pan gravies. Marion Flexner, advocating the use of bottled sauces in *Dixie Dishes* (1941), inadvertently revealed how far down we had come by her day when she wrote that Worcestershire sauce and Kitchen Bouquet were to Southern sauces what powder and lip rouge were to debutantes. I couldn't have put it better myself. It is easy to overdo this culinary face paint, ending up with something that tastes as cheap as too much make up looks. One might add that early-nineteenth-century debutantes didn't wear face paint any more than cooks of their day used commercial condiments.

Three variations of pan gravy are given here. First is a basic pan gravy for roasts; second is one for pan-fried meat; and, finally, true Cream Gravy, which is so seldom seen anymore.

Pan Gravy 1

For Roasted Meat or Poultry:

Roasting pan juices, degreased

1-1/4 cups water, Meat Broth (page 80), or Chicken Broth (page 82)

2 tablespoons fat, skimmed from the roast drippings

2 teaspoons flour or 4 teaspoons Southern Browning (page 110)

Salt and whole black pepper in a peppermill

1/4 cup medium-dry (Sercial) Madeira (optional)

1. Have the pan juices in a large fat separator or measuring cup with a good pouring spout. Put the roasting pan over direct medium heat. Add the water or broth and, stirring and scraping to loosen any of the browned residue, bring to a boil. Let it boil for about 1 minute. Take it off the heat and add the contents of the pan to the roasting juices, making sure that none of the browned bits from the pan are lost.

2. Place a separate pan, preferably a well-seasoned iron skillet (a saucepan will work, though), over the heat and add the fat. When it is hot, rub the flour or Browning into it with a wooden spoon until it is well blended. If using plain flour, cook until it is beginning to color.

3. Gradually stir in the liquid and cook, stirring constantly, until lightly thickened and beginning to bubble. Reduce the heat to a bare simmer, taste and season with the salt and pepper, and simmer for about 5 minutes. For game, pork, or poultry, just before taking the gravy up, you may, if you like, add the optional Madeira and let it simmer 2 minutes longer. Pour into a heated sauceboat and serve at once. Makes about 1-1/2 cups.

Pan Gravy 2

For Pan-Fried Meat and Poultry:

2 tablespoons fat, left in the bottom of the frying pan	1-1/4 cups Meat Broth (page 80), Chicken Broth (page 82), or water
2 teaspoons all-purpose flour or 4 teaspoons Southern Browning (page 110)	Salt and whole black pepper in a peppermill
	1/4 cup port or medium dry (Sercial) Madeira (optional)

1. Reheat the pan with its reserved fat over medium heat and stir in the flour until smooth. If using plain flour, continue stirring it until it has browned to the color you want for the gravy, but be careful not to let it, or any of the residue left in the pan, scorch.
2. Gradually stir in the liquid and cook, stirring and scraping to loosen any browned bits of crust that may be stuck to the pan, until lightly thickened and beginning to bubble.
3. Reduce the heat to a bare simmer. Taste and season the gravy with salt and a few gridings of pepper, add the port or Madeira, then simmer for about 5 minutes more. Pour into a heated sauceboat and serve at once. Makes about 1-1/2 cups.

Cream Pan Gravy

This used to be *the* gravy for Southern Fried Chicken (pages 153 to 154), but it has been more or less supplanted by flour-thickened milk gravy. With a little grated lemon rind or fresh herbs, it is a good sauce for Breaded Veal Cutlets (page 180), fried lamb or pork chops or Sautéed Ham (page 201) instead of red-eye gravy.

1 tablespoon fat, left in the bottom of the frying pan	2 teaspoons minced fresh or 1 teaspoon dry herbs (optional, see step 2)
1 cup heavy cream (minimum 36% milk fat)	Grated zest of 1 lemon (optional)
Salt and whole black pepper in a peppermill	2 tablespoons chopped parsley

1. After removing the meat or poultry from the pan, pour or spoon off all but a tablespoon of the fat. Raise the heat to medium-high, add the cream and bring it to a boil, stirring and scraping the bottom of the pan to loosen any browned bits clinging to it.

2. Season with salt and a liberal grinding of pepper, and reduce the heat to medium-low. Simmer until the cream is lightly reduced and thickened, about 5 minutes. If you like, stir in a tablespoon of minced fresh or a teaspoon of crumbled dry herbs. Thyme and summer savory are good with poultry and game; sage is nice with chicken or pork. Lemon zest is good with game birds.

3. Let the sauce simmer for 2 or 3 minutes to meld the flavors, then pour it into a heated sauceboat, sprinkle the top with the parsley, and serve at once. Makes about 1 cup.

DRAWN BUTTER

"Nothing is more simple than this process, and nothing so generally done badly."

—Mary Randolph, *The Virginia House-wife (1824)*

To echo Mrs. Randolph, there is no sauce more simple or lovely than this melted, but thick butter; yet it is seldom seen in modern American cookbooks, properly executed or otherwise. Drawn butter is just barely melted so that it remains thick on its own—the same thing as beurre blanc in French cooking—but what usually turns up under that name is a pasty white sauce of flour and water with hardly enough butter to justify its name. Most old Southern versions followed eighteenth-century English practice, adding the smallest proportion of flour to aid the thickening and lessen the risk of the butter separating. Later in the nineteenth century, this began to change. The proportions of flour and water (or milk) increased, and most drawn butter recipes were turned into the heavy white sauce that is usual today. For those who have already gone into a cholesterol fit, remember that, needless to say, these rich, gossamer sauces are celebration food, and not something that people would eat every day, then or now.

Before beginning, it helps to keep a few things in mind: Have everything ready for the table before making this sauce; it won't wait for you while you finish anything else up. And if you are using the old technique, never stir the sauce but, rather, shake the pan, swirling gently in a circular motion. Butter sauce by its nature cannot be hot; if it overheats or is allowed to actually boil, the sauce will separate and the delicacy of the butter thickening will be lost.

Plain Drawn Butter is only the beginning. Once you master the technique, it places a myriad of sauces flavored with herbs, shellfish, pickles, and ketchups, at your disposal. A few common variations included here are made with anchovies, capers, and lemon.

All the drawn butter recipes that follow specify a heated sauceboat but it should not be too hot or it will overheat the sauce. You can still handle the sauceboat with your bare hands, so rinse it only briefly with boiling hot water.

Drawn Butter

~

(Master Recipe)

Here I give the historic technique for making this sauce from the days when whisks were rare in home kitchens. The pan is placed over simmering water and shaken gently until the butter is barely melted but still quite thick. It is much easier to control if you use the classic whisking beurre blanc technique that is included at the end of the recipe. The remaining recipes all incorporate that technique, but can be made using the original technique if you are so inclined.

The proportion of flour usually given is about 2 teaspoons, but I find that 1 teaspoon is plenty for a half cup (1 stick) of butter. You may want to practice with the original proportion before cutting it back. Actually, you don't need any flour. Without it the sauce is lighter and more delicate, though it takes finesse. Use the same amount of water and watch it like a hawk.

Other delicious sauces were made by substituting Mushroom Ketchup (page 389), Oyster Ketchup (page 395), or bottled condiments such as Worcestershire Sauce or Oyster Sauce for the water in the master recipe. If the condiment is thick, dilute it with a tablespoon of water.

4 ounces (8 tablespoons or 1 stick) unsalted butter, at room temperature	1 tablespoon water
1 level teaspoon flour (see headnote)	Salt

1. Half fill a pan slightly larger than the saucepan you are using with water. Place it over a medium heat and let it come to a boil. Reduce the heat to a slow simmer.

2. While the water is coming to a boil, put the butter into the smaller saucepan and add the flour. Rub it together with a wooden spoon until the flour is well mixed, then add the tablespoon of water and a healthy pinch of salt to taste.

3. Hold the saucepan just over the simmering water without letting it touch. Shake it gently in a swirling motion until the butter melts and is beginning to bubble, about 4 minutes. Don't ever stir or whisk it; any intrusion could break the fragile liaison and cause the butter to separate. Always shake the pan in the same direction. Pour into a heated sauceboat and serve at once. Makes a little more than 1/2 cup.

Alternative Beurre Blanc (Whisking) Technique: The butter for this technique should still be cold. Omit the flour: it is completely superfluous and even intrusive with this technique.

1. Warm the water and salt in a heavy-bottomed copper or aluminum core saucepan over the lowest possible heat. Meanwhile, cut the butter into small bits.

2. When the water is steaming hot but not bubbling, add 2 to 3 bits of butter to the pan and

whisk until it is almost melted. Add 2 bits and continue whisking until they, too, are almost melted and incorporated. Keep whisking in the butter by bits until it is all incorporated. If at any time the sauce seems to be getting too warm and the butter begins to look at all oily, remove it from the heat and whisk in 3 to 4 bits of butter at once to bring the temperature down. When all the butter is incorporated, pour it into a heated sauceboat and serve at once.

Anchovy Sauce

The intense flavor of salt-pickled anchovies has made them a favorite flavoring agent since antiquity. English and French cooks had been using anchovies for centuries before colonizing America, and continued using them after settling here. Imported Spanish anchovies were used for ketchups, and to lend intense flavor to sauces such as this one.

Salt-cured and packed whole anchovies are the first choice to use here (some Italian grocers sell them), but if you can't find them, buy fillets that are packed in oil in clear jars. That way you can see that the fillets are meaty and pink. The absolute last resort is canned whole anchovies. I don't recommend anchovy paste; having tried it, I don't find it very satisfactory.

4 salt-cured whole anchovies (or fillets)
2 tablespoons water
1 lemon, halved

4 ounces (8 tablespoons or 1 stick) cold unsalted butter, cut into small (1/4 tablespoon) bits

1. If using whole anchovies, split and fillet them before rinsing them thoroughly under cold, running water and pat them dry. If using fillets, rinse briefly, brushing off any fine bones that may be clinging to them, and pat dry. Chop and, using a fork, work them to a paste with the water in a heavy-bottomed copper or aluminum core saucepan.

2. Place the pan over the lowest possible direct heat. Whisk in a squeeze of lemon juice and heat until it is steaming. Whisk in the butter in bits as directed in step 2 of the Alternative Beurre Blanc (Whisking) Technique (page 114). Off the heat, whisk in another squeeze or so of fresh lemon juice. Taste and adjust the lemon juice (good anchovies should sufficiently season it without further additions), and serve at once. Makes about 3/4 cup.

Caper Sauce

Capers were once relished with mutton, and this piquant sauce was usually paired with that meat, but it is also good with roast or poached chicken, and magic on broiled or sautéed fish.

1 tablespoon caper pickling liquor

4 ounces (8 tablespoons or 1 stick) cold unsalted butter, cut into 1/4 tablespoon bits

4 tablespoons nonpareil (small) capers

1. Prepare the sauce following the Alternative Beurre Blanc (Whisking) Technique (page 114), using the caper pickling liquor instead of water.
2. Swirl in the capers and heat the sauce for a few seconds, then pour it into a heated sauceboat and serve at once. Makes about 3/4 cup.

Lemon Butter

An especially nice sauce for vegetables such as asparagus, artichokes, or broccoli, or for dipping shrimp and steamed crab.

1/2 cup water

Salt

1 lemon

4 ounces (8 tablespoons or 1 stick) unsalted butter, at room temperature

1. Put the water and a pinch of salt into a small saucepan and turn on the heat to medium-high. Let it come to a boil.
2. Peel the zest from the lemon and drop it into the water. Let it come back to a boil and cook for 5 minutes. Meanwhile, halve the lemon and squeeze out 2 tablespoons of juice. Drain the zest, discarding the water, pat dry, and cut it into fine julienne.
3. Make the butter sauce according to the Alternative Beurre Blanc (Whisking) Technique (page 114), using 1 tablespoon lemon juice in place of the water. Whisk in the zest and the remaining tablespoon of lemon juice. Pour it into a heated sauceboat and serve at once. Makes about 1/2 cup.

Homemade Mayonnaise

Most Southern cooks would be lost without a jar of mayonnaise in the refrigerator, so thoroughly is it integrated into our cookery. Dishes with a mayonnaise base are such a point of pride, and so commonplace, that one would think more pride and care would be taken with the mayonnaise itself. Yet, rare is the cook who actually makes her own anymore.

Perhaps one reason for this is that classic mayonnaise is made by working oil and vinegar, a drop at a time, into raw egg yolks. It's a lot of hard, time consuming work, but still the way to get the best texture—for a really special occasion or person, I wouldn't do it any other way. However, the food processor makes such respectable mayonnaise with so little effort that I admit I am seldom moved to make it by hand. You can also make mayonnaise in the blender, but I find that it involves a lot of stopping and starting to keep the sides scraped down. Follow the directions for the food processor, but stop the machine and scrape down the sides periodically.

Make sure the eggs are good and cold before you start. Many warm egg-based sauces are ruined because the eggs were not warm enough, but with mayonnaise, the opposite is the case. Some old recipes even went so far as to direct the cook to chill the oil and make the sauce over a basin of ice. I find it is sufficient to have cold eggs and a cool mixing bowl.

2 large egg yolks, or 1 whole large egg (if using the food processor method)

1 teaspoon dry mustard (optional)

Salt and ground cayenne

1 cup olive oil

The juice of 1 lemon, or 2 tablespoons wine vinegar

Traditional Hand Method

1. Put the egg yolks into a mixing bowl with the mustard (if using), a healthy pinch of salt, and a tiny pinch of cayenne. With a wire whisk or pair of forks held together, beat everything together until the mixture is smooth.

2. Have the oil in a pitcher or measuring cup with a good pouring spout. Drizzle about a teaspoon of oil into the eggs, beating constantly, until it is incorporated. Beat in half the oil a few drops at a time, thoroughly incorporating each addition before adding more.

3. Beat in a spoonful of lemon juice or vinegar. Alternately beat in the remaining juice or vinegar and oil in droplets, finishing with oil. Taste and adjust the seasonings. Store covered and refrigerated. Makes 1-1/2 cups.

Food Processor Method

1. Put the whole egg (do not use yolks—they're too delicate to withstand the power and heat of the machine's blade), mustard (which helps the emulsion in this method), a healthy pinch of salt, a tiny pinch of cayenne, and the lemon juice or vinegar into the bowl of a food processor fitted with a steel blade. Process until smooth, about 1 minute.

2. With the motor running, add the oil from a pitcher or measuring cup with a good pouring spout in a very thin, steady stream (it should take about 2 minutes). When the oil is incorporated, stop the machine, taste and adjust the seasonings, and pulse a couple of times to mix. Store covered and refrigerated.

NOTES:

Oil: *Salad oil in the nineteenth century was olive oil; it's the only one to use for a classic mayonnaise. If it's too heavy for your taste, use a mild olive oil or mix it half and half with an oil of less assertive flavor such as corn or safflower. I don't personally care for the current fashion for canola oil in mayonnaise.*

Eggs: *Classic recipes use only the yolks; the consistency is creamier and richer, not unlike softened butter. Whole egg mayonnaise is lighter, but stiffer. Whether I use a whole egg or only the yolks often depends on what I am planning to sauce and whether I am making the mayonnaise with the machine. With salmonella rapidly becoming the health buzz word in this country, I should caution you not to be reckless with the eggs. I use only organically raised, very fresh eggs, and wash them before cracking them. I've never, ever made anyone sick. If you are cooking for someone with an immune-system deficiency, however, and cannot get pasteurized eggs where you live, you shouldn't risk using raw egg mayonnaise.*

To use mustard or not: *Classic French mayonnaise does not contain it, but American and English versions often do. Southern recipes go both ways. Whether I use it depends on what I am planning to sauce. If you are a novice at making mayonnaise, mustard does help insure a good emulsion. Let your own taste preference guide you.*

THREE CLASSIC CREAM SAUCES
White (Cream) Sauce

Whenever I encounter what frequently passes for cream sauce in modern cookbooks, I want to lie down with a bottle of bourbon. Most are horribly misnamed white pastes of milk and flour, into which true cream is seldom admitted. They contribute absolutely nothing of gastronomical interest, serving only to paste up the food over which they are blanketed, and have nothing in common with the real cream sauce that they purport to imitate. The only thing one can say in their favor is that they are foolproof, which can hardly be called compensation. But this fine, venerable recipe is cream sauce as God meant it to be—rich, concentrated white stock thickened with real cream and enriching egg yolks. It is complex and rich, yet subtle, delicate, and never heavy. It turns an ordinary boiled hen into a celebration, and gives leftover vegetables a new lease on life.

This recipe is taken mainly from Mary Randolph, and were I able to get the kind of lovely, thick cream that she used, I would omit the flour called for, since really good cream does not need any help, especially when reinforced with eggs.

3 cups Basic Meat Broth (page 80), made with veal, or Chicken Broth (page 82)

1 small white onion, trimmed, split lengthwise, peeled, and minced

5 or 6 whole peppercorns

1 lemon slice, taken from an end (optional)

1 Bouquet Garni (page 34) (optional)

Salt and whole nutmeg in a grater

2 tablespoons butter rolled in 1 teaspoon flour

2 large egg yolks

1/2 cup heavy cream (minimum 36% milk fat)

1 tablespoon minced parsley

1. Put the broth in a saucepan with the onion, peppercorns, and, if it appeals to you, the slice of lemon and Bouquet Garni, especially if the broth is not highly seasoned. Bring it to a boil over medium-high heat, reduce the heat to medium, and cook until it is reduced by half.

2. Add a pinch of salt and grating or two of nutmeg. Begin adding the floured butter in bits, stirring until it dissolves before adding more. Simmer, stirring constantly, until lightly thickened, about 5 minutes.

3. In a separate bowl, beat the egg yolks together with the cream until they are light and smooth. Temper the cream and eggs by beating in half a cup of the simmering stock. Gradually pour this into the remaining stock and simmer, stirring constantly, until thickened, about 4 minutes. Turn off the heat and stir in the parsley. Pour into a heated sauceboat and serve at once. Makes 2 cups.

NOTES: *The seasonings varied from cook to cook; Mrs. Randolph, for example, suggested lemon and sweet herbs, and even added an anchovy, but was the only Southern source to do so. In short, don't feel bound to the seasonings given here. If the egg liaison troubles you, you may as I often do omit the eggs and double the amount of cream. Simmer in step 3 until the cream is reduced and the sauce thick, about 10 minutes.*

Oyster Sauce

Especially nice with fish and poultry, this rich cream sauce was another universal favorite in the nineteenth century. When making it, let the cream simmer down so that the sauce is slightly thicker than you think it should be so that it won't get too diluted by the liquid thrown off by the oysters as they reheat, and let the oysters barely heat through when they're added or they'll throw off too much liquid.

1 pint shucked oysters, with their liquor

1 blade mace, or a pinch of powdered mace, or whole nutmeg in a grater

Whole white peppercorns in a peppermill

Salt

2 tablespoons unsalted butter rolled in 2 teaspoons all-purpose flour

1 cup heavy cream (minimum 36% milk fat)

1/2 lemon

1. Pick over the oysters to make sure there are no lingering bits of shell. Put the oysters and their liquor into a saucepan with the mace or a grating of nutmeg and liberal grinding of white pepper and turn on the heat to medium. Cook until the gills of the oysters just begin to curl, about 3 minutes. Turn off the heat.

2. Fit a wire strainer over a bowl and pour in the oysters. Let it drain completely. Pour the oysters into a separate bowl, cover, and refrigerate if you're not finishing the sauce right away.

3. Put the oyster liquor in the saucepan, add a tiny pinch of salt, and turn on the heat to medium. As soon as it begins to bubble, add the butter and flour in bits, stirring until each is dissolved. Simmer, stirring, until the liquor thickens, about 5 minutes.

4. Add the cream, bring it back to a simmer and simmer until thickened. Cut the oysters into small pieces, add them to the sauce, and simmer until they are just heated through. Off the heat, stir in a squeeze of lemon juice, taste, and correct the seasonings. Pour into a heated sauceboat and serve at once. Makes about 3 cups.

Shrimp Sauce

Here's another luscious sauce that takes advantage of the happy affinity that shellfish has for cream. Early-nineteenth-century cooks understood what modern cooks are only now relearning: that most of the flavor in shrimp resides in the head and shells. Here, they are boiled to make a richly flavored broth that is reduced to a glaze and then enriched with cream. The delicate shrimp tails are added only at the end, so that they poach to succulent perfection. Though this sauce was originally meant for baked fish, it is a fine thing to put over homemade egg noodles or fried grits as a main course.

3 pounds medium whole shrimp, heads on weight	1 blade mace, crushed, pinch powdered mace, or whole nutmeg in a grater
1 quart water	1 tablespoon unsalted butter, rolled into
1 pint heavy cream (minimum 36% milk fat)	1 teaspoon all-purpose flour
Salt and ground cayenne	

1. Snap off the heads of the shrimp and peel them. Rinse the shrimp, cover, and refrigerate until needed. You may do this several hours ahead of time. Refrigerate the shrimp, but let them sit at room temperature for 30 minutes before proceeding.

2. Bring the heads, shells and water slowly to a boil in a 3-quart pot over medium heat. Watch the pot carefully, as it will boil over easily. As soon it begins foaming up, reduce the heat to low, loosely cover, and simmer until the liquid is reduced by half, about 1 hour. Strain it into a clean saucepan, discarding the shells.

3. Return it to medium heat, bring to a simmer and cook until it is reduced to 1/2 cup. Add the cream, a healthy pinch of salt, a pinch of cayenne to taste, and the mace or a grating of nutmeg. Raise the heat to medium-high and bring it to a boil, stirring constantly. Reduce the heat to medium and simmer until it begins to thicken. Add the floured butter in bits, stirring constantly, and let each bit dissolve before adding more.

4. Add the shrimp and simmer for 3 minutes, or until they have just turned pink and curled. Do not overcook. Serve at once. Serves 6.

NOTES: *If you are able to get really good, rich cream (more than 40% milkfat) omit the butter and flour; the cream won't need any help at all. If you're using this to sauce fish, you may make it up through step 3, but don't add the shrimp to it until the fish is ready to serve. If you are using it to sauce pasta or grits, time them to be ready at the same time that the shrimp goes in to cook. Toss noodles thoroughly in the sauce, but serve it ladled over the grits (not stirred in). It responds well to any homemade egg noodles, but does not marry well with dry factory pasta such as spaghetti.*

Mint Sauce

Forget this minute that dismal green-dyed apple jelly flavored with mint extract that they sell in the supermarket, and try never to think of it again (that ought not to be too difficult). This is mint sauce as it should be—light, fragile, and fragrant as a good clear spring day. The traditional sauce for spring lamb in English cooking, it was popularly served in the Anglo parts of the South with both lamb and mutton, but it is equally good with venison and pork. Mint both complements and softens their sometimes gamy flavor.

If you can't get fresh mint, dried herbs will work if they are of good quality and are allowed to steep in the vinegar in the warmth of the full sun. Though the sauce is most successful with fresh herbs, I've used dried leaves with good results. The kind of mint, by the way, is entirely up to you. The most common one in old Southern gardens was spearmint, and that was likely the type used then, but I first tested the recipe with peppermint, because that's what I had, and got no complaints.

3 tablespoons sugar

1/2 cup white or red wine vinegar

1/4 cup (tightly packed) coarsely chopped fresh mint leaves (or around 2 tablespoons, depending on its pungency, if dried)

1/2 cup unsalted butter

1. Dissolve the sugar in the vinegar. Stir the mint into the vinegar and sugar mixture, cover the bowl, and let it steep, at room temperature, for several hours. If you are using dried mint, put the bowl out in full sunlight for the first hour.

2. No more than half an hour before you plan to serve the sauce, melt the butter over very low heat. As soon as it has just melted, take it off the heat and let it cool slightly. Whisk the butter gradually into the vinegar, pouring in a small, but steady stream, until it has the smooth consistency of a vinaigrette-like emulsion.

3. The sauce can be held in a warm, but not hot, place for up to half an hour. Since it is not really emulsified, it will probably separate. Don't worry if that happens; just beat it again until it is smooth. Makes 1 cup.

Fish and Shellfish

COLERIDGE'S "WATER, WATER, EVERYWHERE," is an apt description of the South. Between the Atlantic seaboard and long arc of the Gulf coast, the South has more seacoast than the rest of the country combined, and our inlands are riddled with many waterways. Where river and sea meet, they nourish an extensive network of wetlands, the natural breeding ground and nursery for shrimp, oysters, and crabs.

What all that water adds up to is an abundance of fish. Commercial fishing has always been a mainstay of Southern coastal economies, and game fishing is a popular pastime for sportsmen and overstressed businessmen alike. The produce of their efforts has long been an important part of our diet. Early cookbooks were full of recipes for all manner of fish and shellfish—trout, rockfish, mullet, perch, flounder, eel, and catfish, crabs, shrimp, oysters, clams, and (less frequently) crawfish. It may seem to those who visit the South today that the only way we know how to cook this bounty is to fry it, but the old books suggest that early Southerners had a broad repertory of fish cookery of startlingly delicacy. Often the recipes were simple almost to the extreme, but in such cases, perfect ingredients and careful cooking was essential; their simplicity actually showed more sensitivity than less. And in any case, the fish was sent to the table with a fine sauce such as Lemon Butter (page 116), Shrimp Sauce (page 121), Oyster Sauce (page 120) and "Dutch Sauce" (Hollandaise), or an exquisitely simple one of puréed tomatoes or sweet red peppers. But in all cases, the balance was superb.

Pan-Fried Fish

For most Southerners, the most popular and satisfying way to cook a fish has always been to fry it. As testament to this fact, Annabella Hill *(Mrs. Hill's New Cook Book*, 1867) began her fish chapter with a detailed recipe for it. Fish fries are a deeply rooted social event in the South, and a sure way to raise money for the church roof. Every time the staff of the Southern Foodways Alliance, centered in Oxford, Mississippi, thinks of circumventing the logistical nightmare of transporting its annual symposium attendees to a catfish fry at the legendary but isolated Taylor Grocery, the protests turn nasty. The whole region is dotted with restaurants very much like Taylor Grocery (once called fish camps) that sell only fried fish, and when I was growing up, the announcement that we were eating out meant we were going to the fish camp. These restaurants still flourish even though we nowadays aren't supposed to admit to liking fried food.

One reason outdoor events and fish camps have always been popular is that frying fish is easier said than done. Also, the fragrance fills the house and may linger in the air for days—appetizing before dinner, but less so when you wake up to it two days later. That said, sometimes nothing but fried fish will do, and it can still be done well at home. The secret to moist, tender fish with a contrasting, crackling crust is simple, but critical: the fish must cook quickly. To insure this, the fat must be fresh, clean, plentiful, and boiling hot.

8 small (8-ounce) whole fish, or 8 (6-ounce) steaks or fillets

Lard or peanut oil, and plenty of it

2 cups breading (see notes)

Salt and whole black pepper in a peppermill

Ground cayenne (optional)

2 large eggs

2 lemons, cut in wedges

1. If you are using whole fish that hasn't already been cleaned, clean, scale, and gut them. You may remove the head, but you'll miss some of the best meat if you do. Rinse well and pat dry.

2. Put enough fat into a deep, wide cast-iron skillet, Dutch oven, or deep fryer to come no more than halfway up its sides, but deep enough to at least half cover the fish. Heat it over medium heat until it is hot, but not smoking, about 375 degrees F. Don't try using higher settings to heat the fat more quickly; iron holds heat and once overheated is hard to cool to the right temperature.

3. Spread the breading on a wide platter, season liberally with salt, pepper, and, if liked, a little cayenne, and toss well to mix. Beat the eggs until smooth in a wide, shallow bowl. Have all this close by the frying pan. One at a time, dip the fish into the egg, let the excess run off, roll it quickly in the breading and slip it carefully into the fat until the pan is full.

4. Fry, turning halfway, until they are a rich gold, no more than 3 or 4 minutes per side for the whole fish, or about 2 minutes per side for the fillets. Blot briefly on absorbent paper, transfer them to a wire rack set over a rimmed baking sheet, and keep warm while frying the remaining fish. Put them on a platter, scatter the lemon wedges around them, and serve at once. Serves 4.

NOTES: *Fried fish, especially fresh-water varieties, are traditionally served with Hush Puppies, (see Cornbread Fritters, page 328), which should be fried in the fat in which the fish have already cooked. Have the batter ready to drop in as soon as you take up the last fish, and keep the fish in a warm oven (about 150 degrees F) while you cook them. As to vegetable accompaniments, I don't remember ever being offered fried fish without some kind of coleslaw. In season, boiled or roasted corn on the cob is also wonderful to have on the side.*

As to breading, you may use dry breadcrumbs, finely powdered cracker crumbs, super fine cornmeal (sometimes called corn flour), or plain all-purpose flour. What Southerners use generally depends on the kind of fish they're frying. Cornmeal is best (and most traditional) with freshwater fish such as bass, bream, carp, catfish, or trout. For saltwater fish, use breadcrumbs or cracker meal. Use plain flour for delicate fillets.

Trout Steaks with Wine and Rosemary

This is a lovely old recipe from the Custis manuscript cookbooks that belonged to Martha Washington from the time of her marriage to Daniel Custis in 1749 until she passed it to her granddaughter, Eleanor Parke Custis, in 1799 (see Karen Hess, *Martha Washington's Booke of Cookery and Booke of Sweetmeats* in the bibliography). The manuscript was probably copied out in England in the mid-seventeenth century, but the recipes are much older. How much it was actually used in Colonial Virginia is uncertain; by Martha Washington's day, the books were little more than family heirlooms. However, this recipe demonstrates the kind of lovely cooking that came from England with the early settlers.

The use of rosemary with oily or freshwater fish is quite old, and pairing it with ginger is a masterful touch. The original manuscript title was "To Boyle a Trout," but of course the fish should never be allowed to actually boil. Until the late-nineteenth century "boil" meant to cook covered in liquid and it was used for anything from a rolling gallop to a poaching simmer.

4 trout steaks, about 6 ounces each, cut 1 inch thick	2 large sprigs fresh (or 1 teaspoon dried) rosemary
Dry white wine (see step 1)	2 slices fresh gingerroot, cut the size of a quarter
8 tablespoons unsalted butter	1 lemon, cut lengthwise into 8 wedges
Salt	Fresh rosemary or parsley sprigs as garnish

1. Wash the fish, pat dry, and put them in a deep, lidded skillet that will hold them in one snug layer. Add enough wine to completely cover, then lift them out and set aside.

2. Add 3 tablespoons butter, a healthy pinch of salt, the rosemary and ginger to the pan. Turn on the heat to medium-high, bring it to a good boil, and then let it boil for 3 or 4 minutes to permeate the wine with the aromatics but not long enough for any of it to evaporate.

3. Add the fish, let it come back to a simmer, then reduce the heat to an imperceptible simmer, cover, and simmer until the fish are cooked through, about 4 minutes. Do not let them overcook; in fact, if the steaks are not as thick as called for here and are boneless, or if you are using fillets, cover the pan and take it off the heat altogether. Let it stand for about 5 to 8 minutes. The residual heat will be enough to finish cooking them. Transfer the fish to a heated platter.

4. Turn up the heat to high and reduce the liquid to a glaze, about half a cup. Remove and discard the ginger and rosemary. (If you have used dried leaves, strain the sauce at the end.) Freshen it with a squeeze or two of fresh lemon juice, and whisk in the remaining butter a little at a time. Garnish with the cut lemons and sprigs of fresh rosemary or parsley and serve at once. Serves 4.

NOTES: *The reduction of the poaching liquid is my suggestion; the manuscript is actually silent on this point, but it seems consistent with the other recipes. You may make it into a classic beurre blanc by gradually whisking in 8 tablespoons of cold butter cut into small bits. My friend and mentor, Karen Hess, supplied the sensible suggestion of removing the pan from the heat when poaching fillets. She also says that this is an excellent recipe for virtually any fish steaks or fillets, and I agree. You might use bluefish, tuna, swordfish, or grouper, which is heaven cooked this way. This is also a very nice treatment for whole rainbow trout, though these would need to poach a little longer, say 10 to 12 minutes, depending on their size.*

Baked Shad Stuffed with Roe

For centuries, all along the eastern seaboard of the United States, the spring run of shad, when they are spawning, has been eagerly greeted. These fish are available, of course, at other times, but early spring, when the females are fat with rich roe, is when they are most highly prized. Here, the roe is used in the stuffing, and the fish bakes in an aromatic bath of garlic, onions, herbs, and red wine. The recipe comes basically from Mary Randolph's *The Virginia House-wife* (1824) and both garlic and red wine are authentic. Mrs. Randolph did not mention the roes, but they have long been used in this way, and since she was not specific about the stuffing, I believe that the roe stuffing used here is consistent with the spirit and intent of her kitchen. The recipe may appear long and daunting, but it is really easier and faster to prepare than it is to describe, so don't be intimidated by it.

When shad are not in season, you can bake any fish using this recipe, substituting a cup or more of oysters, crabmeat, chopped shrimp, or crayfish for the roe.

1 (3-pound) whole shad with roe	2 cups water
4 tablespoons unsalted butter	1/2 cup red wine
1/4 cup minced onion	1/4 cup Mushroom Ketchup (page 389), or 1/4 cup lemon juice
4 large cloves garlic, lightly crushed and peeled, 3 left whole and 1 minced	1 tablespoon red wine vinegar
2 cups breadcrumbs	6 whole cloves
1/2 cup chopped parsley	1 tablespoon Southern Browning (page 110)
Salt	2 lemons, cut into wedges

1. If the fish isn't already cleaned, clean, scale, and gut it, and then cut out the gills, but leave the head attached. Separate the roe and lay them aside.

2. Most fishmongers will bone the fish for you, and if the fish is shad, let them do it, as there are two extra rows of bones down both flanks of a shad that other fish don't have, and it takes practice to learn how to remove them properly. For other fish, it isn't very difficult;

once you get the hang of it, it takes less than 5 minutes. Here's how: make a slit down the belly side of the fish, from the abdominal cavity to the tail. Find the line of center bones and gradually work the knife right against them, gently pulling the flesh back as you go. Keep working until you have loosened the entire side all the way to the back, being careful not to cut through the back. Now insert the knife just under the bones and work them loose from the other side. When the bones are loose, either bend the tail and head until you feel the spine snap or clip it at each end with kitchen shears, and pull it out. Using needle-nosed pliers, gently pull out the rib bones of the abdominal cavity. Lay the fish open and cut out the center row of bones, and, if it's shad, find and cut out the rows of bones running down each flank of the back and belly.

3. Wash the fish inside and out and pat it dry. Lay it on the slice (removable tray) of a large fish poacher, or lay it on a double-folded piece of clean cheesecloth, linen, or muslin.

4. Position a rack in the center of the oven and preheat it to 350 degrees F. Melt 3 tablespoons of the butter in a large skillet over medium heat. When the foaming has subsided, put in the roe and sauté until it's cooked through and opaque. Remove it to a plate and let cool. Add the onion to the pan. Sauté until the onion is translucent, about 4 minutes. Add the minced garlic and sauté until fragrant, about half a minute longer. Turn off the heat.

5. Crumble the roe with a fork and take out any tough connective tissues. Return it to the skillet along with the breadcrumbs and parsley. Add a healthy pinch of salt, a few gridings of black pepper, and a small pinch of cayenne. Toss until the stuffing is well mixed.

6. Fill the fish with the stuffing, being careful not to overfill the body below the abdominal cavity. Sew it shut with twine, skewer it with a few toothpicks, or simply tie the body in several places with twine (that's how I do it myself, but Mrs. Randolph probably wouldn't approve).

7. Put the fish in the poacher or a long, narrow pan that will hold it without bending it. If you don't have a pan long enough, you may have to sacrifice the head. (If you must cut it off, put it in the pan with the fish, since it contains a lot of the best flavor.) Sprinkle with salt and a few grindings of pepper. Mix the water, wine, ketchup or lemon juice, and vinegar and pour it over the fish. It should not quite cover it. Scatter the whole garlic and whole cloves around it.

8. Bake, uncovered, in the center of the oven for 30 to 40 minutes, basting frequently with pan juices, until cooked through (the flesh will be firm when pressed in the center of the back). Carefully transfer the fish to a serving platter. Keep it warm while you finish the sauce. If the head was detached, set it aside to use in a soup. It makes gorgeous chowder.

9. The juices should already be somewhat reduced, but if they aren't, boil them down quickly over medium-high heat and then lower the heat to a slow simmer. Knead the

browned flour into the remaining butter and stir it into the sauce in bits until it is all absorbed. Simmer, stirring constantly, until thickened, about 4 minutes more. Strain the sauce into a sauceboat, garnish the fish with the cut lemons and parsley, and serve at once. Serves 6 to 8.

SOUTHERN BLUE CRAB

Everywhere there is a seacoast in the South, there are ancient recipes for the abundant blue crabs that inhabit our coastal inlets. Crabs were already familiar to the English settlers, and they would certainly have eaten them from the very beginning of the colonial era. Chesapeake Bay blue crabs are venerated in Maryland and Virginia, yet the region's earliest cookery writer, Mary Randolph, made no mention of them in *The Virginia House-wife*, though old English books used in the colonies, such as *The Compleat Housewife* (1727), did make use of crab. Later, *Housekeeping in Old Virginia* (1879) included a number of recipes.

To determine the gender of a crab: This is easier than you think. Look first at the tips of the pincers. The female's pincers have reddish tips, the male's don't. Next flip the crab over belly-side up. The apron (main part of the underbelly shell) of a female is broad and triangular, while the male's apron is pointed and roughly shaped like a T.

By the way, if you are crabbing on your own, you should be aware of state regulations protecting blue crab in their waters. They differ from state to state, so make yourself familiar with the regulations in your area.

To Cook and Pick Crabs

To cook the crab: A dozen medium blue crabs will yield about a pound of picked, cooked meat. In a kettle that will easily hold the crab, bring at least 4 quarts salted water to a boil, and, if you like, throw in 2 tablespoons mixed pickling spice or a mixed "seafood boiling" spice. Drop in the live crabs, cover, and allow to come back to a boil. Simmer until the crabs are a bright orange red, about 10 to 15 minutes. This is shorter than most old books recommended, but overcooking is fatal to the delicate meat. Immediately drain and rinse them in cold water to prevent further cooking.

To pick them: First pull off the legs and large pincers. Crack the pincers with a nutcracker, or shell-cracker designed for the purpose, and carefully lift out the meat. Brush off any bits of shell that may be clinging to the meat and pick out the connective cartilage. Set this meat aside. Now, turn the body onto its back and dig out the little feelers and mandibles at the mouth. Grasping the belly shell at this point, pull it up and off the back fin; the inner body will come with it. Take out the spongy, finger-like gills running along both flanks of the body. These are sometimes called the "dead man's fingers" (not because that's what they look like, but because dead is supposedly what you will be if you eat them). Remove and discard the sand sack and internal organs. If the crab is a female and you are lucky enough to have caught her while she is spawning (and local regulations permit it), there will be a clump of bright yellow or coral-colored roe just inside the belly. Carefully scoop it out and plan right then to have She-Crab Soup. Save any tomalley or fat to use for flavor. Pick all the meat from the inner cartilage (this is the part that is sold at a premium in fish markets as lump "back-fin" meat. When all the crabs have been cleaned, pick over the meat again to be sure you have not missed any shell.

The meat is now ready to be used in any of the recipes that follow, or in St. John's Crab Salad (page 280), or in soups and stews on pages 100 to 103.

Harriott Pinckney Horry's Stewed Crabs

This recipe was among the early entries to Mrs. Horry's household notebook, and may be the oldest Southern one in print. It was published in her niece's book, *The Carolina Housewife*, in 1847, eight years after Lettice Bryan's recipes for dressing crab (*The Kentucky Housewife*, 1839), but Mrs. Horry's recipe long predates her niece's cookbook, probably dating from before the Revolutionary War.

A similar dish survived into this century in Charleston, enriched by the addition of shrimp, oysters, onions, and sweet red pimientos. Served at Henry's Restaurant, over a crisp cake of fried grits, it was something to remember. Though this recipe calls for the crab to be served over toast points, you can try it over Fried Grits (page 286) for a real taste of the old Lowcountry.

Unsalted butter	Salt and whole black pepper in a peppermill
4 toast points	Whole nutmeg in a grater
4 medium crabs, cooked and picked clean as directed on page 129 (about 1 heaping cup of picked meat)	1 level tablespoon fine soft breadcrumbs
	2 large egg yolks
	1 tablespoon white wine vinegar, warmed
1 cup dry white wine	

1. Lightly butter the toast points and arrange them on a heated platter or individual plates.

2. Put the crab and wine into a saucepan and season to taste with salt, pepper, and a good grating of nutmeg. Turn on the heat to medium and bring it to a simmer. Let simmer for 5 minutes and stir in the breadcrumbs. Take it off the heat.

3. Beat the yolks in a small bowl. Beat a couple of spoonfuls of the hot wine into them and gradually beat them into the wine and crab. The residual heat should be enough to cause them to thicken. If not, return the pan to a low heat, and stir constantly until it is lightly thickened.

4. Stir in the warmed vinegar, and ladle the crab and sauce over the toasts. Serve at once, so the toast doesn't get soggy. In fact, it would be a good idea to serve the whole thing from a chafing dish at the table, ladling out one serving at a time. Serves 4 as a first course, or 2 as a main course.

Annabella Hill's Deviled Crab

Virtually everywhere else in the world, "deviled" is an adjective given to food that is highly seasoned with pepper, and literally means "hot as the devil." But here in the South, it more often indicates the presence of mustard. So it is with this old way of cooking crabs. The shells are not a capricious, optional decoration, for they not only seal in the moisture, but also help the meat hold its sweetness. If you are not able to get whole live or precooked crabs in the shell and must be content with packed meat, you may cook the meat in scallop shells or small ramekins, but be careful not to let it overcook and dry out.

Though she lived in LaGrange, an inland river city, Mrs. Hill would have had crabs to work with, though how often is difficult to say. Refrigerated transportation was unknown in the South during Mrs. Hill's heyday as a cook, but crabs and oysters, properly packed, could be kept alive for several days, and were shipped inland when cool weather permitted it. Possibly they were shipped up the Chattahoochee River from the Gulf. But no matter how often she had crabs on hand, it's clear that she knew what to do with them.

The olive oil is original, and a nice touch; it marries very well with shellfish, which is why it's common in Italian cookery. In fact, if you added a few minced garlic cloves—which Mrs. Hill would not have thought out of line—you might think you were somewhere on the Adriatic.

2 dozen medium blue crabs, cooked and picked (See To Cook and Pick Crabs on page 129), 8 back shells reserved, or 2 pounds packed crabmeat

4 tablespoons extra virgin olive oil

1 tablespoon dry mustard, mixed with 1 table-spoon wine vinegar, or 2 tablespoons Dijon mustard mixed with a pinch of dry mustard

Salt and whole black pepper in a peppermill

Ground cayenne pepper

2 tablespoons unsalted butter

1 cup dry bread or fine cracker crumbs

1. Position a rack in the upper third of the oven and preheat it to 400 degrees F. Put the crabmeat in a mixing bowl and mix it well with the oil, mustard, a healthy pinch of salt, a liberal grinding of black pepper, and a pinch or so of cayenne to taste.

2. Fill the reserved shells with the crabmeat, mounding it up a little on the top. Melt the butter in a skillet over medium-low heat and turn off the heat. Add the crumbs and toss

until the butter is evenly absorbed. Sprinkle the crumbs evenly over the crab filling.

3. Put the crabs on a rimmed baking sheet and bake in the upper third of the oven until the tops are nicely browned and they are just heated through, about 20 minutes. Serves 4 as a main course, or 8 as a first course.

> NOTES: *Modern recipes often add garlic, onions, minced bell pepper and herbs to the filling. Allow about 2 minced garlic cloves and 1/4 cup each finely minced onion and bell pepper. Sauté them in the oil over medium heat before adding them, adding the garlic after the onion and peppers are softened. Chopped fresh parsley and/or basil, finely crumbled bay leaves, and oregano or marjoram are all fine choices for the herbs.*

Crab Croquettes

When you have good crabmeat and no back shells, this is a nice variation on Deviled Crab. These croquettes, today called crab cakes, have long been a Lowcountry favorite and are a fixture in modern Southern restaurants—even those who don't specialize in fish. The quality level varies, depending on how much breading the cook adds; there should be just enough of it to hold the cakes together, though some cooks hold that any breading at all is a sacrilege. While not universally used, garlic is included in some old recipes, so I give it as optional.

There's a fashion for serving crab cakes doused in so-called Creole rémoulade sauce that I wish would go away. You might as well be eating cod; the sauce is generally hot enough to clear your sinuses for a week and completely overpowers the fragile taste of the crab. In the years since I first wrote that pronouncement, I'm sorry to say things have only gotten worse. In an effort to be creative (at least, that's all I can figure) they're now mixing hot peppers and other weirdness like wasabi into the cakes themselves. Heaven help us.

24 medium blue crabs, cooked and picked (To Cook and Pick Crabs, page 129), or 2 pounds commercially packed crabmeat

1 tablespoon dry mustard, mixed with 1 tablespoon wine vinegar, or 2 tablespoons Dijon mustard mixed with a pinch of dry mustard

Salt and whole black pepper in a peppermill

Ground cayenne pepper

2 cups fine cracker crumbs

1 tablespoon minced parsley

2 tablespoons unsalted butter (or, following Mrs. Hill's lead, olive oil)

1/2 cup minced shallots or yellow onions

1 large clove garlic, lightly crushed, peeled, and minced (optional)

2 large eggs, well beaten

Lard or oil, for frying

1. Toss together the crabmeat, mustard, a large pinch of salt, a liberal grinding of black pepper, a small pinch of cayenne, 1 cup crumbs, and the parsley in a large mixing bowl. Put the butter and onion in a skillet and turn on the heat to medium. Sauté the onion, tossing frequently, until softened and transparent, but not browned, about 5 minutes. Add the garlic, if using, and sauté until fragrant, about 1 minute. Mix the onion, garlic and eggs into the crabmeat.

2. Spread the remaining crumbs on a plate. Mold the crab mixture into 8 round, flat cakes about 3/4 inch thick, roll them carefully in the crumbs, and lay them in one layer on a clean plate.

3. Put enough lard or oil into a skillet to cover the bottom by 1/2 inch. Turn on the heat to medium-high. When the fat is hot, but not quite smoking, slip enough croquettes into the pan to fill it without crowding. Fry 2 or 3 minutes, or until the bottoms are nicely browned, carefully turn, and fry until uniformly browned, no more than 3 minutes.

4. Take them up with a slotted spatula, blot briefly onto absorbent paper, and transfer them to a warm serving platter. If you cook them in batches, keep the first batch in the oven set at 150 degrees F (or the warm setting). Don't cover them, or their steam will make them soggy. Serves 4 as a main course, or 8 as a first course.

NOTES: *As John Martin Taylor observed in* Hoppin' John's Low Country Cooking, *few good Southern cooks make crab cakes the same way twice. You can vary them by changing the seasonings. A healthy pinch of Mrs. Hill's curry is quite good, as is a spoonful of Mushroom Ketchup or Worcestershire sauce. I often add fresh basil or a pinch of crumbled dried thyme, and substitute minced green onions for the onion. Like Deviled Crab (page 131), modern cooks often add a little chopped sweet bell pepper, either green or red.*

OYSTERS

Oysters once flourished all along the eastern seaboard and Gulf rim and native North Americans were enjoying them long before the European conquest. In all probability, they were also the ones to inaugurate what may be the South's oldest social institution, the oyster roast. They reputedly had a great relish for oyster, and believed them to be a powerful aphrodisiac, a popular belief in the South even today.

Popular histories claim that oysters were not popular with the upper classes of England and America until the nineteenth century, at least partly because they were cheap and popular with commoners. But a casual glance at printed and manuscript cookbooks, most of which were written for or by upper-class housewives, shoots that full of holes. Oysters in some form were commonplace in both printed and manuscript recipes.

Creamed Oysters Carolina Housewife

Of all the nineteenth-century food writers, Miss Rutledge gives oysters the most sympathetic treatment. In this recipe, they are lightly poached in their own liquor, then removed promptly to keep them from being overcooked by the preparation of the sauce. The thickened oyster liquor is then enriched with nutmeg, pepper, and cream, and the oysters are returned to the pan just long enough to heat them through. Modern Charlestonian cooks sometimes add sherry and mushrooms to Miss Rutledge's recipe, but the sensible core survives unchanged.

Creamed oysters were a popular supper party dish, and figured prominently on the table of many Lowcountry ball suppers. But they were not unknown at dinner or even breakfast.

1 quart oysters, well drained	Whole nutmeg in a grater
1 cup strained oyster liquor	Whole black pepper in a peppermill
2 tablespoons unsalted butter	Salt
1 tablespoon flour	Crisp buttered toast points
2 cups heavy cream (minimum 36% milk fat)	

1. Bring the oysters and liquor to a simmer in a heavy-bottomed pot over medium heat. As soon as the oysters are plump, lift them out with a slotted spoon and set aside in a covered bowl.

2. Bring the remaining liquor to a boil. Roll the butter in the flour until it is well mixed, and, when the liquor begins to boil, add it in small pieces, stirring after each addition, until it is all incorporated and the liquid begins to thicken.

3. Stir in the cream, a good grating of nutmeg and a liberal grinding of pepper. Let it come to a boil, stirring constantly, then reduce the heat to low and simmer until thickened.

4. When ready to serve, lift the poached oysters from their bowl, leaving behind any liquid they may have thrown off, and add them to the sauce. Let them just heat through, but do not let the sauce boil again or the oysters will overcook. Off the heat, taste and adjust the seasonings, adding a pinch or so of salt if needed.

5. Arrange the toast on individual plates, ladle the oysters and sauce over them, and serve at once, or serve them from a chafing dish with the toasts in a basket. Serves 6 to 8 as a first course.

A Fine Oyster Pie

And a fine pie indeed! That was the title of the variation of this recipe that appeared in *The House-keeper's Friend* in 1896 and I saw no reason either to dispute or change it. The roots of this pie are almost certainly medieval English, where fish pies of all sorts have been popular for centuries. Variations appeared in virtually every source, and even the earliest called for "puff paste." Far from the supposition that puff pastry is something new to Americans, it was old hat to most antebellum Southern cooks. In some recipes, the oysters cooked in the pastry, but other cooks prepared them separately and then poured them into a precooked shell, as is done here.

1/2 recipe Puff Pastry (page 354), or 1 pound frozen pastry

1 recipe Creamed Oysters Carolina Housewife (page 134), not made ahead

1/2 cup fine but soft breadcrumbs

1. Preheat the oven to 450 degrees F. Divide the pastry into two parts, one a little larger than the other, and roll out the larger piece into a fairly thick crust (about 3/16-inch). Line a deep-dish pie plate or casserole with it, pick it well with a fork, and bake it blind as directed on page 356. Let it cool.

2. Meanwhile, roll out the remaining paste and cut it to fit the top of the pie. Put it on a baking sheet, decorate it with ornamental shapes cut from the scraps, and bake as directed on page 355.

3. Make the creamed oysters as directed in the recipe, adding the crumbs with the oysters in step 3. As soon as they are ready, pour them into the prepared shell, and carefully lay the top crust over the pie. Serve at once; it will not hold and should not be reheated. Serves 4 as a main course, or 6 as a first course.

Scalloped Oysters

"Scalloped" here means to cook in the manner of scallops. Though that shellfish seems to have been unknown to most nineteenth-century Southerners (they are never mentioned in any Southern cookbooks until after the turn of the century), the shells, at least, must have been known, since many recipes called for them—"either real or of tin." Later recipes did away with the shells altogether and used, instead, a deep casserole. It is in that form that this recipe survives today. Both methods are given here, since scallop shells are readily available today, and make convenient individual portions.

8 large scallop shells, or one deep pottery
casserole

7 tablespoons unsalted butter

1 quart shucked oysters

2 cups finely crushed crackers

Salt, whole black pepper in a peppermill, and
cayenne pepper

1/4 cup oyster liquor, strained and reserved, or
heavy cream

To Bake in Scallop Shells:

1. Preheat the oven to 450 degrees F. Lightly butter the shells and set them aside. Melt the
remaining butter in a saucepan over medium heat and set aside to cool slightly.

2. Put the oysters in a bowl with 1-1/2 cups of the cracker crumbs and season to taste with
the salt and pepper. You may use a little cayenne if you like, just don't overdo it. The
mixture should be dry, but if it seems too dry, moisten with the reserved liquor or cream.

3. Put a layer of rock salt in the bottom of a shallow pan to stabilize the shells and place the
shells on top (or cradle them in crinkled foil). Divide the oyster and crumb mixture among
the shells, dust the top of each with the remaining crumbs, and pour the melted butter
over them.

4. Bake the shells until the tops are brown and the oysters are just cooked through, about 10
to 15 minutes, and serve at once. Serves 8 as a first course, or 4 as a main course.

To Bake in a Casserole:

1. Preheat the oven to 375 degrees F. (The slower heat is necessary to keep the larger
casserole from getting too brown on top before the middle is done.) Lightly butter the
casserole and cut the remaining butter into bits.

2. Strew a layer of cracker crumbs over the bottom of the casserole and cover it with oysters.
Top the oysters with more crumbs and dot them with bits of butter. Season with a little
salt and pepper and then put on another layer of oysters, repeating with crumbs, butter,
and seasonings until all the oysters and all but half a cup of crumbs and 2 tablespoons
butter have been used. Moisten with the oyster liquor or cream.

3. Melt the remaining butter in a small pan over low heat and mix in the remaining crumbs
until the butter is evenly absorbed. Sprinkle them evenly over the casserole and bake for
about half an hour, or until the top is golden and the oysters are just heated through. Serve
at once.

Fried Oysters

"Ask any man what would be his favorite luncheon and he will answer, without hesitation, 'fried oysters.'"

—Newspaper clipping pinned into the household
notebook of Kate McPheaters Glascow, c. 1880.

When oysters are rolled in crumbs and fried quickly, they fulfill as at no other time the succulent promise instilled in them at creation. Crisp and hot outside, creamy and tender inside, there is no better way to cook them and certainly no more satisfying way to eat them. As the quote above suggests, nineteenth-century Southerners were of like mind.

Many older recipes directed that the oysters be fried only in butter—an extravagant glory that could only have been available to wealthy households or to those who kept cows. Unless it has been clarified, butter can burn before you realize it and spoil the flavor. Lard was more universal, gives a crisper crust, and does not burn as readily. You may substitute peanut or another vegetable oil if you really must avoid animal fat.

Buy the biggest oysters you can find, and keep the fat as hot as is possible without smoking.

4 dozen large oysters	Salt and pepper to taste
2 large eggs	Lard, clarified butter, peanut oil, or vegetable
1/2 cup all-purpose flour	oil, for frying
2 cups fine cracker or dry bread crumbs	2 lemons, cut into quarters
(I prefer cracker crumbs)	

1. Drain the oysters and spread them on two layers of paper towels. Have the eggs, flour, and crumbs ready in separate shallow bowls. Season the crumbs lightly with salt and pepper.

2. Put enough lard or oil in a deep skillet or Dutch oven to come up the sides at least 1/2 inch. Turn on the heat to medium. When it is hot, but not smoking (around 375 degrees F), roll half the oysters, one at a time, in the flour, shake off the excess, dip them in beaten egg, and then roll them in the seasoned crumbs. When they are all coated, slip them into the fat and fry until the bottom is brown, about 2 minutes.

4. Meanwhile, bread the remaining oysters. When the frying oysters are browned on the bottom, turn and let them brown on the other side, about 2 minutes longer.

5. When the frying oysters are done, lift them from the fat with a wire frying skimmer, blot briefly on absorbent paper, and transfer them to a wire cooling rack set over a baking sheet. Slip the second batch into the fat and fry them in the same way, about 2 minutes per side. Drain them quickly and serve at once with lemon wedges on the side. Serves 4 as a main course, or 8 as an appetizer.

An Oyster Roast (Broiled Oysters)

This is truly ancient shellfish cookery. Live oysters in their shells are laid on a gridiron and heated over coals until they just pop open. That's all there is to it. Along the Georgia and Carolina coasts, an oyster roast is our equivalent of a clambake, the invitations to which indicate the beginning of the winter social season. Everyone dresses casually, because oyster liquor ends up everywhere, including your lap. The oysters come to the table steaming in galvanized buckets, along with plenty of absorbent napkins, melted butter, and cocktail sauce. In Savannah, they were once followed by great bowls of Hoppin' John and baskets of hot biscuits, but most modern menus include red rice, cole slaw, and barbequed or fried chicken.

The cooking method has evolved somewhat. Modern cooks often lay a sheet of corrugated galvanized steel roofing over the heat, spread the oysters over it, and cover them with the moistened burlap sacks in which the oysters were packed. The most flavorful way to roast them is over a charcoal fire, omitting the blanket of wet burlap, but you can make do with a very hot oven, if you really have no other alternative.

8 dozen (96) whole, live oysters, well-scrubbed

1 cup melted, clarified unsalted butter, seasoned to taste with salt, freshly squeezed lemon juice, or Worcestershire sauce, or a mixture of all three seasonings

1 cup seafood cocktail sauce (see note)

2 lemons, cut into wedges

1. Prepare a large grill or pit with enough charcoal to make a thick layer over the entire bottom. Light and let them burn down to a bright red glow. Position a rack about 6 inches above the heat.

2. Spread the oysters on a pan and place the pan directly on the grill rack. If they don't all fit on the rack at once, cook them in batches. Grill until the shells are hot and you see them pop open slightly. (Alternatively, to roast them in the oven, position a rack in the upper third of the oven and preheat it to 450 degrees F. Spread them on a rimmed baking sheet and roast until the shells pop.)

3. Immediately remove them from the grill or oven, pile them in buckets or on a deep-rimmed platter, and serve them at once, with the sauces offered in separate bowls. Serves 4 (or only 2 if you invite me).

NOTES: *Seafood cocktail sauce was not a part of the old oyster roasts, being a mid-twentieth century addition, but it is considered an essential today. To make it, mix tomato ketchup in equal parts with prepared horseradish and season to taste with lemon juice, pepper, and hot sauce.*

SHRIMP

Along the eastern seaboard and Gulf rim, the vast marshlands are an ideal nursery for spawning shrimp. The small brown, intensely sweet inlet or creek shrimp from these waters are highly prized during their season (late spring to early December) and figure prominently in the cookery of coastal cities. Though small, they are big on flavor, and, when very young, can be eaten whole, shell and all. The larger pink and white shrimp from deeper waters are not as intensely flavored, but are almost as delicious and are equally loved.

Breakfast Shrimp

This recipe is Southern cooking at its most glorious and simple best. The shrimp are done in less time than it takes to scramble an egg and are bathed in lots of sweet butter, which soaks up their elusive flavor and becomes a rich sauce for their traditional accompaniment, hominy grits. It is not, by the way, something to feed people with a phobia about cholesterol.

The dish comes from the Lowcountry of South Carolina and Georgia and has sensibly survived into this century. Some of its descendants, particularly in so-called nouvelle restaurants, are heavy with spicy sausage, peppers, onions, and lots of odd seasonings, but those later recipes don't seem to have the spirited elegance nor reverential treatment that is contained in this one.

The quantities given are for two servings, but you may make as many as four at a time. Don't try to make more than that per batch, or the pan may get too crowded and you will end up steaming the shrimp in the excess juices they throw off.

Although this recipe uses raw shrimp, some traditional ones called for them to be boiled first. Provided they have not been boiled to death, precooked shrimp will work almost as well, and this does make an excellent way to get rid of leftovers from a party tray. But whether you use precooked or raw shrimp, be sure they are at room temperature when you start.

16 to 20 small shrimp (or 12 large shrimp), headed

4 tablespoons unsalted butter

Salt and whole black pepper in a peppermill

1 cup Basic Boiled Grits (page 285)

1. Peel and devein the shrimp. If using large shrimp, cut them in half. You may do this the night before and keep them covered in the refrigerator overnight, but always allow them to return to room temperature before cooking them. If they are ice cold, the outside will be overcooked and rubbery before the inside is done.

2. Have ready a warm plate for each serving. Over medium heat, melt the butter in a sauté pan or skillet large enough not to crowd the shrimp. When it is bubbling nicely, add the shrimp and toss them with a fork until they are pink—about 3 minutes, and not a minute

longer. If you are using precooked shrimp, sauté just long enough to heat them through and season the butter, about 1, and no more than 2, minutes.

3. Remove the pan from the heat, season them with salt to taste, and continue tossing the shrimp to arrest further cooking.

4. Quickly place a serving of grits into each warm plate. Spoon the shrimp and butter over the grits and serve at once. Serves 2.

Savannah Shrimp-Stuffed Peppers

Sweet bell peppers and shrimp are nice to put together, and are often coupled in old Savannah recipes. Here, peppers make a flavorful casing that enlivens the sweet flavor of the shrimp with a distinctive, herbal tartness. The recipe is from *The Savannah Cook Book*, where Harriet Ross Colquitt recorded it verbatim from a then-old manuscript cookbook. Mrs. Colquitt unaccountably called it temperamental and naïve, but it is a lovely and perfectly clear recipe.

4 green bell peppers (see notes)	Whole nutmeg in a grater
1-1/2 pounds (headless weight) peeled, raw shrimp	Salt and whole black pepper in a peppermill
	1/4 cup medium-dry (amontillado) sherry
1/2 cup fine soft breadcrumbs	1 cup heavy cream
1 tablespoon unsalted butter, softened	1/4 cup dry breadcrumbs

1. Bring enough water to cover the peppers to a boil in a large kettle. Add the whole peppers (do not peel or seed them) and boil rapidly for 4 minutes. Drain and let them cool. Slice off the stem end and scoop out and discard the seeds and connective membranes.

2. Position a rack in the center of the oven and preheat it to 350 degrees F. Put the shrimp into a large mixing bowl with the soft crumbs, butter, a grating of nutmeg, a pinch or so of salt, and a light grinding of black pepper. Toss lightly, then add the sherry and cream and mix well.

3. Lightly butter a casserole that will comfortably hold all the peppers and put them in it, cut side up. Divide the shrimp filling equally among the peppers. Sprinkle the dry crumbs over the tops of each and bake in the center of the oven until the shrimp filling is cooked through and bubbly and the tops are golden, about half an hour. Serves 4.

NOTES: *This makes a nice dish for a buffet, and can be doubled or tripled without damage. Green peppers were called for in the original recipe, but it's even better when made with ripe red bell peppers, though green peppers do make a nice presentation mixed with Gulf Shrimp-Stuffed Tomatoes (recipe following), alternating the red and green vegetables on the same tray.*

Gulf Shrimp-Stuffed Tomatoes

Tomatoes and shrimp have a great affinity for one another, and their marriage in any dish is usually a happy one. That's particularly true here, because this is shrimp with tomato and not much else. The recipe comes from *The Texas Cookbook* (1883), and takes full advantage of the seasonal Gulf shrimp that Southeast Texans enjoy. The baking here is necessarily brief, to keep the shrimp tender, so the tomato casing stays slightly underdone and doesn't altogether lose its fresh flavor. I have changed only one thing from the original recipe: the onion and tomato pulp undergo a brief preliminary cooking so that the stuffed tomatoes spend only a brief time in the oven—just enough to brown the crumbs and heat everything through.

1 pound (headless weight) small shrimp	Salt and whole black pepper in a peppermill
6 large, firm, ripe tomatoes	1 tablespoon parsley
1 small yellow onion, minced	3/4 cup fine cracker or dry breadcrumbs
4 tablespoons unsalted butter	

1. Bring about 3 quarts salted water to a boil in a large kettle and drop in the shrimp. Cover and count 2 minutes, and immediately drain and douse them with cold water to arrest the cooking. They should be a little underdone. Shell and devein them.

2. Position a rack in the center of the oven and preheat it to 375 degrees F. Gently wash and dry the tomatoes. Cut out the stems and then scoop out the seeds and inner pulp, being careful not to puncture the outer flesh. Discard the seeds and roughly chop the pulp.

3. Put the onion in a skillet or sauté pan with 2 tablespoons of the butter. Turn on the heat to medium and sauté until the onion is soft, but not browned, about 5 minutes. Add the tomato pulp, a healthy pinch of salt, and a few grindings of black pepper. Bring it to a boil, then reduce the heat and simmer for 5 minutes. Off the heat, mix in the parsley, 1/2 cup of the crumbs, and the shrimp.

4. Butter a baking dish that will hold all the tomatoes and put in the shells. Spoon the shrimp mixture into them. Wipe out the pan in which the onion and pulp cooked and melt the remaining butter over low heat. Off the heat, add the remaining cracker crumbs and toss until the butter is evenly absorbed. Sprinkle the crumbs evenly over the tops of the stuffed tomatoes and bake until just heated through, and their tops are golden, about 20 minutes. Serve warm. Serves 6.

A Savannah Shrimp and Tomato Pie

Here shrimp with tomatoes are paired up again, layered with milk-soaked crumbs and seasonings and gently baked. The affinity that tomatoes and shrimp have for one another is allowed to work uncomplicated by a lot of seasoning. This kind of simple casserole was a common dish for supper or tea, especially on Sunday, which was commonly the cook's afternoon off. Those who have written this cooking off as too fattening please note that, in this dish, there is virtually no fat at all.

8 large, ripe tomatoes	1/4 cup whole milk
1 small onion, minced	Salt and whole black pepper in a peppermill
1 pound (headless weight) raw shrimp	Ground cayenne pepper
2 cups soft breadcrumbs	1/4 cup fine dry bread or cracker crumbs

1. Blanch, peel, quarter, and seed the tomatoes as directed on page 262, reserving their juices, and then chop.

2. Put the tomatoes, reserved juices, and onion in a saucepan and turn on the heat to medium-high. As soon as it begins to boil, reduce the heat to a bare simmer and cook until the onions begin to soften, about 5 minutes. Turn off the heat.

3. Peel the shrimp and set aside in a covered bowl. Put the soft crumbs in a bowl and pour the milk over them, tossing so that they absorb it equally. Set aside.

4. Position a rack in the center of the oven and preheat it to 375 degrees F. Choose a casserole that will hold all the ingredients in two layers, and lightly grease it with butter. Put half the milk-soaked crumbs in the bottom of the dish, followed by half the shrimp, then half the tomatoes. Season liberally with salt, cayenne, and a few grindings of pepper. (Go easy on the cayenne; it gets hotter when mixed with tomatoes.) Repeat with remaining crumbs, shrimp, and tomatoes and season with a little more salt, cayenne, and pepper.

5. Dust the top evenly with the dry crumbs, and bake in the upper third of the oven until nicely browned and the shrimp are cooked through, about 20 to 30 minutes. Serves 4.

NOTES: *This recipe, from a Savannah household notebook, is almost identical to the one in* The Carolina Housewife *(1847), a book that enjoyed wide circulation in Savannah and Tidewater, Georgia despite the sometimes unpleasant rivalry between Charleston and Savannah, I suspect a link, though the dish was already common when Miss Rutledge set it down. Her recipe didn't call for the milk, but each layer was enriched by dotting it with butter. Her version turns up frequently in later Southern cookbooks, appearing with only incidental changes in such publications as New Orleans'* The Picayune's Creole Cook Book *(1900).*

Poultry and Game

WE ARE TODAY SO INUNDATED WITH inexpensive, farm-raised chickens, ducks, and turkeys that we take for granted that they have always been an everyday part of the American diet. But these birds have only recently been cheap and plentiful. In the not too distant past, when each family raised its own fowl, domestic birds, particularly tender young chickens, were luxury food.

The early European settlers of America did, however, find a wealth of game birds—wild doves, ducks, geese, marsh birds, pheasant, pigeons, quail, and turkeys. Some of these were eventually domesticated, but imported European poultry was the most common inhabitant of Southern barnyards. Since domestic birds were expensive to raise and young hens were more important for the eggs they produced, they were reserved for special occasions, and, even then, tended to be served in much smaller portions than is common nowadays.

Game was therefore important in Southern diets, especially of poorer families. During the War Between the States, when meat was often in desperately short supply, it became highly prized indeed, though, ironically, birdshot and other ammunition was in shorter supply than meat. Game meat is still popular on Southern tables, though often it is from farm-raised breeds of animals that were once found only in the wild and it lacks some of the complex flavor natural to animals that have fed on wild nuts and berries.

ROASTING POULTRY

Though fried chicken is indubitably a hallmark of Southern cooking, the way of cooking this bird that satisfies me the most is roasting. Nothing else preserves the rich succulence of the flesh, encased as it is in the golden bronze crispness of its own skin, scented with the dusky aroma of sage, and spiced with fresh black pepper. Basting and turning, deglazing the pan for a gravy rich with browned bits of drippings, I always end up singing, even when the inevitable perspiration runs down my glasses and makes them slip to the end of my nose. Usually, I scorch one or more of my fingers, but seldom notice or care.

Roasting is one of the oldest ways of cooking, and yet, one of the least understood by modern cooks. Before the advent of iron cookstoves, roasting was done before a clear, very hot fire. The cooking time required was considerably less than given today. In T*he Virginia House-wife*, Mrs. Randolph provided a superb recipe for very young chickens (weighing under two pounds), done in a quarter of an hour. Yes, fifteen minutes. We, with our steamy, uneven ovens and oversized chickens are incredulous, but had we Mrs. Randolph's clear, hot fire and young birds; it would still be a viable recipe. As iron cookstoves became common, open hearths were bricked up; roasting and baking became hopelessly confused. A few traditional cooks, such as Annabella Hill and Theresa Brown, continued to advocate open-hearth roasting, but their voice was eventually drowned by the clamor of technology. By the end of the century, the knowledge of true roasting had all but disappeared along with Mrs. Randolph's quick cooking times.

With everyone in a panic over salmonella, I have made no attempt to reproduce Mrs. Randolph's recipe here. If nothing else, few of us could get the tender young broilers for which it was intended. But even the large roasters so prevalent today can be safely cooked in a very short time; a three-pound chicken will roast in three-quarters of an hour. The secrets are simple and few, but critical:

* The oven must be completely preheated and very hot.

* The bird must be at room temperature. If it is still cold when it goes into the oven, it will not cook evenly, increasing rather than inhibiting the chance of salmonella infection.

* A stuffing, when used, must be hot when it goes into the bird, or it will slow the cooking down and cause the flesh to cook unevenly. In no case should any bird be stuffed and then refrigerated; that's an open invitation to salmonella poisoning.

* Choose an oval roasting pan with sides about 2 inches deep that is only a little larger than the bird. This keeps the juices from drying out and burning in the corners of the pan.

* If you do not rotate the bird frequently, most of the roasting should be done breast down. The breast muscles are largest and leanest; therefore, they are also the driest. If the bird roasts for the entire time on its back, the juices will flow away from the meat that needs it most into the abdominal cavity, where they will do no good at all.

* Once the roasting begins, keep the heat high and turn and baste the bird frequently to imitate spit-roasting. This can make a mess of the oven, so if you are a clean freak, brace yourself.

Roast Young Chicken

(Master Recipe)

Young chickens are the easiest to begin mastering the high-temperature method for roasting poultry. Precise cooking times will vary from bird to bird, but once you have young chickens down, most other poultry follows the same basic method. I prefer chicken without stuffing, but if you like, any of the forcemeats given in this chapter (pages 148 to 152) would be good.

For the Broth:	1 medium carrot, peeled and thinly sliced
The neck and giblets from the chicken	2 to 3 sprigs parsley
1 medium onion, trimmed, split lengthwise, peeled, and quartered	6 to 8 whole peppercorns
	1 quarter-sized slice fresh ginger
1 rib celery, thinly sliced	Salt

For the Chicken:

1 young chicken weighing no more than 2-1/2 to-3-pounds (often labeled "fryers" in the South)

Salt and whole black pepper in a peppermill

5 to 6 dried sage leaves, crumbled (about 1 rounded teaspoon)

1/3 recipe (about 2-1/2 cups) stuffing (pages 148 to 152), made at the point indicated in step 3 (optional)

About 2 tablespoons unsalted butter or lard

1/4 cup medium dry (Sercial) Madeira (optional)

1. While the bird is losing its chill, make the broth: put the neck and giblets, onion, celery, carrot, parsley, peppercorns, ginger, and a healthy pinch of salt in a medium saucepan. Add 4 cups water, turn on the heat to low, and bring it slowly to a simmer. Skim it carefully and simmer until the liver is cooked through, about 10 minutes. Take out the liver, and simmer for at least 1 hour.

2. Position a rack in the center of the oven and preheat it to 500 degrees F. Wash the chicken and pat it dry. Liberally rub it inside and out with salt and pepper. Rub the inside of the abdominal cavity with the sage. (If you are stuffing the bird, omit the salt, pepper, and sage on the inside. If you are not stuffing it, skip to step 4.)

3. To stuff the chicken, make the dressing according to the chosen recipe and loosely spoon it into the bird while it is quite hot. Close the cavity with a trussing needle and twine, small metal skewers, or toothpicks.

4. Tie or skewer the legs together and bend the tips of the wings back behind the shoulders at the back. If there is any loose skin from the neck, tuck it under the wing tips to hold it in place. Lightly grease a heavy oval roasting pan that is slightly larger than the chicken with lard, butter or chicken fat. Rub the breast lightly with a little butter and place the chicken on the pan breast up. Put it on the center rack of the oven and roast, undisturbed, for 10 minutes to sear the skin.

5. Baste with a little butter and, using tongs and a carving fork, turn the chicken carefully onto one side. Reduce the heat to 450 degrees and roast for another 10 minutes. Carefully turn it onto the other side, baste with pan juices, and roast 10 minutes more. If it is getting too brown, reduce the heat to 400 degrees. Gently turn it breast down, baste with pan juices, and cook for about 15 to 20 minutes more, or 25 to 30 minutes if the chicken has been stuffed. To be sure that the chicken is done, a meat thermometer inserted between the thigh and body should register 160 degrees. Turn it breast up and if its skin is not brown enough (I find it usually is), let it roast about 5 minutes more.

6. Take up the chicken onto a warm serving platter. Draw off as much fat as possible from the drippings, and make Pan Gravy 1 (page 111), using the broth from the neck and giblets and the optional Madeira. If you like, the liver can be chopped and added to the gravy when it is ready. Serves 4.

NOTES: *For a change from pan gravy, you may serve the chicken with White (Cream) Sauce (page 119), Oyster Sauce (page 120), or Creamed Onions for Roast Poultry (page 234). As mentioned in the introduction to this recipe, the frequent turning is designed to imitate spit-roasting. If you have an oven fitted with a rotisserie, you naturally won't need to turn it by hand. If you have trouble handling the turning, or if your attention is likely to be occupied elsewhere, turn the chicken breast down after the initial searing (it is usually not yet too hot to handle) and let it roast for the entire time in that position. Shake the pan or wiggle it from time to time to keep the skin from sticking. If it sticks anyway, don't fret over it. Just slip a metal spatula under the bird and gently work it loose. It may not be as pretty, but it will still taste wonderful, and that's what is important.*

Roast Turkey

A young turkey is anatomically no different from a chicken, and roasts in exactly the same way. All it requires is a little more time. Please read the master recipe before beginning.

Broth prepared as for Roast Young Chicken (see previous recipe), using the neck and giblets of the turkey

All the ingredients for Broth as listed in Roast Young Chicken (page 145), using the neck and giblets of the turkey

1 all-natural young turkey (10 to 12 pounds), not "self-basting"

Salt and whole black pepper in a peppermill

1 recipe Annabella Hill's Wild Mushroom and Ham (page 150), Southern Cornbread, Sage, and Onion Dressing or Stuffing (page 149), or Sausage or Oyster Stuffing (page 150)

About 3 tablespoons unsalted butter, melted

1/2 cup medium dry (Sercial) Madeira

1. Make the broth and prepare and stuff the turkey for roasting following steps 1 through 4 of Roast Young Chicken, the Master Recipe.

2. Position a rack as close as possible to the center of the oven (allowing enough headroom for the turkey) and preheat it to 500 degrees F.

3. The roasting of the turkey is pretty much the same as for Roast Chicken: it only requires more time between turnings. Roast for 15 minutes before basting it with butter and turning it onto one side (wear oven mitts and use two carving forks, or a fork and tongs); turn it on one side and then the other, allowing 30 minutes on each side. If at any time you feel that the turkey is browning too quickly, turn down the heat to 400 degrees. If it still seems to be browning too quickly, reduce the temperature to 375 degrees.

4. Finally, baste well with butter, turn it breast down, and roast for about 30 to 40 minutes more, or until the juices at the thigh run clear, and a meat thermometer inserted between the meaty part of the thigh should read 160 degrees (the stuffing should register 165 degrees). Turn to the breast side back up and roast until the top is nicely browned, about 5 to 10 minutes more. Take the turkey up to a warm serving platter and let it rest 15 minutes before carving. If you've stuffed it, remove the stuffing as soon as possible after that.

5. Make a double recipe of Pan Gravy 1 (page 111), adding the chopped turkey liver and Madeira as directed in the master recipe. Serves 6 to 8.

NOTES: *If you are roasting a larger turkey, or have trouble handling a large bird, you may omit the quarter turns after the initial searing and roast the bird breast down for the entire time, turning it up at the end to let the breast skin brown (I often find that it's brown enough without doing that). The breast skin may stick and tear a little and not look as spectacular when you take the bird to the table, but it will be so moist and succulent that you won't care. Since taste is the most important thing, don't worry too much if it does.*

FORCEMEATS, OR STUFFINGS, AND DRESSINGS

Forcemeat is an ancient name for the savory fillings for sausage casings or the cavity of poultry or boned meat; it need not actually contain meat. Today, the term has disappeared from the American lexicon, but it was in common use until the end of the nineteenth century. Today, two terms are used in the South: stuffing and dressing. They describe virtually the same mixture, but are not interchangeable. What might elsewhere be "stuffing" inside the bird is, in the South, often cooked in a cake apart from the meat and served, cut into squares, as a side dish. Since it was never stuffed into anything, we call it dressing, to the endless confusion of outsiders. Though the two words are becoming entangled, and one sometimes hears a Southerner refer to stuffing as dressing, never does one hear it the other way around.

Southern Sage and Onion Dressing or Stuffing

Sage and onion is a classic English combination for stuffing that has been so completely adopted by Southern cooks that to call it "sage and onion" dressing is almost redundant. When traditional Southern cooks say dressing, this is what they mean. If it is made with any other ingredients, they will elaborate. The mixture can be used as a true stuffing, as well; directions are included for using it both ways.

2 large yellow onions, trimmed, split length-wise, peeled and chopped fine

2 tablespoons unsalted butter (4 if making dressing and not stuffing)

3 cups crumbled stale (day old) Soda Cornbread (page 324)

3 cups (tightly packed) stale breadcrumbs, preferably from Soda Biscuits (page 319)

1 tablespoon crumbled, dried sage

Salt and whole black pepper in a peppermill

Whole nutmeg in a grater (optional)

Grated zest from 1 lemon (optional)

2 large eggs, well beaten (optional0, see step 2

About 1/2 to 1 cup Chicken Broth, or broth made from the neck and giblets of the fowl (see step 1 of Roast Young Chicken, page 146)

1. If you are baking the dressing in a pan separately from the roast, position a rack in the center of the oven and preheat it to 350 degrees F. Put the onion and 2 tablespoons of the butter in a large skillet (for stuffing, it should be large enough to hold all the dressing at once) over medium heat. Sauté until soft and transparent, but not browned, about 5 minutes. Turn off the heat.

2. Put both kinds of crumbs in a large bowl. Add the onions, sage, a healthy pinch of salt, a few grindings of black pepper, and, if liked, a generous grating of nutmeg and the lemon zest. Toss until well mixed. Add the eggs and toss again until the crumbs are evenly coated. (If using it as stuffing, you may omit the eggs; the stuffing will be looser, but lighter.) Moisten it with broth—not so it's soggy, but wet and yet still loose and slightly crumbly. If you are cooking it as stuffing, skip to step 4.

3. To bake as dressing, lightly butter a 9 x 13-inch baking pan or dish that will hold it in a layer about 1-inch deep. Pour in the dressing and pat it flat. Dot the top with the remaining butter and bake until the center is set and the top is golden brown, about 30 to 45 minutes.

4. To use as stuffing, have the bird ready to stuff before proceeding. Put the stuffing in the pan in which the onions were sautéed and turn on the heat to medium. Toss until it is just hot and turn off the heat. Loosely spoon the hot stuffing into the cavity of the bird, leaving room for it to expand, and truss it well to hold the stuffing in. When properly stuffed,

a bird should arrive at the table with no evidence that there is anything inside it. Any leftover stuffing that doesn't fit can be baked as for dressing in a small, covered dish. Makes about 7 cups, stuffing 1 turkey or 3 chickens, or serving 12 as dressing.

> NOTES: *Lemon and nutmeg are rarely seen in modern recipes, but were frequently used by antebellum cooks. Why they disappeared is incomprehensible; they make a delicious difference. Many modern Southerners add celery to this dressing but it is almost never mentioned in the old recipes. If you like, add 1 cup of chopped celery to the pan with the onion in step 1.*

Sausage Dressing or Stuffing: Omit the butter; substitute marjoram for the sage (especially if the sausage contains sage). Crumble 1 pound bulk sausage (see Southern Country, or Bulk Sausage, page 195) into a skillet and sauté it until it is browned, crumbling it well with a fork. Drain off all but 2 tablespoons of fat, add the onions, and proceed from step 1.

Oyster Stuffing For Turkey or Fish: Make the stuffing according to the recipe, omitting the sage and adding 1 pint shucked, drained oysters and 1/2 cup chopped parsley with the sautéed onions in step 2. Substitute 1/2 to 1 cup strained oyster liquor for the broth.

Annabella Hill's Wild Mushroom and Ham Stuffing for Turkey or Gamebirds

An antebellum cook would be puzzled by references to "wild" mushrooms; wild ones were the only kind they knew. Mushrooms have a particular affinity for all manner of poultry, and are here used in forcemeat that is especially compatible with turkey or quail. It is taken from *Mrs. Hill's New Cook Book* (1867) with only one change: though most other antebellum recipes for turkey stuffing contained suet, Mrs. Hill's stuffing was fried in lard. Forgive my tinkering, Mrs. Hill, but the suet is better. You may make the stuffing ahead of time up through step 3 and refrigerate it, covered, but it is better to wait until you are ready to use it before putting it together.

1 pound fresh wild mushrooms, or 1 ounce imported dried *boletus edulis* (porcini or cêpes), reconstituted and soaking liquid reserved (see notes), and 1/2 pound fresh cremini or portobello mushrooms

1 cup chopped shallots

1/4 pound suet, shredded

1/2 cup minced parsley

5 cups (tightly packed) finely crumbled day-old Wheat Bread (page 312) or other home-style bread

1 cup cubed dry-cured (country) ham

Salt and whole black pepper in a peppermill

Whole nutmeg in a grater

2 large eggs, well beaten

1. Wipe the mushrooms clean with a clean, dry cloth, and then slice them. Cut large slices into bite-size pieces. Put the shallots and suet in a pan large enough to hold all the stuffing and turn on the heat to medium. Sauté, tossing, until golden, but not browned, about 5 minutes. Add the mushrooms and toss until they are heated through, about 4 minutes. Turn off the heat.

2. Put the bread in a large mixing bowl. Add the shallots, suet, mushrooms, parsley, and ham. Season well with a healthy pinch of salt, a few grindings of black pepper, and a liberal grating of nutmeg. Add the eggs and toss well. Moisten it with a little broth, or soaking water from the dried mushrooms, but don't make it soggy. If you make it ahead, cover and refrigerate it.

3. When you are ready to fill the fowl, put the stuffing into the skillet in which the shallots and mushrooms cooked (or use two if you don't have one big enough) and turn on the heat to medium. Tossing constantly, heat it thoroughly and spoon it loosely into the bird. Truss up the bird as directed in the individual recipes and immediately roast it. Makes about 7 1/2 cups, stuffing a 12-pound turkey, 3 young chickens, or 12 to 15 quail.

NOTES: *To reconstitute dried mushrooms, soak for half an hour in 1 cup of room temperature water (you can speed up the soaking by using boiling water; soak 10 to 15 minutes). Dip them in the soaking water several times to loosen any sand that is clinging and lift them out. Strain the water through an un-dyed paper towel or coffee filter and reserve it to use in step 2.*

Sweet Potato Stuffing

Potatoes were once a popular stuffing, both in England and in this country, especially for geese and suckling pigs. Most antebellum recipes specifically call for white potatoes, but there are occasional Southern ones using our favored sweet potatoes. They make an especially delicious stuffing for pork or for ducks or other game.

2 tablespoons butter

1/2 cup minced shallots, or yellow or green onion

2 cups (about 1-1/2 pounds) boiled sweet potatoes (see notes) or Oven-Roasted Sweet Potatoes (page 246), peeled and mashed

2 cups dry breadcrumbs

10 to 12 chopped fresh, or 6 to 8 crumbled, dried sage leaves

1 tablespoon chopped parsley

The grated zest of 1 lemon or orange (see note below)

Whole nutmeg, in a grater

Salt and whole black pepper in a peppermill

1. Put the butter and shallots in a skillet that will hold all the stuffing, and turn on the heat to medium. Sauté until soft and transparent, but not brown, about 5 minutes.

2. Put the potatoes and crumbs in a large mixing bowl. Add the sage, parsley, and zest and mix well. Season well with a few gratings of nutmeg, salt, and a liberal grinding or so of pepper. Mix in the seasonings, then put the stuffing into the skillet with the shallots and butter.

3. Turn on the heat to medium. Stirring constantly, heat until the shallots are thoroughly mixed in and the dressing is quite hot, but don't let it scorch. Stuff it into the bird, truss it and immediately roast it according to the individual recipe. Makes slightly more than 4 cups, enough for 2 ducklings or chickens.

NOTES: *To boil sweet potatoes, scrub them under cold running water but do not peel them. Put them in a heavy-bottomed pot that will hold them in one layer and cover by 1-inch with cold water. Bring it to a boil over medium-high heat, reduce the heat to a steady simmer, and cook until the potatoes are easily pierced with a fork. Drain well before using.*

In north Georgia, sweet potato stuffing was once commonly used with opossum (Yes, it is spelled with an o). This is also a fine stuffing for domesticated ducks or turkeys. For larger birds, you may have to increase the recipe by half or even double it. It is also good with chicken, boned leg of pork or for thick pork chops, and gives character to bland little Cornish hens. If you are using this as a stuffing for ducks, use orange zest instead of lemon.

SOUTHERN FRIED CHICKEN

Fried chicken—so simple, so golden, so savory and pristine, yet in every way elegant—encapsulates in its flawless conception and simple execution everything that is good about a Southern kitchen. Hot from the pan, at once both crisp and juicy, cold from a picnic basket, so succulent, tender, and savory. Always special and festive, yet ever comfortable and familiar—and altogether satisfying.

And here it is; no book on Southern food can be called complete without it, any more than an Italian cookbook could do without veal scaloppini. And yet, I offer the recipe with reservations; you may be shocked, but there is not and never has been any single such thing as "Southern" fried chicken. Oh, yes, all over the South, in homes and fast-food diners, disjointed chickens are rolled in breading and fried in deep fat—just as all over Italy, scaloppini are floured and sautéed quickly—but that's as far as the similarity goes. As there are countless recipes for scaloppini, so every town in the South (indeed, every cook) produces a version of fried chicken that is claimed as the only authentic one, and few of them are exactly alike. Some claim that salt and pepper are the only appropriate seasonings; others lace the breading with a collection of herbs and spices. Some claim that only flour may be used as breading; others mix in cornmeal; there are even old recipes that use cracker crumbs. Those who advocate dipping the chicken in milk are equally divided between sweet (fresh) milk and buttermilk; still others hold that to use any milk at all is blasphemy. There are those who want only a crisp, crackling crust; others unabashedly steam their chicken, covering the skillet to make the crust "tender" (read, "soggy"—now you know where I stand).

Two recipes are given here. It goes without saying that they are only a sampling of the variety gleaned from household notebooks and cookbooks from all over the nineteenth-century South. They are by no means definitive; believe me, this entire book could be filled with recipes for fried chicken, and still there would be a barrage of letters saying that none of them are right! In fact, when, after this book was first published, I actually did an entire book on fried chicken, that's exactly what happened!

A word about the chickens: in all the old recipes that actually gave a weight for frying chickens, that weight was no more than 1-3/4 pounds—very young, tender birds. If you are using commercially raised chickens, you will probably not be able to get them weighing any less than 2 pounds, if that. Commercial chickens have a short, but accelerated lifespan, and fully-grown ones might be twice the weight of a naturally raised bird the same age. If you have access to naturally raised chickens and are able to get young ones weighing in at less than 2 pounds, by all means use them. Count on a 1-3/4-pound chicken feeding two to three modern appetites. A 2-1/2- to 3-pound bird will feed four polite people these days, three honest ones.

Basic Fried Chicken With Cream Gravy

This recipe appeared, with very little variation, in almost every printed cookbook from Mrs. Randolph in 1824 through to Mrs. Dull in 1928. If any recipe can be said to be THE one, true Southern fried chicken, this one probably comes the closest. Please note the word *probably*. All the old cookbooks included cream or rich milk gravy as a part of the recipe for frying the chicken. Even today, it is almost never (except at picnics) served without a bowl of gravy on the side. Of the few variations on the common theme, none followed Mrs. Randolph's example, who poured the gravy over the chicken before sending it to the table; later books strenuously objected to the practice.

All of the old recipes used lard, then the most commonly used fat for frying, and it is still the best choice for this recipe. Don't argue; it's the only way to make decent fried chicken. If you're that worried about fat, why are you thinking of fried chicken in the first place?

2 young fryers, preferably less than 2 pounds, but not more than 2-1/2 to 3 pounds each, cleaned, disjointed, and cut up

Salt and whole black pepper in a peppermill

3 cups unbleached all-purpose flour

Lard (all right, vegetable oil, if you must), for frying

1-1/2 cups light cream or half-and-half

1. Put the chickens in a basin of cold water and soak them for a few minutes. Drain well and pat dry with a clean towel. Season them liberally with salt and pepper and set aside.

2. This is a modern adaptation that produces a thicker coating than either old method (the flour was at first "dredged"—that is, sprinkled over the bird—and later, spread on a plate and the chicken was rolled in it). Put the flour in a medium-sized brown paper bag, fold over the top, and give it a quick shake to loosely dust the inside of the bag with the flour.

3. Put enough lard to come no more than halfway up the sides into a large, deep cast-iron skillet or Dutch oven that will hold both chickens in one layer without crowding. (If you don't have a large enough pan, use two or cook it in batches.) Heat over medium-high heat until the lard is melted and hot, but not smoking, around 325 to 350 degrees F.

4. Beginning with the legs, thighs, and wings and finishing with the breasts, drop 2 to 3 pieces at a time into the bag, fold over the top, and shake until it's well coated. You may need to add a little more flour after the first few batches—check after each batch. Shake off the excess and slip them into the hot fat, beginning with the dark meat, which takes longer to cook. Repeat until all the chicken is coated and in the pan.

5. Fry slowly until the bottom is a rich golden brown, about 12 minutes. Carefully turn and fry until golden brown on all sides and just cooked through, about 12 minutes longer. The juices of a punctured piece should run clear, but try not to test it this way more than you can help or you'll dry the chicken out. Some recipes direct that it's done when it no longer "sizzles" as you turn it over, but that will only lead you to certain disaster. If it doesn't sizzle at all, it's already overcooked. Remove the chicken with tongs, letting it drain well, blot briefly on absorbent paper, and transfer to a wire rack set over a rimmed baking sheet. If you're serving it hot, keep warm.

6. When all the chicken is cooked, carefully pour or spoon off all but 2 tablespoons of cooking fat into a heatproof bowl. Put the pan back over the heat and add a tablespoon of flour left over from coating the chicken. Cook, scraping the bottom to prevent scorching and loosen any bits of cooking residue, until it is lightly browned. Slowly stir in the cream and cook, stirring constantly, until lightly thickened. Let it simmer gently for 3 or 4 minutes, but don't let it get too thick. If that happens, thin it with a little milk (not more cream). Season to taste with salt and pepper and pour into a sauceboat without straining it: The little bits of crust are an essential part of the flavor. Put the chicken on a serving platter and serve at once. Serves 6 to 8.

Chicken Kentuckian

This traditional recipe for chicken sautéed with bourbon comes from the family of The Reverend William H. Ralston, for many years the rector of St. John's Church, Savannah, and a devout churchman and Kentuckian—I *think* in that order. The recipe first appeared in print in a collection prepared by the Episcopal Church Women, but it is a very old dish with French roots that have been firmly planted in the Kentucky hill country. Like everything else Father Ralston did, it is absolutely forthright and unpretentious, and yet it glows with the refined elegance of the polished silver that once graced the rectory. Father Ralston is no longer with us, but whenever I make this chicken, I feel him close by.

Once again, this recipe demonstrates the versatility of Kentucky's national beverage. It does something very nice to the chicken, and is especially complemented by the earthy flavor of wild mushrooms. Of course, you may make this dish with white button mushrooms, but their mild flavor is not nearly as satisfactory as wild ones. When domestic white mushrooms are the only kind available, or when the wild ones are out of season, I mix the domestic ones in equal parts with reconstituted dried boletus or shiitake mushrooms, which gives reasonable results.

If you want to have some fun and educate someone at the same time, invite a Yankee over for a Kentucky fried chicken dinner and put a platter of this in front of him.

2 young frying chickens, no more than 2-1/2
  to 3 pounds each, disjointed as for frying
Salt
1/2 cup all-purpose flour
8 to 10 large, wild mushrooms, sliced thick, or
  1/2 pound cremini or portobello mushrooms
  and 1/2 ounce dried boletus edulis mushrooms (porcini or cêpes)

1/4 cup unsalted butter
1-1/2 tablespoons extra virgin olive oil
2 teaspoons chopped scallion
1/2 cup well-aged bourbon
1 cup heavy cream

1. Wash the chickens, pat them dry and spread them on a platter. Lightly dust them with salt and flour. Wipe the fresh mushrooms with a dry cloth and slice them thickly. If you are using dried mushrooms, put them in a bowl, pour 1 cup of boiling water over them, and soak 15 minutes.

2. In a large, heavy skillet that will hold all the chicken without crowding, heat the butter and olive oil over low heat. Add the chicken and scallion and sauté, turning frequently, until golden and tender, about half an hour. While it cooks, baste every few minutes with spoonfuls of the bourbon, being careful to add it in small amounts so there is never any liquid accumulated in the pan: it should sauté, not steam. When the chicken is cooked through and golden and all the bourbon has been used, remove it to a warm platter.

3. Turn up the heat to medium-high. If you are using reconstituted dried mushrooms, first lift them out of their soaking water, dipping them to loosen any sand that is clinging to them, and put them in the pan. Filter the soaking water through a paper towel or coffee filter and pour it into the pan. Bring it to a boil, stirring frequently, and evaporate all the liquid. Add the fresh mushrooms and sauté, tossing constantly, for about 3 minutes.

4. Add the cream and scrape loose any residue that may be stuck to the skillet. Simmer until it is just heated through and starting to thicken. Taste the sauce and correct the seasonings, then pour it over the chicken. Serve at once. Serves 6.

FRICASSEE

"Fricassee" is an old French name for a kind of stew that dates back at least to the late Middle Ages. The usual explanation of the name is that it derives from *frire* (to fry) and *casser* (to break). Fricassees were composed of disjointed fowl or the cracked joints of larger animals, fried, then simmered in a rich gravy enlivened with vinegar or verjuice (the fresh juice of under-ripe grapes), and, later, lemon. The bones were cracked to expose the marrow, thus adding body and richness. The thickening liaison varied, but in the earliest recipes, it was usually egg yolks. Not all classic French fricassees were finished in this manner, but the early English recipes almost invariably were, and in Italy, a *fricassea* is by definition finished with egg and lemon. In English and American cookery, egg liaisons began to disappear in the eighteenth century. At first, they were supplemented with flour, which eventually replaced eggs altogether.

A Classic Fricassee for Chicken, Duck or Rabbit

This fricassee is true to the older method. The sources are *Martha Washington's Booke Of Cookery and Booke of Sweetmeats*, E. Smith's *The Compleat Housewife* (1727) and Harriott Horry's household receipt book (circa 1770–1819—see Hooker in the bibliography for the transcription). It is a fine recipe for chicken, rabbit, duck and whole small game birds. Mrs. Horry suggested a garnish of fried oysters, crisp bacon, and forcemeat balls—rather fussy and complicated without help in the kitchen. The Washington recipe was the only one in which the fowl stewed in the gravy. For the nouvelle crowd, who think they invented flower garnishes; the one included here was in Mrs. Horry's manuscript.

For the gravy:

1/4 pound small cremini mushrooms

2 cups Chicken Broth (page 82) or Basic Meat Broth (page 80)

3 to 4 Pickled Oysters (page 394, optional, see note for substitutes)

3 salt-packed whole anchovies

2 shallots, coarsely chopped

3 sprigs each fresh sweet marjoram and parsley

1/4 cup claret (Bordeaux) or other dry red wine

Salt

1 teaspoon whole black peppercorns

For the fricasee:

1 chicken (2-1/2 to 3 pounds) or 2 rabbits or small ducklings (about 1-3/4 pounds each)

Salt and whole black pepper in a peppermill

1 blade mace, crushed, or a pinch of powdered mace, or whole nutmeg in a grater

1 tablespoon all-purpose flour

4 ounces (8 tablespoons or 1 stick) unsalted butter

1 lemon

2 large egg yolks, beaten

For the garnish:

1/4 pound bacon, fried crisp (optional)

8 edible flowers, such as nasturtiums or pansies (optional)

8 sprigs parsley

1 lemon, cut in wedges

1. To make the gravy, wipe the mushrooms with a dry cloth and trim off the stems. Set aside the caps and put the stems with all the gravy ingredients into a pot and turn on the heat to medium. When it comes to a boil, skim off the scum and reduce the heat to a bare simmer. Simmer until it is well flavored and slightly reduced, about 1 hour. (This can be made a day or so ahead.)

2. Disjoint the chicken and dust it with a little salt, a few grindings of black pepper, the mace or nutmeg, and flour.

3. Put the butter in a skillet that will hold all the chicken and turn on the heat to medium. When it is melted and the foaming has subsided, add the chicken and fry until it is nicely browned on all sides and nearly cooked through, about 20 minutes.

4. Meanwhile, strain the broth, discarding the solids. Cut the zest from the lemon and cut it into fine julienne. Seed and chop the pulp fine. When the chicken is nearly done, add the mushrooms and cook for a minute. Pour off most of the fat and add the broth, lemon zest, and pulp. Give it a stir and simmer for 2 minutes. The flour should partially thicken the sauce. Turn off the heat.

5. Beat about 1/2 cup of sauce into the egg yolks. Add them to the pan, shaking constantly, until the sauce is lightly thickened. Remove the chicken to a warm platter, pour the sauce over it, and garnish with the bacon, flowers, parsley, and lemon wedges, or with the last 2 items alone. Serves 4.

NOTES: *The broth can be made several days ahead; indeed, the entire dish can be made ahead up to step 4. Don't add the lemon and thicken the sauce until you are ready to serve it. A tablespoon of Oyster Ketchup (page 395) or Oriental oyster sauce may be substituted for the pickled oysters.*

GAME

Game hunting is getting a reputation these days as a barbaric and uncivilized practice. Frankly, the reasoning eludes me. I don't hunt myself, but mainly because I couldn't hit the broad side of a barn with a cannon, and not because of any dainty reservations about shooting things. Quickly killing a bird that has lived happily in its natural habitat with a single, well-aimed shot is certainly more humane than the conditions under which we raise and slaughter many chickens in this country. Besides, nourished on a diet of wild seeds, nuts, and berries, game animals are infinitely more interesting to eat. We are so far removed from killing with our meat entombed in plastic-wrapped trays in the market that we forget that to kill is necessary in everything we eat, including plants. There is no way to escape it, and we would do well to get used to it again.

SQUAB, OR PIGEONS

We Americans are an odd bunch. Mention eating pigeons and most of us will run screaming for the door, but the same squeamish bunch will put it away with gusto if you call the same bird a "squab"—which is just another name for young pigeons. Go figure.

One of our forebearer's favorite game birds is missing from this book and from modern American tables. Passenger Pigeons were too popular: loss of habitat and wholesale slaughtering made them extinct. We may only guess at what culinary appeal these dove-like birds possessed, but probably their popularity was due in part to availability. Once, migrating flocks literally blackened the sky over entire communities. All one had to do to secure a brace was to load a gun with birdshot and point it skyward. But no more: the supply that had seemed endless unfortunately was not.

Old American recipes for squab are pretty flexible, adapting beautifully to quail, dove, and pheasant, if you can get them, but they also work with the young squab that are being raised domestically. Most of these old recipes had to be adaptable. Game hunting is a lot like going to the market in Moscow; you take what you can get and are glad of it. On the other hand, a New York friend pointed out to me that the city is practically teeming with—er, squab. Yes, well.

A Fricassee of Squab, or Young Pigeons

This lovely stew is fine not only for squab, but quail or other small game birds, and breathes life into farm-raised "game" birds of any kind. It even makes something respectable of those bland little Cornish hens. It is an old English fricassee, thickened with eggs and garnished with lemon, one of the most beautiful that I know.

For the herb butter:

2 ounces (1/4 cup or 1/2 stick) unsalted butter, softened

4 to 5 whole cloves, crushed to a powder in a mortar

1 blade mace, crushed to a powder in a mortar

1 teaspoon each minced fresh thyme, parsley, and marjoram

Salt and whole black pepper in a peppermill

For the fricassee:

4 large squab or other game birds

1 pint rich Basic Meat Broth (page 80)

1/4 cup dry white wine

1 tablespoon Mushroom Ketchup (page 389)

5 to 6 whole peppercorns

2 blades mace or a good pinch powdered mace or grated nutmeg

Zest of 1/2 lemon

3 tablespoons minced onion or shallot

3 sprigs each fresh thyme, parsley, and marjoram

Salt

1 tablespoon butter

3 egg yolks, well beaten

1 lemon, cut into wedges

1. Position a rack in the center of the oven and preheat it to 500 degrees F. Make the herb butter by kneading all the ingredients together, seasoning it to taste with salt and pepper. Wash the birds inside and out and pat dry. Divide the herb butter equally among each cavity. Tie the legs together, wrap a length of string around them, and another around the wings to hold them in place. Put them breast up in a flameproof casserole that will comfortably hold them in one layer.

2. Roast 10 to 15 minutes, or until or seared and golden. Meanwhile, bring the broth to a boil. Turn off the oven, remove the casserole, and slowly add the boiling broth.

3. Put the pan over direct medium heat, and bring the broth back to a boil. Add the wine, ketchup, peppercorns, mace, lemon zest, onion, herbs, and a healthy pinch of salt. Loosely cover, reduce the heat to low, and simmer slowly until the birds are tender, about half an hour. Take the pan from the heat and remove the squab to a warm platter. Cut off and discard the trussing string.

4. Beat half a cup of hot cooking liquid into the egg yolks to temper them, and add them to the remaining broth, shaking the pan or stirring with a wooden spoon until the sauce thickens. The residual heat should be enough to do this, but if it isn't, put the pan back over the heat for half a minute or until the sauce just thickens, being careful not to let it curdle. Pour the sauce over the birds, garnish with the cut lemon, and serve at once. Serves 4.

NOTES: *The original recipe called for pickled mushrooms, which were similar in flavor to the ketchup. If you don't have Mushroom Ketchup, you may substitute a teaspoon of Worcestershire sauce mixed with a teaspoon of vinegar and one or two pieces of dried boletus mushrooms crushed to a powder. Sometimes, marinated mushrooms are available in specialty groceries; you might try substituting a dozen of them for the ketchup, or just omit the mushrooms altogether.*

QUAIL, OR BOB WHITE

Of all the game birds that flourish in the southeastern meadows and woodlands, quail, I think, are the loveliest. Also known throughout the South as "bobwhite" because their plaintive call sounds like someone calling "Bob, Bob White," the beautiful patterns of their soft, brown plumage conceal a delicately flavored, succulent flesh. Quail are Native American partridges, similar to the partridges that early settlers had known in England, but more closely related to the continental European birds from which we derive the name. Their generous numbers and delicate flavor has made them popular with hunters and cooks alike.

Since they are small, quail are easy to overcook when they're grilled or roasted. Recipes directing that they be roasted for an hour are disastrously wrong, as an hour of true roasting will produce something that resembles quail only in appearance. It certainly will no longer have the delicate flavor and texture that these birds ought to have. Old cooks cooked them quickly, and compensated for their fragility by giving them self-basting stuffings such as oysters or by wrapping them with fat ham. Quail that are roasted or grilled should not be skinned. If you are presented with skinned birds, roasting is possible only if they are thickly wrapped in bacon, but it's safer to quickly fry them in order to keep them moist and tender, or to treat them to a slow, gentle braising, where slow-cooking is not only possible, but desirable.

Our great-grandparents had to rely on the prowess of the family hunter in order to enjoy quail, but today they are widely available from commercial farms, of which Carolina quail are reputed to be the finest. Hunters and some serious cooks eschew commercial birds, saying they lack flavor—and they're right: birds fed on wild seeds and berries are sure to be more flavorful than ones fed on chicken feed, but for the city-bound and bad shots like me, farm raised birds are fine. Besides, they never contain the unpleasant surprise of a stray ball of birdshot. I know; I lack a sense of adventure. But I am not, so far, lacking any teeth.

Grill-Broiled Quail (or Other Game Birds)

This may be one of the most satisfying ways to cook game birds of any kind. The aromatic smoke from hardwood coals is the ideal enhancement for their slightly wild flavor.

8 medium quail, or 4 large squab or other game birds, dressed but not skinned

1/2 cup (4 ounces or 1 stick) unsalted butter, melted

Salt and whole pepper in a peppermill

2 tablespoons chopped parsley

1 tablespoon Mushroom Ketchup (page 389), Asian oyster sauce, or 1-1/2 teaspoons each Worcestershire sauce and red wine vinegar

1 whole lemon, cut lengthwise into 8 wedges

1. Wash the birds inside and out and dry them. With kitchen shears or a very sharp knife, split each bird up the back and flatten it gently so that the keel (breast) bone snaps. Lay them on a pan without touching, brush them with a little melted butter, and sprinkle them generously with salt and a few grindings of black pepper.

2. Prepare a grill with hardwood coals. (If you use charcoal briquettes, light them and, after they are ready, throw on them a handful or so of hardwood chips or grape vine clippings). When the coals are bright red and very hot, spread them and position the rack about 5 inches above them.

3. Turn the birds skin-side down and brush the cavity side with some of the melted butter and sprinkle them with salt and pepper. Place them on the grill skin-side up, brush the tops with more of the butter, and grill about 10 minutes.

4. Turn them, brush well with butter, and grill until they are cooked through and the skin is nicely browned, about 5 to 8 minutes more. If you find that the skin is getting too dark before the meat is done, turn them cavity side down and finish the cooking with the skin facing away from the heat. Watch carefully and don't let them overcook.

5. Remove the quail skin-side up to a warm platter. In a small saucepan, warm the remaining butter over low heat and stir in the parsley and ketchup. Pour the sauce over the birds, scatter lemon wedges among them, and serve at once. Serves 4.

Roast Quail with Oysters

Coastal cooks have long understood the natural affinity that oysters have for game birds; the combination turns up again and again wherever both can be found. The pairing in this recipe, however, has an especially practical side. The juices thrown off by the oysters as they cook naturally baste the tender little birds, making them exceptionally moist and flavorful. This is a delicate treatment for two very delicate foods, and careful timing is essential. Overcooking will dry out the quail and reduce the oysters to hard, tasteless little knots.

Probably this recipe was derived from the old European ones that employ a forcemeat of oysters and grated breadcrumbs, but I have found nothing that uses only the oysters without bread or vegetables, as this one does, anywhere outside the South. I've also failed to find forcemeat that was better suited to the tender, delicate meat of quail. It's so simple and ingenious that everyone you serve it to is bound to swear it's some kind of clever "nouvelle" concoction.

8 dressed quail

18 to 24 large oysters

1/4 cup butter, melted and cooled

1/4 cup unbleached all-purpose flour

Salt and whole black pepper in a peppermill

1. Position a rack in the upper third of the oven and preheat it to 500 degrees F. Wash the quails and pat dry. Drain the oysters in a sieve set over a bowl (the liquor can be saved to use in stock or soup).

2. Spread the flour on a dinner plate to cover the entire bottom and have it and the butter ready beside a casserole that will just hold the quail in one layer. Dip each oyster in the melted butter and roll it in flour. Shake off the excess. Stuff the body cavity of each quail with 2 to 3 oysters each, completely and tightly filling it. Tie the legs together with twine.

3. Rub the quail well with melted butter, place them in the casserole, and season lightly with salt and liberally with pepper.

4. Roast, uncovered, 15 to 20 minutes, basting midway with more melted butter. Serve at once. Serves 4.

Grilled Quail with Oysters: Quail prepared in this manner can also be grilled as in Broiled Quail (page 161). Prepare the birds as directed through step 3, then grill them as directed in steps 2 through 4 of Broiled Quail, allowing about 10 minutes per side. Don't hold that time as gospel: a lot will depend on the size of your birds, so watch carefully and don't overcook them.

Roast Quail with Sweet Potato Stuffing: Another very pleasant variation is accomplished by stuffing the quail with Sweet Potato Stuffing (page 152). Roast about 20 to 25 minutes, or until just tender.

RABBIT AND SQUIRRELS

For early Southerners, a hunter returning home with a brace of rabbits in late fall was a welcome sight. They're still popular quarry for modern hunters, even where fully farm-raised rabbits are available already dressed in the market. Like other farm-raised "game," commercial rabbits lack some of the complex, gamy flavor acquired by a diet of wild nuts and greens. Some don't care for this "wild" taste and prefer instead to catch them alive, so they can be purged on cereal and lettuce. But rabbits are beautiful, gentle animals, and this carries with it the very real risk that you'll get too attached to them to be able to kill them. It's easier to do that in the field, when you can think of them as the varmints that ruined your crop of early lettuce.

Now, squirrels are a different matter. First, let's get rid of a few modern preconceptions. Perhaps you think they are too cute and playful to eat. Obviously, you have never had them nest in your attic and chew everything in it to shreds, or attack the cat or dog—or you—with green nuts, which they can easily turn into a lethal weapon. They can be as mean as Lucifer. Squirrels are rodents—rats with bushy tails—and if you live in a city with a park, you already know that they are some of the greediest little beggars around. Just ask anyone who keeps a bird feeder or pecan tree in their back yard how gentle and cute they think squirrels are; you'll get an earful.

All foolishness aside, the early settlers did not have cartoons in which game animals were personified into cuddly heroes, or parks where they could be treated as pets; they had little of our modern inhibitions about eating them. For them, both these critters were welcome meat, and, fattened on wild fodder and nuts, they can be very good to eat. Well into the twentieth century, they were enjoyed fried, roasted, and stewed (squirrels were the original bases for two of our most famous regional stews, Burgoo and Brunswick Stew, and my grandmother used to make delicious dumplings with them).

By far the most popular way of cooking both rabbits and squirrels, however, was to flour and fry them to golden, crisp perfection as you would a chicken. Skin and disjoint the rabbit and follow the recipe for Basic Fried Chicken (page 154), adding, if you like, a tablespoon of dried thyme and a healthy pinch of cayenne to the flour mixture before coating them. Grill-broiling was also a popular way of cooking rabbits. Split them down the back and lay them flat as you would a chicken for grilling. Use Annabella Hill's Basting Sauce (page 203) and grill about 20 minutes per side, basting frequently with sauce. Another excellent way to cook them is the following stew.

Mary Randolph's Rabbit Stew

Mrs. Randolph noted that squirrels make soup "equally good, done the same way," and so they do. In fact, this is an excellent stew for any small game, or even large game birds or young chickens. Birds will need far less cooking time, about 1 hour. Unlike roasted fowl, stewed birds should be meltingly tender and practically falling off the bone.

2 large rabbits, dressed, or 4 squirrels or 6 game birds such as squab	1/2 teaspoon whole cloves, ground to a powder in a mortar or spice mill
1/4 pound lean sliced salt-cured pork or country ham	1 blade mace, ground to a powder in a mortar or spice mill
2 large sprigs fresh thyme (or 1 teaspoon if dried)	2 large white onions, thinly sliced
2 large sprigs fresh parsley	2 tablespoons butter
Salt and whole black pepper in a peppermill	1 tablespoon Southern Browning (page 110)
Ground cayenne pepper	1/4 cup red wine
	2 tablespoons chopped parsley

1. If you are using wild rabbits, skin and disjoint them as you would for frying. Wash them under cold, running water and drain. Rinse the salt pork, especially if it appears to be very salty, and pat it dry. If using fresh thyme, tie it into a bouquet garni with the parsley.

2. Put in a layer of rabbit on the bottom of a heavy-bottomed Dutch oven or stew pot. Sprinkle with a little salt, pepper, cayenne, and a pinch of the spices. If using dried thyme, sprinkle in half of it. Put in a thick layer of onions, then pork, and repeat until all the ingredients are used up.

3. Bring a quart of water to a boil in a teakettle and pour it over the rabbit. Add the herb bundle or parsley sprigs. Bring it just to a boil over medium heat, skimming it well, and reduce the heat to a bare simmer. Cover loosely, with the lid slightly askew, and simmer until the rabbit is very tender and the broth is somewhat reduced, about 2 hours.

4. Remove and discard the herbs and pork and skim off the excess fat. Knead the butter and Browning together and stir it into the stew in bits. Let simmer until thickened, about 3 or 4 minutes more, then stir in the wine and simmer 5 minutes. Garnish with parsley and serve. Serves 6.

NOTES: *You may make the stew a day or so ahead up through step 3. In fact, like most stews, it is better made ahead, and is easier to degrease when cold, as the fat will be congealed on the top. However, wait until you are ready to serve it before proceeding with step 4 and finishing it with the thickening and wine.*

VENISON

Venison was once so prized in England that cookery books gave recipes for dressing beef and mutton in imitation of it, and the choice bucks were reserved for the king. The early English settlers brought their fondness for this meat with them, and found to their delight that it was plentiful in the New World. Its sometimes-gamy flavor may be an acquired taste for people raised on corn-fed livestock, but venison is still prized by many Southerners, who believe it is a taste worth acquiring.

Deer once roamed all over the South, but automobiles and spreading suburbanization have limited their range to the few remaining uninhabited woodlands and reserves. In some places, they are protected and are becoming so numerous and tame that they come right into heavily populated neighborhoods, drawn by the plentiful food supply in gardens and flowerbeds. In neighborhoods where the city-bred have settled, the suggestion that the herd be controlled by hunting inevitably raises controversy. But that's no problem in old rural neighborhoods.

Most of my deer meat when I was writing this book came from Mr. Ludean Falagan, who lived in Guyton, Georgia. Every summer, the deer came in from the woods that border his property and raided Mr. Falagan's garden. For years, he tried everything he could think of to scare them off, to no avail. Finally, he just gave up and let them graze—even planted a row of peas in the deer's favorite grazing spot. But every fall, when the season opened, Mr. Falagan loaded his hunting rifle, went down to the hunting stand in the trees near his garden, and waited for one of those nice, pea-fattened deer to come back . . .

Baked Leg of Venison

In the sealed chamber of a modern oven, meat will not actually roast, but will bake in its own steam. While roasting can be approximated with very high temperatures, unless venison is especially fat and tender, I prefer to let the oven do what it does best and gently bake it.

Until well into the eighteenth century, most baked meats were cooked in a hard pastry crust, a practice that survived into the nineteenth century in many parts of America. This continued to be the prescribed method in many books until mid-century, and most early recipes for baked venison were so treated. Here, however, the meat bakes in an open pan, its own moisture supplemented with wine and perfumed with aromatic herbs. Many old recipes added wine only at the end, but I like to let it cook with the meat from the beginning and freshen the sauce with port or Madeira at the end. Though seldom mentioned in old recipes, the wine and herb mixture makes a fine marinade, and you may want to try using it that way, following the alternate instructions included in step 3.

1 leg venison, about 7 to 9 pounds	Salt and whole black pepper in a peppermill
2 cups dry red wine	Lard, or unsalted butter for rubbing the meat
3 bay leaves, crumbled if dried, chopped if fresh	3 cups thinly sliced yellow onions
3 large cloves garlic, crushed and peeled	1/2 cup port or medium-dry (Sercial) Madeira
8 whole cloves, crushed in a mortar or spice mill	1/2 cup red currant jelly or Cranberry Preserves (page 384) (optional)
6 to 8 whole dried sage leaves, crumbled or 1 tablespoon chopped fresh sage	2 tablespoons unsalted butter

1. Trim the meat, removing the skin if it has not been done, and wash it well.

2. Put the red wine in a mixing bowl and add the bay leaves, garlic, cloves, sage, a large pinch of salt, and a few liberal grindings of pepper. Mix together well. If you would like to marinate the venison, proceed with step 3. Otherwise, skip to step 4.

3. Put the meat in an oval enameled or stainless steel roasting pan, pour the seasoned wine over it, and marinate, basting and turning occasionally, for 4 to 8 hours, or overnight, refrigerated.

4. Preheat the oven to 500 degrees F. If you have marinated the meat, drain off but reserve the marinade. Wipe the meat dry, and rub it well with lard or butter, salt, and freshly ground black pepper. Put half the onion on the bottom of the pan and put the meat on top.

5. Bake in the upper third of the oven for about 15 minutes, or until well seared. Pour the seasoned wine over it, cover with the remaining onions, and reduce the heat to 350 degrees F. Bake until the meat is cooked to the level of doneness you prefer, 20 minutes per pound for medium (160 degrees F), basting often with pan juices. If it begins to get too brown, or if the juices are evaporating too quickly, cover the pan.

6. Take up the meat to a platter and let it rest for half an hour before carving. Meanwhile, degrease the pan juices and bring them to a simmer in a saucepan over medium heat. Simmer until reduced by about half. Deglaze the roasting pan with the port or Madeira and add it to the pan juices. Stir in the optional jelly or preserves until dissolved and simmer until lightly thickened. Off the heat, swirl in the butter in bits, and pour it into a warm sauceboat.

7. Slice the venison thinly at a 45 degrees angle to the bone, beginning at the shank. Arrange it on a warm platter, drizzle with gravy, and pass the remaining gravy separately. Serves 10 to 12.

NOTES: *The garlic may surprise you, as it is often supposed that Southerners have never liked or eaten it before the late twentieth century. Actually, it could more accurately be said that some Southerners are rediscovering garlic. Another herb commonly used with baked venison was thyme. You may substitute it for the sage if you like. I am not crazy about currant jelly with venison and personally never use it, but it is traditional.*

Venison Stew

This simple, earthy stew is a very satisfying thing to eat when the autumn weather turns crisp or when winter nights get nasty and wet. Served with its traditional accompaniment of Basic Boiled Grits (page 285), it is startlingly like the game and polenta feasts of northern Italy. In some parts of the South, it was also accompanied by Fried Grits (page 286) or Boiled Rice (page 289)—any of which would be fine.

The recipe is adapted from several sources, since recipes could and did vary. My maternal grandmother would have added a couple of grape leaves, as she did when she made goat stew. Creole cooks added a bouquet garni, bay leaves, and mushrooms. Some of the old English recipes that were likely used by the early colonists included a bit of lemon peel, a practice that virtually disappeared by the mid-nineteenth century, but one well worth reviving. Some finished the stew with wine, but it was not universal. Occasionally, currant jelly was included, but that's pushing it, for my taste, so it is not included here. Some old recipes added potatoes or turnips—or both. In short, there were as many recipes as there were cooks.

The recipe serves four, but can be expanded easily. Like most stews, it's pretty flexible.

3 pounds venison, bone in, preferably from the shoulder or neck, or 1-1/2 pounds, if using boneless venison

2 tablespoons unsalted butter

1 cup sliced yellow onion

1 clove garlic, lightly crushed, peeled, and minced

Salt and whole black pepper in a peppermill

Ground cayenne

2 or 3 large sprigs parsley

2 fresh or brine-cured grape leaves, well rinsed

Zest of 1 lemon, cut in several large pieces

2 tablespoons Southern Browning (page 110), dissolved in 3 tablespoons water or kneaded into 2 tablespoons butter

1/4 cup claret, port, or medium dry (Sercial) Madeira

1. Bring a teakettle filled with water to a boil. Rinse the meat well in cold water and pat it dry. Cut it into 2-inch pieces.

2. Put the butter in a large, heavy Dutch oven or flameproof casserole over medium-high heat. When it is melted and hot, add the venison and brown it well on all sides. Remove the meat and add the onion and cook until it turns a pale gold, about 4 minutes. Add the garlic and sauté until fragrant, about half a minute. Return the meat to the pan and season well with salt, a liberal grinding of pepper, and a pinch of cayenne.

3. Add enough boiling water to completely cover the venison. Let it come to a boil, add the parsley, grape leaves, and lemon zest, and reduce the heat to a bare simmer. Cover and simmer slowly until the meat is very tender, about 2 hours.

4. Skim off any excess fat and raise the heat to medium. Let the juices reduce slightly, but not too much: there should be at least a cup. Add the Browning mixture gradually to the stew, stirring constantly, and then stir in the wine and simmer until the stew is thickened, about 4 minutes. Serves 4.

NOTES: *In the Carolina or Georgia Lowcountry, this dish is served with Basic Boiled Rice (page 289). Elsewhere you might get Mashed Potatoes (page 242) or Basic Boiled Grits (page 285), but never macaroni. Harriott Horry added a handful of morels near the end of the simmer. You could follow her lead, finishing it with a splash of red wine or port if you wanted to dress it up.*

In the modern South, this dish is made with cubed steak — that is, steak that has been put through a tenderizer. It is available regionally in most markets. If you use cubed steak, you'll of course omit the pounding in step 1. Many cooks (myself included) add caramelized onions. First, thinly slice 2 medium onions and fry them in 2 tablespoons of drippings in a large skillet over medium heat until golden brown. Remove them from the pan and proceed with the recipe, adding the onions back with the browned meat in step 3.

Beef Olives

I have no idea why "olive" is the name given to these rolls of beef and forcemeat. This is medieval English cookery, which some historians suggest was devised to be eaten with the fingers in the days before forks were common. The rolls were called "olaves" in the old English recipes, but that appears to have been an older spelling variation of olive. The Oxford English Dictionary gives three archaic uses for the word for things other than olive fruit. One is this dish, one is an oval shaped horse bit, and the last is an oval mollusk native to the English Channel. The Medieval English would certainly have known about olive fruit, so the safest presumption is that the name denotes anything roughly oval in shape.

Almost every Southern cookbook until the early-twentieth century included some version of beef olives, often under the simpler name "Rolled Steak." But, by the time of Mrs. Dull's *Southern Cooking* in 1928, they were nowhere to be found. Veal olives linger as "Veal Birds" in general-purpose American cookbooks, but seldom have the spirited finesse of the old recipes.

2 pounds beef round, cut across the grain in slices about 1/2 inch thick	1 tablespoon chopped parsley
Salt and whole black pepper in a peppermill	3 tablespoons minced onion
2 cups fine soft, but stale, breadcrumbs	2 large egg yolks, beaten
2 tablespoons minced beef suet	1-1/2 cups Basic Meat Broth (page 80)
1 teaspoon crumbled dried sage	1 to 2 tablespoons unsalted butter
1 teaspoon freshly grated nutmeg	1 tablespoon Southern Browning (page 110), kneaded into 1 tablespoon butter

1. Position a rack in the upper third of the oven and then preheat it to 350 degrees F. Lay the beef on a flat surface and pound it with a textured mallet until 1/4 inch thick. Season well with salt and pepper.

2. Mix the crumbs, suet, sage, nutmeg, parsley, onion, and egg yolks. Moisten, if needed, with a little broth, but don't make it soggy. Spread evenly over each piece of beef, roll them up tightly, and tie in at least two places with butcher's string dipped in water.

3. Melt a tablespoon of butter over medium heat in a flameproof lidded casserole that will hold the olives in one layer. Add the olives and brown well on all sides. Add the broth, cover, and bake for about 1 hour, or until the beef is fork tender and the forcemeat hot through.

4. Remove the olives to a platter. Put the casserole over direct medium heat, bring the broth to a boil, and reduce it to about 1 cup. Stir in the Browning and butter, reduce the heat to a simmer, and cook, stirring, until just thickened, about 4 minutes. Pour it over the olives and serve at once. Serves 6.

VEAL

With the prices that veal nowadays fetches in our markets, and the limited choice of cuts generally available in the South, it seems hard to imagine that veal was once commonplace, relatively inexpensive, and even considered inferior to other meats. Mrs. Hill wrote that it "of itself is an insipid meat." The authors of *The Texas Cook Book*, published in Houston in 1883, noted that veal "is not as nutritious as beef or mutton, but in many places is much cheaper." This was pretty much true until well into the twentieth century. John and Karen Hess, in *The Taste of America* (1977), remind us of mid-century scandals in which unscrupulous purveyors were caught trying to pass off veal as chicken. Modern attempts to make turkey and chicken imitate veal are a turn of events that Mary Randolph, Sarah Rutledge, and Lettice Bryan, not to mention Mrs. Hill, would have found truly strange.

There is some debate about what veal was like in the early-nineteenth century. A few historians claim that few actually had true milk-fed veal, that most of it was actually from older calves. But surely true veal was available; Mrs. Hill and Lettice Bryan were both clear as to what proper veal was, and a common practice among dairy farmers was to take the calves early to keep the cow lactating. Milk-fed veal is pale, creamy pink, lighter sometimes than raw chicken breast, and very tender, ideally no more than three months old. As the calf matures and begins to eat grass, the meat deepens in color and gets tougher, not only because of the change in diet, but because the animal is more active. Shop with a reliable butcher to be sure you are not getting older calves' meat that has been bled to make it pale.

Annabella Hill's Curried Veal Stew

Curry, that exotic mixture of spices that is the trademark of so much far-eastern cuisine, became quite popular in England when British trade and, later, the Empire, spread into India and other parts of Asia. Its popularity reached to the American colonies, where it became a common seasoning, especially in the South. Curry is also widely known in the Caribbean, where communities of Indian immigrants have settled. The thing that became popular was, of course, a blend of spice that didn't exist as such in India, but never mind.

The Southern classic, Chicken Country Captain, which we most likely borrowed from England, is widely known. This stew is perhaps less so, and is nowadays rarely seen, but it's every bit as good.

3 pounds veal in one piece, bone-in, from the neck, shoulder, or shank, or 1-1/2 pounds boneless	2 large cloves garlic, lightly crushed, peeled, and minced (optional)
Salt and whole black pepper in a peppermill	1 tablespoon Mrs. Hill's Curry Powder (page 37)
2 large yellow onions, trimmed, split lengthwise, peeled, and thinly sliced	1 tablespoon unbleached flour
	1 tablespoon butter
	1 cup heavy cream

1. Bring a teakettle full of water to a boil. Meanwhile, rinse the meat under cold water and wipe it dry. Rub it lightly with salt and a few grindings of pepper, and put it in a snug-fitting Dutch oven. Strew the onions over the meat, and, if you like it, the optional garlic.

2. Add enough boiling water to barely cover the meat and onions. Bring it to a boil over medium heat, skimming any scum that rises, and reduce the heat to low. Loosely cover and simmer gently until the veal is fork tender, about 1-1/2 to 2 hours. Remove the meat to a warm platter.

3. Raise the heat and bring the broth to a boil. Let it boil until it is reduced to 2 cups. Meanwhile, mix the curry powder and flour in a small bowl, add the butter, and blend

it evenly with a spoon or fork. Bring the cream to a boil in a small saucepan over medium heat. Let it simmer, stirring it occasionally, until slightly reduced. Turn off the heat, but keep it hot.

4. When the broth is reduced, lower the heat to medium and add the seasoned butter and flour in pieces, stirring constantly. Let it simmer for 5 minutes, stirring often, until it is thickened and the flour has lost its raw, pasty taste. Slowly stir in the hot cream, let it come back to a simmer, and simmer until thickened. Turn off the heat.

5. Slice or cut the veal into small pieces, removing and discarding the bones. Spread a little sauce on a warm platter, arrange the veal over it, and cover with the remaining sauce. Serve at once. Serves 4.

NOTES: *Though less flavorful, this stew can also be made with 2-inch pieces of boneless stewing veal. The smaller pieces cook faster, usually in about 1 hour. When I tried them, my natural laziness took over and I left the meat in the broth while it reduced and thickened. Though no doubt Mrs. Hill would not approve, today I brown the veal first, then sprinkle the curry spices into the pan and let them toast until fragrant, and then proceed with the stew as directed.*

To Ragout a Breast of Veal

If printed cookbooks are any indication, this was one of our favorite dishes of veal, not only in the South, but all over America. No wonder: the breast may be spare and prone to gristle, but no other meat is more succulent and flavorful.

In all but a very few of the old recipes, the meat was browned by roasting it in front of a clear fire. It was then added to a rich gravy and braised slowly until tender. To simplify things, and to keep from heating the oven, the rack is here browned on top of the stove in the braising pan. Note the use of garlic, bouquet garni, and lemon zest. The original recipe was garnished with veal sweetbreads sautéed in butter. Since sweetbreads are often hard to come by, they are omitted here, but you should try them if you are lucky enough to find them.

4 pounds veal breast, bone in, about 4 ribs from the thick brisket end

Whole black pepper in a peppermill

Unbleached all-purpose flour

2 tablespoons unsalted butter

1 medium yellow onion, trimmed, split lengthwise, peeled, and chopped

1 medium carrot, peeled and chopped

1 large, or 2 medium cloves garlic, lightly crushed, peeled, and minced
2 cups Basic Meat Broth (page 80) made with veal bones, or water

1/2 cup dry white wine

Salt

Zest of 1 lemon, removed in large pieces

1 slice lemon, cut from the center

1 Bouquet Garni (page 34) or 1 teaspoon each dried thyme and marjoram, 1 bay leaf, and 2 sprigs parsley tied up in cheesecloth or a large tea ball

Parsley sprigs and 1 lemon, cut into 8 wedges, for garnish

1. If the butcher hasn't already done so, trim the veal, paring away the skin and scraps from the ends of the rib bones. Cut through the joints, but do not separate the ribs. Very lightly season it with a few grindings of black pepper and dust it with a little flour.

2. Melt the butter in a flameproof casserole or enameled iron Dutch oven that will comfortably hold the breast over medium-high heat. When it's hot, but not browning, put in the veal and brown it on all sides. Remove it from the pan.

3. Add the onion and sauté until golden, about 5 minutes. Add the carrot and sauté until softened, about 2 minutes, then add the garlic and sauté until fragrant, about half a minute more. Add the broth and bring to a boil, stirring and scraping the pan to loosen any browned bits that are sticking to it, then add the wine and let it come back to a boil.

4. Return the veal to the pan, season with a healthy pinch of salt, and add the zest, lemon slice, and bouquet garni. Let it come back to a simmer, loosely cover, and reduce the heat to low. Simmer gently, turning occasionally, until very tender, about 2-1/2 to 3 hours.

5. Remove the veal to a warm platter. Let it rest 15 to 20 minutes and carve between the ribs into individual portions. Skim off any excess fat from the pan juices, and, if they aren't thick enough, raise the heat briefly to medium-high and boil until lightly reduced and thickened. Pour the gravy over the veal, garnish with the parsley and lemon wedges, and serve at once. Serves 4.

NOTES: *This is similar to Milanese* osso bucco, *both in concept and execution, and veal shanks are wonderful done this way.*

The kind of wine originally used is not clear. At least one recipe for veal specifically says claret (Bordeaux wine), and there are occasional references to sack (sherry). There was a thriving wine industry in this country by the middle of the nineteenth century, but wine was also imported. Claret, Madeira, port and sherry were all advertised in Southern newspapers. The cook probably used whatever she had on hand, which, I rather suspect, was more often than not sherry. With few exceptions, I prefer white wine in veal dishes and so have used it here. Whatever you use, a word of caution: Don't be tempted to substitute more wine for the stock on the mistaken notion that more is always better. There is too much liquid required here to substitute wine; 2-1/2 cups would over-power the veal and give the whole thing a sour bite.

VEAL CUTLETS AND COLLOPS

In old American and English cookery books, cutlet and collop both describe the same cut—a thin slice taken from the fillet end of the round. Usually—though not always—"cutlet" was used when it was breaded and fried, and "collop" when treated like scaloppine. Recipes for both were universally popular in American cookbooks of the nineteenth century; Southern ones were no ex-ception. Here are two classics that once graced our tables.

Breaded Veal Cutlets

Breaded cutlets have suffered much at the hands of frozen food vendors and modern cafeterias. When I was in college, much of what we were offered in the cafeteria was questionable, but their cutlets, I think, were the worst: Dry slabs of ground meat and filler entombed in a tough, coarse breading, fried until it both felt and tasted like sawdust, slathered with canned tomato sauce, and blanketed with squares of vinyl-like "mozzarella." We called them "dreaded" veal cutlets.

This is Italy's justly famous Milanese cutlet—thin slices of veal, lightly breaded and fried to golden perfection. The Milanese may be justified in their claim to its creation, but it has long been an international dish. Popular stories would have us believe it was mostly unknown in America until recent years, but a glance at period cookbooks does not bear this out. Most have contained the basic recipe. If there's a more satisfying way to cook and eat veal, I've never found it.

For frying the cutlets, clarified butter produces the best flavor and is by far the easiest to work with since there are no milk solids to burn. Modern Italian cooks raise the burning temperature of butter by mixing it with olive oil. Lard is the fat most used in Southern recipes and the least likely to burn. It produces a fine crust, but the flavor isn't as distinctive as butter. If you can't use animal fat, olive oil lends the most satisfying flavor. I favor the Italian butter and oil mixture, mainly because I am lazy.

1-1/2 pounds veal cutlets, sliced 3/8 inch thick
Salt and whole black pepper in a peppermill
1 cup dry breadcrumbs
2 large eggs, well beaten in a wide shallow bowl

Clarified butter, lard, or equal parts unsalted
   butter and oil, for frying
1 lemon, cut into 8 wedges

1. Lay the cutlets out on a flat work surface and pound them with a mallet until 1/4 inch thick. Sprinkle lightly with salt and a few grindings of pepper.

2. Spread the crumbs on a plate. Roll each cutlet in the egg, let the excess flow back into the bowl, and lay it on the breadcrumbs, turning and pressing the crumbs into it until both sides are well coated. Spread them on a wire rack or a plate and let them dry for at least half an hour. (You may make them several hours ahead.)

3. When you are ready to cook the cutlets, put enough fat into a wide skillet to cover the bottom by at least 1/4 inch. Turn on the heat to medium-high. When the fat is melted and quite hot (but not smoking) slip enough cutlets into the pan to fill it without crowding. Fry for about 2 minutes per side, or until both sides are a rich golden brown.

4. Blot briefly on absorbent paper and transfer them to a warm serving platter. If you have to fry them in batches, keep the first batch warm until all the cutlets are ready. Garnish with lemon wedges and serve at once. Serves 4.

Annabella Hill's Curry Sauce for Cutlets

Though the best possible sauce for a cutlet is a squeeze of lemon juice, they were often accompanied by tomato sauce, just as they sometimes are in Italy. Mrs. Hill's curry sauce is another nice accompaniment. The savory-sweet combination of apple, onion, and curry spices is an inviting contrast to the crackling crust and delicate meat. It is also delicious with cutlets of turkey or chicken breasts, and a fine sauce for pork or mutton, especially with a handful of raisins or currants thrown in. A splash of Madeira wouldn't hurt anything, either.

1 medium onion	1-1/2 cups half-and-half
1 tart apple	1 tablespoon unsalted butter
2 level teaspoons flour	Salt
2 teaspoons Mrs. Hill's Curry Powder (page 37)	

1. Peel the onion and peel and core the apple. Cut both into dice the same size. Mix together the flour and curry in a small bowl, dissolve it in a little of the half-and-half, and set it aside.

2. Put the onion, apple, and butter in a 1- to 1-1/2-quart saucepan over medium heat. Sauté, tossing and stirring frequently, until they are golden, about 5 to 8 minutes.

3. Pour in the half-and-half and let it come to a boil, stirring constantly to prevent it from scorching. As soon as it begins to boil, stir the curry paste to mix it and gradually stir it into the pan. Bring it to a boil, stirring constantly, and reduce the heat to low. Season to taste with salt. Simmer until it is thick and the flour has lost its raw taste, at least 5 minutes. Pour it into a heated sauceboat.

4. While the sauce simmers, cook the cutlets according to the previous recipe and arrange them on a heated platter. Drizzle a little sauce over them if you like and serve at once, passing the remaining sauce separately.

Scotched Collops

"Scotch" here is not a reference to Scotland or whiskey, but to an old method of tenderizing meat by cutting diagonal scores into it. It has nothing to do with Scotland unless you subscribe to the notion that the crisscross pattern of the scoring resembles a tartan plaid. If you do, you have the kind of imagination that makes a good Southerner.

There is a close kinship here to the wine-sauced *scaloppine* of Italy. It's a fast, tasty, and elegant way to do veal, so it seems odd that it did not survive the nineteenth century. No modern Southern cookbooks mention this delectable dish, and the latest recipe that I have found, called Scotch Collops, in Harriet Ross Colquitt's *The Savannah Cook Book* (1933), had nothing but name in common with this one. An unspeakable mess of ground beef boiled in tomato juice and served over rice, it was a sad corruption of Minced Collops, a dish popular in the eighteenth and nineteenth centuries. Clearly, more had been lost than the original meaning of the word "collop."

The seasonings varied: the oldest, Harriott Horry's, contained anchovies and sweet marjoram and was garnished with oysters, mushrooms, sweetbreads, and forcemeat. Whew. Sage, nutmeg, and lemon were usual, and are included here. The thickening agent varied, as well. Some used flour, others, egg yolk. I've used the latter because it makes a more elegant finish.

Like scaloppine, scotched collops must not be overcooked or they will take on a texture not unlike dried buffalo.

2 pounds veal scallops cut from the round, across the grain, 1/4 inch thick	1 teaspoon freshly grated lemon zest
1/2 teaspoon crumbled dried sage	1 tablespoon chopped parsley
Whole nutmeg in a grater	1/4 cup Basic Meat Broth (page 80)
5 tablespoons unsalted butter	1/2 cup dry red or white wine (see notes)
Salt and whole black pepper in a peppermill	Juice of 1 lemon
2 tablespoons minced shallot, or 2 teaspoons minced garlic	1 large egg yolk, beaten

1. Lay the veal scallops on a work surface and pound them to 1/8 inch thick. Score each lightly in a crisscross with a sharp knife, being careful not to cut all the way through the meat, and rub well with sage and nutmeg.

2. In a heavy skillet, melt 4 tablespoons of the butter over medium-high heat. When it starts to bubble, put in some of the scallops and sauté until barely cooked through, about 1 minute per side. Take them up onto a warm platter and repeat until all the meat has been cooked. Season with salt and pepper to taste, cover the platter, and keep warm.

3. Add the shallots to the pan and sauté until they begin to color. Add the lemon zest and parsley and pour on the broth. Let it boil up, stirring and scraping the pan to loosen any browned residue, and add the wine and lemon juice. Let it come back to a boil and remove the pan from the heat. Beat in the egg yolk. The residual heat should be enough to thicken the sauce. If not, return the pan to low heat and stir constantly until the sauce lightly thickens. Off the heat swirl in the rest of the butter, taste and adjust the seasoning, and pour the sauce over the veal. Serve at once. Serves 6.

NOTES: *Few recipes specify the kind of wine, but at least one source calls for claret (Bordeaux wine). I tend to prefer white wine in this recipe, but a dry red or Madeira will work if you would like to try it. The garlic is authentic: Mrs. Randolph made wide use of it, especially with veal, and her recipe included a healthy dose.*

MUTTON AND LAMB

Medieval and Renaissance England's main export commodity was wool, so it should be no surprise that mutton was a staple of the English diet. As England established its permanent colonies in America, they naturally brought sheep with them, and mutton and lamb became a commonplace part of the New World's table. Both remained popular throughout the nineteenth century, but in our own century, lamb remained popular in most places while mutton began to disappear. In her 1928 book, Mrs. Dull practically ignored mutton, but referred to lamb as "plain, everyday food." While the fondness for mutton has faded in other parts of America, it has remained strong in Kentucky, where it never lost its central place in the local diet. It is in *The Kentucky Housewife* that we find the most varied and sympathetic mutton and lamb cookery.

Unfortunately, what most of us get in the market today is neither lamb nor mutton. The old cookbooks are specific, from Amelia Simmons through to Mrs. Hill: Lamb is very young sheep, taken when it is under six months old, and mutton is mature sheep no less than two years old. What is sold as lamb in our markets is almost always somewhere in between. Unless you have had very young lamb, you have no idea how tender, delicate, and sweet it can be. And true mutton has a distinctive, savory flavor that puts our modern halfway between meat to shame. But even though it is a far cry from the lamb and mutton of a century ago, commercial lamb can be respectable, and with a little care, even quite good. The recipes that follow are a sampling of the wide variety and high level of quality of mutton cookery in the South's early days.

Roast Leg of Lamb or Mutton

Though the difference in size and age makes roasting times for mutton and lamb vary, the method is exactly the same. The preference for most roasted meat through the third quarter of the nineteenth century was rare, but lamb was usually cooked a little longer, to about medium. Only when boiled or braised did it appear on the table with no hint of red remaining.

If the size of a whole leg of lamb intimidates you, or isn't practical for your household, you may, of course, roast a smaller piece of meat (such as the shank or butt half) using this recipe. Adjust the cooking times according to the weight of the meat. But keep in mind that large roasts mean lots of lovely leftovers, which can be used for sandwiches and such savory dishes as Lettice Bryan's Mutton Casseroles (page 187).

1 whole leg of lamb, or the shank half of a leg of mutton, about 7 pounds

Salt and whole black pepper in a peppermill

Mint Sauce (page 122), Caper Sauce (page 116), or Georgia Apple and Tomato Chutney (page 392)

1. Position a rack in the upper third of the oven and preheat to 500 degrees F. Wash the meat and pat dry. Don't trim off the fat, even if there appears to be a lot. Most butchers have already trimmed off too much as it is.
2. Put the meat, fat side up, on a rack fitted into an oval or oblong roasting pan that will hold it comfortably. Dust it lightly with salt and pepper. Roast, undisturbed, for 15 minutes.
3. Reduce the heat to 400 degrees F, and roast, basting frequently with the pan drippings, until done to your taste, about 15 minutes per pound for medium-rare.
4. Transfer the roast to a serving platter and let it rest at least 15 minutes before carving. If you feel there is too much fat, you may trim some of it away before carving. Serve with the sauce of your choice passed separately. Serves 12 to 15.

NOTES: *If the meat is getting too brown before it's done, tuck a piece of cooking parchment or foil around it, being careful to leave it loose enough to vent the steam. Personally, I like the fat to be crispy and well browned.*

Grilled Mutton or Lamb Chops

This is a lovely recipe that does nice things to the neither-nor meat that passes for lamb in many American markets. Mrs. Bryan changed the parchment wrap after cooking, so the chops would come to the table encased in pristine white. Frankly, I'm too lazy and have never cared to fuss over them at the last minute, so have never bothered with this fastidious step. With care, you can omit the paper casing altogether and the crust will be crackling crisp and brown.

The same recipe was frequently used for veal chops, and it is a delicious treatment for them. If you are not able to grill the chops, you may omit the paper casing and oven broil or fry them (see the notes).

8 mutton or lamb rib chops (about 3/4 inch thick)	Whole nutmeg in a grater
Grated zest from 1 lemon	1 cup dry breadcrumbs
Salt and whole black pepper in a peppermill	2 large eggs, well beaten in a wide, shallow bowl
	4 to 5 tablespoons unsalted butter

1. Prepare a grill with hardwood coals and let them burn down to an intense red glow. Meanwhile, trim the chops, stripping the rib bone of its fat and scraps of meat, but leaving it attached to the eye or medallion. Lightly flatten the eye of each and season with lemon zest, a little salt, a liberal grinding of black pepper, and a sprinkling of freshly grated nutmeg.

2. Spread the breadcrumbs on a plate and have them ready beside the eggs. Dip each chop in the egg, letting the excess run back into the bowl, then roll them in the crumbs. Lay the chops on a rack until you are ready to cook them, but for no less than half an hour to let the breading set.

3. When the coals are ready, melt the butter in a small saucepan over medium heat. Don't let it bubble up or brown, but turn it off as soon as it has melted.

4. Lay each chop on a square of parchment, fold it over, and twist the paper around the bone to hold it together. Position the grill rack 4 to 6 inches above the coals and put the chops on it. Baste lightly with melted butter and grill for about 4 minutes. If the paper starts to brown, raise the rack further from the heat. Baste again, turn, and baste the cooked side liberally. Cook for another 4 minutes. Quickly take the chops from the grill, loosen the paper to prevent them from steaming, and serve immediately. Serves 4.

NOTES: *This recipe can also be used with loin chops and either loin or rib veal chops. Cut the parchment large enough to completely encase the loin chops and fold it tightly. The veal chops should cook in about the same length of time if they are no thicker than called for above.*

If you choose to omit the paper casing, grease the rack well to keep the breading from sticking to it and position it a little higher above the heat. How much will depend on the intensity of your coals. Before putting the chops on the grill, brush them lightly with the melted butter, and baste them again halfway through the cooking. This is a delicious treatment for loin chops.

These chops are also delicious fried in clarified butter or butter mixed with olive oil. Omit the paper wrap and double the amount of butter if using clarified butter or allow 1/4 cup of olive oil with the amount of butter called for above. Heat the fat over medium-high heat until hot but not smoking and fry the chops about 3 minutes per side. Be careful not to overcook them; a great deal of their charm lies in having a crisp outer crust contrasted with a juicy pink interior.

Lettice Bryan's Mutton Casseroles

This is a nice way to use up leftover boiled or roasted leg of mutton or lamb. It is essentially a light shepherd's pie, seasoned with lemon peel and tomatoes and baked in individual ramekins. The potatoes must be quite stiff or the gravy will dissolve them and make the bottom mushy and uninteresting. If you don't have cooked country ham, raw slices of country ham or prosciutto are preferable to those dull boiled ham sandwich slices.

1 recipe Mashed Potatoes (page 242)	Whole black pepper in a peppermill
2 large, ripe tomatoes	Whole nutmeg in a grater
1 pound leftover Roast Leg of Lamb or Mutton (page 185) or other leftover lamb	Grated zest of 1 lemon
	Salt
1/4 pound cooked or raw country ham or prosciutto	3/4 cup leftover Pan Gravy 1 (page 111)

1. Position a rack in the center of the oven and preheat it to 350 degrees F. Put on a teakettle of water to boil. Lightly butter four large ramekins or individual gratin dishes and line them with half the potatoes.

2. Blanch, peel, and core the tomatoes as directed on page 262. Cut them crosswise into 8 to 10 even slices. Seed and drain them in a colander set over the sink.

3. Chop the meat by hand with a knife or in the food processor, pulsing the machine to keep from completely pulverizing it. Chop the ham separately.

4. Pat the tomatoes dry and put a layer of them over the potatoes, about 2 slices per dish.

Divide the meat evenly between the dishes and season with a few grindings of pepper, a grating of nutmeg to taste, and the lemon zest. If your ham isn't very salty, add a little salt. Portion the gravy among each dish, and sprinkle them evenly with ham. Cover with the remaining potatoes and smooth with the flat of a knife or spatula.

5. Bake until nicely browned and heated through, about half an hour. Serves 4.

NOTES: *Do not substitute canned tomatoes for the fresh ones. If you are using Italian-style plum tomatoes, such as Roma, you will need about 4. Cut them about 1/4-inch thick, and cover the bottom layer of potatoes with them.*

Resist the temptation to add onions or garlic; the fresh balance between tomato, lemon zest, ham, and nutmeg is pretty near perfect. Mrs. Bryan doesn't say so, but I don't think she would fuss too much if you topped each casserole with a sprinkling of freshly grated Parmesan.

PORK

Swine are not native to North America, but were early imports to the American colonies. In much of the South, they were allowed to run loose and forage for roots and wild nuts among the underbrush of the virgin forests. The wild hogs of the Appalachian Mountains and coastal barrier islands are descended from imported domestic animals that got loose. This casual sort of animal husbandry was seen as shockingly lazy to visitors of the colonies in the eighteenth century; however, the flavor of the meat must have been extraordinary. (Too bad we can't see fit today to feed pigs in part on the acorns that are raked from our cities' parks.)

Pork is widely supposed to have been the staple meat of Southern households, but in some parts of the South, fresh pork was not as commonplace as veal or mutton. Salt-cured and smoked pork, however, was omnipresent, and the pickling and curing was an important responsibility of the women of the household. A little discussed enterprise common among the wives of upper-class planter and plain farmer alike was the selling of their surplus home-cured hams, lard, butter, and eggs (hence the expression "butter and egg money"). In 1856, Martha Goode Tucker (mistress of Rose Hill, Milledgeville, Georgia) recorded the sale of 170 pounds of ham and 48-1/2 pounds of lard.

Pork does not keep as well as other fresh meat, so, before refrigeration, cured pork was the staple, and ham, for many, was an everyday food. Fresh pork was therefore a cold weather treat, particularly in the hog-killing and curing season of late autumn.

Pork and sage are a classic combination, both in English and Southern cooking, but I didn't realize until after this book had been published for several years that every blessed recipe included on these pages had sage in it. You needn't sing on one note like that: feel free to experiment with other herbs—such as winter savory, marjoram, or rosemary.

Baked Pork Loin with Sweet Potatoes

Pork and sweet potatoes, both of which come into season in autumn, are a classic pairing in the South, and they are naturals together. When a leg or loin was roasted before the fire, sweet potatoes were often laid in a pan underneath it, where they naturally basted in the juices that fell from the roast. They were also frequently baked together, as this recipe does them, in a Dutch oven. You can use any cut of pork: The shoulder (Boston butt), or even a fresh leg, but the loin is especially nice and possibly the best cut to choose.

Our modern obsession with fat has led to the breeding of leaner pigs, and most butchers compound the felony by trimming off the skin and most of the fat; this adds to the danger of drying out the meat by overcooking. Be sure that the meat you buy has not been trimmed too much, but has a healthy layer of fat all round to keep it moist. You can usually get rid of the excess fat at the end.

1 pork loin roast weighing 4 to 5 pounds, preferably not boneless	Extra virgin olive oil
6 to 8 crumbled, dried sage leaves	6 medium sweet potatoes (or use quartered winter squash for a nice change)
Salt and whole black pepper in a peppermill	1/4 cup medium-dry (Sercial) Madeira (optional)

1. Position a rack in the lower third of the oven and preheat it to 450 degrees F. Trim some of the excess fat from the pork but leave a thin layer to keep the meat moist. Rub it with sage, a healthy pinch of salt, and a few grindings of black pepper. Choose a covered roaster that will hold the pork and sweet potatoes at once. Fit it with a metal rack or trivet that will leave room for the potatoes around it. Rub the rack or trivet with olive oil and put the pork loin on it, fat side up. Drizzle it with a tablespoon or so of olive oil.

2. Bake for 15 minutes, then reduce the heat to 350 degrees F, baste again with olive oil, and add a cup of water to the pan. Bake for about 1 hour, basting occasionally with the pan juices.

3. Meanwhile, scrub the sweet potatoes under cold, running water and dry thoroughly. After the first hour of baking, place the potatoes around the pork and baste well with pan juices. Bake until the potatoes and pork are cooked through and tender, basting frequently, about 1-1/2 hours more. The meat juices should run clear and the potatoes should yield easily when gently squeezed.

4. Take up the pork and potatoes onto a warm platter and put the roasting pan on top of the stove. Skim off the excess fat and make gravy as directed for Pan Gravy I (page 111), using the fat and roasting juices. If you are using Madeira, add it to the gravy and simmer until thickened, about 4 minutes more. Taste and adjust the seasonings and pour into a heated sauceboat. Serves 6.

Green Ham with Sage, or Fresh Leg of Pork

No, this isn't about moldy pork; just cut that out. In many parts of the South, a fresh leg of pork that has not been cured is called a "green" ham. The name arose in the days when all hind-leg cuts, regardless of treatment, were called hams. As the word came to mean only cured meat, Southerners began to refer to an uncured leg as they would un-ripened fruit or vegetables, as "green." The practice is still common in the Carolina Piedmont region, where it is also used for fresh (as opposed to dried) corn and, oddly enough, for freshly harvested shrimp. It remains practical in our day, since the old words for cured pork have come to have other meanings in American English. "Bacon" in old English meant any kind of pickled pork, but now means one particular smoked cut of meat. And in modern meatpackers' jargon, "ham" is used for all kinds of products: It can (and often does) mean just about anything and may not be describing the leg or even pork. Old time Southerners wouldn't have known how to deal with something called turkey ham—nor, I suspect, would they have wanted to learn.

A green, or fresh, ham was a great luxury in the days when slaughtering was done only in the cool weather of late fall. Since curing had to be done as soon as possible and the leg was usually put aside for it, to eat a fresh ham right away was a real indulgence. For many families (my own included), green hams were as traditional at autumnal holiday feasts as was cured ham or turkey.

Probably the best and most satisfying way of doing a fresh ham is to roast it as Annabella Hill directed: seasoned with sage and onion stuffing, liberally basted with olive oil and spit-roasted before a clear, brisk fire. That isn't possible with a modern range; however, with high temperatures and a little care, one can come close. The seasonings here are the traditional Southern and English ones for pork—sage and plenty of freshly ground black pepper. The cooking begins in a very hot oven to brown and seal the outside, then the heat is reduced for the slow cooking that pork takes to so well. This method produces a lovely brown skin and moist, juicy meat without burning the fat.

In some old recipes, the ham was boned and stuffed. I prefer to leave the bone in, but if you would like to try it, boning and stuffing directions are included in the notes at the end of the recipe.

1 fresh, uncured leg of pork (sometimes labeled fresh ham), about 10 to 12 pounds

2 to 3 tablespoons extra virgin olive oil

10 to 12 dried sage leaves, crushed to a powder (about 1 tablespoon)

Salt and whole black pepper in a peppermill

1/2 cup medium-dry (Sercial) Madeira or port

Fresh Peach Sauce (page 379), Cranberry Preserves (page 384), Georgia Apple and Tomato Chutney (page 392), or applesauce

1. Position a rack in the upper third of the oven and preheat it to 500 degrees F. Put the pork in a roasting pan fitted with a rack and rub all sides with olive oil and dust it well with the sage, a large pinch or so of salt, and liberal grindings of black pepper. Roast for about 15 minutes without opening the oven.

2. Reduce the heat to 400 degrees F. Baste with a little more olive oil, and then roast, basting frequently thereafter with the pan juices, until the meat is well done and the juices run clear, about 25 minutes per pound. If the outside appears to be getting too brown, you can lay a sheet of cooking parchment over it and reduce the heat to 350 degrees F.

3. Take up the ham and allow it to rest for about half an hour before carving. Meanwhile, make gravy as directed for Pan Gravy I (page 111) with the fat and roasting juices. Add the Madeira and let it simmer until thickened. Pour the gravy in a warmed bowl or sauce-boat and pass it separately with one of the sauces suggested above. Serves 12 to 14.

NOTES: *If you like, whole sweet potatoes or quartered winter squash can be placed around the ham during the last hour. Baste them whenever you baste the pork. The leg can also be stuffed. Cut out the bone with a fillet knife, being careful to keep the outer skin and flesh intact. Fill the bone cavity with a half recipe of Southern Sage and Onion Stuffing (page 149), or with Sweet Potato Stuffing (page 152), and tie it with twine to help hold its shape. A boned and stuffed leg will cook more quickly than one with the bone in—about 20 minutes per pound after boning.*

Braised Pork Chops

Here is pork with sage again in a very simple dish whose flavor depends on the forthrightness of sage, pepper, and browned crust, unadulterated by other spices or vegetables. It's a simple, unsophisticated way to do chops, but an extremely good one.

Don't use canned broth for this; it's too strongly flavored and will throw out the delicate balance of flavors. If you don't have homemade broth on hand, use water instead.

2 cups Basic Meat Broth (page 80) or water
4 pork chops (about 3/4 to 1 inch thick)
1 teaspoon crumbled dried sage leaves
Salt and whole black pepper in a peppermill

1/4 cup plain, all-purpose flour, spread on a plate
1/4 cup medium-dry (Sercial) Madeira, optional
1 tablespoon unsalted butter

1. Bring the broth or water to a boil. Trim the excess fat from the chops and dust them with sage, salt and pepper.

2. Put the fat trimmings into a deep skillet over medium heat. Cook, turning and pressing the fat, until you have about 2 tablespoons of rendered fat (if you don't have enough, supplement it with lard or olive oil). Remove and discard the browned cracklings. Roll the chops in the flour, shake off the excess, and slip them into the skillet. Brown both sides well and spoon off the excess fat.

3. Add enough hot broth or water to half cover them. Reduce the heat to a bare simmer, tightly cover the pan, and simmer until fork tender, about 1 hour.

4. Remove the chops to a warm platter, raise the heat briefly, add the Madeira, if using, and, stirring and scraping the pan, boil the gravy until slightly reduced and thick. Turn off the heat and swirl in the butter. Spoon the sauce over the chops and serve at once. Serves 4.

NOTES: *You could also add to the gravy 3 tablespoons minced onion that have been simmered to a golden brown in a little butter and a spoonful of cider vinegar, in which case, definitely omit the Madeira. This recipe is also an excellent way to braise other kinds of chops, such as mutton or venison.*

A PAIR OF PORK TENDERLOIN RECIPES
Tenderloin Steaks, or Medallions

This was once the favorite breakfast dish on the autumn days that hogs were butchered. The tenderloin is sliced crosswise into medallions (the old books called them steaks), gently flattened, dusted with sage and pepper, then pan-fried very quickly in a little lard. Stuffed into hot biscuits, or sauced with pan gravy and served with fried apples or Fried Sweet Potatoes (page 248), they make awfully good eating at any time.

If you're afraid of the lard or really must avoid it, olive oil is a legitimate substitution. Mrs. Hill, whose recipe follows this one, took a cue from Dr. Kitchiner and used olive oil for basting roast pork, so the combination is consistent with her kitchen and intent. I often use it, mainly because I am lazy and the bottle is always close at hand.

1 pair pork tenderloins, about 2 pounds
10 to 12 whole dried sage leaves, crushed fine
Salt and whole black pepper in a peppermill

1 rounded tablespoon lard, unsalted butter, or olive oil
1 rounded teaspoon flour

1. Rinse the tenderloins, pat dry, and cut them crosswise into 1/2-inch-thick medallions. Lightly beat them with a mallet until 1/4 inch thick. Rub sage, salt, and freshly ground pepper into both sides of each medallion.

2. Heat the lard or oil in a cast-iron skillet that will hold the steaks in one layer over medium-high heat. When the fat is quite hot (the edge of the meat should sizzle when dipped into it) put in the medallions. Fry quickly, turning once, until they are just cooked through, about 3 minutes per side. Don't overcook them; tenderloin cooks more quickly than other pork cuts and is safely done cooked to medium.

3. Take up the medallions onto a warm serving platter and pour off all but a tablespoon of the fat. Sprinkle the flour into the pan and let it brown, stirring constantly to prevent scorching. Add a cup of water very gradually, stirring and scraping the pan constantly, and let it come to a boil. Reduce the heat to a bare simmer and cook until thick, about 5 minutes. Pour the gravy over the medallions and serve at once. Serves 4 to 6.

Annabella Hill's Grilled Tenderloin Medallions

Grill broiling is another simple and beautiful way of doing pork tenderloins. They are again cut into medallions and seasoned the same as the previous recipe, but then broiled quickly over aromatic hardwood coals, which of course lends a wonderfully rich flavor. There are no alternate directions for the oven broiler since fragrant wood coals are the whole point to this recipe. You might as well pan-fry them and save yourself the trouble of stooping to the broiler.

1 pair pork tenderloins, about 2 pounds
Salt and whole black pepper in a peppermill
4 tablespoons unsalted butter, softened

10 to 12 fresh sage leaves, chopped, or 8 to 10 whole dried sage leaves, crumbled

1. Prepare a grill with coals, light them, and let them burn to a glowing bright red. Meanwhile, rinse the tenderloins, pat dry, and cut crosswise into 1/2-inch thick medallions. Lightly beat with a mallet until 1/4-inch thick. Rub salt and freshly ground pepper into both sides of each medallion.

2. Melt 2 tablespoons of butter and brush the medallions with it. Mix the sage with the remaining butter on a warm serving platter. Have it ready by the grill.

3. Position a grill rack about four inches above the coals and place the steaks on it. Grill about 3 or 4 minutes to the side, until they are browned and just cooked through. Take up immediately onto the platter, turning to coat them with the sage butter, and serve at once. Serves 4 to 6.

NOTES: *Though these medallions really don't need anything else, applesauce or Fresh Peach Sauce (page 379) are excellent accompaniments, as are Oven-Roasted Sweet Potatoes (page 246). Or, since you have the grill fired up anyway, try Grill-Broiled Sweet Potatoes (page 248).*

Southern Country or Bulk Sausage

"While some ignore pepper and the different spices as highly injurious to the tender coats of the stomach, others require such tremendous quantity of Cayenne, spice, brandy, the combustibles generally, that, as has been well observed, 'only a fire-proof palate lined with asbestos can endure.'"

—Annabella P. Hill, *Mrs. Hill's New Cook Book* (1867)

In most places, the word "sausage" describes highly seasoned, chopped meat stuffed into an edible casing and tied off into links. But here in the South, we often use "sausage" generically, as has long been done in England, to describe finely chopped bulk forcemeat that was never stuffed into a casing. True stuffed sausages are—and always have been—known to the South, and might be made from a number of meats and even fish (that should surprise the nouvelle crowd, who think they invented fish sausages). However, bulk sausage was usually made from pork. Though highly seasoned with herbs and pepper, it needn't always, as Mrs. Hill noted, be hotter than Hell's gate-hinges.

Because of our humid, warm climate, sausages were seldom tied into links in the Deep South, as mold tended to grow at the link. When they were stuffed, the sausage was looped (without twisting the casing into links) and then smoked. The old way to smoke sausages was to hang them in loops from the open kitchen rafters, without touching. In the days of open-hearth cookery, the sausages lightly smoked as they hung above the hearth. In our hearth-less, overheated houses, this is no longer possible. With a modern refrigerator and freezer on hand, you can link sausages and omit smoking them without worrying about mold.

In making any sausage meat, the lean is trimmed of every scrap of fat, so that the ratio of fat to lean can be strictly maintained. The classic proportion is two parts lean to one part fat; this gives the sausage its essential texture and moisture. If that really sends you into a panic, you can up the proportion to four to one, but no more; otherwise the meat will not be tender and moist, but grainy, tough, dry, and of no gastronomical interest whatever. Always bear in mind that while sausage is rich, portions are and should be small, and besides, much of the fat melts away when it's cooked.

If you have genuine health problems that require you to limit your fat intake, just forget sausage altogether. There are too many other good things that you can eat rather than settle for a dry, faded substitute of the original article.

For the Seasoning Mix:

2 tablespoons freshly ground black pepper

3 tablespoons salt

2 teaspoons crushed cayenne pepper flakes

4 tablespoons ground dried sage (see notes), or 2 tablespoons each sage, thyme and marjoram

Grated zest of 1 lemon (optional)

4 pounds lean, well-trimmed pork, preferably from the neck or shoulder

2 pounds soft pork fat (preferably back fat, not the grainy leaf fat), using the trimmings from the meat

1. Combine the seasonings mix and put it into a shaker (such as a grated cheese jar) with holes large enough for the cayenne to pass through. Have it close at hand.

2. Using a meat grinder with medium holes, grind first the meat and then the fat, separately. Mix them together and put them through a second time. Sprinkle with half of the seasoning mix and put it through the grinder again. Sprinkle with half the remaining seasoning and run it through the grinder once more. Transfer it to a mixing bowl and knead until the seasoning is uniformly distributed.

3. Pinch off a 2-inch diameter ball of meat and flatten it into a thick cake. Put it into a small skillet over medium-low heat. Cook slowly, turning it frequently, until it is nicely browned and cooked through, but not dry. Taste it for seasoning; if it needs more, knead in another sprinkling and fry another test piece. Keep doing this until you hit the right combination, keeping track of your additions for future reference. You may need to make more seasoning mix if the sausage isn't seasoned enough to suit you. Makes 6 pounds.

NOTES: *Bulk sausage will keep, well covered and refrigerated, for about two weeks. It also freezes fairly well, either in one pound pieces or molded into individual cakes, which is more convenient, though individual cakes do not keep as well. My great-grandmother's preserving method was to fry the sausage in cakes, stack them in sterilized jars, and cover them with hot rendered fat. The fat made an excellent seal when it cooled and hardened, keeping out mold and bacteria.*

The sage and pepper in sausage meat is classically English, but Southern cooks have made it their own, adding to it our easily grown, inexpensive cayenne. This unique flavor combination has been a standard in the South for nearly two centuries. For bulk sausage, the sage must be dried, ground to a powder and sifted to remove any stem. You can buy powdered, sifted sage, but it will not have as much flavor; far better to powder it yourself for the best results.

Older recipes made a use of a wider variety of herbs and spices, including rosemary, thyme, marjoram, parsley, allspice, cloves, mace, and nutmeg. If you want to experiment with these, first grind them to a powder with a mortar and pestle or spice mill.

The zest and juice of lemons, as well as pickled lemons, were once more widely used as seasoning in English cookery, and it was still common practice when America was first colonized. For a time, lemons would surely have been used this way in America; however, their appearance in American books is rare. The last Southern reference I have found to lemon in sausages is The Kentucky Housewife (1839), so I suspect it was becoming archaic by the beginning of the nineteenth century. Lemon zest lends an unusual, but lovely Mediterranean perfume to sausages.

Pan-Fried Southern Sausage

1 pound Southern Country, or Bulk Sausage (page 195), or other bulk sausage

2 teaspoons all-purpose flour

1/2 cup brewed coffee or tea and 1/2 cup water, or 1 cup whole milk

Salt and whole black pepper in a peppermill

1. Divide the sausage into 8 to 12 equal balls and lightly flatten into thick round cakes. Put them into a cast-iron skillet or heavy-bottomed sauté pan over medium heat.

2. Slowly fry the sausage, turning frequently, until all sides are nicely browned and they are just cooked through, about 15 to 20 minutes. Spoon off the excess fat as it is rendered to help prevent grease pops and splattering. They are done when firm but still springy when pressed with a finger at the center. It must be completely done, but don't overcook it or it will be hard and dry. Drain on absorbent paper and transfer the sausage to a warm serving plate.

3. Drain off all but 1 tablespoon of fat from the pan. Raise the heat to medium-high and add the flour, stirring until it is smooth and beginning to color. Slowly stir in the coffee, tea, or milk and bring it to a boil, stirring constantly. If you are using coffee or tea, slowly add the water after it is simmering and bring it back to a simmer, stirring. Season well with salt and pepper, reduce the heat to low, and simmer, stirring occasionally, until thick, about 4 minutes. Taste and adjust the seasonings, pour it into a warmed sauceboat, and pass it separately with the sausage. Serves 4.

ABOUT OLD OR "COUNTRY" HAMS

These somewhat picturesque names for Southern dry-cured hams are directly related to their origins in the smokehouses and cellars of the plantations and farms of largely rural Carolina, Georgia, Kentucky, Virginia, and Tennessee. They are called "old" because they're air-cured for at least ten months, and "country" because, until recently, they were always cured on the farm in airy, clapboard smokehouses. Each family cured their own, and friendly rivalries developed in every community. In Grassy Pond, where I grew up, the champions were the Sarratt sisters and their elder brother, who live on the farm out beyond the schoolhouse. The farm and the sisters are still there, but sadly, their hams are only in our memories.

Country hams are cured by first rubbing the meat with salt and allowing them to lie until the salt has been mostly absorbed. Some packers stack the hams so as to press out the moisture. Modern processors often mix in brown sugar or molasses, but it's not a very old practice. The hams are wiped clean, rubbed with spices, and hung to air dry. The method is very old, and is the same one used to make prosciutto. Usually, Southern hams are smoked and these were the most highly prized, but the family ham might be air cured without smoking. In either case, they are finally rubbed with more salt and spices and sometimes hardwood ash (or wrapped in cloth sacks) to protect them from nesting flies, and hung in an airy, sheltered place to age for no less than ten months. Most families allowed their best hams to age for at least a year and some as many as three (hence the name "old"). There is a popular belief lingering among the few who still cure hams that they must go through the July "sweats" to be any good.

Because these hams are dry salt-cured, they are much saltier than brine-cured hams and benefit from a preliminary soaking in cold water for at least 12 hours; 24 is better, and 48 may be necessary for hams that are more than a year old. A long, slow simmer in water further leaches out excess salt, but even then, they are so rich that they are served in small, paper-thin slices, never in the great thick slabs that those lifeless, brine cured and water injected hams are today.

Some Notes on Cooking Old Country Hams

"Although there are very few Southern kitchens in which the [ham] pot is not made to boil every day, yet in the fewest number is it well done. The process is simple enough, and the failures are the result of irregularity and inattention. The cook, as a general thing, places her [ham in the] pot over a fierce fire, which starts the water boiling with a gallop. The scum rises to the top, and is permitted to remain. Other business engages her attention. The pot for a while is forgotten, and when at length it is remembered, and looked into, the liquor is found too much reduced. This is replenished with cold water and the fire stirred, and the boiling goes through the same process. With this kind of management, is it strange that even our favorite everyday dish of boiled ham is seldom put upon the table well cooked?"

—Annabella Hill, *Mrs. Hill's New Cook Book*, 1867

Almost nothing needs to be added to that. The water in which an old ham cooks must never boil hard, or the ham will be soggy, stringy, and lifeless. The steam bubbles must rise and come just shy of breaking the surface, the slowest simmer you can manage—really a gentle poaching. But the simmering must be steady: the ham may start in cold water, but once the water begins to simmer, it is replenished as needed only with water that is just off the boil so that the temperature inside the kettle is never lowered.

The recipe given here cooks the ham in a bath flavored with wine or whiskey, but keep the flavoring agents subtle. A well-cured ham is already seasoned to a turn, and does not take kindly to being doused with sugary soft drinks, or spiked with a lot of strong spice.

Notes on glazes: I have not been able to pinpoint when the sweet glazes now popular all over America first began to be used, but do not find them in any of the antebellum Southern sources. 1879 is the earliest mention that I have found of any sugar at all, and it was white sugar—not the brown that is usual today. These glazes begin to appear early on in the twentieth century; Mrs. Dull (1928) is the first (Southern) mention I find of brown sugar glazes with those awful canned pineapple and cherry decorations. They kept getting sweeter and gooier as the century progressed. In spite of their modern popularity, I find them obtrusive with a really good old ham, and out of place with the intent of antebellum cooks, so you won't find one here.

Carving country ham: The first and most important secret to successfully carving a ham is a razor-sharp knife. The second is to let the ham cool and recompose itself for at least half an hour before you start. Place the ham sideways in front of you, skin side up, the shank to the left if you are right-handed, to the right if you're left-handed. Hold the knife at a 45-degree angle to the bone, pointing toward the shank, and start cutting away the fat in thin slices until you reach lean meat. Gently cut it into paper-thin slices, always working at a 45-degree angle with a slight sawing motion of the knife. The slices will, of course, be small at first. Don't let them get too large, and always make sure they are as thin as you can get them. Once you can grasp the shank without risking the knife slipping and cutting into your hand, it helps to hold the shank bone with your free hand.

Country Ham in Champagne

This is a luxurious way of doing a fine old dry-cured ham that has, unfortunately, nearly been lost. We know of it mostly from later recipes that the author claimed made the ham taste as if it were cooked in champagne. Why it disappeared is hard to understand; it is shamefully easy and extremely good. By gently poaching in the acidic wine bath, the ham surrenders much of its salt and acquires a delicacy that no pig ever dreamed it could have. It need not cost a ton, either: a good, dry domestic champagne made by the true methode champenois, and not artificially carbonated, works just fine. Another gorgeous alcoholic bath for an old ham is bourbon. Substitute 2 cups of well-aged Kentucky whiskey for the champagne in this recipe.

Serve country ham with prepared English or French Dijon-style mustard, and Georgia Apple and Tomato Chutney (page 392).

1 whole country ham, about 11 to 13 pounds	1 large egg, well beaten
1 bottle dry champagne	1 cup fine, dry breadcrumbs or cracker crumbs

1. Under, cold, running water, scrub the ham all over with a stiff brush to remove all mold. Put the ham in a large tub and cover it completely with cold water. Soak it for at least 8, or for as long as 24 to 48 hours, if the ham is especially old, changing the water three times during the process.

2. Drain the ham and put it in a large, deep oval pot that will hold it and enough water to cover it. Pour the champagne over the ham and add enough cold water to completely cover. Turn on the heat to medium-low and let it come slowly to the boiling point, skimming off the scum as it rises.

3. Reduce the heat to a barely perceptible simmer. The steam bubbles should just break the surface of the water so that it hardly moves. Never allow it to actually boil. Simmer gently until it is just tender, about 3 to 4 hours. Turn off the heat and let the ham cool in the cooking water.

4. Position a rack in the center of the oven and preheat it to 400 degrees F. When the ham is cooled, lift it from its cooking liquid. With a sharp knife, remove the rind and some of the fat, but leave a good layer on all sides. Score the fat in crisscross and put the ham into a baking pan, skin side up. Resist the temptation to stud it with cloves or goop it up with sugar. Brush the egg over the ham with a pastry brush and dust all sides well with crumbs, pressing them to help them stick.

5. Bake, uncovered, until the crumbs are toasty and brown, about 45 minutes. Let it rest for half an hour before carving, and cut it with a razor-sharp knife into the thinnest possible slices (see "Carving country ham," page 199). Serves 25 to 30.

Sautéed Ham with Red-Eye Gravy

This is a traditional breakfast dish in the South, but when we were children, we were just as likely to get it for supper during the winter. Grits are an indispensable accompaniment and should be cooked until they are dry enough to handle the gravy. At breakfast, eggs fried in rendered ham fat are often served along with it.

The secret to success is to cook the ham lightly and quickly. Don't worry about trichinosis—no self-respecting amoeba would live through what that ham has been through, and besides, it is safely cooked in a couple of minutes.

1 pound thin-sliced uncooked country ham	1/2 cup boiling water
About 1/2 cup plain, all-purpose flour	Whole black pepper in a peppermill
1/2 cup strong tea or coffee	

1. If the ham is especially old and rich, soak it in water to cover for about 10 minutes. Drain and pat it dry. Trim the fat from it and cut each slice into medallions about 2 inches across. Spread the flour on a plate and put it by the stove.

2. Rub a cast-iron or heavy-bottomed skillet with a piece of the fat trimmings, put them into it, and turn on the heat to medium. When the fat is rendered, take up the cracklings. Turn the ham slices lightly in the flour, shake off the excess, and add them to the pan. Sauté quickly, no more than 2 minutes per side. It should be just cooked through and tender, like veal scaloppini. Overcooking will make it tough and rubbery. Take it up onto a warm serving platter.

3. Deglaze the pan with the tea or coffee and bring it to a boil, add the water, scraping and stirring to loosen any cooking residue in the pan, and continue cooking until the gravy is lightly reduced and thickened. Season to taste with pepper and pour the gravy into a sauceboat and serve at once. Serves 4.

NOTES: *You can also fry slices of boiled or baked country ham. Slice it thin and trim off most of the fat. Put the fat in a skillet—enough to make about a tablespoon of fat per serving of ham—over medium-low heat. When the fat has all been rendered, take up the cracklings and add the sliced ham. Cook slowly for about 5 minutes, turning frequently, until it's heated through and tender. Drain off most of the fat and make red-eye gravy as directed in step 3 of the main recipe.*

CLASSIC SOUTHERN BARBEQUE

If anything that could be called the "national dish" of the South, perhaps barbeque, even more-so than fried chicken, would be it. Southerners are passionate about it, almost to the point of being downright fanatical. Yet, when many people today speak of barbeque, what they are often describing is a sauce rather than the cooking method our ancestors knew. Modern cookbooks, including some Southern ones, have all sorts of recipes for things that they call "barbequed"—that is, meat baked or fried and slathered with a thick, vinegary-sweet tomato sauce. They may be good, but they are not barbeque, and no one in the South during the last century would recognize them. True Southern barbeque is *not a sauce*, but a cooking method. The meat is placed on a spit or gridiron, washed with an aromatic basting sauce and cooked over a pit of banked, slow-burning hardwood coals until the meat is falling-apart tender and permeated with the rich flavor of wood smoke. It is a cooking method as old as time.

In other parts of the country, grill-broiling is called barbeque, but true Southern barbeque differs from it in several critical ways. Grilling depends on clear, intense heat to seal in the juices and cook the meat quickly. Smoke is there, but it is neither encouraged nor essential. A slow, smoky fire is, however, the key to a good barbeque, and green hardwood is sometimes added to the pit in order to produce a slow smolder and as much fragrant smoke as can be managed.

Basting sauces were commonplace by the beginning of the nineteenth century, but unlike the thick tomato sauces common today, early ones were usually simple compositions of butter and water lightly seasoned with salt and hot pepper. Vinegar, which acts as a tenderizer, was added by mid-century. In 1867, Annabella Hill gave a lucid description of the proper method for barbequing meat with a basting sauce of vinegar, mustard, pepper, and butter, a combination that was to be what constituted "barbeque sauce" in Georgia until after the turn of the century. Sauces with a tomato ketchup and molasses base are modern and, in the beginning, were added only after the meat had been removed from the fire. (The earliest recipes, all from this century, give testimony to this fact in that they were usually called dipping sauce.) There's good reason not to use sweetened tomato sauce for basting; its high sugar content burns easily, leaving a thick, acrid coating of carbon on the meat that is neither appetizing nor flavorful. Even good pit-masters who swear by a tomato ketchup–based sauce know enough to leave it off until the last half hour of the cooking, just enough to let the sauce sink into the meat without burning.

Traditional barbeque was inextricably connected to crowds and large parties because nothing, except spare-ribs, can be properly barbequed in small pieces, and it is a lot of hard work. Often the meat was started the evening before, and the men stayed up all night, swapping stories (and usually a bottle) as they kept watch over it. It is easy to see why good pit-masters are so few and far between. But, fortunately, real barbeque stubbornly survives in our century, even though it has mostly been relegated to restaurants. But no matter how skilled the cook, and no matter how magical the basting sauce, a restaurant barbeque, for me, will never be the same. I'd like to take you back a few years. We'd put on our best summer cottons, pack an old quilt, and head for some remote Baptist church. We'd spread the quilt under a big shade tree and dig into a plate piled high with real, honest-to-God barbeque that had been slow-cooked all night over a real pit of hickory wood, and finish it off with a big slab of lemon meringue pie. There, in those days, was heaven, and we didn't know enough to recognize it.

Barbequed Spareribs with Annabella Hill's Classic Georgia Basting Sauce

The most popular and common meat for a nineteenth-century barbeque in Georgia was a whole shoat. In case you don't know, shoats are young, male pigs killed when they are less than a year old and weighing in at around forty pounds. They are very tender and much easier for the cook to manage than a full-grown hog. The animal is split along the belly, gutted, flattened, and iron rods are often run through it to hold the carcass rigid and facilitate turning it over the pit.

For the entire six years of this book project, I tried—and failed—to devise a recipe that could be managed on a home grill with the satisfying flavor and texture of true pit barbeque. My patient friends endured some pretty awful stuff. Spending a lot of time with pit-masters in the decade since this book was first published has taught me a lot, and I've since helped make some very decent barbecue. But you don't need to be a pit master to manage these spareribs, and they have the rich, satisfying flavor and succulence that one expects from good barbeque. They can even be managed on a hibachi.

Traditional accompaniments for barbeque are Mama Macie's Cole Slaw (page 272), Roasted Corn (page 218), and your favorite potato salad.

2 full racks spareribs, about 8 pounds

Mrs. Hill's Classic Georgia Basting Sauce:

1/2 pound (1 cup or 2 sticks) unsalted butter

1 cup cider vinegar

1/2 cup water

1 teaspoon cayenne pepper

1 teaspoon black pepper

2 teaspoons salt

2 tablespoons dry mustard

1 tablespoon crumbled dried sage leaves, optional (my own addition)

1. Put 1 cup of hardwood chips (preferably hickory or pecan) in a bowl with water to cover them and let them soak until they are saturated, at least 2 hours. Fill the bottom of your grill with a thick layer of hardwood coals, light it, and let them burn down to a good, glowing red.

2. Meanwhile, wash the ribs under clear, cold water and pat them dry. Careful cooks trim away the tough membrane that covers the inside of the ribs; restaurants seldom can give them that much hands-on detail. You'll win points with the Southerner in your life if you do it.

3. While the coals burn down, melt the butter in a small saucepan that will hold all the sauce ingredients comfortably and stir them into the butter. Keep it warm, but not hot, over very low heat—don't ever let it bubble.

4. Now, spread the coals and let them ash over. Spread half the soaked wood chips over them and place the ribs on a grill about 8 inches above the heat. Let them get hot and start to color, then turn them. When both sides are hot, begin basting with the warm sauce. If the coals start to flame up from the fat, spray them with water and raise the rack a little until the fire settles again.

5. Turn and baste the ribs every 10 to 15 minutes until the meat is very tender and the outer fat is crisp, brown, and smoky—about 2 hours; longer won't hurt. Add more moistened wood chips as needed to keep a good fragrant smoke coming up off the coals, and lightly spray any coals that flame up with water. You may need to replenish the coals by adding a few around the edges. When they've burned down, move them to the center. But use caution: Never add lighter fluid to them, and don't put red-hot coals under the meat; the heat must be steady, but low. Serves 6.

The Southern Way with Vegetables

"[Spinach] should be cooked so as to retain its bright green color and not sent to the table . . . of dull brown or olive color; to retain its fresh appearance, do not cover the vessel while it is cooking."

—*The Savannah Cook Book*
(The Ladies of Westminster Presbyterian Church,
Savannah, Georgia, 1909)

SOUTHERN VEGETABLE COOKERY has developed an undeservedly bad reputation. If we were to believe the most commonly propagated myths, early Southerners were a largely carnivorous lot who ignored vegetables in general, and gave the few we did eat indifferent treatment—that is, they were tastelessly overcooked and swimming in hog fat. This myth is regularly perpetuated by the dismal cooking of tourist trap diners that advertise "country cookin'" without the g, and has been around for so long that even Southerners have begun to believe it. Fortunately, it is a myth that is as false as it is popular, as the spinach recipe quoted above clearly demonstrates.

The earliest records from Virginia, Carolina, and Georgia tell of a veritable Garden of Eden, brimming with all manner of vegetables that were carefully prepared and apparently relished. William Byrd, in *The Natural History of Virginia* (1737), recorded a luscious variety of vegetables and fruits in Virginia, from asparagus and artichokes to sorrel and tomatoes. Among the lists are several varieties of garlic and onions. Of fruits, there were hundreds—more than two dozen varieties of apples alone—many of which have disappeared from modern orchards. Later, Thomas Jefferson kept a record of the vegetable markets in Washington between 1801 and 1809 (his tenure as President), wherein he noted nearly forty varieties, many of which—such as sorrel, salsify, and fava beans—are nowadays considered almost exotic and rare. All the varieties mentioned by Mr. Jefferson appear in the earliest Southern cookbooks, from his cousin's book, *The Virginia House-wife* in 1824, to *Mrs. Hill's New Cook Book* (which bordered on encyclopedic) in 1867. Each treated vegetables with the same care and attention that marks the spinach recipe quoted above. In some, vegetable cookery occupies the largest portion of the text. This is only logical: the South has a longer growing season than any other part of the country, and because of its mixed climate, can sustain far more variety than other places. At any rate, that wide variety of produce, freshly gathered and carefully prepared, is at least part of the reason for the almost mythic reputation that Southern cookery once enjoyed among travelers and writers of the nineteenth century.

There are more than fifty recipes for over twenty varieties of vegetables offered here, making this the longest and most comprehensive chapter in this book. The classic recipes for artichokes and asparagus are included, along with several for onions (so much for the notion that early Southerners didn't eat them), mushrooms, and eggplant. They are only a sampling—space limitations prevented me from including dozens of wonderful dishes—but perhaps they are enough to finally banish some of those tired old myths.

ARTICHOKES

An English historian named Thomas Fuller (1608–1661) once remarked that "it was a very valiant man who first embarked upon the eating of oysters." My money has always been on the one who first ate thistles. Nothing looks less promising as a prospect for food, but for the truly valiant it has a luscious reward.

Perhaps you are surprised to find artichokes in a cookbook about antebellum Southern food, since many popular accounts claim that Americans did not know of this vegetable until the latter part of the nineteenth century. James Beard asserted with authority in *American Cookery* that there was no printed record of artichokes in America before the third quarter of that century; other popular histories date them even later. This would surprise William Byrd, who wrote of their growing in Virginia in 1737, or Thomas Jefferson, who grew them at Monticello and recorded their presence in Washington's markets as early as 1801, or Amelia Simmons, author of what is widely believed to be America's first cookbook (1796). Mary Randolph wrote quite casually of artichokes in *The Virginia House-wife*, as did every Southern writer to follow her.

Artichokes were cultivated and eaten in England as early as the sixteenth century, and, by the seventeenth century, were popular with the English (at least of the upper classes), who enjoyed them both cooked and dressed raw, as a salad. It seems probable that artichokes were among the European vegetables transplanted by the early colonists.

Basic Cooked Artichokes

This is how all the old cooks prepared this deceptively delectable vegetable. The method was almost universal throughout America. Of the Southern writers, only Sarah Rutledge (*The Carolina Housewife*, 1847) deviated by simmering trimmed artichoke bottoms in white sauce.

4 medium-sized artichokes	1 recipe (1/2 cup) Drawn Butter (page 114),
Salt	not made ahead, but at the point indicated
	in step 3, below

1. Wash the artichokes and trim off the small, tough leaves at the base. Some recipes suggest cutting off the stem, but you'll lose some of the artichoke's most succulent flesh if you do. The better plan is to peel its tough, reedy skin, and rub it with lemon juice to prevent discoloring.

2. In a kettle that will hold all the artichokes, bring enough water to completely cover them to a rolling boil over high heat. Add a small handful of salt, put in the artichokes, cover, and let the water come back to a boil. Reduce the heat to medium and simmer, uncovered,

until the artichokes are tender, about half an hour. They're done when a gently tugged outer leaf easily comes away. Immediately drain and put them in a warm serving dish.

3. Make the butter according to the recipe, pour it into a sauceboat or into four individual cups, and serve at once with the artichokes. Serves 4.

JERUSALEM ARTICHOKES

This little root vegetable is completely misnamed: it is neither an artichoke nor from anywhere near Jerusalem. It is the root of a Native American sunflower whose flavor is reminiscent of true artichokes. Though truly American in origin, its curious name probably derives in part from the Italian word *girasole* (literally, follow the sun) that was gradually corrupted into a more familiar English word. Oddly enough, the vegetable has an entirely different name in Italy. There are various explanations for the artichoke part, from the notion that they taste (vaguely) like one, to the fact that the unopened flower buds, which Native Americans may have eaten as a vegetable, look like one. Unaccountably, modern growers renamed them "sunchokes," a name I find just as confusing as the old one while wholly lacking its charm, but when you shop for them that is probably how they'll be labeled.

This fine vegetable was enjoyed in the South for hundreds of years, first by Native Americans and later by European settlers. Once, it was so popular that older cookbook authors simply called them "artichokes" and distinguished the real thing by calling it a "burr" artichoke. Sadly, in this century this delicate vegetable has fallen unaccountably out of favor, and has been relegated mostly to the pickle jar. Maybe their renewed popularity among the "foodie" crowd will encourage all of us to rediscover the delights of this truly native vegetable.

Basic Cooked Jerusalem Artichokes

Almost any root vegetable that is boiled is better off when it is allowed to cook in its skin, and Jerusalem artichokes are no exception. Not only does the skin keep the boiling water out, it holds the natural juices and flavors in. Most of the early books directed that Jerusalem artichokes were to be prepared in the same way as potatoes, and the same basic rules for boiling potatoes apply, as well:

* Select tubers that are roughly the same size.

* Have them at room temperature.

* Drop them into water that is just below boiling.

* Only use as much water as is needed to barely cover them.

2 pounds Jerusalem artichokes   Unsalted butter, melted

Salt

1. Gently scrub the artichokes under cool, running water. If they're just out of the refrigerator, let them warm to room temperature, about an hour.

2. Put the artichokes in a large, heavy-bottomed pot, add water until they are just covered, then lift out the artichokes and set them aside. Cover and bring to a boil over medium-high heat.

3. Add a small handful of salt and then the artichokes. Loosely cover and let it return to a boil, uncover, reduce the heat to medium, and simmer to the level of tenderness that the individual recipe requires. To eat them plain or as a salad they should be just tender, with a little resistance to the bite, and may take as little as 10 minutes; for creamed (mashed) artichokes, they should be as soft as boiled potatoes and may take as much as half an hour.

4. Drain well and, if you prefer, peel them while still hot. Serve warm with lots of melted butter, or make Mashed Jerusalem Artichokes following the recipe for Mashed Potatoes (page 242) or Baked Jerusalem Artichokes, following the first variation for Mashed Potatoes, Lettice Bryan's Baked Potatoes (page 243). Serves 4

Jerusalem Artichokes in Cream

Here is another nice thing to do with these tasty roots. Don't overdo the cream; it should thoroughly but lightly coat the artichokes. If they're swimming in it, their delicate flavor will be smothered. This same recipe was also used to dress trimmed artichoke bottoms that have been cooked as for Basic Cooked Artichokes (page 207).

2 pounds Jerusalem artichokes, boiled as   1/2 cup heavy cream (minimum 36% milk fat)
    directed in previous recipe until just tender   Salt and whole black pepper in a peppermill
1 tablespoon unsalted butter

1. As soon as the artichokes are just tender, drain and quickly peel them. You may let them cool just enough to handle, but don't let them get cold, and under no circumstances put them in cold water to hasten their cooling—which will make them soggy.

2. Wipe out the pot in which they were cooked and put in the artichokes, butter, and cream. Return the pot to a medium heat and cook, tossing frequently, until the cream has thickened and is lightly coating the vegetables. Season to taste with salt and pepper and transfer to a warm serving dish and serve at once. Serves 4.

ASPARAGUS

"Asparagus is a nice vegetable, and requires equally as much nicety in preparing it."

—Lettice Bryan, *The Kentucky Housewife*, 1839

"The whole point of asparagus is the taste and texture and scent of springtime."

—Karen Hess

Asparagus has been growing in the America almost from the beginning of European colonization. As early as 1737, William Byrd, in *The Natural History of Virginia*, noted splendid asparagus growing in Virginia and, if early cookbooks are any indication, it was universally popular. Lightly and quickly cooked, it is the nicest of vegetables, as Mrs. Hess so aptly observed, the essence of spring. But you wouldn't know Southerners thought so from looking at many of our contemporary cookbooks. It used to elude me how so many nice people could do such awful things to this lovely vegetable, but at last, it occurred to me: any good cook knows that the best way to prepare fresh asparagus is to cook it quickly and sauce it simply with melted butter. All those pasty casseroles, mushy croquettes, and smothering white sauces were merely attempts to make something palatable out of canned asparagus.

Southern cooks from the early days of the nineteenth century treated this vegetable with appropriate reverence. Mary Randolph, in *The Virginia House-wife* gave rather a long cooking time (25 minutes) but the asparagus was tied together in a bundle, and she did caution to watch for the exact instant that the asparagus became tender, admonishing that a minute or two more would destroy both flavor and color. Lettice Bryan, quoted above, avoided time altogether.

Unfortunately, as the century progressed, such reverence faded. By the time of *Housekeeping in Old Virginia* (1879), half an hour of hard boiling was pretty much the standard, with little of Mrs. Randolph's carefulness remaining. As anybody with one eye and half sense knows, such treatment will reduce asparagus to a gray-green, water-logged mush of absolutely no gastronomical interest whatsoever.

Buying and storing asparagus: Few of us will be able to enjoy the luxury of our own homegrown asparagus. Shop carefully and try to buy it locally grown in season. Supermarket chains often ship vegetables from all over the country; theirs may never be local or fresh. But smaller grocers and vegetable vendors often buy only local stock when it's in season. You can usually tell that it has been locally grown by price. When the price drops, you know you are no longer paying for shipping and warehouse storage; when it skyrockets again, the season is over. Find out when the vendor takes delivery, and try to buy and cook it that day. As soon as you get it home, trim off the cut part of the stems, and put the asparagus in a vase of water, like flowers. Let it stand for at least an hour. This helps refresh the vegetables and restore some of the moisture they have lost in storage. If you can't cook it the same day, refrigerate it, but take it out an hour before you cook it, change the water, and let it stand until you are ready to cook it.

Preparing asparagus for cooking: Generally, the younger the asparagus, the more slender and tender the stems are, though a lot depends on the variety. True spring shoots seldom need more than a little trimming, but once the stalks begin to mature and the stems turn fat and white at the bottom, they will also need to be peeled. The inside of this tough part is every bit as tender and succulent as the rest of the stem. Moreover, some varieties may be slender and lovely looking, but the outer skin is tough halfway up the stem. If you broke off the tough part, you'd lose nearly half the asparagus; it would be a shame to throw it away when it is so easily peeled.

Have ready a basin of clean, cold water and spread the work surface with newspaper (the peelings tend to go in all directions). Lay the stalk on a cutting board with the tip hanging off one side. Rolling the stem as you go, lay a vegetable peeler on the stem and lightly peel only the tough part of the stalk—about one-third of the way up. This is what the old cookbooks meant by "scrape them nicely." Drop it into the water and continue until all the stalks are prepared.

Basic Cooked Asparagus

Here is the classic recipe. It varies only in detail from the basic methods of early English books. Choose a large, wide kettle that will hold the asparagus without trimming off too much stem. A fish poacher is perfect for the job.

1-1/2 pounds asparagus, prepared as directed above

6 slices bread (preferably homemade), cut on the diagonal into triangles and toasted crisp

1 recipe (1/2 cup) Drawn Butter (page 114), not made ahead but where indicated in step 4

Salt

1. Put at least 2 quarts of water in a large pot wide enough to hold the asparagus without breaking the stems. Cover and bring it to a boil over high heat. Throw in a small handful of salt.

2. Divide the asparagus into two equal bundles and tie them with twine or cotton ribbon in two places. Slip the bundles into the water, cover the pot, and bring it back to a good boil. Uncover and cook until the asparagus is just tender but still bright green. Keep an eye on it; this can be in as little as 5 or as long as 10 to 15 minutes. Meanwhile, spread the toast on a warm platter.

3. As soon as the asparagus is done, lift out each bundle with a kitchen fork or tongs, untie, and spread over the toast, leaving the points of the toast exposed on either side. (Early cooks dipped the toast in the cooking liquor, but this makes it rather insipid for my taste.)

4. Make the Drawn Butter according to the recipe. Pour some of it over the platter and serve, with the remainder of the sauce passed separately. Serves 4.

GREEN BEANS

Any beans harvested before they're mature, whose pods are still green and tender enough to eat, can be called green beans. Lumping them together like that is somewhat misleading. Just as mature beans are very different and of many varieties, so are their young pods, and what is a suitable method for one type may not work at all with another. For example, the slow simmer required by broad tough pole beans will reduce tender young snaps or French haricots to mush, as early-nineteenth-century cooks understood quite well. *The Kentucky Housewife* had three recipes for beans, giving each variety its own treatment, and Mrs. Randolph implied that beans that took longer to cook than her prescribed 15 minutes were not eaten by nice people. Such discernment was not to remain for the duration of the century. By the 1870s, most cookbooks gave only one method for all beans: slow-boiling with a piece of salt pork. There are any number of reasons why this might have happened—the popularity of one bean, for example, or the advent of canning as a means of preservation, but we can never really know for certain.

Most green beans of the nineteenth century had tough, woody strings down the seams of the pod, hence the name "string" beans. With the development of stringless varieties, most of the old ones have disappeared. Unless you grow your own, you will be lucky to get anything but blue lakes, the recently developed hybrid that most supermarkets carry. They are not suitable for slow-cooking. Southern markets sell broad flat beans, called "pole" beans because of their pole-climbing vines. They aren't universally available, but are preferable for slow-cooking.

Mary Randolph's Quick Cooked Young French Beans

"To send up the beans whole, when they are young, is much the best method, and their delicate flavor and color is much better preserved. When a little more grown, they must be cut across, in two, after stringing; and for common tables, they are split, and divided across; but those who are nice, do not use them at such a growth as to require splitting."

—Mary Randolph, from the original recipe in *The Virginia House-wife*, 1824

This is a gorgeous and careful recipe. Mrs. Randolph was meticulous, down to specifying soft spring water instead of hard well water for soaking beans that were not quite fresh. The next time someone tries to tell you that early Americans didn't care about vegetables, throw this recipe back at them. Admittedly, Mary Randolph had the advantage of close contact with the French-trained cooks at Monticello, from whom she probably got this recipe, but even so, such is not the way of someone who was indifferent about beans.

Not only French haricots but any slender young, tender beans respond well to this recipe, even those indifferent supermarket blue lakes. The water must really boil, and hard, or the beans will lose their color.

1 pound young green beans (see notes on types, above)	2 tablespoons (more or less to taste) unsalted butter, melted
Salt	

1. Have ready a basin of cool water. Snap off the stem end of the beans, pulling off the strings (if there are any) as you go, then snap off the pointed tails and make sure that all the string has been removed (if it's a stringless variety, don't tail them—it's not necessary). Drop them as they are trimmed into the water and let them soak for at least 15 minutes to freshen them.

2. Put 2 quarts of water in a large, heavy-bottomed pot and bring it to a boil over medium-high heat. Throw in a small handful of salt.

3. Drain the beans in a colander and add them to the pot. Let it come back to a boil and cook until the beans are tender but firm to the bite and still bright green, between 5 and 10 minutes.

4. Drain at once; never allow them to sit in the water after they are done or the color and flavor will be ruined. Toss with the melted butter and serve at once. Serves 4.

Slow-Cooked Pole Beans with Ham

Here they are, those beans that have made Southern vegetable cookery infamous, boiled to Hell and back with a ham hock. I used to suppose they were probably not very nutritious, but they actually have a lot to offer nutritionally, and, besides, they're awfully good if they're done right. Pay attention to the title: this method is meant for sturdy, thick-skinned beans, any variety requiring a long, slow simmer to make them tender. Generic supermarket green beans will be reduced to a truly un-nutritious mush if subjected to this treatment.

Though all the old recipes call for bacon, that didn't mean smoked meat like our modern breakfast bacon; the older meaning of bacon is pickled (brine-cured) pork. If you can't use pork, try substituting a well-scraped piece of Parmesan cheese rind. Onions appeared in old recipes from time to time, but weren't universal, so I've included them as optional.

2 pounds pole beams or other thick-skinned green beans	1/2 cup finely chopped white onion (optional)
1/4 pound salt pork or dry-cured (country) ham, in one thick piece, or a country ham hock	Salt and whole black pepper in a peppermill

1. Wash the beans thoroughly in cold water and drain them. Have ready a fresh basin of cold water. Snap off the stem and tail of the beans and string them carefully. Break or cut them into 1-inch lengths and drop them into the water.

2. Rinse the pork or ham well, pat dry, and put it in a 4-quart pot. Cook, turning frequently, over medium heat until it has thrown off most of its fat. If you are using the onion, add it to the pot and sauté until golden, but not scorched. Add enough water to completely cover the beans and bring to a boil. Turn the heat to low, cover, and simmer for 15 minutes.

3. Add the beans, raise the heat, and bring it back to a boil. Reduce the heat to low, skim off any scum that rises, then cover, and simmer for at least an hour-—2 hours won't hurt anything if the beans are the old-fashioned kind. They should be meltingly tender but not falling apart or mushy.

4. By the time the beans are done, their liquor should be considerably reduced. However, if there is still a lot, raise the heat to medium-high and cook until the liquid is reduced and mostly absorbed by the beans, stirring often to prevent scorching. Pour the beans into a warm serving dish and season to taste with salt and pepper. If you like, chop the pork and stir it in before serving. Serves 4 to 6.

Two Variations for Slow-Cooked Beans

I. With New Potatoes

This was a popular way to cook those lovely new potatoes that were once a late spring or early summer treat. Freshly dug young potatoes were rubbed to remove the dirt and skin and laid on top of the green beans to steam. When they are truly fresh, the skin will rub right off in your hands. Unfortunately, this seldom happens with the "new" potatoes that most of us have to be content with. Nowadays, all that means is that they are small; they've usually been in cold storage for so long that they've lost most of their delicacy, much less the claim to be called "new." I would leave the peeling intact, but if you do remove it, it will have to be done with a peeler. Still, cooked in this way, they do regain some of their spring freshness.

1 recipe Slow-Cooked Pole Beans with Ham (page 243), prepared through step 3

8 to 12 small red potatoes, each about 1-1/2 inches round, well scrubbed

Salt and whole black pepper in a peppermill

1. When the beans are nearly done, peel the potatoes quickly and lay them on top of the beans (you may omit peeling them, especially if they're not very fresh, though this is not traditional). Tightly cover and steam until they are tender, about 20 to 30 minutes.

2. Remove the potatoes to a warm bowl, season lightly with salt, cover, and keep warm. Quickly finish the beans as directed in step 4 of the recipe. Pour them into a warm serving bowl, arrange the potatoes around the edges, and dust with several grindings of pepper. Serve at once. Serves 4 to 6.

II. With Steamed Young Vegetables

I used to assume that this was a family dish, never having eaten it away from our family's table. But when I began working on this book, many recalled their mothers and grandmothers cooking beans and little vegetables in this way, and it became obvious that it had been in the South for generations. Simple as it is, it is really a remarkable dish, for two completely different vegetables undergo very different treatment in the same pot. The beans get their tenderizing long simmer, while immature vegetables steam in the evaporating aromatic juices. The earthy flavor of the beans enrobes the vegetables, which lend their delicate freshness, in turn, to the beans.

Marcella Hazan is fond of recounting that Italian cooks are very lazy, but, after an afternoon in my kitchen, she conceded that Southern cooks were even lazier. This recipe proves the point. A Southern dinner used to be considered incomplete without at least three vegetables, and this dish provided the variety in a single pot with very little effort on the part of the cook. Of course, lazy isn't the same thing as careless, and this does require that you pay close attention to that one pot.

1 recipe Slow-Cooked Pole Beans (page 213), prepared up through step 3

1 pound immature vegetables (each no longer than 2 inches), such as yellow crookneck squash, okra, carrots, spring onions, or even zucchini or eggplant, either alone, or in combinations (use your imagination)

2 tablespoons unsalted butter, melted (optional)

Salt and whole black pepper in a peppermill

2 tablespoons chopped parsley

1. While the beans are cooking, wash and trim the other vegetables but leave them whole. When the beans have cooked for at least 1 hour and are nearly done, lay the vegetables on top in a single layer. They must not touch any liquid or their bottoms will boil instead of steam and cook unevenly. Tightly cover the pot and steam until the vegetables are tender, about 10 minutes. Begin testing them after 8 minutes; they should be cooked through but still firm.

2. The moment they are done, take the vegetables up into a warm serving bowl. Toss them, if you like, with melted butter and season to taste with salt and a few liberal grindings of pepper. Sprinkle them with parsley. Finish the beans as directed in step 4 of the recipe, take them up into a separate bowl, and serve at once. Serves 4 to 6.

CABBAGE AND ITS RELATIVES

Cabbage was once a winter staple, not only here in the South, but everywhere it was grown. Packed in straw and kept in a cool, dark cellar, the tight heads would keep almost all winter, and were a reliable source of vitamins when other green vegetables were not available. Cabbage was also pickled in salt to make sauerkraut, an ancient European way of preserving it that the colonists brought with them to America, where it remained popular.

From the beginning, Southerners enjoyed this vegetable cooked all kinds of ways—with salt-pickled pork, much like corned beef and cabbage; in simple wedges sauced with butter; or stewed, mixed with onions, and fried in cakes. Another frequent recipe is cabbage pudding, what we would recognize as stuffed cabbage. Mostly these are English recipes, little changed by their transatlantic migration, but after four centuries, we have made them our own.

One such dish that has come to seem wholly American is coleslaw. One household note-book I encountered had half a dozen recipes for slaw dressing—every page well splattered from use. Coleslaw came to us by way of England, but its name is an Americanism derived from Dutch *kool sla*, *kool*, meaning cabbage, later Anglicized to the old English word for cabbage, *cole*, and *sla* meaning salad—literally, cabbage salad. The name was further Americanized as "hot slaw" became popular, beginning in the South as early as The *Kentucky House-wife* in 1839, and cole was corrupted to cold. Slaw was sometimes (though rarely) spelled *slaugh*.

Broccoli and cauliflower, two other members of the cabbage family, were also popular in Southern books, despite the commonly held belief that broccoli was unknown in the South until this century, and that cauliflower was known only to Northerners. Yet, Thomas Jefferson and other early Southerners wrote of them in an offhand way, suggesting that they were not a novelty. There were even several varieties of broccoli available. Clearly, they have both been enjoyed here in the South at least since the early days of the republic. Recipes for these vegetables seldom varied: They were boiled quickly in much water and served whole with melted butter, not much different from the way they are prepared today. To include detailed recipes here would be superfluous. But their universality in antebellum Southern books tells us that they have long been enjoyed here and deserve a place in the history of Southern food.

Boiled Cabbage

This was a universal recipe for small, tight heads of white (i.e. pale green) cabbage. Contrary to the notion that Southerners always cooked cabbage until it was watery mush, all the early books directed that it be cooked in quartered wedges that remained intact and firm. Lettice Bryan even wrote that they should be sent to the table standing up in the dish, a nice touch, but not one that could be accomplished with a cabbage that has been overcooked. I offer this recipe as an antidote to those popular misconceptions.

> 1 small, fresh cabbage, about 6 inches in diameter
> Salt
>
> 2 to 4 tablespoons unsalted butter, melted
> Whole black pepper in a peppermill

1. Pull off the cabbage's outer deep green leaves and discard them or save them for vegetable soup. Wash the cabbage thoroughly under cool running water and cut it into quarters.
2. Bring 2 quarts of water to a boil in a deep 4-quart pot. Add a small handful of salt, let it come back to a boil, and add the cabbage. Skim off any scum rising to the top. Boil briskly until the wedges are tender, but still holding together, about 10 to 15 minutes.
3. Take them up with a slotted spoon to a warm serving bowl, arranging them upright like the petals of a flower, the wedges pointing up and out. Drizzle with melted butter, making sure some of it gets between the leaves. Liberally grind pepper over it and serve at once. Serves 4.

Lettice Bryan's Fried Cabbage

This is the identical treatment given onions by Mrs. Bryan in her recipe on page 238. In fact, I often mix onion with the cabbage when I cook it this way (see the variation at the end of the recipe). Don't be put off by the name, since it does not actually fry. Properly done, there is very little fat per serving, and the cabbage is transformed, surrendering its green crispness for a mantle of pale gold. Its natural sweetness is concentrated and lightly caramelized to a rich, delicate flavor that is the perfect complement for roast poultry or pork.

> 1 small, fresh cabbage
> 2 tablespoons lard or unsalted butter
>
> 1/4 cup water
> Salt and whole black pepper in a peppermill

1. Pull off the tough, dark outer leaves of the cabbage and discard them or set aside for soup. Wash it under cold, running water and cut it in half lengthwise. Cut out the core and slice each quarter across into thin strips no more than a quarter of an inch wide.
2. Put the cabbage, fat, and water into a large, heavy lidded skillet and cover tightly. Turn on the heat to low. Cook slowly, stirring from time to time, until the cabbage is very tender, about 3/4 to 1 hour. If it gets too dry, add a few spoonfuls of water, but no more than is absolutely necessary.
3. When the cabbage is very tender, remove the lid and raise the heat to medium high. Cook, stirring constantly, until all the moisture is evaporated and the cabbage is evenly golden, being careful not to let it scorch. Turn off the heat, season with salt and pepper, and serve warm. Serves 4.

CORN

Many nowadays are surprised when they find out that the antebellum South's largest single crop was not cotton. Every farm and plantation (even the rice plantations of Carolina) had to devote more than half its acreage to something that was far more important: the native grain maize. In those pre-machine days, a large plantation could have a hundred slaves, dozens of plow-mules, and innumerable chickens and pigs. Maize was the staple that kept everyone going, and it thrives in the mild, humid Southern climate. It was so important to Americans that the English word for grain, "corn," is in the United States used exclusively to mean maize.

Native Americans introduced European settlers to the value of this native grass at the very beginning. At first it was the only thing that stood between many settlers and starvation, and some of the first conflicts between Native Americans and settlers, one at Plymouth as early as 1622, and at Jamestown even earlier, were over the colonists' raids on tribal cornfields. No other single foodstuff can contribute such variety to the table and yet be so commonplace. Until recently, most Southerners ate corn in some form every day, at virtually every meal. Fresh corn might appear stewed, roasted, or "fried" in place of potatoes or rice, or work its way into a main course savory pie, both alone and laced with seafood or ham. Dried whole kernels are ground to make meal that was used for dozens of breads and sweets, and both whole grains and lye hominy are coarsely ground into that infamous Southern hot cereal, grits. No other grain—except perhaps, for the rice of Asia—has been as integrally a part of a culture.

Roasted Corn

This is perhaps the nicest way there is to prepare fresh corn. The ears cook in the husk, not only sealing in the natural moisture, but protecting and enhancing the delicate flavor in a way no other wrapping can. Originally, the corn was roasted in the hot, banked ashes of the kitchen hearth. A modern oven lacks the romance, perhaps, but it does the job well enough. The recipe has rarely been written down; we know of it mostly through letters, diaries, and journals. For example, we know it to have been enjoyed at Monticello only because Jefferson recorded the first appearance of "roasting ears" in his garden journals.

The most flavorful roasted corn is pulled fresh from the field and thrown directly into the oven. It needs no cleaning or silking; the silks will slip right off with the husks when they are done. But if you are not sure of the origin of your corn, it is better to pull back the husks to partially silk and wash them as directed here, to be sure that there are no lingering pesticides.

8 large fresh ears sweet corn
Unsalted butter

Salt and whole black pepper in a peppermill

1. Position a rack in the upper third of the oven and preheat to 400 degrees F. Put the corn in the sink and fill it with enough cold water to completely cover and soak them for about 10 minutes.

2. Lift out an ear and carefully pull back the husks just enough to expose the tip. Dislodge any unwanted tenants and cut out any brown spots or wormholes from the tip of the kernels. Rinse well and pull the husks back up as much as possible as they were originally, and give the top a twist to seal. Repeat with the remaining ears.

3. Roast in the upper third of the oven until just cooked through, about 20 minutes.

4. Wearing a pair of insulated kitchen mitts or gloves, take the corn out of the oven, quickly pull off the husks and silks, brush off any silks that remain and pile them into a warm serving bowl. Serve at once, passing butter, salt, and pepper separately. Serves 4 healthy appetites, or 8 light ones.

Fried Corn

This traditional way of doing fresh corn appears at first to be misnamed, since it does not fry in the usual sense. Here, "fry" hearkens back to an ancient, rarer meaning of the word—that is, "to boil." The corn stews slowly in its own milk and a little butter (or rendered salt-pork fat) until the natural starches thicken. The corn turns out rich and creamy, its natural sugars concentrated and intensified by the slow cooking.

There are two secrets to making this dish well, both simple. First, the kernels must be both cut and scraped as described so that there is a lot of milk. And you must be vigilant with the stirring, or the corn will stick to the pan and burn.

8 young, tender ears of sweet white corn

2 tablespoons unsalted butter (or bacon drippings)

Salt and whole black pepper in a peppermill

1. Shuck and carefully silk the corn, breaking off the stem. Over a large bowl, cut the outer half of the kernels from the ears with a sharp knife, leaving half the kernel still attached to the cobs. Then thoroughly scrape the cobs with the blunt side of the knife blade to force out all the milk from the cut kernels into the bowl.

2. Put the butter or drippings in a large, well-seasoned iron skillet or heavy-bottomed non-stick pan. Turn on the heat to medium-high. When the fat is just melted, add the corn and its milk. Bring to a boil, stirring and scraping the pan to keep it from sticking. Turn the heat down to medium and continue cooking and stirring until the milk begins to thicken, about 5 minutes.

3. Reduce the heat to a slow simmer. Cook, stirring constantly and carefully scraping the bottom to keep it from scorching, until it is very thick and tender, about 5 minutes more. Taste and season accordingly with salt and pepper, and allow a minute or so more of cooking for the seasonings to meld. Turn off the heat and serve at once. Serves 4 to 6.

NOTES: *In* The Kentucky Housewife *Mrs. Bryan cooked the corn in a covered skillet, a practice still used by some traditional cooks, but I find that method harder to control. There are other cooks who allow a crust to form on the bottom of the pan and then scrape it up and stir it into the corn. This is repeated over and over until the mixture is thoroughly laced with browned bits of crust. It requires constant supervision, or the crust will scorch and give the dish an unpleasant acrid taste, but it's a lovely variation that really brings out the sweetness of the corn.*

Indian, or Green Corn Pudding

This variation of English savory custard puddings survives surprisingly unscathed from Maine to Florida. It is a delicate, delicious treatment for fresh corn. The name "Indian" pudding can be confusing in the older books because it was quite often used to describe both this dish and a baked sweet pudding made with cornmeal. In both instances, it had nothing to do with Native American cookery, but was only a foreshortening of the names "Indian corn" and "Indian meal," both of which had fallen into disuse by the middle of the nineteenth century.

You may be surprised to learn that this pudding was sometimes served with a sweet sauce as a dessert, with no added sugar. Fresh corn is naturally sweet, but its sugars begin to break down into starch the moment the ear is pulled from the stalk. Added sugar began to appear in recipes for it as soon as freshly picked corn began to be supplanted by canned corn and fresh ears that had spent days in a refrigerated warehouse. With good, fresh corn, however, to add sugar is incongruous and intrusive.

The other odd name, "green corn," did not mean corn of that color; it was just the old way of differentiating tender, young ears from fully matured or dried corn. The name is rare outside Georgia and the Carolina Piedmont, and even there it has all but faded from use.

2 cups sweet white corn kernels with milk, freshly cut from the cob as in step 1 of Fried Corn (page 219)

2 large eggs, lightly beaten

1/2 cup light cream or half-and-half

Salt and whole black pepper in a peppermill

Whole nutmeg in a grater

1 tablespoon unsalted butter, softened

1. Position a rack in the lower third of the oven and preheat it to 350 degrees F. Put on a teakettle of water to boil. Combine the corn, eggs, and cream in a mixing bowl. Season lightly with salt, pepper, and a grating of nutmeg, and mix until thoroughly combined.

2. Lightly butter a 1- to 1-1/2-quart ceramic casserole or soufflé dish and pour in the batter. Place the casserole in the center of a large, deep pan and put it in the lower third of the oven. Pour boiling water carefully into the larger pan until it comes halfway up the sides.

3. Bake until the pudding is set, about 1 to 1-1/2 hours, depending on the shape of the casserole. The wider and shallower the pan, the quicker the pudding will cook. Be careful not to overcook it, or the custard could break and become watery. Serve hot or at room temperature. Serves 4.

Corn Oysters, or Fritters

Vegetable fritters were common to all early-nineteenth-century cookbooks, Southern ones not excepted. Corn fritters were especially universal and sometimes went by the name "corn oysters" or "mock oysters," presumably because they resembled fried oysters. Fritters made from squash, salsify, and eggplant were also known, and Annabella Hill gave us okra fritters, one of the earliest fried okra recipes in print.

Mrs. Hill understood that all vegetable fritters tended to get soggy if the inner moisture and steam had no place to escape, and instructed that the fritters be served flat, without stacking, on a folded napkin. It says something unfortunate that later recipes which otherwise copied Mrs. Hill omitted the nicety of this careful detail.

2 large eggs

4 ears tender white corn, cut from the cob as directed in step 1 of Fried Corn (page 219)

1 tablespoon unsalted butter, melted and cooled

Salt and whole black pepper in a peppermill

Whole nutmeg in a grater

2 tablespoons all-purpose flour

Lard, or peanut or other vegetable oil, for frying

1. Position a rack in the upper third of the oven and preheat it to 150–170 degrees F (the warm setting). Fold a large linen or cotton napkin to fit a platter that will hold the fritters in a single layer and fit a metal rack over a rimmed baking sheet and put it into the oven.

2. Separate the whites and yolks of the eggs, setting the whites aside in a metal or glass bowl. Put the yolks in a large mixing bowl and lightly beat them. Add the corn, butter, a large pinch of salt, liberal grinding of black pepper, and generous grating of nutmeg. Sift the flour gradually into the corn with a sifter or wire sieve, beating constantly until it is well mixed.

3. Put enough lard or oil in a deep skillet to come up the sides at least 1/2 inch (but no more than halfway). Turn on the heat to medium-high. While the fat is getting hot, beat the egg whites in a separate bowl until they form stiff, but not dry peaks.

4. When the fat is hot, but not smoking (365–375 degrees F) briefly beat the corn batter to mix it and fold in the egg whites. Drop the batter by tablespoonfuls into the fat and fry until the bottoms are golden brown, about 2 minutes. Turn and cook until both sides are uniformly brown. Drain well, blot briefly on absorbent paper, and transfer the fritters to the wire rack in the oven while you fry the remaining batter. Arrange the fritters on the napkin-lined platter and serve at once. Serves 4 to 6.

NOTES: *For a change, I like to add about 2 tablespoons of minced onion or green scallion. Simmer over low heat in the butter called for in the batter until they are softened, but not brown and fold them into the batter in step 2. You might also experiment with herb combinations.*

Fritter Variations:

Okra Fritters: Cook the okra as directed for Stewed Okra (page 231), omitting the butter and seasonings from the recipe. Trim off the tough, woody stems and roughly mash the pods with a fork. Substitute the okra for the corn in Corn Oysters, increasing the amount of flour to 1/2 cup.

Squash fritters: Cook the squash as directed in steps 1 and 2 of Creamed Squash (page 254). Trim off the stem and blossom ends, crush the squash to a rough pulp with a potato masher, and substitute it for the corn in Corn Oysters.

Eggplant Fritters: Cook 2 medium eggplants (about 3/4 pound each) as you would the squash, above. Trim off the stem, peel and mash to a pulp, and substitute it for the corn in Corn Oysters.

GUINEA SQUASH, OR EGGPLANT

Imagine eggplant as a mind-altering drug. As were many nightshades, eggplants were, for a time, thought to be poisonous, and even to induce insanity. The Italian name, *melanzana*, from Latin *mala insana* (literally, insanity), or possibly *mela insana*, "crazy apple," is a lingering reminder of the old European name "mad apple." Originating in the Far East, they were introduced to Europe and Africa by the Arabs. That, at least, is pretty clear. But how (and when) they came to America is a subject of considerable confusion and debate.

According to pop-culture historians, eggplants were supposed to have been introduced to America by way of late-nineteenth-century immigrants from Spain and Italy, but this does not stand up to close examination. Evidence suggests that the more likely route was by way of the African trade—more significantly, West African slave trade—whence came the early American names "guinea squash," and, occasionally, "guinea melon." The oldest recipes I find are from areas where slavery was both legal and common—that's to say, the South. In these places, early Italian and Spanish immigrants were rare. There was a Spanish presence, to be sure, in Florida, Texas, South Georgia and (for a time) Louisiana, but any real culinary influence was minimal, and while some early Southern cookbooks show some knowledge of Mediterranean cookery, it was sparse and, for the most part, indirect.

Eggplants have been growing in the South (at least in Virginia) since at least 1737. The first known Southern cookbook, *The Virginia House-wife* (1824), included eggplants, and it should be noted that the cooking Mrs. Randolph recorded was from her heyday as a housekeeper—that is, the 1790s. Thomas Jefferson had eggplants at Monticello and recorded their presence in Washington markets as early as 1801. Clearly, this vegetable has been on Southern tables for a lot longer than pop-culture historians would have us suppose.

As to their common English name, "eggplant," Karen Hess speculates that it most likely derives from the fact that some varieties of eggplant are white and about the size and shape of a swan's egg (she quotes at least one such early English description of "Madde Apples"). Though today we're most familiar with the purple-skinned variety, to the extent that many paint companies use the word "eggplant" to describe a deep purple color, both white and purple ones are mentioned in Southern cookbooks as late as 1879. Most books said that purple varieties were superior, and the white eggplants eventually fell out of use. Today, thanks to heirloom vegetable growers, some of the older white varieties are again available.

For the cook, eggplant presents two problems: A tendency to bitterness and an alarming ability to absorb fat. To combat them, cooks have, over time, employed a number of methods. The oldest one was to parboil them whole in salted water; later, they were sliced and soaked in cool salted water. Today, they are most often sliced, salted and left to stand—the method that I prefer, and still do despite arguments from scientists that it isn't necessary.

Fried Eggplant

Fried eggplant, coated with crumbs and cooked quickly in boiling fat, is a truly international dish. A lingering legacy of the old Turkish domination of the region, it is practically indigenous to virtually every Mediterranean country, and small wonder: it was, and still is, one of the most satisfying things you can do with eggplant.

Mrs. Randolph was careful to instruct that the breading must be allowed to dry before the eggplant are fried, going so far as to bread one side at a time as directed here. It is still a sound practice.

2 large firm purple eggplants	1 to 1-1/2 cups dry breadcrumbs spread on
Salt	a dinner plate
1 large egg, well beaten, in a shallow bowl	Lard or peanut oil, for frying

1. Wash the eggplants and cut off the stem, but don't peel them. Slice crosswise into rounds about 1/2 inch thick. Sprinkle all sides liberally with salt and put them in a colander to drain for half an hour. Beads of moisture will form on the eggplant and it will discolor slightly. Press them gently to squeeze out the excess moisture and pat dry, wiping away any salt that remains.

2. One at a time, dip one side of each slice in the egg, let the excess flow back into the bowl, and press it into the breadcrumbs. Put them breaded side up on a wire rack to dry, about half an hour. Bread the other side in the same manner and let it dry on the rack. (You can do both sides at once if you are in a hurry. It's a little messier, but it won't hurt anything.)

3. Position a rack in the upper third of the oven and preheat to 150–170 degrees F (or the warm setting). Fit a wire rack over a rimmed baking sheet and put it in the oven. Put enough fat in a deep cast-iron or heavy nonstick skillet to come up the sides about 1/2 inch. Heat it over medium heat until hot, but not smoking (around 375 degrees F). Add enough eggplant to fill the pan without crowding. Cook until the bottoms are golden, about 3 minutes, turn them carefully and fry until evenly brown. If they begin to brown too quickly, turn the heat down slightly. Blot briefly on absorbent paper, put them on the rack in the oven, and repeat with the remaining eggplant.

4. Fold a large cotton or linen napkin over a large platter that will hold the eggplant in one layer. Put the eggplant on it without stacking and serve at once. Serves 4 to 6.

Stuffed Eggplant

Virtually every antebellum Southern cookbook had some variation of stuffed eggplant, the fillings ranging from the elegant simplicity of this recipe to rich, complex stuffings of ham, poultry, tongue, or veal, seasoned with mace, pepper, sage, and lemon. Either way is wonderful. All stuffed vegetables in open-hearth days were either stewed in gravy or baked in a Dutch oven, but as the cast-iron stove displaced the hearth, oven baking replaced the older methods.

This recipe follows *The Carolina Housewife* and *Mrs. Hill's New Cookbook*, and suggests that a simpler approach was favored in the Deep South, although Mrs. Hill did give us an alternate forcemeat stuffing.

2 medium-sized, purple eggplants, about 3/4 pound each	Whole black pepper in a peppermill
Salt	1 tablespoon chopped parsley
1 small onion, trimmed, split lengthwise, peeled, and minced	1 tablespoon chopped fresh basil, mint, or thyme, or 1 teaspoon dried mint or thyme (optional)
3 tablespoons unsalted butter	1 egg, lightly beaten
1 cup dry breadcrumbs	

1. Wash the eggplants, but do not peel or stem them. Put enough water in a large kettle to cover them and bring it to a boil over medium-high heat. Add a small handful of salt and the eggplants. Let it come back to a boil, reduce the heat to medium, and cook until they begin to soften, about 15 minutes. Drain and let them cool enough to handle.

2. Position a rack in the center of the oven and preheat it to 400 degrees F. Cut the eggplants in half length-wise and make a deep cut half an inch in from the skin. Using a sharp spoon or melon baller, scoop out the pulp, leaving a half-inch thick shell on all sides. Coarsely chop the pulp and sprinkle lightly with salt.

3. Put the chopped pulp, onion, and 2 tablespoons of the butter in a skillet over medium heat. Simmer until the onion is softened, but not browned, about 5 minutes. Turn off the heat. While the pan is still warm, add two-thirds of the crumbs, a liberal grinding of pepper, the parsley, and optional herbs. Toss until all is well mixed.

4. Lightly butter a baking dish that will hold all the eggplant in one layer. Pat them dry, put them in the dish cut side up, and divide the filling among them. Brush the tops with egg.

5. Wipe out the skillet and melt the remaining butter over medium-low heat. Stir in the crumbs until the butter is evenly absorbed. Sprinkle them over the eggplant, patting into place, and bake in the center of the oven until heated through and browned on top, about 20 to 30 minutes. Serves 4.

MUSHROOMS

To talk of "wild" mushrooms in the context of these recipes would have seemed redundant to the cooks who first recorded them. Even though mushrooms were available in markets early on (Jefferson's records of the Washington markets shows them for sale as early as 1801) and were also advertised in some newspapers (according to historian Richard Hooker, such ads appeared in *The South Carolina Gazette*), they weren't cultivated commercially until later in the nineteenth century. A few odd horticulturalists like Jefferson experimented with them (but then, he experimented with just about everything), however most cookbook authors presumed that their readers would gather their mushrooms in the wild, since every early recipe began with instructions of identifying and gathering edible types.

It has been suggested that mushrooms were not eaten much by early settlers because of problems with identification, but this hardly seems likely. Many edible varieties common to Europe are also indigenous to America—*Boletus Edulis* (*cèpes* and *porcini*), chanterelles, morels, and common field mushrooms, to name a few—all of which are easily identified. Harriott Pinckney Horry mentions morels in her household notebook in entries that probably predate the Revolution, and morels are found in old forests of the area. Of course, she also mentions truffles, which are not found in Carolina, so there's always a possibility that the recipes were copied out verbatim from a European cookbook. Possible, but not, I think, likely. By the mid-eighteenth century, Charleston was a wealthy, cosmopolitan city, and truffles may easily have been imported, as such exotic things often were—or Mrs. Horry may have known another fungus as a truffle; there are native varieties of puffball, for example, that grow underground. At any rate, mushrooms were so commonplace in nineteenth-century sources, long before commercial cultivation, that they must have been widely used.

Most of these older recipes for mushrooms were lovely, and remained so until the advent of the canned variety. As these became the norm, the recipes deteriorated hopelessly. A case in point is "Parisian Stuffed Mushrooms" from the *Tested Recipes Cook Book* (1895), which demonstrates how far mushroom cookery had sunk by that time: "If the mushrooms have not been cooked or canned," it begins, "peel the cup and *put in water and vinegar to soak . . .*" (emphasis mine)—in other words, make them like canned mushrooms. It goes without saying that the rest of that recipe is not included here.

Types of Mushrooms to Use

> "*Gather grown mushrooms, but such as are young enough to have red gills.*"
>
> —Mary Randolph, *The Virginia House-wife* (1824)

"Those proper for food are only found in open ground . . . they are a dull pearl-colored white . . . while the under part is tinged with pink."

—Lettice Bryan, *The Kentucky Housewife* (1839)

"The upper part and stalk are white; the under a salmon color . . . and are found in open fields or pastures."

—Annabella Hill, *Mrs. Hill's New Cook Book* (1867)

What these ladies are describing is *Agaricus campestris*, common field mushrooms, easily identified and plentiful during summer and autumn in open meadows and pastures. Because of the ladies' aversion to shade-loving mushrooms, they missed our native *Boletus edulis*—the prized *cèpes* of France and *porcini* of Italy. Field mushrooms are not sold commercially, but they are easy to find throughout the eastern section of the country—or, they were before the rampant development of the last century. If you are inexperienced at foraging for mushrooms, don't try to learn on your own—take an experienced gatherer with you and stick to easily identified varieties, such as boletus, chanterelles, chicken mushroom (sulfur shelf), morels, oyster mushrooms, puffballs, and those common field mushrooms, which are closely related to the cultivated white champignon and brown mushrooms found in the market. Each variety reacts differently to heat, but most of them will work fine in these recipes, as will cultivated mushrooms. When gathering, don't pull the mushrooms up, but cut the stalk just above the ground. Many varieties depend on the roots remaining in place for them to propagate.

If you'd rather rely on cultivated or commercially gathered mushrooms, there is a growing variety of them available aside from the ubiquitous champignons, cremini, and portobellos—including *boletus*, chanterelles, chicken, morel, shiitake, and oyster mushrooms, mostly in specialty grocers and natural food stores. We forget, thanks to commercially-raised mushrooms, that they are seasonal in the wild—and the availability of wild varieties varies from early spring to late autumn. I often mix cremini or portobello mushrooms with reconstituted dried boletus mushrooms for flavor, though they are no real substitute for the real thing. The secret to most mushrooms is absolute freshness, and commercial ones seldom are. Look for tight, dry caps with no damp spots, whose underside membranes still mostly cover the gills. My own preference is for smaller mushrooms such as little button cremini and the so-called "baby" portobellos, since they have the most flavor.

To clean mushrooms: Regardless of the variety of mushrooms that you choose, it is important that they never be exposed to water. Modern scientists contradict this caution, because the flesh of mushrooms is naturally full of water. They are, but that's the very reason to avoid exposing them to more: once its surface is moistened, it tends to stay damp. Wipe the caps and stems clean with a dry cloth or paper towel, and use a soft vegetable brush for any clinging dirt on the base of the stem (or trim the base of the stem away).

Stewed Mushrooms

"Gather grown mushrooms, but such as are young enough to have red gills . . . red wine may be added, but the flavour of mushrooms is too delicious to require aid from any thing."

—Mary Randolph, *The Virginia House-wife*, 1824

Amen, Mrs. Randolph. This was a universal recipe, with occasional variations including spices (even—I shudder to mention it—cloves), vinegar, and, as Mrs. Randolph noted, red wine, but few display that lady's understanding and reverence. This follows her recipe, with Lettice Bryan's dollop of cream added as an option. They are nice enough without it, so you can leave it out if you feel cream would make it too rich.

Stewed Mushrooms can be served over toast as an elegant first course, but I like them best as is, or as a sauce for fish and roasted poultry or as a filling for an omelet.

3/4 pound wild or cremini mushrooms (see headnote above)

Salt and whole black pepper in a peppermill

2 tablespoons unsalted butter

1/2 teaspoon all-purpose flour

1/4 cup heavy cream (minimum 36% milk fat) (optional)

1. Clean the mushrooms as directed on page 227. Trim off any tough stems. Cut large caps into halves, quarters, or thick slices, but leave the smaller ones whole.

2. Put the mushrooms into a lidded pan that will comfortably hold them in no more than two layers (such as a straight-sided sautoir pan). Sprinkle with a healthy pinch of salt and liberal grinding of pepper. Cover tightly and put over medium-low heat. *Do not add water*; they will make their own juices as they cook.

3. Stew gently, shaking the pan occasionally to keep them from sticking, until tender, about 20 minutes. Try not to lift the lid while they're cooking so that their natural juices won't evaporate.

4. Meanwhile, roll the butter in the flour. When the mushrooms are tender, remove the lid and add the floured butter in bits, shaking the pan until it is just melted and the juices are lightly thickened. If you like, you may add 1/4 cup cream and let it heat until lightly thickened, about 4 to 5 minutes more. Turn the mushrooms out into a warm bowl and serve at once. Serves 4.

NOTES: *With a little finesse, you can thicken the juices with the butter liaison without the flour—and it is so much better without it. Omit the flour and swirl in the butter, off the heat, shaking—and never stirring—until it is barely melted and the sauce is thick. Properly done, this will produce a sauce like pure silk, but it cannot be reheated, so serve it at once.*

Mushrooms with Cream

These are not merely a variation of the previous recipe. Mushrooms cooked in real cream are one of the world's great gastronomical inventions. Properly done, they need nothing but a little salt and pepper to bring out their flavor. This dish has gotten a rather bad reputation from all those graceless concoctions of canned button mushrooms gooped up with floury white sauce. Button mushrooms are bad enough; canning makes them altogether insipid. Good cream thickens on its own and does not need to be gooped up with flour.

3/4 pound wild or cremini mushrooms

2 tablespoons unsalted butter

Salt and whole black pepper in a peppermill

1 cup heavy cream (minimum 36% milk fat)

4 thick slices home-style bread, buttered and toasted crisp

1. Clean the mushrooms as directed on page 227 and, if they are very large, slice them crosswise 1/4 inch thick. Leave small mushrooms or morels whole.

2. Put the butter in a sauté pan that will hold the mushrooms in a single layer and place over medium-high heat. As soon as it is melted, add the mushrooms and toss to coat. Sauté, tossing frequently, until shiny but slightly underdone (not yet coloring).

3. Season with a healthy pinch of salt and a few grindings of pepper. Add the cream, let it come to a boil, and cook, tossing or stirring until the cream is lightly thickened, about 3 or 4 minutes more. Remove it from the heat.

4. Arrange the toast on a platter, or, if you are serving it as a first course, on individual salad plates. Pour the mushrooms over the toast and serve at once. Serves 4.

NOTES: *One of my favorite additions to this dish is about 1/4 cup finely julienned country ham or prosciutto. Add it after the cream is thick in step 3 and barely heat it through, about 1 minute more. Though seldom mentioned, 1 tablespoon minced shallot can be added to the butter in step 2. Sauté for about 4 minutes, until softened, before adding the mushrooms.*

Annabella Hill's Baked Mushrooms

Baking does nice things for mushrooms of almost any sort. It concentrates their flavor and intensifies their earthy aroma as no other method can. Even commercial white mushrooms benefit from it, acquiring a respectable flavor and texture that you would not expect them to have on their own. For this recipe, the most successful wild mushrooms are large field mushrooms, shiitake, boletus, or portobellos; oyster mushrooms are too delicate.

Mrs. Hill served these mushrooms on toast, but they are at their best eaten just as they are from the dish.

3/4 pound wild, or 1 pound cremini or white button mushrooms
Salt and whole black pepper in a peppermill

1 tablespoon Southern Browning (page 110) kneaded into 3 tablespoons unsalted butter, softened

1. Position a rack in the center of the oven and preheat to 375 degrees F. Clean and trim the mushrooms as directed on page 227.

2. Butter an earthenware or ceramic dish that will hold the mushrooms in one layer. Put in the mushrooms, stems up. Sprinkle lightly with salt and a few grindings of pepper, and dot with the butter/browning mixture. Bake until are tender, about 20 minutes. Serves 4.

OKRA

Okra is an annual flowering hibiscus (*Abelmoschus esculentus*) native to Africa. Its flowers, whose bright yellow petals deepen to rich burgundy red at their center, are some of the loveliest of all the hibiscuses. Of course, okra isn't grown for its ornamental qualities, but for the mucilaginous seedpods that develop after the brilliant flower has faded.

How and when okra got to the South isn't altogether clear, but it almost certainly was introduced by the African slave trade, and was popularized by the slaves themselves, as only they knew how to cultivate and cook it. Both its American names, "okra" and "gumbo," have African origins. According to Jessica Harris, "okra" derives from the West African name *nkru-ma* of the Ghanan Twi language, and gumbo from Angolan kingombo. The local preference for each name probably goes back to origins of the African slaves in a given region, as Karen Hess has suggested in *The Carolina Rice Kitchen*. After okra was introduced to Euro-American tables, "gumbo" came almost exclusively to mean the African stews in which the okra was the principal ingredient, and now names thick Creole stews that may ironically contain a variety of shellfish, pork, beef, chicken, or sausage and no okra at all.

We tend to think of this vegetable as peculiarly Southern and African-American, but it can be found in Central and South America wherever Africans were settled and is also known to the cooking of the Middle East. Marcella Hazan startled me by exclaiming that she loved okra, until she gently reminded me that, after all, her family had once lived in Egypt and had Lebanese connections.

I've been told that okra is an acquired taste. It may very well be, but, if so, I acquired mine early on. What I think people really mean is that okra is rather slimy when overcooked and that takes some getting used to. Frankly, there's nothing worse. But you won't have that problem if you are careful not to overcook it. In fact, you needn't cook it at all. My mother recalls that in her girlhood, they made okra salad—yes, from raw okra. It is wonderful.

Stewed Okra

This is the dividing line for true okra lovers. People who will otherwise eat it fried, in soup, gumbo, or cooked with tomatoes, draw the line here. Their prejudice is based on years of badly stewed okra, boiled until the pods are a mushy, slimy mess, a prejudice that usually disappears when they are served okra that is stewed using this method. Mrs. Randolph called this "Gumbs—a West India Dish," hinting at the route that okra most probably took on its way into North America.

My original interpretation of this recipe was to cook the okra in abundant boiling water, as is done in step one of the recipe following this one, a method used by many old cookbook authors. While that accomplished a similar result, it was not as flavorful as this method, and Karen Hess has persuaded me that the method given here was Mrs. Randolph's original intent.

1 pound young, tender okra pods	2 tablespoons unsalted butter
Salt and whole black pepper in a peppermill	

1. Gently wash the okra under running water, rubbing away the fine fuzz that covers its surface. Trim the stem cap, but leave it intact to hold the okra's mucilage inside during the cooking.

2. Put the okra in a heavy-bottomed, lidded pan in one layer. Add about 1/4 cup of water, a large pinch of salt, and a liberal grinding of pepper. Cover tightly and place over medium-high heat. Cook, shaking the pan occasionally, until the okra is just tender but still bright green, about 3 to 5 minutes. Remove it from the heat, uncover, and swirl in the butter, shaking the pan until it has melted into the pan juices and coated the okra. Pour into a warm serving bowl and serve at once. Serves 4.

Fried Whole Okra

This is one of the most satisfying ways of preparing okra that I know. Tender, young pods are blanched, lightly breaded in cornmeal or crumbs and quickly fried in very hot fat. Like oysters and other delicate shellfish, okra is ruined if the fat is not hot enough and if they cook for too long. To be completely successful, the okra pods must be as fresh as possible and no longer than two inches, and the fat must be clean and very hot.

I have seen and sampled recipes for fried okra that use more mature pods that are cut into short pieces. Frankly, I don't care for them very much, not only because the mature pods are not as tender, but because the cut end releases some of the natural moisture, resulting in okra that is not as succulent when cooked. There are also commercially packaged breaded and frozen okra pieces available in some parts of the South. If you think you hate fried okra, it's probably because that is the only kind that you have had.

24 small, young okra pods, no longer than 1-1/2 to 2 inches
Lard or vegetable oil

2 eggs, well beaten in a shallow bowl
1 cup cornmeal or fine, dry breadcrumbs or cracker meal, spread on a dinner plate

1. Position a rack in the upper third of the oven and preheat it to 150–170 degrees F (the warm setting). Fit a wire rack over a rimmed baking sheet and put it in the oven. Bring a large pot of salted water to a boil over high heat. Wash the okra and drop it into the boiling water. Let it come back to a boil and cook until crisp-tender but still bright green, about 3 or 4 minutes. Drain well.

2. Put enough fat into a heavy iron skillet or a deep nonstick pan to come up the sides by 1/2 inch and turn on the heat to medium-high. Have the eggs and breading ready by the skillet.

3. When the fat is very hot, dip the okra, one at a time, in the egg, turning until well coated. Lift it out, to allow the excess to flow back into the bowl, and quickly roll it in the breading, making sure it is lightly, but thoroughly, coated. Lightly shake off the excess and slip it into the fat. Repeat with the remaining okra until the pan is full but not crowded.

4. Fry quickly until golden, about 2 minutes. Drain well, blot briefly on absorbent paper, and transfer to the wire rack in the oven. Repeat until all the okra is cooked. You may serve it as Mrs. Hill would have done, on a platter lined with a folded napkin, but serve it quickly, so that it is piping hot. Serves 4.

Okra and Tomatoes

This is one of the key foundations on which so much of classic Southern cooking is built. From this basic trunk, any number of vines sprout—soups, vegetable side dishes, even sauces for meat. Variations on the common theme are universal from Virginia to Texas. The basic recipe certainly predates the 1824 edition of *The Virginia House-wife*, which is its first appearance in print, and is included in virtually every Southern book thereafter. Sometimes there is no mention of onions, or the cook will substitute salt pork for the butter, but the basic method and proportions remained consistent. In her 1867 book, Annabella Hill made the first, ominous mention of sugar, which was to become a fixture in almost all later tomato recipes. This recipe, however, follows Mrs. Randolph; sugar does not belong here.

The pairing of these two vegetables has all the makings of a great love story. No match was ever more tenuous or improbable, and no lovers were ever more clearly meant for one another. Tomatoes are Central American and okra, African—for thousands of years half a world away from one other until the colonization of the West began and they were finally brought together. What they do for one another must be tasted to be fully understood; tomatoes lend their sunny tartness while the okra, in turn, enrobes with its silken texture, blunting the acid bite of the tomatoes. The liaison is a perfect balance of flavor, texture, and color.

2 cups fresh tomatoes (about 4 to 5 medium), blanched, peeled, and seeded (page 262), and coarsely chopped, or 2 cups Italian canned tomatoes, with their juices

2 cups sliced tender young okra pods

1/4 cup chopped yellow onion

2 tablespoons unsalted butter or bacon drippings

Salt and whole black pepper in a peppermill

1. Put the tomatoes and their reserved juice, okra, onion, and butter in a deep heavy-bottomed pan over medium-high heat. Bring it to a boil, stirring occasionally to prevent sticking and scorching, then reduce the heat to a slow simmer.

2. Season with a healthy pinch of salt and a few liberal grindings of black pepper. Stir well and let it simmer, uncovered, until thick, about 1 hour. Check the pot and stir it occasionally to be sure that the vegetables have not become too dry and begun to stick. Just before serving, taste and correct the seasonings and let simmer about 2 minutes longer to meld them. Serves 4.

ONIONS

In this century, onions have become big business in Georgia, where the soil around the town of Vidalia produces a large and uniquely fragrant sweet onion. Though not the only sweet onions grown in the South (Texas 1015s and Wadmalaw Sweets are two notable examples), they are, by far and away, the most famous, and are so important to the area's economy that the name is one of only a few to be protected and regulated by laws similar to the laws that protect Parmigiano cheese and champagne.

But onions were relished in Georgia, and in the rest of the South, long before the famous Vidalia sweets were developed. The myth that these pungent members of the lily family have only been eaten around here in recent times can be discredited by even the most casual glance at early Southern cookbooks and household notebooks. Through these records, it is apparent that Southern cooks and gardeners both knew of and used many members of the onion tribe. Spanish yellow onions, delicate silver-whites, shallots, and leeks are just a few varieties that are frequently referenced. There is even a variety of wild onion called ramp that has been enjoyed in parts of the South for generations. So have the recipes given here.

Creamed Onions for Roast Poultry

Unlike most modern "creamed" vegetables, which are usually bound in an uninteresting flour-thickened white sauce, these onions are truly finished in cream. They are delicious as a sauce or side dish for all kinds of roasted fowl or other game. Mrs. Randolph used them as a sauce for roast ducks, a fine combination. For many Southern families, creamed onions are traditional as an accompaniment for the Thanksgiving turkey.

1-1/2 pounds small white onions, no more than 1-inch round

2 cups Chicken Broth (page 82)

1 teaspoon all-purpose flour

2 tablespoons unsalted butter

1 cup heavy cream (minimum 36% milk fat)

Salt, whole black pepper in a peppermill, and whole nutmeg in a grater

1 tablespoon chopped parsley

1. Blanch the onions in a large kettle of boiling water for 2 minutes, immediately drain them and plunge them into cold water. Cut off the roots and the top stem and slip the onions out of their skins. Make a deep cross-shaped cut in the root end of each onion as you go.

2. Bring the broth to a boil in a large pot over a medium-high heat, and slip in the onions. There should be just enough liquid to cover them. If it doesn't, add a little water, but don't add more broth. Let it return to a boil, then reduce the heat to a bare simmer. Loosely cover and simmer until the onions are almost tender, but still firm, about 15 to 20 minutes. They'll

undergo further cooking, so don't let them get too soft. Raise the heat to medium-high, uncover, and quickly reduce the cooking liquid by slightly more than half.

3. Meanwhile, knead the flour into the butter until it is well mixed. When the broth is reduced, lower the heat to medium and stir in the floured butter. Simmer until thickened, about 3 or 4 minutes. Pour in the cream, raise the heat again to medium-high, and let it come back to a boil.

4. Reduce the heat as low as possible, add a pinch of salt, a liberal grinding of pepper, and freshly grated nutmeg to taste, and simmer until the sauce thickens slightly and the seasonings are blended, about 4 minutes more. Pour into a warm bowl, sprinkle with parsley, and serve at once. Serves 6.

Lettice Bryan's Spring Onions in Cream

Green, or spring onions are any young onion that still has tender green sprouts. Scallions are virtually the only type of green onion available today, but when I was growing up, the spring onions we had were actually young shallots, as they once were for many Southerners. They have a distinctive flavor that no scallion could ever hope for. This is probably why green scallions are sometimes called shallots in the South, and why there's so much confusion when they are called for in old recipes. Mrs. Bryan made a distinction between them, but later writers often did not.

This is an especially nice treatment for any green onions; it is fine thing to do with leeks and transforms mild little scallions. But if you should be so lucky as to have your own garden where you can pull shallots that are still green, it will put a little bit of heaven on your dinner table.

1-1/2 pounds small green onions or scallions	Whole black pepper in a peppermill
Salt	Whole nutmeg in a grater
1 cup heavy cream (minimum 36% milk fat)	1 tablespoon chopped parsley

1. Trim off the roots and any browned or withered leaves from the onions. Cut off just enough of the green tops to make them all of a uniform length and drop them into a basin of cold water.

2. Put a cup of water into a wide, shallow pan that will hold the onions in no more than two layers, and bring it to a boil over medium heat. Drain the onions from their cold bath and drop them into the pan. Cover loosely and let it come back to a boil, then uncover, and add a healthy pinch of salt. Reduce the heat to medium, and let them cook, uncovered, until tender. This should take no more than 10 minutes and may take as little as 5, so keep an eye on them. If they overcook, they will lose their color and much of their delicate flavor.

3. Remove the onions from the pan with a slotted spoon or spatula to a warm platter. Raise the heat to high and reduce the cooking liquid to about 2 tablespoons, about 3 to 4 minutes.

4. Pour in the cream and let it come back to a boil. Return the onions to the pan. Taste and add another pinch of salt, as needed, a liberal grinding of pepper, and a few gratings of nutmeg. Simmer until the cream is thick and lightly coating the onions, about 4 minutes more. Transfer them back to the platter, garnish with parsley, and serve at once. Serves 4.

Mrs. S. C. Manning's Stuffed Spanish Onions

You would never think that this recipe comes from New Orleans, but so it does. Mrs. Manning was the mother of my late friend the Reverend Robert H. Manning. She copied a number of older recipes into her household notebook sometime around 1900. There is no mention of herbs, but they were there—just hidden. Mrs. Manning's was an Anglo, not Creole, kitchen; it is likely the chicken had been simmered with sweet herbs and nutmeg, and so required very little additional seasoning. If the meat you are using is from a simple roast or stew, you may punch up the flavor with a few minced herbs, such as sage, thyme, basil, or parsley, and, of course, a little nutmeg.

4 large sweet yellow onions, such as Bermuda or Vidalia Sweets

1 cup minced cooked chicken

4 tablespoons soft breadcrumbs

1 tablespoon unsalted butter, melted

Salt and whole black pepper in a peppermill

1 tablespoon minced herbs, such as sage, thyme, basil, or parsley (optional)

1 blade mace, crushed, or pinch of powdered mace, or whole nutmeg in a grater (optional)

2 cups Chicken Broth (page 82)

A doubled recipe (1 cup) Drawn Butter (page 114), not made ahead but at the point indicated in step 5

1 tablespoon chopped parsley

1. Peel the outer skins from the onions, but don't cut off the root or stem. Bring a large kettle of water to a boil, add the onions, and bring back to a boil. Reduce the heat and simmer until they are nearly tender. Depending on the size and age of the onions, this could take from as little as 20 minutes to as long as 45.

2. Position a rack in the center of the oven and preheat it to 350 degrees F. While the onions simmer, mix together the chicken, crumbs, butter, seasonings, and herbs and spices to taste.

3. Drain the onions and let them cool enough to handle. Scoop out a little of the center of each. Fill the resulting cavity with a tablespoon or so of the stuffing, and then work a little in between the layers of flesh until it is all used up. Be careful not to break the onions' layers.

4. Lightly butter a casserole that will just hold the onion and put them in root side down and stuffed side up. Pour the broth around them and bake them until the tops are golden and the stuffing cooked through, about half an hour.

5. Carefully lift the onions onto a shallow serving dish. Make the drawn butter according to the recipe and pour some of it over the onions. Sprinkle with parsley and serve at once, passing the remaining sauce separately. Serves 4.

NOTES: *In Mrs. Manning's original recipe, the onions were tied in cheesecloth and simmered in broth to cover, but I find them less likely to get soggy and better tasting when they are baked.*

Instead of drawn butter, you can finish the sauce as for Creamed Onions For Roast Poultry (page 234), using the broth in which they baked. You may also like to vary the stuffing, using whatever leftover meat is on hand, or use minced ham or 1/2 pound of crumbled, browned Southern Country, or Bulk Sausage (page 195), or commercial bulk breakfast sausage.

Annabella Hill's Onion Custard

This delicate and lovely custard is close kin to the savory flans of Spain. Though Mrs. Hill had no direct connections to that country, she had an extensive library of European and American cookbooks, including Dr. William Kitchiner's *The Cook's Oracle* and Alexis Soyer's *The Modern Housewife or Ménagère*. The recipe is almost certainly European, as it is not common in American books, but Mrs. Hill seems to have thought Southerners should know about it. I think so, too.

10 medium white onions, trimmed, split lengthwise, peeled, and thinly sliced

3 tablespoons unsalted butter

4 large eggs

2 cups half-and-half, or whole milk

Salt and whole black pepper in a peppermill

Whole nutmeg in a grater

1. Position a rack in the center of the oven and preheat it to 350 degrees F. Put the onions and butter in a large iron or heavy nonstick skillet and turn on the heat to medium. Simmer, stirring frequently, until the onions are a rich gold. Take them up with a slotted spoon, spread them on a cutting board, and chop them fine.
2. Break the eggs into a large mixing bowl and beat until they are light and smooth. Gradually beat in the half-and-half, a little at a time, and stir in the onion, a healthy pinch of salt, a few grindings of pepper, and freshly grated nutmeg to taste.
3. Pour the custard into a shallow earthenware or glass casserole (about a 9 x 9-inch square, or 10-inch round one). Bake in the center of the oven until the custard is set, but still slightly runny in the center, like an omelet, about 15 minutes. Serve it in the baking dish. Serves 6 to 8.

Variation: Mrs. Hill was specific about using white onions, but yellow onions work as well. She made no mention of a water bath around the casserole, which is usual with modern custards, and given her short cooking time of 15 minutes, it seems doubtful that she used one, but intended the earthy texture produced by the method outlined. However, it does make a nice variation. Bring a teakettle of water to a boil while you fry and chop the onions in step 1. Set the casserole in a larger pan with 2-inch-deep sides (such as a sheetcake pan) and place it on the oven rack. Carefully pour the boiling water around it until it comes halfway up the sides of the casserole. Bake the custard until it is set, about 45 minutes.

Lettice Bryan's Fried Onions

When I first came across this recipe, I was startled by its resemblance to a traditional Italian onion sauce for pasta. While that dish contains wine and parsley and this one does not, the treatment is identical. In fact, this was not meant to serve as a vegetable, but as a sauce for meat. It is superb with broiled steak or chicken, any roasted poultry or game, and even simply roasted or broiled fish. Its secret is simple; the onions undergo a long, slow simmer with a little fat, then their liquid is quickly evaporated to concentrate the natural sweetness. The onions finally do "fry" in the end to a rich golden brown. The choice of lard isn't arbitrary; it imparts the best color and flavor, but if you prefer not to use it, substitute equal parts olive oil and butter.

1-1/2 pounds yellow onions, trimmed, split lengthwise, peeled, and sliced thin

3 tablespoons lard (or 1-1/2 tablespoons each butter and olive oil)

1/4 cup water

Salt and whole black pepper in a peppermill

1. Put the onions, fat, and water into a large, well-seasoned iron skillet, cover tightly, and turn on the heat to low. Let the onions simmer slowly until they are very tender—in fact, almost falling apart—about 45 minutes.

2. Remove the lid and raise the heat to medium-high. There will be a lot more liquid in the pan than the amount you put in at the beginning, but don't worry about it. This is supposed to happen. Let all the liquid evaporate, stirring frequently to prevent scorching.

3. When all the liquid has evaporated, continue cooking, stirring constantly, until the onions have taken on a deep, rich golden color. Be careful not to let them scorch or they will be bitter. Turn off the heat. Season with a healthy pinch or so of salt, and a few liberal grindings of pepper. You may make this several hours ahead. Reheat gently, over low heat, stirring frequently. Serves 4 to 6.

POTATOES

Potatoes originated in the Andes Mountains of Peru, in South America, where they had been cultivated at least since 6000 BC. The Incas called them *papas*, and cultivated them as a staple crop. When the Spanish Conquistadors overran Peru in the sixteenth century, they were more interested in Incan gold than in vegetables, and potatoes were at first hardly noticed. When the Europeans did take notice, they confused *papas* with *batatas*, the sweet potatoes of North America, which had already been introduced to Europe. This confusion of the names has made the early history of potatoes in Europe difficult to document.

Ironically, the two plants are not even distantly related. Potatoes (*Solanum turberosum*) belong to the botanical family *Solanaceae* that includes many poisonous and hallucinogenic plants, including nightshades. This probably accounts for the Europeans' early belief that potatoes were unwholesome, much as they had been said to be leery of its cousins, tomato and eggplant. Until the seventeenth century, potatoes were little more than a horticultural curiosity.

Sweet potatoes (*Ipomoea batatas*) on the other hand are not even remotely related to nightshades, and were believed to be a powerful aphrodisiac, so they gained acceptance more quickly. Widely grown in Spain by the end of the sixteenth century, they were the tubers that the English knew as "potatoes" until late in the seventeenth century. (When Shakespeare's Falstaff cried "let the skye raine potatoes" in *The Merry Wives of Windsor* he was referring to sweet potatoes and is actually making a ribald joke about their reputation as an aphrodisiac.) During the seventeenth century, potatoes were gradually accepted as food for the poor (that was when they were first cultivated in Ireland), but didn't win wide acceptance until the mid-eighteenth century.

The earliest days of the potato in North America are obscure and the subject of debate among historians. A few early English accounts of Virginia report that the natives were already cultivating a tuber called *openauk* which some, including Thomas Jefferson, believe were potatoes, but this is disputed. In *The Herball or General Historie of Plantes*, 1597, John Gerard wrote that he had received from Virginia the roots of white potatoes, which the natives called *pappus*, but Gerard's authenticity is often questioned. (Also, some Englishmen tended to refer to the entire New World as "Virginia.") All the same, wild potatoes have been found as far north as Nebraska, and there was more intercommunication among the Native peoples of America than is often supposed, so there is every possibility that Gerard and Jefferson were right. But, whether white potatoes were already growing in Virginia or not, they had no place in the diet of the European settlers until late in the eighteenth century. In the South, the preference for sweet potatoes continued, and for many Southerners, until well into my living memory, "potato" meant a sweet one; whites were called "Irish" potatoes to distinguish them.

Today, there are more than five thousand potato varieties cultivated worldwide. Of the fifty-odd varieties grown in the United States, only a dozen hybrids account for about 85% of the harvest. There are lingering regional preferences, but those few hybrids are the most widely available to us. Unfortunately, they are seldom identified by name, but are usually generically labeled "red," "round white," or "russet." Regardless of what might be printed on that bag in your supermarket, there is no such critter as an all-purpose potato. What may be a fine cooking method for one may not be suited to another. In general, young, waxy potatoes are best for boiling, steaming, and frying; more mature, mealy ones are better for baking or mashing. In either case, I prefer organically grown potatoes, when they are available, because—at least, to me—they taste better. If you have a natural food grocer in your area that sells organic produce, it is worth seeking out.

Types of Potatoes

Russets: (Also "Burbank Russets") This oblong, rough russet-skinned potato was developed by Luther Burbank in 1872. Today, there are a number of hybrid russets such as Norgold and Belrus. Sometimes called "California longs," the most famous russets come from Idaho, and the association is so ingrained that they are called "Idaho" potatoes even when they weren't grown in that state. They may also be marketed simply as "baking" potatoes, and when mature, they are ideal for that method. They are also good mashing potatoes, and mature ones are excellent for frying; young, newly harvested russets are moisture rich and not as suitable for frying.

Round whites: Accounting for most of America's potato harvest, "round white" is a loose name for dozens of varieties, some of which are not even round. The lion's share goes into processed products—chips, frozen fries, and other potato products. Several round-white strains have even been specifically developed for potato chips. Most round whites available today are recent hybrids such as Superior, Kennebec, and Katahdin. They are usually what you'll find in that bag generically labeled "white potatoes."

Yellow (or gold) potatoes: A number of fine yellow-fleshed potatoes are now available, even in supermarkets, the most common being Yukon Gold. When young, these potatoes have a fine, waxy flesh colored a delicate yellow, hence their name. They are excellent steamed whole or boiled in their skins. Very mature Yukon Golds are good mashed and have a fine, buttery flavor. These are today available in regular markets, but in my area, at least, the best are still found at Natural food and specialty grocers.

Red-skinned potatoes: There are a number of red-skinned varieties, though, unfortunately they are almost never marketed by name, but simply as red, or worse, "new" potatoes (they are seldom actually new; this only means that they were harvested while still immature). Compounding the felony, some "new" potatoes are even dyed red to fool shoppers. True new potatoes have a skin so fragile it rubs off in your hands, and flesh that is waxy, succulent, snow-white, and vaguely

The Guides to Understanding Southern Cooking—some of the historical cookbooks and manuscripts in the author's library.

Shrimp Paste, page 69, Dishes for Teas, Receptions and In-Betweens

Southern Vegetable Soup, page 87, Soups

Cream Pan Gravy, page 112 (with Fried Chicken, page 153), Savory Sauces

Trout Steaks with Wine and Rosemary, page 126, Fish and Shellfish

Chicken Kentuckian, page 155, Poultry and Game

Baked Pork Loin with Sweet Potatoes, page 189, Meats

The Southern Way with Vegetables, page 205

Mary Randolph's "To Dress Salad," page 270, Salads

Shrimp Pilau, page 297, Grits, Rice, and Noodles

Soda Biscuits, page 319, The Southern Baker's Art

A Rich Fruitcake (center), page 335, The Southern Baker's Art

Wine Jelly, page 372, Desserts

Candied Citrus Peel, page 387, Conserves

sweet. Cooking them any way other than steaming them seems almost a sacrilege. As red-skinned potatoes mature, the skin darkens and they lose much of their moisture. Mature red-skins are good for boiling, frying, and mashing, but are not very good bakers.

Storing Potatoes: The ideal storage environment for any potato is a cool, dry, but airy, bin where no light is admitted. The refrigerator is not ideal (some believe this makes them sweet), but in warmer climates, like Savannah, it may be the only choice.

Basic Boiled Potatoes

To Serve Plain or Use in Salads, Croquettes, and Other Dishes

"Pour [the boiled potatoes] into a colander; skin rapidly, putting them into a hot dish. Some cooks pour them from the hot water into cold water; this is done to make the skinning easier. After this, the next step should be to throw [the potatoes] to the pigs, as they absorb the water, and are rendered hard and sodden, and unfit for the table."

—Annabella Hill, *Mrs. Hill's New Cook Book* (1867)

No boiled potato destined for Mrs. Hill's table, whether it was to be simply mounded into a heated serving bowl, fried in croquettes, or mashed with butter and milk, was ever peeled before it was cooked. The same was true of every cook until the middle of the nineteenth century. One obvious reason is that the peeling protects the inner meat of the potato from absorbing water. But it also contains much of the potato's flavor, which goes down the drain when they are peeled before cooking.

Most people presume that boiling a potato is the one thing any idiot can do, requiring no special skills or real attention from the cook. Mary Randolph and Annabella Hill knew better. One of the longest and most detailed recipes in both these ladies' books was for boiled potatoes. "First assort them, and boil together those of the same size. Common sense teaches that this ought to be done," Mrs. Hill advised; Mrs. Randolph cautioned that "most boiled things are spoiled by having too little water, but potatoes are often spoiled by having too much." Nothing will affect your potato recipes more adversely than will indifferent boiling. If the potatoes have been badly treated at the beginning, no amount of art in the subsequent recipe will give you back the flavor you have robbed from them. Here, therefore, are some basic things to remember:

• Start with good potatoes. Again, there is no such thing as an all-purpose potato (see the notes above), so experiment until you find the best types available in your area for boiling, baking, and frying.

* The potatoes should all be roughly the same size. You needn't weigh or put a ruler to them; just keep them fairly uniform. Cooking times will depend on the size, as Mrs. Hill aptly observed. Don't cut them to a uniform size, as this exposes the inner flesh to water.

* Resist the temptation to rinse the potatoes in cold water to speed up the peeling. Mrs. Hill was right about what they were good for after such treatment, and almost nobody keeps pigs anymore.

> 2 pounds potatoes (of a uniform size)
> Unsalted butter, melted (optional, to be used only if serving the potatoes as is)
>
> Salt and whole black pepper in a peppermill (optional, only if serving the potatoes as is)

1. If the potatoes are refrigerated, take them out of the refrigerator at least half an hour before you cook them. Wash them under cold, running water, scrubbing off any dirt without breaking the skin, and put them in a large pot that will easily hold all of them. Add enough water to cover them by an inch. Remove the potatoes, cover the pot, and turn on the heat to medium-high.

2. When the water is nearly, but not quite, boiling, add the potatoes. Let the water come to full, rolling boil. Reduce the heat to medium or medium-low (a steady bubble but not a hard boil) and simmer until tender, from 10 to 30 minutes, depending on the size and age of your potatoes.

3. Drain and let sit, uncovered, in a warm place for about 5 minutes. Have ready a heated bowl. Quickly peel the potatoes with your hands (don't use a knife or potato peeler), the skins will slip right off. Put them in the bowl as they are peeled. Serve them tossed with melted butter, salt, and a liberal grinding of pepper, all to taste, or use them in one of the following recipes. Serves 4.

Mashed Potatoes

> 2 pounds Basic Boiled Potatoes (previous recipe), cooked quite soft
> 4 to 6 tablespoons unsalted butter, softened
>
> About 1/4 to 1/2 cup cream or milk, heated to the boiling point
> Salt and whole black pepper in a peppermill

1. As soon as the potatoes are peeled, mash them coarsely and rub them through a colander (or put them through a potato ricer) back into the pot in which they were cooked. Over low heat, gradually beat in the butter, then the cream, and a healthy pinch of salt.

2. Stir until they are smooth and the liquid is incorporated. If they appear to be too dry, add a spoonful or so more cream, but don't overdo it. Taste and adjust the seasoning, going easy if you are serving the potatoes with a highly seasoned gravy or stew. Mound them in a warmed serving bowl, dust the top with a little black pepper, if liked, and serve at once. Serves 4.

Two Variations for Mashed Potatoes

Lettice Bryan's Baked Potatoes

What we nowadays know by this name was called roasted potatoes by early-nineteenth-century cooks. This is what they knew as baked potatoes.

2 large eggs
1 recipe Mashed Potatoes (page 242, omitting step 2)

About 1/4 cup heavy cream (minimum 36% milk fat)
Whole black pepper in a peppermill

1. Position a rack in the upper third of the oven and preheat it to 400 degrees F. Lightly grease a shallow, 9-inch-square or -round earthenware baking dish.
2. Break the eggs into a large bowl and beat them until they are light and well mixed. Add the mashed potatoes and cream and mix well. If the mixture still seems stiff, add a little more cream or milk and mix it in. Season with a few grindings of pepper and mix well. Spoon them into the casserole, smooth the top, and bake in the upper third of the oven until set and lightly browned. Serves 4.

Potato Balls or Croquettes

This recipe combines two versions of croquettes. The first version is practically universal to all antebellum cookbooks and manuscripts. The second, with its crumb coating, was given only by Mrs. Randolph.

2 large egg yolks
1 recipe Mashed Potatoes (page 242)

1 cup all-purpose flour, or dry bread or fine cracker crumbs
Lard or peanut oil, for frying

1. Fold a large linen or cotton napkin to fit a platter and set it aside. Beat the egg yolks in a small bowl until they are light and smooth. Add them to the potatoes and mix well.
2. Spread the flour or crumbs on a plate and have it close by the stove. Put enough lard or oil in a deep skillet to come halfway up its sides (about an inch deep) and put it over medium-high heat.

3. While the fat is heating, shape the potatoes into balls or cakes, the former no larger than 1-1/2 inches in diameter, the latter no larger than an inch thick and 2-1/2 inches across. Roll them in the flour or crumbs until coated.

4. When the fat is hot but not quite smoking (around 375 degrees F), add as many croquettes as will fill the pan without crowding. Fry until the bottoms are golden brown, about 2 minutes, turn carefully, and fry until uniformly browned, about 2 minutes more. Blot briefly on absorbent paper, put them on the napkin-lined platter, and repeat with the remaining croquettes. Serve hot. Serves 4.

NOTES: *The croquettes can be fried in a deep-fat fryer, and there are several advantages to using one if you have it. For one thing, they seldom have to be turned over, and the risk of splattered grease and broken croquettes is lessened. Moreover, you can usually cut down the frying time, so less fat is likely to be absorbed by the potatoes. Most deep fryers come with a thermostat, so the heat can be more evenly and easily controlled—but don't take for granted that the thermostat is accurate. Always test it with a candy/frying thermometer that you know is accurate.*

Fried Potatoes

". . . or cut them in shavings round and round, as you would peal a lemon; dry them well in a clean cloth, and fry them in lard or drippings."

—Mary Randolph, *The Virginia House-wife*, 1824

There is a popular legend that George Crum, a chef at a hotel in Saratoga Springs, New York, "invented" potato chips in 1853 in response to a patron's complaint that his fried potatoes were not crisp enough. It is reinforced by the fact that many recipes from later in the century are titled "Saratoga Potatoes," and is so popular that I am almost reluctant to point out that potato chips precede Crum by half a century. It is possible that he really thought he'd invented something new; possibly, in the way of true businessmen, the hotel's management merely wanted people to believe it, and for a long time, they have. Yet here is Mary Randolph—in black and white—telling us exactly how to do it nearly thirty years before the frustrated Mr. Crum.

Beef tallow is by far and away the best fat for frying potatoes, but lard is the one most often mentioned in the old recipes, and makes a very good second to tallow. It stands up well to the high heat and lends a lovely crispness that vegetable oil can't imitate. However, if you prefer not to use animal fat, you may use vegetable oil. Of them, I find peanut oil the most satisfactory.

2 pounds mature white potatoes   Salt
Lard, or peanut or other vegetable oil, for frying

1. Position a rack in the upper third of the oven and preheat to 150–170 degrees F (the warm setting). Fit a wire rack over a rimmed baking sheet and put it in the oven. Have ready a basin of cold water. Wash, scrub, and peel the potatoes. With a very sharp knife, or, if you don't have a very sure aim, a mandolin or food processor, cut them into rounds no thicker than a quarter of an inch, or shave them into paper thin slices with a vegetable peeler or mandolin. Drop the sliced potatoes into the basin of water and let them stand for at least half an hour.

2. Put enough lard or oil in a deep cast iron pot (such as a Dutch oven) or deep fryer to come no more than halfway up the sides, never more, as the fat could easily boil over. Heat it over medium-high heat until very hot, but not smoking (around 375 degrees F).

3. Meanwhile, drain and thoroughly dry the potatoes, making sure that no moisture remains on them or it will cause the fat to explode and splatter all over everything, including you. Believe me, I know.

4. Slip the potato a few at a time into the fat and fry, stirring frequently to prevent their sticking together and to aid crisping, until they are crisp and golden brown. Take them up with a wire frying skimmer, drain well over the pot, and spread them on the wire rack in the oven. Repeat until all the potatoes are fried. Sprinkle them with salt and serve immediately. Serves about 6.

NOTES: *The French double-frying method, which is not mentioned in old Southern books, makes for lighter fried potatoes and sometimes makes the rounds puff up (pommes soufflées). For the first frying, the fat should not be as hot as given above, around 260–290 degrees F. Fry the potatoes for 8 minutes, or until they are soft. Take them from the fat, drain, and let cool. Raise the temperature of the fat to 375 degrees F, and fry the potatoes to a golden brown.*

To Make Potato Chips: Paper thin slices of potato cook in a flash, so once they go into the fat, don't turn your back, even for an instant. They also tend to stick to one another. Carefully separate them before you drop them into the fat, and fry only a few at a time, or they will stick together no matter how much stirring you do. Potato chips cool as quickly as they fry, and will never be hot by the time they get to the table, so don't bother trying to hold them in the oven. You can blot them briefly on absorbent paper, but don't let them lie on it long or they could get soggy. Spread them well apart to drain on the wire rack set over a rimmed baking sheet.

SWEET POTATOES (OR YAMS)

Sweet potatoes are native to the Americas and were being cultivated in the Caribbean islands when Columbus first landed. The Natives called them *batata*, a name that, as has already been noted, the Spanish probably confused with *papas*, combining the two into a common name that has confused historians ever since. Sweet potatoes are not at all related to white potatoes, nor to African yams, which they resemble and with which they are often confused. However, sweet potatoes are often called "yams" here because African slaves thought that was what they were. The name passed from servant to master and has become thoroughly ingrained in the Southern lexicon. Many Southerners find the notion that their sweet potatoes are not yams nearly as amusing as they do the sixteenth century belief that they were a powerful aphrodisiac.

In the lean years of the War Between the States and period of Reconstruction following, sweet potatoes were the only thing that kept many impoverished Southerners alive. Most post-reconstruction Southerners were heartily sick of them—sick, but not, mind you, done with them. They've remained a staple in our diet and a distinguishing feature on most Southern tables.

Most of the traditional recipes have survived right along with the potatoes virtually unchanged by modern ranges. With the exception of that overly sweet, marshmallow-topped mess called with complete inaccuracy and overstated elegance sweet potato soufflé, most modern recipes have nineteenth century roots.

Today many varieties of sweet potatoes are available, though they are not usually sold by name, except in specialty groceries. In shopping for them, use caution where the word "yam" is concerned, especially outside the South: real yams are sometimes sold in Northern West Indian markets. They resemble sweet potatoes in shape only: their flesh is paler, finer textured, not nearly as sweet, and has much more starch. They can be boiled, roasted, or fried as potatoes are, but will not be as successful in any of the recipes that follow, so be careful of what you buy.

Oven-Roasted Sweet Potatoes

"To Roast Sweet Potatoes—Sweep the hearth well; lay on the potatoes; cover with hot ashes; let them remain until tender. Irish potatoes may be cooked in the same way."

——Annabella Hill, *Mrs. Hill's New Cook Book*, (1867)

These potatoes are as Deep South as it gets. Originally, they really roasted, as Mrs. Hill faithfully recorded, smothered in the banked coals of a good wood fire. This method survived well into the twentieth century. When my father was growing up, he and his brothers used to bank the fires for the night and then shove sweet potatoes into the hot ash. The next morning, they rolled out their perfectly cooked potatoes before building the day's fire. He says he hasn't had a breakfast that good since.

Of course, the potatoes don't really roast in a modern oven, and lose something of the distinctive flavor my father remembers without the hardwood ash. But, with a baking stone or a *Romertopf* (an unglazed clay baking dish, see page 30) and a little care, they can still be delicious. Or, better still, if you have a wood-burning fireplace, give the original way a try.

6 large sweet potatoes	Unsalted butter, softened

1. If the potatoes have been refrigerated, let them come to room temperature before baking them, at least 1 hour. Position a rack in the center of the oven and preheat it to 400 degrees F. If you have a baking stone, terracotta baking tiles, or a *Romertopf*, put it in while the oven is cold and preheat it for at least half an hour.

2. Scrub the potatoes with a soft brush under running water to remove all dirt and dry carefully. If you are not using the *Romertopf*, put the potatoes on a rimmed baking sheet and place the sheet directly on the stone or tiles. If you are using the *Romertopf*, take it out of the oven with heavy mitts, put in the potatoes, replace the lid, and return it to the oven. Bake, turning every 15 minutes to keep them from getting too brown on the bottom, until the skin is crisp and the potatoes yield easily when pressed, about 1 to 1-1/2 hours.

3. Remove the potatoes, slit them down the center of the top, wrap a towel around, and press gently until they "pucker." Put a lump of fresh butter into each and serve at once. Serves 6.

Lettice Bryan's Baked Sweet Potato Puffs

Mrs. Bryan intended these puffs to be for the tea-table, but allowed that they were equally good for breakfast, and so they are. Go easy on the sugar, as the potatoes are naturally sweet and will need very little added to them.

4 medium-sized sweet potatoes	1/4 teaspoon ground cinnamon
1 tablespoon butter	1/4 teaspoon freshly grated nutmeg
1/4 cup sugar, more or less, to taste	

1. Scrub the potatoes with a soft brush under cold running water. Put enough water to cover them into a large heavy-bottomed pot and bring to a boil over high heat. Add the potatoes and bring back to a boil, then reduce the heat to a gentle simmer, and cook until they are quite soft, about 45 minutes. Drain the potatoes and let them cool slightly.

2. Position a rack in the center of the oven and preheat it to 400 degrees F. Peel the potatoes and force them through a potato ricer into a large bowl. Mix in the butter, sugar, and spices.

3. Butter a baking sheet well. Drop the potato puree from a spoon in 1-1/2-inch rounds onto the sheet, about 1/2 inch apart. Bake the puffs until light brown, about 25 minutes, transfer them with a spatula to a warm serving plate, and serve at once. Makes about 24.

Fried Sweet Potatoes

In recent years, Southern restaurants have begun serving sweet potato fries and chips, believing that they were doing something clever and new. Actually, they go back into the eighteenth century. Sarah Rutledge knew that there was nothing new about them when she relayed the method in *The Carolina Housewife*, as did Annabella Hill in *Mrs. Hill's New Cook Book*. Both these ladies would have thought fried sweet potatoes old hat. So much for avant-garde.

Some of the old recipes called for parboiled potatoes. They are lighter, of course, because they are already partially cooked, and so spend less time in the fat. Naturally, you can fry left-over cooked sweet potatoes; it's a nice way to rejuvenate leftovers.

2 pounds sweet potatoes   Salt
Lard or peanut oil, for frying

1. Position a rack in the upper third of the oven and preheat it to 150–170 degrees F (the warm setting). Fit a wire cooling rack over a rimmed baking sheet and put it on the oven's top rack. Scrub the potatoes with a soft brush under cold running water and peel them. With a very sharp knife (or mandolin or food processor), cut the potatoes into rounds no thicker than 1/4 inch, or shave them into paper-thin slices with a vegetable peeler, mandolin, or food processor. Separate them on towels or absorbent paper and let them air dry for a few minutes.

2. Put enough lard or oil in a deep cast-iron pot (such as a Dutch oven) or deep fryer to come no more than halfway up the sides, never more, as the fat could boil over. Heat it over medium-high heat until very hot, but not smoking (around 375 degrees F).

3. Slip the potatoes a few at a time into the fat and fry, stirring frequently to prevent their sticking together and aid the crisping, until they are crisp and golden. They will not get as crisp as regular fried potatoes. Take them up with wire frying skimmer, drain thoroughly, and spread them on the wire rack in the oven to keep them hot while the next batch cooks. When all the potatoes are fried, sprinkle them with salt and serve immediately. Serves 6.

Grill-Broiled Sweet Potatoes

Broiling *under* a flame is a recent development, made possible by the advent of our gas and electric ranges. All early-nineteenth-century cooks broiled on a gridiron over the fragrant hardwood coals of the kitchen hearth, a method as old as time. The difference in flavor is extraordinary. If you can't get real hardwood coals and must be content with compressed briquettes, you can still come reasonably close to the original flavors by strewing the prepared charcoal with hardwood chips. When the chips flame up and burn out, they make fine, fragrant coals, but they won't last very long, so be prepared to work quickly.

Two variations are given at the end of the recipe: mushrooms (yes, mushrooms) and tomatoes were universally popular for grill broiling in old cookbooks, but you can also use this method for sliced summer squash, eggplant, and halved Vidalia Sweet onions.

If you are doing more than one vegetable at a time, take into account the different cooking times. Start with the vegetables that take longer to cook and add the quicker-cooking ones later so they will all be done at the same time.

4 medium sweet potatoes (about 2 pounds)   Salt and whole black pepper in a peppermill
About 4 tablespoons unsalted butter, melted,
   plus softened butter for serving

1. Prepare a grill with enough charcoal, preferably hardwood, to cover the bottom in a single layer, and light it. While the coals are burning down, scrub the potatoes with a soft brush under cold running water, pat dry, and slice crosswise in 1/2-inch-thick rounds.

2. When the coals are ready, spread them out and, if using briquettes, strew them with wood chips. The chips will burst into flame after a minute or so. Let them burn down to glowing coals. Lightly grease a gridiron and position it about 4 inches from the coals.

3. Brush the potatoes with melted butter, lay them on the grill buttered side down, and grill broil about 5 to 7 minutes, or until the bottoms are brown, turn, brush with more butter, and grill broil until they are uniformly brown and tender. Take them up onto a warm platter and serve at once, passing salt, pepper, and softened butter separately. Serves 4.

Grill-Broiled Mushrooms: Allow 8 to 12 large mushrooms such as portobellos, shiitake, or, if you're really in luck, *cèpes* or *porcini*. Wipe them clean with a dry cloth. Brush the caps with butter and lay them on the grill stems up. Broil about 3 minutes, or until they are hot and beginning to color, then brush with butter, turn, and broil until tender, about 2 minutes more.

Grill-Broiled Tomatoes: Allow 4 medium or 2 large, ripe tomatoes. Wash and cut them in half lengthwise. Brush the cut side with butter and lay them on the grill, cut side down. Broil about 2 minutes, or until they are beginning to brown. Brush with butter, turn, and broil until the skin crinkles, about 10 minutes more.

SALLET

At one time in the Carolinas and Georgia, you would have heard most leafy vegetables referred to as "sallet" (pronounce the t). This was not an affectation or mispronunciation, but a holdover from the early Elizabethan settlers. Sallet is the old English word for greens, obviously an early spelling of the modern word salad, which now means only greens that are served raw. The family of Southern sallets includes the leaves of the mustard plant, some of the cabbages (such as kale), the leaves of such root vegetables as beets and turnips, as well as spinach, dandelions, watercress, land cress, and a wild plant known locally as poke (or "polk") sallet.

Most often nowadays, these vegetables are cooked by stewing them in meat broth made with dry salt-cured pork such as a country ham hock. This is definitely an acquired taste, but one on which most Southerners thrive. Another traditional method still in common use is to either sauté the youngest, most tender leaves, or wilt them with Red-Eye Gravy (page 201), and then toss them with a little vinegar that has been spiked with hot peppers, what we in the South call Wilted Salad (page 278). Many sallet greens (except poke sallet, which must be cooked before it's eaten, and collards, of course) can also be included in raw salads.

Until the advent of freezers, most sallets appeared on Southern tables only in the summer, except for the hardier ones like turnips and collards, which are actually supposed to be more tender after they have been nipped by the first frost.

Stewed Winter Greens

Back in the 1980s, a trendy food magazine proclaimed Southern food "in" and devoted the better part of an issue to what they saw as the high points of Southern food. One of the dishes presented was stewed greens, erroneously referred to as "winter greens with potlikker." Not only do Southerners not call the dish by that name, they do not, except perhaps in tourist trap diners, spell liquor phonetically. However named or spelled, this broth is both delicious and nutritious. It isn't traditionally served as a soup in a separate course, as that same magazine suggested doing, but it is so good that you may be tempted to do so.

This is the method used for hefty winter greens such as collards, fall kale, and even cabbage. Stewed collards are traditional New Year's Day fare in many Southern households, particularly when mated with black-eyed peas or Hoppin' John (page 292). Though commonplace on tables in the country and in poorer households, many upper-class Southerners considered stewed greens unfit for formal dinner tables, and eating such humble fare on New Year's Day was supposed to bring good luck and prosperity. I suspect this dainty attitude about greens arose out of the days of post war (you know, *the* War) poverty, when absolutely everybody ate them because they had to.

1 country ham hock, or 1/2 pound lean salt pork

1 medium yellow onion, trimmed, split lengthwise, peeled, and sliced (optional)

2 pounds collards, kale, or cabbage leaves

Salt and whole black pepper in a peppermill

1. Put the ham hock or salt pork, optional onion, and 2 quarts water in a large kettle that will comfortably hold all the greens at once. Bring it slowly to a boil, carefully skimming the scum as it rises. Cover, reduce the heat as low as possible, and let it simmer for about half an hour.

2. While that simmers, wash the greens in several changes of water, rubbing off any soil that clings to them, and drain well. Cut out the coarse stems and slice the leaves across into ribbon-like strips about 3/4-inch wide.

3. Raise the heat under the broth to medium-high and bring it back to a boil. Drop in the greens by large handfuls, bring back to a boil, and reduce the heat to a bare simmer. Cover and cook until the greens are tender, about 15 minutes for young, tender greens such as kale, as much as an hour for mature collards or cabbage. Taste, adjust the salt, and add a few gridings of pepper. Simmer a few more minutes to allow the flavor to blend. Serves 4 to 6.

NOTES: *Stewed greens hold up well to being made ahead and may be made several days before and reheated. Pepper Vinegar (page 36) or cider vinegar, passed separately, and Crackling Bread (page 325) are the traditional accompaniments.*

Stewed Turnip Sallet

Turnip greens, the leafy tops of the turnip root, are supposed by popular belief to have been eaten only by really common people. The same historians who propagate this myth conversely insist that the authors of early Southern cookbooks were rich women who were out of touch with what common people were eating. If they would only look: Mary Randolph, Lettice Bryan, and Annabella Hill all included recipes for stewed turnip sallet in their books. These "rich" women did not seem to think these greens too coarse for *their* tables, and certainly could not be said to be out of touch with common kitchens.

Unlike more delicate greens, such as spinach, turnip sallet cannot be wilted in a small quantity of moisture and butter. All three ladies caution against this, indicating that there must be a great quantity of water or the greens will be tough, bitter, and lose their color. They are also better stewed with salt pork in the broth instead of butter. Mrs. Randolph claimed this as the Virginia way, but it seems to have been pretty much universal. Mrs. Bryan is the first to mention vinegar as table seasoning, which is nowadays always offered whenever any greens are served. Of the three, only Mrs. Hill suggested a garnish of sliced, boiled eggs; today, Southerners only do that with spinach, but she more or less said that it was indispensable.

1 country ham hock, or 1/2 pound lean salt pork	Salt and whole black pepper in a peppermill
2 pounds young turnip sallet	Pepper Vinegar (page 36) or cider or red wine
2 hard-cooked eggs, peeled and sliced (optional)	vinegar

1. Put the ham hock and 2 quarts water in a large heavy-bottomed pot. Bring it slowly to a boil over medium heat. Skim it well, reduce the heat to as low as possible, and simmer half an hour.

2. While the meat is simmering, wash the greens in several changes of water, until they are free of all dirt and sand, and drain well.

3. Raise the heat to medium-high and bring the broth back to a boil. Add the greens, cover, return to a boil, and remove the lid. Skim well, reduce the heat to medium-low, and cook, uncovered, until tender, about 15 minutes for young greens; older ones may take as long as 30.

4. Lift the greens out of their liquor with a slotted spoon, and put them in a warm bowl. (Many Southerners swear by the pot liquor as a restorative tonic, but it is not served with the greens.) You may chop the meat and garnish the greens with it or with sliced boiled eggs, as Mrs. Hill suggested. Serve at once, passing salt, pepper, and any or all of the vinegars separately. Serves 4 to 6.

SQUASH AND OTHER EDIBLE GOURDS

The squash family includes not only the familiar yellow crooknecks, patty-pans (cymlings), and zucchini, but also pumpkins and gourds. Actually, they are a part of a much larger botanical family that even encompasses melons and cucumbers. Though popularly believed to be—like corn—truly American in their origins, parallel forms of edible gourds have been known throughout Europe and Asia for thousands of years (there are even Biblical references to them). Native Americans were cultivating many varieties of squash when Europeans first landed on this continent, many of which, according to early accounts, closely paralleled European varieties. This branch of the plant world is thought to have originally come from Asia, but has been dispersed so widely, and for so long that botanists can really only speculate on this point. Our modern name "squash" is, at least, American, from a native dialect. However, Europeans were quick to recognize these vegetables for what they were—edible gourds, and were soon cooking them according to traditional European methods.

The earliest squashes mentioned in Southern cookbooks were cymlings (patty-pan squash) and pumpkins. Cymlings, with their flat, round bodies and scalloped edges, look a little like a flying saucer. Their flavor can vary depending on the variety, but it mostly is a cross between yellow crooknecks and acorn squash. Though nowadays their color can range from white to yellow to deep zucchini green, the most common variety in the early nineteenth century appears to have been white. Pumpkins were treated mostly as a vegetable, but might also be put to work in their more familiar role as a sweet pie filling. There were other types, loosely called "winter squashes," but they were seldom given by name. Probably, they included native varieties of acorn and butternut squash. Later cookbooks give recipes for cashaws (very large gourds) by name, and for yellow crooknecks (usually called summer squash). Zucchini, perhaps the most ubiquitous summer squash in American gardens and markets today, have not always been as common as they are now. When this book refers to summer squash, yellow crooknecks or young yellow or white cymlings are intended. Zucchini (except for the strain of yellow ones available in some areas) cannot be substituted unless the recipe specifically says so.

Creamed Squash

This is probably the oldest Southern recipe known for squash. It has been in continuous use since Mrs. Randolph set it down in *The Virginia House-wife*, appearing in virtually every ante-bellum Southern cookbook, and has survived into our century unchanged. So standard was it that Lettice Bryan even went so far in *The Kentucky Housewife* as to say that it was the *only* nice way to prepare summer squash. It's certain that there is none better.

In selecting squash for this recipe, choose young white cymlings or yellow crooknecks whose skin is still tender and easily pierced with your fingernail. Their color should be clear and light and the surface smooth. Yellow zucchini will also work, but not the green ones. Mature summer varieties and winter squash can be used, following the notes at the end of the recipe.

3 pounds summer squash (yellow crooknecks, cymlings, or yellow zucchini)
2 tablespoons unsalted butter

1/2 cup heavy cream (minimum 36% milk fat)
Salt and whole black pepper in a peppermill

1. Wash the squash thoroughly under cold, running water, gently but thoroughly rubbing off any soil. If there are any blemishes or brown spots, cut them off, but don't trim off the stem and blossom ends until after they are cooked.

2. Put enough water to completely cover the squash in a heavy-bottomed pot and bring it to a boil. Add the squash, let the water come back to a boil, and reduce the heat to medium. Simmer until tender, about 15 or 20 minutes. Drain and let them cool enough to handle.

3. Dry out the pan in which they cooked and add the butter. Trim off the stem and blossom ends of the squash, cut them in large chunks, and put them in the pan and mash them up roughly with a potato masher. Turn on the heat to medium and heat, stirring frequently, until they are bubbly. Mix in the cream, a healthy pinch of salt, and simmer, stirring often, until the squash are dry and creamy, about 4 minutes.

4. Taste and adjust the salt. Turn them out into a warm bowl, lightly sprinkle the top with a few grindings of black pepper, and serve at once. Serves 6.

NOTES: *This same recipe can also be used for winter squash or pumpkin. Peel them with a vegetable peeler, halve them, and remove the seeds. Cut them up into 2-inch-sized chunks and use very little water—only as much as it takes to keep them from sticking and scorching. Winter squash will take a little longer to cook, about 20 to 25 minutes. When they're tender, instead of draining them, turn up the heat and boil away any remaining liquid, stirring constantly. Proceed as directed from step 3.*

Squash Pudding

(Squash Casserole)

This old recipe is still a faithful standby at Southern family reunions and Church covered-dish suppers. It is as good at room temperature as it is hot, and holds well; therefore it can be made hours ahead without damage. As with fried chicken, most modern Southern cooks have their own version, incorporating herbs, cheese, and even ham. This recipe goes back at least to the 1870s, and may have antebellum antecedents, but none have survived in print. My grandmother's squash pudding varied from the oldest one I know, in *Housekeeping in Old Virginia*, only in detail, so it has been in continuous use for more than a century.

Choose yellow crooknecks, white or yellow cymlings, or yellow zucchini for this dish.

2 pounds small young summer squash	2 large eggs, well beaten
3 tablespoons unsalted butter (1 only if omitting crumb topping)	1/2 cup cream or milk
1/2 cup minced white or yellow onion	Salt and whole black pepper in a peppermill
1 cup soft breadcrumbs	1/2 cup dry breadcrumbs or fine cracker crumbs (optional)

1. Position a rack in the center of the oven and preheat it to 350 degrees F. Wash the squash under cold, running water, gently but thoroughly rubbing off any soil. If there are any blemishes or brown spots, cut them off, but don't trim off the stem and blossom ends until after they are cooked.

2. Put enough water to completely cover the squash in a large, heavy-bottomed pot and bring it to a boil over medium-high heat. Add the squash, let it come back to a boil, and reduce the heat to medium. Simmer until tender, about 15 to 20 minutes. Drain and let them cool enough to handle. Trim off the stem and blossom ends, cut them into large chunks, and put them in a large mixing bowl. Roughly crush the squash with a potato masher or large fork, but don't mash it into a puree—they should be fairly chunky.

3. Heat a tablespoon of butter and the onion in a small pan over medium heat. Sauté, stirring constantly, until the onion is transparent and soft, but not colored, about 5 minutes. Add the onion and soft crumbs to the squash and mix well.

4. Beat together the eggs and cream and mix them into the squash, with a healthy pinch of salt and a few good grindings of pepper. Lightly butter a 2-quart casserole and pour in the squash.

5. If you're using the crumb topping, wipe out the pan in which the onion cooked and melt the remaining butter in it over low heat. Add the dry crumbs and stir until the butter is evenly absorbed. Sprinkle them over the casserole and bake in the center of the oven until the top is golden brown and the pudding is set and firm in the center, about 30 minutes. Serve hot or at room temperature. Serves 4 to 6.

Variation: If you want to try the more modern version with herbs and cheese, mix in a tablespoon each of chopped fresh sage and thyme (or a teaspoon each if dried) and half a cup of grated sharp cheddar, Parmigiano-Reggiano, or Cheshire cheese when you mix in the seasonings in step 3.

MaMa's Stuffed Summer Squash

My grandfather would keep the yellow crookneck squash in the garden cut before they got very big, but every now and then, a few of them would escape his vigilant eye. Whenever that happened, this was invariably how my grandmother would cook them. The ingredients are the same as for squash pudding, but here the squash becomes its own casing. During the baking, the natural sugars in the outer flesh become concentrated, giving them an extra boost of flavor.

Though the squash for this recipe are larger than I use for other summer squash recipes, they should still be quite young and tender, with the seeds, as Mrs. Bryan put it, hardly more than blisters. Select yellow crooknecks that are clear, unblemished yellow whose bodies are about 2-1/2 inches in diameter. You can also use cymlings (patty-pan squash), which should be creamy white or delicate yellow, and no more than 4 inches in diameter, or small young zucchini.

4 yellow crookneck squash (preferred), or cymlings or zucchini (either yellow or green)	2 large eggs, well beaten
	Cream or milk
1/2 cup minced green onion	Salt and whole black pepper in a peppermill
3 tablespoons unsalted butter	1/2 tablespoon each chopped fresh sage and
3/4 cup soft breadcrumbs	thyme, or 1/2 teaspoon if dried (optional)

1. Position a rack in the center of the oven and preheat it to 350 degrees F. Wash the squash under cold, running water, gently rubbing off any soil. Don't trim off the stem and blossom ends.

2. Put enough water to cover the squash in a large pot and bring it to a boil over medium-high heat. Add the squash, let it come back to a boil, and reduce the heat to medium. Simmer until the squash are tender, about 15 or 20 minutes. Drain and let them cool enough to handle.

3. Lay the squash on a cutting board so that they lie flat without rolling. Cut off 1/4 inch of the side that is facing up. Using a melon baller or spoon, carefully scoop out the center pulp, leaving about 1/4 inch of the outer flesh intact, taking care not to puncture the shell. Lightly grease a rimmed baking sheet or 9 x 13-inch casserole and arrange the hollowed out squash on it, not touching, open side up. Roughly chop the pulp and top slices and put them in a mixing bowl.

4. Heat the onion and 1 tablespoon of the butter in a shallow pan over medium heat. Sauté, stirring constantly, until the onion is transparent and soft, but not colored, about 2 to 4 minutes. Add the onion and crumbs to the bowl. Mix in the egg and moisten with a little cream or milk, if needed; the filling should be moist but not soggy. Add a healthy pinch of salt, a few grindings of pepper, the optional herbs, and mix well.

5. Spoon the filling into the squash shells, carefully packing to prevent air pockets, and mound it on the top. Dot with the remaining butter and bake in the center of the oven until the filling is set and the tops are lightly browned. Serve hot, warm, or at room temperature. Serves 4.

Fried Summer Squash

Any young summer squash—yellow crooknecks, zucchini, or cymlings—can be fried in this way when they are picked while still very young and tender. Mrs. Hill directed that squash prepared this way be parboiled, but that step isn't necessary or even desirable when the squash are truly young, fresh and sliced thin.

You may use any breading given below and still be authentic; there are old recipes using all of them. But the cornmeal coating is the one that tastes most peculiarly Southern and satisfies me the most—probably because it's the way my mother and grandmothers did it.

1-1/2 pounds young, tender summer squash (any variety)

2 large eggs, well beaten, in a wide, shallow bowl

1 cup cornmeal, dry breadcrumbs, or fine cracker crumbs, spread on a dinner plate

Lard, or vegetable oil, for frying

Salt and whole black pepper in a peppermill

1. Position a rack in the upper third of the oven and preheat it to 150–170 degrees F (the warm setting). Fit a wire rack over a rimmed baking sheet and put it in the oven. Fold a large cotton or linen napkin to cover a serving platter.

2. Carefully wash and dry the squash and cut them into slices a little less than 1/4 inch thick—crosswise, in rings, if the squash are long and thin, or lengthwise if they are small crooknecks or zucchini.

3. Have the eggs and crumbs or meal close at hand. Put enough lard (or oil) in a wide, cast-iron skillet to come up the sides by at least 1/4 inch. Heat over medium-high heat until it is hot, but not smoking. Dip the squash one slice at a time in the egg, roll them in the breading, gently shake off the excess and slip them into the hot fat until the pan is full, but not crowded.

4. Fry until the bottoms are golden brown, about 3 minutes, turn and fry until they are uniformly brown. Take them up with a frying skimmer or tongs, drain well, and put them on the wire rack in the oven. Add more squash to the pan as soon as there is space until all of it is fried. Season lightly with salt and a few good grindings of pepper, transfer the squash to the napkin-lined platter in a single layer (do not crowd or stack them) and serve hot. Serves 4.

NOTE: *With all fried vegetables, I find it best to drain them, as directed here, on a wire rack set on a baking sheet rather than on the usual butcher paper or paper towels. Squash are full of moisture that seems naturally drawn to absorbent paper, resulting in a bottom crust that is limp and soggy. If you like, you can blot the squash on absorbent paper to absorb some of the fat, but then get it quickly off the paper and onto the rack.*

Stuffed Winter Squash Kentucky Housewife

If your idea of a "gourmet" recipe is a list of ingredients a foot long requiring two sous chefs, a lay-reader, and a Fort Knox-sized bank account, you might as well skip this one. There are only two ingredients, both embarrassingly inexpensive, and the basic preparation is so completely artless that you would never believe how good it is anyway. But, if you're looking for a quick, hearty and delicious winter supper that can be thrown together in minutes, go easy on the family budget, and taste like a holiday feast—this is it.

This is another of Lettice Bryan's incomparable recipes from *The Kentucky Housewife*. I have done absolutely nothing to it but add a conventional temperature for her "moderate" oven.

2 acorn or other small round winter squash, each about 5 inches in diameter	1 pound Southern Country, or Bulk Sausage (page 195), or any bulk breakfast sausage

1. Position a rack in the center of the oven and preheat it to 350 degrees F. Lightly grease a baking dish large enough to hold the squash whole. Scrub the squash, pat dry, and split them in half lengthwise, using the ribbed lobes as guides. Scoop out and discard the seeds and membranes.

2. Pack the cavities of each half with sausage meat, leveling off the meat with the edges of the squash. Press the halves back together so that they are held together by the sausage and place them in the baking dish with the seams horizontal.

3. Bake in the center of the oven until the squash are tender and yield easily when pressed with your finger, about 1 to 1-1/2 hours. The sausage will be cooked through after that time, but a meat thermometer inserted into the center should register 180 degrees F. Serves 4 as a main course.

Variation: I often do a variation of this that is only slightly more complicated and wonderfully good. It also has less fat, if you worry about those things. Use half the amount of sausage and brown it over medium heat with 1/2 cup of chopped onion. Take it off the heat and add 1/2 pound lean ground beef, 1/2 cup of dry breadcrumbs, and a beaten egg. Mound the stuffing into the squash halves, sprinkle over them about 1/2 cup of dry breadcrumbs, and proceed as above, baking the squash open-face instead of pressing the halves together, for about 1 hour. Be careful not to overcook this one, or the squash and filling will be dry.

TOMATOES

A lot of misconceptions about the history of tomatoes are regularly propagated in American news-papers, magazines and cookbooks. Each summer, someone reports with authority that tomatoes were not eaten in this country until the middle of the nineteenth century, and even then were supposed to have been thought poisonous if eaten raw. I once watched a "history" on television that made the hilarious assertion (with the utmost seriousness and great authority) that Americans didn't eat tomatoes until well into the nineteenth century, at first as a medicinal, no less, and ketchup, they explained, was first made as a tonic. *Where* the heck do they get this stuff?

None of these stories has a shred of foundation. Thomas Jefferson grew tomatoes at Monticello as early as the 1780s, and they appear in American editions of English cookery books as early as the mid-1700s. Perhaps the most telling record is that of Harriott Pinckney Horry, a Charleston matron who recorded in her household notebook a recipe "To Keep Tomatoos for Winter use," possibly as early as 1770. If, by that time, Carolina housekeepers were concerned about storing them for winter use, we must accept that tomatoes had been eaten for at least a generation. According to Karen Hess, the first known printed American recipe appears in the 1790s, a virtual lift of an older English one. By 1824, they figured prominently in the cookbook of Jefferson's cousin, our Mary Randolph. As for eating them raw, Mrs. Randolph gave us a recipe for classic gazpacho, and little more than twenty years later Sarah Rutledge, in *The Carolina Housewife*, asserted with authority that tomatoes could safely be eaten raw.

Tomatoes are native to Central America, where they have been cultivated for food since Pre-Colombian times—at least a thousand years. They were introduced to Europe early in the sixteenth century by the Spanish, supposedly not as an edible fruit, but as a curiosity for orna-mental gardens. This may be true, since tomatoes actually are supposed to have been thought poisonous; but, poisonous or not, their journey from the front garden to the kitchen was a quick one. As early as 1597, English travelers reported Spaniards eating them with relish. Their pop-ularity may have been speeded by a belief that, like many plants from the New World, they had great aphrodisiacal powers. (The French name *pommes d'amour*, or love apples, is a lingering reminder of this reputation.) By the beginning of the seventeenth century, tomatoes appeared regularly in the cookery of Spain, Italy, and Southern France. The English, who continued to believe they were poisonous despite traveler's reports to the contrary, were slower to accept them. They don't appear in English cookery books until the end of the century.

The exact time of their introduction into North America is somewhat fuzzy. Thomas Jefferson credited one of his neighbors, a Dutch doctor, but this hardly seems likely given Mrs. Horry's record from South Carolina. Spanish colonials, who remained in close proximity to the South in Mexico, Texas, Cuba, Florida, and (for half a century) Creole Louisiana, traded with early America. Their influence, while undocumented, can't be completely discounted. There is a folk legend that African slaves brought tomatoes to North America by way of the Caribbean. Many historians now accept that the Portuguese had long since introduced tomatoes to the West Coast of Africa; so that legend is entirely possible. Folk legends do have a peculiar way of telling the truth. But of truth, we may never really know. Meanwhile, the spell of the love apple endures. So loved and deeply ingrained has it become in western cooking, it is difficult to imagine American, Spanish, Italian, and Provençal cookery without it.

Buying and keeping tomatoes: I used to think that those awful tomatoes in supermarkets that look and taste like boiled Styrofoam were picked too green to ripen properly. But now I know better: harvesting has little to do with their unfortunate texture and lack of flavor. They are a special hybrid developed specifically for their long shelf life and resistance to bruising. The flavor has literally been bred right out of them. They are hopeless; the only time they are at all edible is when they are fried while still green. If you are not fortunate enough to be able to grow your tomatoes, buy carefully, only when they're in season, and avoid fruit that doesn't have a distinct tomato fragrance, or any with an off, washed-out color. Pinpoint white speckles on the skin are a dead giveaway that the tomatoes are shelf hybrids that have been ripened by gas. Look for deep red color, a rich fragrance, and remember that bigger is not necessarily better.

As with any other fruit, tomatoes do benefit from being allowed to mature before they are picked. That's why vendors make a point of the label "vine ripened." However, if they are still a little green, put them stem up on a bright spot that gets plenty of indirect sunlight (but none that is direct) until the color deepens to a deep, full red, and they become fragrant.

When you find a reliable vendor with good stock, buy and freeze what you can for off-season use. Freezing will irreparably damage their texture but, unlike canning, frozen tomatoes require no added salt or acid, and so maintain much of their summer-fresh sweetness. It requires no special art: Just wash and dry them, seal them in airtight plastic bags, and pop them in the freezer. As long as you keep them well-sealed, they'll last all winter. Once they are thawed, the peeling slips right off, so no blanching, peeling, or precooking is needed. They are then ready to use in any way you would use fresh tomatoes, except for salad. My great-grandmother, who knocked herself out canning every year, would have loved it.

Several of the recipes following can be made off-season with good-quality canned Italian San Marzano tomatoes or with several good varieties of American-packed organically grown tomatoes. Check with your local natural food store for the brand available to your area. Occasionally, pretty good plum tomatoes (marketed as "Roma") are available off-season, too, and can be substituted in any of the recipes.

To peel tomatoes for cooking by blanching: Bring a large teakettle of water to a boil. Put the tomatoes in a large, heatproof bowl and pour the boiling water slowly over them until they're covered. Let them stand for 1 minute, drain, and rinse the tomatoes with cool water. Cut an X in the base, core them, and then slip off the peelings.

To peel tomatoes for eating raw: Use a vegetable peeler, preferably one with a serrated blade designed for soft-skinned fruit.

Stewed Tomatoes

"The art of cooking tomatoes lies mostly in cooking them enough."

—Sarah Rutledge, *The Carolina Housewife,* 1847

From its first appearance in the second edition of *The Virginia House-wife* (1825) to John Egerton's *Southern Food* in 1987, this recipe has been a standard in virtually every Southern cookbook. Seasonings varied, from the simple salt and pepper in Mrs. Randolph's recipe, to the onion, thyme, parsley, and bay leaf in the *Picayune's Creole Cookbook,* but the basic method remained untouched. Slow cooking brings out their natural sweetness, and properly done, the tomatoes need no further embellishment. By 1860, sugar began to appear and was applied in ever increasing doses as canned tomatoes supplanted fresh ones in the recipes, but it has no reason to be here if the tomatoes are fresh and of good quality.

5 or 6 medium, ripe tomatoes

1 medium onion, trimmed, split, peeled, and minced (optional)

2 tablespoons unsalted butter

Salt and whole black pepper in a peppermill

NO SUGAR— FORGET IT!

1. Scald and peel the tomatoes as directed above. Over a wire sieve set in a bowl to catch the juices, cut the tomatoes into thick slices or quarters and scoop out the seeds. Put the tomatoes into the bowl with their juices.

2. If you're not using onion, skip to step 3. Put the onion and butter in a 3-quart stewing pan over medium heat and simmer until it is softened, but not colored, about 5 minutes.

3. Add the tomatoes and their juices, a healthy pinch of salt, a liberal grinding of pepper, and bring the mixture to a boil. Reduce the heat to a bare simmer, loosely cover, and simmer until the tomatoes are meltingly tender, about 1 hour.

4. Uncover and raise the heat briefly to medium-high. Let it boil until the juices are thickened, stirring often to keep them from scorching. Serve either hot or at room temperature. Serves 4.

NOTES: *You could use good-quality Italian canned tomatoes for this dish if you cannot get fresh ones (in fact, they are better than the boiled Styrofoam supermarket variety), but it will only have a ghost of the fine flavor that good, ripe fruit will bring. Since onions were not universal, I give them as an option, but if you are using canned tomatoes, I would definitely include them.*

Stewed Tomatoes à la Creole: Include the onions and add a Bouquet Garni (page 34) of fresh thyme, parsley, and bay leaf, in step 3. Remove and discard it before serving, and thicken the juices with a small handful of soft breadcrumbs.

Baked (Scalloped) Tomatoes

This is another universal way of doing tomatoes, appearing with only minor variations in virtually every cookbook from the second edition of *The Virginia House-wife* (1825) forward. Except for the occasional recipe using canned tomatoes with their invariable seasoning of sugar, it has changed little. Those later recipes notwithstanding, this dish should only be made with fresh tomatoes; canned ones are already cooked and, no matter how they are seasoned, have an acid harshness that can't be counteracted or masked. Naturally, the breadcrumbs should be from good bread, preferably a homemade loaf.

4 large, ripe tomatoes

Salt and whole black pepper in a peppermill

1 blade mace, crushed to a powder or pinch powdered mace, or whole nutmeg in a grater (optional)

4 tablespoons unsalted butter

1 generous cup soft breadcrumbs

1. Position a rack in the center of the oven and preheat it to 350 degrees F. Scald and peel the tomatoes as directed on page 262. Cut them crosswise in 1/4-inch-thick slices.

2. Lightly butter a 2-quart ceramic or glass baking dish. Cover the bottom with tomato slices, overlapping them slightly. Sprinkle with a pinch of salt, a liberal grinding of pepper, and, if you like, a bit of mace or nutmeg. Dot with bits of butter and cover with crumbs. Continue layering the tomatoes, butter, seasonings and crumbs until the tomatoes are used up, finishing with a liberal covering of crumbs on top. Dot the top with the remaining butter.

3. Bake in the center of the oven and until the tomatoes are cooked through and the crumb top is well browned, about 45 minutes to 1 hour. Serves 4.

Baked Whole Tomatoes

This exquisitely simple recipe comes from *The Texas Cookbook* (1883), compiled by the Ladies' Aid Society of the First Presbyterian Church of Houston, Texas—believed to have been the first cookbook printed in Texas. It's the first, and only, time that I know of that this recipe appears in print; however, it has been used in my family for at least four generations. There is no added fat, seasoning, or liquid; nothing, in fact, but tomatoes and a hot oven left alone to interact and do their magic. The result is a wonderfully concentrated tomato flavor, enhanced by the slight caramelizing of the fruit's natural sugars.

Whenever I am asked to demonstrate how Southern cooking can be simple and sublime all at once, this is one of the recipes I always mention. There are many other, more complex and educated ways of cooking tomatoes, but none that are any better.

4 large, ripe tomatoes (I'm not kidding;
    that's all)

1. Position a rack in the upper third of the oven and preheat it to 375 degrees F. Gently wash the tomatoes and pat dry. Put them stem side up in a glass or ceramic baking dish that will hold them all without crowding.

2. Bake in the upper third of the oven until the skins wrinkle, about half an hour. Serve hot. Serves 4.

NOTES: *You may pass salt, black pepper, and butter at the table for those who think they'll need it, but try to persuade everyone to at least try them plain.*

Annabella Hill's Stuffed Tomatoes

That modern dieter's lunch of raw tomato stuffed with cottage cheese always seemed a little weird for those of us who were raised on baked tomatoes stuffed with savory fillings. Vegetable casings in general go back a long way, and stuffed tomatoes turn up in nineteenth-century books from both sides of the Atlantic. The oldest Southern recipe I found was this one, in *Mrs. Hill's New Cook Book* (1867). Mrs. Hill's stuffed tomatoes were simmered in a pan lined with fresh meat (probably pork or ham), but as wood and, later, gas ranges became commonplace, the tomatoes were invariably baked in the oven.

If you have only had one of those bland commercial tomatoes stuffed with frozen spinach soufflé, you probably think that stuffed tomatoes are an awful mistake. That's because what you've *had* was an awful mistake, and not because there's anything the matter with the idea. Give them a try and see for yourself.

3 or 4 thin slices lean country ham or prosciutto

4 large, ripe tomatoes

2 cups minced cooked country ham or prosciutto, or any leftover meat

1 medium white onion, trimmed, split lengthwise, peeled, and minced

1 tablespoon minced parsley

Salt and ground cayenne pepper

1 large egg

1/2 cup dry bread or fine cracker crumbs

1. Position a rack in the center of the oven and preheat it to 375 degrees F. Lightly butter a casserole that will hold the tomatoes in one layer without crowding them. Line it with the sliced ham. Wash the tomatoes and cut them in half crosswise. Scoop out the seeds and set them, cut side up, on top of the ham.

2. Mix together the minced ham or meat, onion, and parsley, and season it with salt and cayenne to taste, going easy on the salt or even omitting it if you are using ham (it's usually salty enough by itself). Stuff the filling into the seed pockets of the tomatoes and mound it evenly on top of each.

3. Wipe out the bowl and break the egg into it. Beat it until smooth and brush it lightly over the tomatoes. Melt the butter in a small sauté pan over low heat and mix in the crumbs until the butter is evenly absorbed. Sprinkle the buttered crumbs evenly over the tomatoes. Carefully add just enough water around them to come halfway up their sides.

4. Bake until the tomatoes are tender and the crumbs are browned, about half an hour. Let them sit for a few minutes to allow the flush of intense heat to dissipate, then lift them out of the casserole with a slotted spatula and transfer to a warm platter. Serve warm. Serves 8.

Fried Tomatoes

Shortly after the motion picture version of Fanny Flagg's novel *Fried Green Tomatoes at the Whistlestop Café* came out, a so-called Southern social historian asserted with great authority that fried green tomatoes were merely apocryphal, that nobody really ate them, at least, not anymore. Poor thing; she's never been to my house, or to any of the farmhouses in the Carolina and Georgia piedmont where I grew up, or she would've known better. Today, they are commonplace on fancy restaurant menus throughout the region, but I wouldn't try them, as one restaurant did, as a carrier for beluga caviar. What a silly idea.

The love of fried food remains alive and strong here the South, in spite of the fat panic, and the path to many a Southerners' heart is still through a cast-iron frying pan. My long-standing suspicion that Southerners would eat fried shoe leather and love it was confirmed by the recent craze for fried pork rinds. It should be no surprise, then, that this dish is still a popular way of dealing with the surplus bounty of the summer tomato patch.

There are several basic recipes for fried tomatoes combined here. The one immortalized by Fanny Flagg is included at the end, with its traditional cornmeal breading and bacon fat for the frying, though it may not be as old or traditional as we think. Without exception, all the old books call for firm, ripe fruit, and most of them are coated with bread crumbs. Not one of them mentions cornmeal. Since the method is always the same, I've given alternate ingredients so you can try several traditional combinations without wading through the same directions repeated ad nauseam. If you are frying ripe tomatoes, use butter and cracker crumbs.

4 to 6 ripe or green tomatoes	2 large eggs, lightly beaten in a wide, shallow bowl
Salt and whole black pepper in a peppermill	
1 cup fine cracker or dry breadcrumbs, or corn meal, spread on a dinner plate	About 1 cup clarified butter, lard, bacon drippings, or vegetable oil

1. Position a rack in the upper third of the oven and preheat it to 150–170 degrees F (the warm setting). Fit a wire rack over a rimmed baking sheet and put it in the oven. Stem, core and slice the tomatoes crosswise about 3/8 inch thick. Don't peel them, even if using ripe ones.

2. If the tomatoes are ripe, gently remove the seeds without squeezing and drain briefly in a colander. If they are green, lightly salt them and let them stand in a colander for 20 to 30 minutes, then wipe them dry. Season lightly with salt and a few grindings of pepper.

3. Have the breading and eggs ready by the stove. Heat the fat in a well-seasoned iron or non-stick skillet over medium heat. When hot, but not smoking (or, if butter, browning), dip the tomatoes one at a time in the beaten egg, let the excess flow back into the bowl, and

roll quickly in the breading. Gently shake off the excess, and slip them into the pan until it is full. Fry until they are golden on the bottom, about 3 minutes, turn, and fry until both sides are golden.

4. Blot briefly on absorbent paper, then transfer them to a wire rack and keep them warm in the oven while you are cooking the next batch. Repeat until all the tomatoes are cooked. Serve piping hot. Serves about 6.

Classic Fried Green Tomatoes: This is the one that yes, by golly, Southerners still eat. For this version, the tomatoes must be very green without even a blush of pink, or they won't have their trademark crisp tartness. Follow the recipe, breading the tomatoes with fine corn meal, and fry them in a cup of bacon drippings, or mix 1/4 to 1/2 cup of drippings with vegetable oil, but yes, you must use *some* bacon drippings.

TURNIPS

People outside the South make great sport of the Southern relish for green turnip tops, which we call sallet (page 251). An otherwise charming and sensible New York friend of mine is fond of recounting that Southerners throw out the only part of the turnip that is edible and eat "the part that everybody else in the world throws away." This is far from being true, however. To the contrary, all parts of the turnip have always enjoyed a regular place on Southern tables. This recipe has been a favorite for two centuries.

Creamed Turnips

The tart, peppery flavor of raw turnips is blunted by the heat of cooking, but it does not altogether disappear. Here, it is further softened by an enrichment of butter and cream. The resulting dish is velvety and rich, but still has enough of the sharpness to keep it lively. Turnips have an affinity for almost any game meat and roasted poultry, and in England, where this dish originated, it once frequently accompanied them. In my family, it is still traditional with the Thanksgiving turkey.

2 pounds medium-sized fresh turnips, as much of the same size as is possible
2 tablespoons unsalted butter

1/2 cup heavy cream
Salt and whole black pepper in a peppermill

1. Scrub the turnips with a brush under cold running water and trim off the taproot and most of the green top, but leave some of it attached. Put them in a pot that will hold them comfortably and add enough water to cover them by an inch. Lift out the turnips.

2. Bring the water to a brisk boil over medium-high heat and add the turnips. Cover until it starts boiling again and skew the lid slightly. Lower the heat to medium and cook until the turnips are very tender, about 20 to 30 minutes. Drain and let them cool enough to handle.

3. Lightly skin the turnips with a vegetable peeler, trim off the remaining green tops, and slice them about 1/2 inch thick. Wipe out the pot in which the turnips cooked and return them to it. Add the butter and turn on the heat to low. Mash the turnips with a potato masher until they are roughly puréed and the butter is incorporated. Gradually add the cream a little at a time, mashing and mixing until it is incorporated and the turnips are velvety, but still slightly lumpy—having a few little lumps is part of the charm. Season with a pinch or so of salt and mix it in.

4. Pour into a serving bowl, dust with a few grindings of black pepper, and serve at once. Serves 6.

Salads

TO DRESS SALAD

"To have this delicate dish in perfection, the lettuce, pepper grass, chervil, cress, &c. should be gathered early in the morning, nicely picked, washed, and laid in cold water, which will be improved by adding ice; just before dinner is ready to be served, drain the water from your salad, cut it into a bowl, giving the proper proportion of each plant; prepare the following mixture to pour over it: boil two fresh eggs ten minutes, put them in water to cool, then take the yelks [sic] in a soup plate, pour on them a table spoonful of cold water, rub them with a wooden spoon until they are perfectly dissolved, then add two table spoonsful of oil; when well mixed, put in a teaspoonful of salt, one of powdered sugar, and one of made mustard; when all these are united and quite smooth, stir in two table spoonsful of common, and two of tarragon vinegar; put it over the salad and garnish the top with the whites of the eggs cut into rings, and lay around the edges of the bowl young scallions, they being the most delicate of the onion tribe."

—Mary Randolph, *The Virginia House-wife,* 1824

VEGETABLE AND GARDEN SALADS

CONTRARY TO THE POPULAR BELIEF that early Americans paid little attention to cooked vegetables and even less to raw ones, period cookbooks suggest that raw green salads were both known and relished all along the eastern seaboard. In the South, Mary Randolph, (an aptly named) Lettice Bryan, and Annabella Hill all provided recipes for salads of great delicacy and balance, suggesting that they were a regular part of the antebellum Southern diet. As for period recipes, I can do no better than Mrs. Randolph, and begin with her recipe verbatim.

Notes on Mrs. Randolph's Ingredients

Salad oil throughout this period was olive oil. Surprising quantities of it were imported into Richmond, Savannah, and Charleston during the eighteenth and nineteenth centuries, and newspapers of the day advertised "the best Florence Oil" for sale. Tuscan oil was then the most prized, and "Florence oil" was used generically, as we use some brand names today, to mean the best quality oil available. It didn't necessarily mean the oil was actually Tuscan, though the inference was probably not lost on the vendors.

"Powdered" sugar meant pulverized loaf sugar. The closest equivalent in modern terms would be superfine granulated, not modern powdered, or confectioners' sugar, which is actually too fine and contains cornstarch as an anti-caking agent.

We think that herb-flavored vinegars were only discovered in the foodie movement of the last century, but Mrs. Randolph is casual in her mention of tarragon vinegar.

Notice the wide variety of greens, some of which are rarely seen in modern salad bowls. Try to find chervil in the average market. The exotic-sounding peppergrass is *lepidium sativum* (sometimes called "creasies" in the South), or common garden cress—at least, it was common at one time; today it is rare. Related to watercress, its flavor is more peppery, hence the name. It was widely used in salads, and was also cooked as a vegetable, like spinach. The late Edna Lewis recalled that her mother fed them cooked land cress as a medicinal whenever they were ailing. For those who think that nineteenth-century Americans did not eat onions, let alone raw ones, note the scallions that garnish the edges of the bowl.

Jerusalem Artichoke Salad

When my mother was a little girl, about five, she would arm herself with a kitchen spoon and go out front to the flowerbed where my great-grandmother grew ginger lilies and Jerusalem artichokes. She would dig up an artichoke, brush off the dirt, and eat it on the spot—raw. Everyone thought she was weird. The practice of eating them dressed with oil and vinegar, as salad, had all but disappeared by then, so Mamma had no way of knowing that her childish relish for the sweet, delicate taste and crunchy texture of raw Jerusalem artichokes hearkened back hundreds of years.

Annabella Hill (1867) provided the earliest of only a few recipes I found for Jerusalem artichoke salad in Southern books. Nevertheless, she wrote that the dish was a popular one, and considered particularly good. (The popularity did linger into the twentieth century; Mrs. Dull included them in a duck salad in her 1928 book, *Southern Cooking*.) But radishes were the only root vegetables Mrs. Hill mentions serving raw; for her salad, the artichokes are boiled first.

Mrs. Hill had a penchant for sweet-sour salad dressings, as did most later Southerners. Since her recipe didn't specify an exact dressing, I have taken the liberty of omitting the sugar I'm sure she used, as I find it obtrusive with Jerusalem artichokes. If this infidelity offends you, add 1/2 to 1 teaspoon of sugar to the dressing before tossing it with the artichokes. That should put you in Mrs. Hill's good graces.

2 pounds Basic Cooked Jerusalem Artichokes (page 208), omitting the butter

2 large hard-cooked egg yolks

1/2 teaspoon dry mustard

1/4 cup wine vinegar

2 tablespoons olive oil

Salt and whole black pepper in a peppermill

2 tablespoons chopped parsley

4 to 6 fresh lettuce leaves, washed and drained

1. Remember not to overcook the artichokes; they should still be quite firm. Let them cool enough to just handle and slice them into thin rounds. Peeling is not necessary, but you may peel them first if you like. Keep warm.

2. Put the egg yolks in the bottom of a salad bowl with the mustard and mash them smooth with a fork. Gradually beat in the vinegar, using a fork or whisk, until it forms a smooth paste. Beat in the oil, a few drops at a time, until it is incorporated and emulsified.

3. Add the warm artichokes to the bowl and toss until they are well coated. Season with salt and a few grindings of pepper, and add the parsley. Toss gently to mix. Taste and adjust the seasonings, and give it a final toss. Let stand until the artichokes cool completely, and serve at room temperature on a bed of fresh lettuce leaves. Serves 4.

NOTES: *Notice that the proportions here are two parts vinegar to one part oil—the opposite of a classic French vinaigrette. This probably developed because olive oil was dear and vinegar was mostly homemade (and therefore cheaper); possibly the homemade vinegar was not as strong. We don't really know, but at any rate, most Southern cooks developed a preference for tart dressings.*

Mamma Macie's Coleslaw

Macie Queen was one of the last of the old-style matriarchs of Grassy Pond, a largely Baptist farming community in Cherokee County, South Carolina, where I spent my early years. Both a formidable cook and natural-born humorist, Mamma Macie's kitchen was always full of laughter and good things to eat. We cut our teeth on her coleslaw and on her wry view of life. Just as no one was safe from her belief that eating was the closest we got to heaven without dying (which, of course, made feeding us her moral responsibility), none was spared her quick wit. Once, the local minister (my father), teasing her for choosing to sit and do her crochet-work while everyone else had gone to walk, asked her to remember what the "Good Book" said. Without dropping a stitch, a recently widowed Macie fixed him with a wry look and quipped, "Preacher, it says be good to the widows."

Macie's coleslaw is a delicately balanced trilogy of fresh cabbage, homemade mayonnaise, and black pepper. If you are accustomed to slaw thick with pickles and sugary dressing, the light, fresh taste of this one will be a revelation. The recipe is a very old one; while I have not been able to date it exactly, it precedes Macie, who was born around the turn of the century, by at least a generation.

1 small head of cabbage, about 4 to 5 inches in diameter

About 1 cup Homemade Mayonnaise (page 117), see notes

Salt and whole black pepper in a peppermill

1. Sit down at the kitchen table to make this slaw or you'll wear your shoulders out. Using a sharp knife on a large cutting board, cut the cabbage first into quarters and then into small chips, no longer than 1 inch and no wider than 1/4 inch. Macie did this without a board, sitting with the bowl in her lap. You can't use a machine, because there isn't one that will chip the cabbage to the right size. Now you know why you have to sit down.

2. Put the chipped cabbage in a large mixing bowl and stir in just enough mayonnaise to lightly but completely coat it. They should not cake together, so add the mayonnaise a little at a time until you have just the right consistency. Season to taste with salt and a few grindings of pepper and mix them in. Let it stand for a few minutes, then taste and adjust the seasonings. Transfer the slaw to a serving bowl, and garnish the top with a few liberal grindings of black pepper. Serves 6.

NOTES: *If you are not accustomed to working with homemade mayonnaise, a word of warning. Commercial mayonnaise has been pasteurized, and is much less likely to spoil than the homemade variety. Uneaten portions of this slaw must be refrigerated promptly, and, if you are making it ahead, it should be kept cold until served. If you are preparing this for persons who are fragile or who have immune-system deficiencies, do not use raw egg mayonnaise unless you can get pasteurized eggs, but use a commercial one instead (Macie used Duke's).*

Granny Fowler's Hot Potato Salad

Hot potato salads turn up from time to time in the old Southern cookbooks, and were considered by some writers superior to cold ones. Most have the simple elegance of this traditional family recipe. Granny, in this case, was my paternal grandmother. Her ability to stretch the cheapest ingredients into something delectable served her well during the Depression, when she managed to feed her large family on the income of a cotton mill loom-worker. The recipe is much older than Granny; it varies from mid-nineteenth century ones only in detail. Once you've had this salad, plain mashed potatoes will never be the same again.

2-1/2 pounds Basic Boiled Potatoes (page 241)
1/2 cup Homemade Mayonnaise (page 117)
Light cream (see step 2)
1/2 cup chopped scallions or other green onions, including the green tops

Salt and whole black pepper in a peppermill
Chopped fresh chives or parsley, for garnish (optional)

1. While they are still very hot, peel the potatoes and mash them up with a potato masher or press them through a ricer into a mixing bowl.

2. Quickly beat in the mayonnaise until the potatoes have the consistency of creamed potatoes, adding a little cream if they appear too dry. Stir in the green onions, season with salt and pepper, and mound them in a warm serving bowl.

3. You may sprinkle chopped chives or parsley over the top if you must, but Granny would have said you were pushy. Serves 4 to 6.

Green Bean Salad

My mother anticipated the craze for "baby" vegetables by at least thirty years. This is her version of an old, lovely salad of green beans that sometimes was called "pickled beans." They came to our table mounded on a rectangular, cut glass relish dish, neatly aligned like chord wood and garnished with finely minced onions—as lovely to look at as they were to eat.

The beans you want for this salad should be as young as possible, very thin and small—preferably no more than three inches long—such as true young French haricots verts.

1-1/2 pounds thin, immature green beans

3 tablespoons minced mild onion, preferably Vidalia Sweet

Salt and whole black pepper in a peppermill

About 2 tablespoons cider vinegar

1 teaspoon sugar (optional)

Extra virgin olive oil

1. Bring two quarts of water to a boil in a large pot over high heat. Meanwhile, trim the stems from the beans, but don't "tail" them. If they are properly young and tender they will not need it. Wash and drain them thoroughly. Have ready a basin of ice water.

2. Drop the beans into the boiling water, cover, and bring back to a boil. Remove the lid at once and parboil the beans for about 2 to 4 minutes, or until crisp-tender but still bright green. Older beans and true haricots verts may require a few minutes more. Drain and immediately immerse them in the ice water to arrest the cooking. Let them get cold and then drain them well.

3. Put the beans in a bowl and strew 2 tablespoons of the onion over them. Sprinkle over them a pinch or so of salt, a few grindings of pepper, and a couple of spoonfuls of vinegar. My mother often adds a little sugar for a sweet-sour flavor at this point. If you like, add a teaspoon or so of sugar, to taste. Toss well, taste, and correct the vinegar and seasonings—go easy; the flavor will intensify as they marinate. Cover and marinate for at least 1 hour. You may make the salad several hours ahead and refrigerate it, but take it out of the refrigerator for at least half an hour before serving.

4. When you are ready to serve the salad, drizzle it with a little olive oil—just enough to give the beans a nice gloss—and toss until they are evenly coated. Arrange the beans on a shallow serving dish, sprinkle the top with the remaining onion, and serve at once. Serves 4.

To Dress Raw Cucumbers

Aside from coleslaw, this is my father's favorite salad, and when I was growing up, seldom was anyone else in the family allowed to make it. Once the cucumber vines began bearing fruit, it was a standard fixture on our table at home. But it is much older than my family, dating back nearly two hundred years. It's a wonderful, cooling salad to have during the searing days of July and August, and a fine accompaniment for fish or fried meat at any time.

4 small, firm cucumbers, preferably the "pickling" variety

2 tablespoons minced mild onion, preferably Vidalia Sweet

Salt and whole black pepper in a peppermill

Extra virgin olive oil

2 to 3 tablespoons wine or cider vinegar

4 broad lettuce leaves (optional)

Chopped fresh chives or green onion tops (optional)

1. If you are lucky enough to get unwaxed cucumbers, there is no reason to peel them. Just scrub them lightly under cold, running water. If, however, the cucumbers are unnaturally glossy and greasy looking, they have been waxed and should be peeled. Using a vegetable peeler, pare them as lightly as possible, so that there is still a blush of pale green on the surface. Cut them crosswise into thin rounds and place them in a large bowl.

2. Add the minced onion and season liberally with salt and a few grindings of black pepper. Toss well.

3. Sprinkle on a little olive oil, just enough to give the cucumbers a nice gloss, and toss again until they are well coated. Taste them and see if more oil is needed, but go easy; they should not be greasy tasting.

4. Sprinkle on a generous 2 or 3 tablespoons of vinegar—how much will depend on the strength of your vinegar and individual taste. Toss well and taste the salad again, adjusting the vinegar and seasonings as needed. Toss once more, cover, and marinate until you are ready to serve the salad, but not for less than 1 hour. It can also be made ahead and refrigerated, but take it out at least half an hour before serving.

5. Just before serving, arrange the lettuce on a serving platter, toss the salad again to redistribute the dressing, and pour it over the lettuce. You may also omit the lettuce and serve the salad directly from the bowl. Either way, sprinkle the top generously with chives or green onions. Serves 4.

To Dress Raw Tomatoes

"Tomatoes may be eaten raw." —Sarah Rutledge, *The Carolina Housewife*, 1847

Food mythology maintains that early Americans didn't eat raw tomatoes because they believed them to be poisonous. One popularly circulated story features some American luminary such as Thomas Jefferson eating a raw tomato on the steps of the county courthouse to prove that it wasn't lethal. Yet, despite those legends, American recipes for dressing raw tomatoes go back at least to 1824, when Jefferson's cousin, Mrs. Randolph, included a classic raw tomato gazpacho in *The Virginia House-wife*. Virtually every antebellum Southern book that followed included a recipe for this salad.

Fresh tomatoes once figured so prominently on Southern tables throughout the summer months that the first frost was met with a certain relief that we were finally done with them. Raw tomatoes could and did appear at every meal, even breakfast. My mother, who can eat tomatoes at every meal for the entire summer, keeps alive an old country tradition by serving thick, cool slices for breakfast, a tradition predating her by at least a century. Lettice Bryan, in giving the recipe in *The Kentucky Housewife*, called this "a delicious breakfast dish."

2 large, or 4 small, ripe tomatoes

4 flat lettuce leaves, such as romaine or Bibb

Salt and whole black pepper in a peppermill

Extra virgin olive oil

Wine or cider vinegar

2 tablespoons minced mild onion (such as Vidalia Sweet) or scallions

1. Cut the tomatoes crosswise into slices about 1/4 inch thick. You may peel them if you like, (see notes). Put them in a colander and let most of the seed pulp and juice drain from them. Wash and drain the lettuce.

2. Just before serving, arrange the lettuce on a platter or individual salad plates, and lay the tomato slices over them. Season lightly with salt and pepper. Drizzle olive oil over the tomatoes in a thin, steady stream, about 2 tablespoons in all, and sprinkle with a few drops of vinegar. Go easy on this last, especially if the tomatoes are very acid; they won't need much.

3. Strew the onion or scallion over the top of the tomatoes and serve at once. Serves 4.

NOTES: *You may peel the tomatoes with a serrated vegetable peeler or peel each slice, if you like, as follows: slip the tip of a sharp paring knife just under the skin of each slice and slide it around to separate the peeling. I find this is easier than peeling the tomatoes whole.*

Though fresh basil was rarely used in the nineteenth century, few modern Southern cooks would omit it. Scatter it generously with 8 to 10 torn fresh basil leaves.

A Southern Wilted Salad

Most of the time, we expect lettuce to come to the table raw, but in many cuisines, these greens are sometimes cooked. In the South, it may be lightly cooked in what we call wilted salad. The greens were traditionally wilted in two ways—either by drizzling them with boiling hot red-eye gravy, or, as is done in this recipe, by tossing them briefly in a hot pan with rendered salt-cured pork drippings. When Annabella Hill recorded this recipe, it had long been in general use in Georgia, and remains popular here today.

This is a fine recipe to use for any leaf lettuce, and may also be used for watercress, young spinach, sorrel (if you can find it) or blanched poke sallet. Iceberg lettuce, which is not long on character or flavor, can actually become respectable when subjected to this treatment.

While the most authentic taste is lent by cider vinegar, I generally use wine vinegar, especially if I'm making it with olive oil (see the variation at the end of the recipe), and have been known to squeeze in a little lemon juice. My granny would have a stroke.

1 large head romaine or other leaf lettuce or salad greens (see headnotes)	Salt and whole black pepper in a peppermill
1/4 pound thick-sliced dry-salt-cured pork or bacon	Cider or wine vinegar

1. Wash and tear the lettuce as you would for raw salad. Set it aside to drain in a colander.

2. Rinse the salt pork well under cold, running water, and wipe dry. Put it in a large, heavy skillet (preferably cast-iron) that will comfortably hold the lettuce in one batch. Fry it over medium heat until it's browned and all its fat is rendered. Drain the pork on absorbent paper. Drain or spoon away all but 2 tablespoons of the fat.

3. Turn up the heat to medium-high and add the lettuce. Sauté, tossing constantly, until each leaf is lightly coated with fat and beginning to wilt. Don't let it get soggy and limp; there should still be a distinct crunch to the bite. Turn off the heat and transfer the lettuce to a serving bowl.

4. Taste and season it with salt (if needed), a liberal grinding of pepper, and a sprinkling of vinegar. The vinegar and other seasonings should be light, just enough to enliven, but not so much as to make the lettuce sour. Crumble some of the pork over the salad and serve at once. Serves 4.

Variation: For those who have problems with pork fat, this is delicious made with a good, fruity olive oil. Though not at all traditional, I sometimes do it that way in my own kitchen. Allow a little more oil, about 3 tablespoons, and omit step 2. To compensate for the salty depth that the drippings lend, and to enliven it, I add a few minced fresh herbs, such as marjoram, thyme, or sage, and sometimes throw in a handful of minced green onions.

SALADS OF POULTRY AND FISH

Theresa Brown's Chicken Salad

The oldest Southern chicken salads were a simple triad of chopped cold chicken, celery, and dressing. Sometimes, a little onion or pickle might be admitted, though this was rare. Miss Brown's recipe, from *Theresa C. Brown's Modern Domestic Cookery* (1871), with its olives, capers, and chopped egg, is perhaps a little unusual but by no means unique. The nasturtium blossoms are part of the original recipe; contrary to popular belief, edible floral garnishes have been around a long, long time, and were not invented in modern California.

1/2 teaspoon celery seeds and 1 teaspoon vinegar, or 1/4 cup minced celery (see step 1)

2 cups chopped cold boiled or roasted chicken

1/2 cup Homemade Mayonnaise (page 117), made with olive oil, mustard, and egg yolks

Whole black pepper in a peppermill

4 large hard-cooked eggs

1/2 cup whole brine-cured green or black olives (such as Greek or Italian), or both, mixed

2 tablespoons small brine-cured capers

Salt

4 white (inner) lettuce leaves

8 nasturtium blossoms or other edible flowers (optional)

1/4 cup chopped green onion or fresh chives

1. Put the celery seeds and vinegar in a mortar or bowl. Bruise them with a pestle or wooden spoon to release their oils, and let it steep 20 minutes. Strain the vinegar, discarding the seeds. (You may omit this and substitute 1/4 cup finely chopped celery, including a few minced leaves.)

2. Put the chicken and mayonnaise into a large mixing bowl and toss until well coated. Season with liberal grindings of black pepper and the strained vinegar (or add the chopped celery).

3. Slice the eggs into thin rounds, setting aside 12 rings of egg whites for garnish. Pit the olives and slice them into thin strips or rings. Add the eggs, olives, and capers to the salad and gently but thoroughly toss to mix. Taste for salt and adjust it accordingly.

4. Arrange the lettuce on individual serving plates, divide the salad among them, and garnish each serving with 2 flowers, if you have them, 3 rings of egg whites, and a sprinkling of green onion or chives. Or, cut the lettuce into fine chiffonade. Mound the salad into the center of a glass serving platter or bowl, edge it with the lettuce, and garnish with the flowers, egg white rings, and a sprinkling of green onion or chives. Serve 4.

St. John's Crab Salad

Along coastal Virginia, Carolina, and Georgia, where Atlantic blue crabs are plentiful and relatively inexpensive, crab salad has become a specialty. This recipe comes from an old collection from Saint John's Church, Savannah. It makes a spectacular first or main course for a summer lunch or dinner.

Part of the charm of this salad is the container in which it is served—the bright orange-red back shells of the crab—but you can make a respectable crab salad from commercially packed crabmeat, serving it instead in scallop shells or lettuce leaves. The same recipe was used with other kinds of fish, particularly salmon, and today is used for the shrimp salad that is served at the parish's annual bazaar. Onions are seldom mentioned in the old recipes, but they are a fine addition, so I included them here as optional.

Though not of the period, a garnish of finely julienned red radish and slivers of chive adds wonderful color and flavor to the salad.

1 dozen large blue crabs, or 1-1/2 pounds (3 cups) commercially packed crabmeat

About 1 cup minced celery hearts, see step 2, including some of the leafy tops

About 1 cup minced green onion (optional), see step 2

Salt and ground cayenne pepper

About 1 cup Mayonnaise (page 117), see step 3, made with olive oil and egg yolks, and omitting mustard

6 flat lettuce leaves, such as romaine

12 small sprigs parsley

1 lemon, cut into 6 wedges

1. Cook and pick the crab (see "To Cook and Pick Crabs," page 129), reserving 6 whole back shells. Clean the shells and dry them.

2. Measure the crabmeat into a glass or stainless steel bowl. For every cup of meat, add 1/3 cup each of minced celery hearts and optional onions. Season with a healthy pinch of salt and a pinch or so of cayenne to taste. Don't overdo the pepper; it should enliven, not inflame. Add the mayonnaise a little at a time until the crab is lightly, but thoroughly, coated.

3. Divide the salad among the reserved shells, mounding it in the centers. Arrange the lettuce on a platter, top with the shells in a pinwheel pattern, garnish with the parsley and lemon wedges, and serve at once. Serves 6.

NOTES: *Though the onion was not universal in all the old recipes, I prefer crab salad with it. Some old recipes use capers; if that appeals to you, allow about 3 tablespoons or more, to taste.*

Fish Salad: To make fish salad, substitute 3 generous cups of flaked cooked fish for the crab. Salmon and flounder are the most frequently mentioned, but you might also try grouper or even chunks of fresh tuna. For shrimp salad as they still make it at St. John's, substitute 1-1/4 pounds cooked shrimp, peeled and cut into small pieces.

Theresa Brown's Lobster Salad

Lobster salad has always been popular, appearing in nearly every Southern cookery book since *The Kentucky Housewife.* No wonder: nothing is as elegant or satisfying to eat in celebration of a clear summer day. Miss Brown's is an especially good one, tossed with celery, onion, and colorful bits of baked beet.

Old friend Jim King, who was subjected to the testing of many recipes in this book, used to say, whenever I hit on a particularly good one, "Well, it'll do 'til lobster salad comes along." This recipe was and is for him.

For the dressing:

2 large egg yolks

1 tablespoon heavy cream (minimum 36% milk fat)

1 teaspoon dry mustard

Salt and whole black pepper in a peppermill

4 tablespoons extra virgin olive oil

3 tablespoons wine vinegar

1 large (about 2 pounds), or 2 small (1 to 1-1/4 pounds) cooked lobsters

1/4 cup chopped celery

2 tablespoons minced mild onion, such as Vidalia Sweet

1 large baked beet (see notes, below)

1 small head Boston or other leaf lettuce

2 large hard-cooked eggs

1 tablespoon minced parsley (optional)

1 lemon, cut into wedges

1. To make the salad dressing, put the egg yolks in a small glass or stainless bowl and beat them until they are light. Beat in the cream, mustard, a pinch of salt, and a liberal grinding of pepper. Gradually add the olive oil in droplets, beating well between each addition until it is incorporated, then beat in the vinegar a spoonful at a time.

2. Take the lobster meat from the shell and cut it into small cubes. Toss it in a glass salad bowl with the celery and onion.

3. Peel the beet, slice it 1/4 inch thick, and cut each slice into decorative shapes such as crescents and stars or into cubes. Put them in a separate bowl. You may make the salad several hours ahead up to this point. Cover the dressing, lobster, and beets, and refrigerate.

4. When you're ready to serve the salad, wash and dry the lettuce. Reserve the nicer outer leaves for garnish and cut the inner white head into narrow strips. Toss the cut lettuce with the lobster.

5. Peel the eggs, cut them into thin rounds, and remove the yolks, setting them aside for another use. Arrange the lettuce leaves on individual plates or a shallow glass bowl. Pour the dressing over the salad and toss until it is evenly coated. Add the beets and lightly toss to mix them. Turn the salad out onto lettuce leaves, garnish with the egg white rings, parsley (if desired) and lemon wedges. Serve at once or the beets will bleed and turn the whole thing bright pink. Serves 4.

NOTES: *The salad is every bit as good without the beets, though not nearly as nice to look at. To bake beets (they are so much better than boiled ones), preheat the oven to 400 degrees F. Wash the beets and trim the root and top, leaving a little of both attached to keep the juices from bleeding. Dry and wrap them in foil, put them on a shallow baking dish, and bake until tender, about 1 hour. Loosen the foil and let them cool enough to handle. The peeling should slip off easily.*

How often inland cooks actually had lobsters is difficult to say. In later books, it is clear that the critter came from a can. Miss Brown and Mrs. Hill may have used so-called Florida lobsters, the large warm-water crayfish of the Caribbean and Gulf of Mexico, though what Mrs. Hill describes is a real, cold-water lobster and she clearly knew what to do with it. Real lobsters were once found off the coast of both Carolinas. They could be kept alive for several days, and therefore might easily have been shipped inland.

Shrimp Salad: Excellent compensation for the family whose food budget does not allow for lobster. Allow 1-1/2 to 2 pounds (headless weight) of medium shrimp, cooked, shelled, and deveined. Make the salad as directed for lobster salad, above, omitting the beets, which are never mentioned with shrimp in the old recipes, and substituting a ripe tomato, cored and cut into 1/4-inch thick slices, seeded, and drained in a colander before cutting into 1/4-inch dice.

Grits, Rice, and Noodles

"Many of the nations' palates, of course, are too coarsened to appreciate [grits'] delicate but full-flavored qualities. One can only pity them, but one doesn't feel obliged to put up with their lip."

—Lydel Sims

GRITS VERSUS HOMINY GRITS

DON'T ASK ME WHETHER GRITS IS SINGULAR OR PLURAL, and don't write to educate me: I don't care. But, once and for all, let me clarify what it/they is/are, since so many people don't seem to know. First of all, there are two kinds—hominy grits and whole corn grits. The former is made from hominy—dried corn kernels treated with lye, hulled, and dried a second time for storage—a preserving method that originated with Native Americans. The lye acts not only (or even primarily) as an agent for removing the hull; it actually changes the structure of the starch and adds to the grain's nutritive properties, making it more versatile and nutritious. Whole corn grits are, obviously, made from the whole dried kernels. The latter has acquired a certain snob appeal in the last twenty years—and it is delicious, but not necessarily superior. In fact, pellagra, a disease largely unknown among Native Americans for whom corn was a staple, became a serious health problem among some Colonials and in certain European countries, simply because the Europeans didn't know to make corn into hominy. When corn is milled, three grades result, the finest of which is corn flour — silky and about the texture of semolina flour. Next is fine corn meal, and then, the coarsest of all, "grist," which most historians believe was corrupted to "grits" (although, there is another explanation that grits is a corruption of a Medieval English word such as "grytt" or "groats"). Grits are not polenta: the grind is rougher and coarser, and polenta is milled from a hybrid yellow corn developed over the centuries in Italy and is very different from the corn used in our region. Moreover, polenta is never made from hominy.

If you live in any kind of civilized area, you'll find three kinds of hominy grits in the market. Mind, only one type is worth buying, but here is a little about all of them. "Instant grits" are precooked and dehydrated; all they need is boiling water. They've also been de-flavored, which is why instant grits are often sold with some kind of flavoring added to make them palatable. They are positively foul and no one with any self-respect ought to eat them. A package labeled "quick grits" contains grits that are processed to reduce the cooking time from an hour to 10 minutes. The flavor suffers in the process, but they'll do in a pinch. A package labeled "hominy grits," with a required cooking time of more than 30 minutes is the real thing. There's only one type of whole corn grits; while they often have more flavor than commercial hominy grits, they are not necessarily better in all applications. You can get them by mail order from a few traditional millers and at a few specialty food stores (see The Classical Southern Kitchen, page 50).

It was disheartening to see grits disappear from Southern tables, the victim of regional American homogenization and unjust malignment by those who have never eaten properly prepared grits. Where once they were a staple so taken for granted that restaurants put them on your plate whether you asked for them or not, today they are almost an afterthought alternative for something called "hash browns," which can apparently be anything from diced boiled potatoes pan-fried with onions to a fried grated potato cake. "Yankee food" is the kindest thing one can say about them. The low-point was when one actually had to ask for grits instead of potatoes in, of all places, Atlanta. Today, whole corn grits have become chic with the haute foodie crowd, thanks in part to the de rigueur appetizer of nouvelle Southern restaurants, shrimp and grits. Perhaps that popularity will lead to a revival of good grits not just on white-cloth restaurant tables, but everywhere, and with it, a relenting of the snob prejudice against hominy grits, and a return to their rightful place: on the breakfast table.

Basic Boiled Grits

Exact measurements for grits are difficult. The usual proportion is four to one, but the amount of water needed can vary. Generally, whole corn grits are thirstier than hominy grits and require more water. Keep a teakettle of water simmering close at hand in case the grits become too dry and stiff before they get tender. Though polenta and grits are not remotely the same, some demented individuals are now calling grits "Southern polenta;" if that appeals to you, I'd really rather not know about it.

4 cups water   Salt
1 cup raw hominy or whole corn grits

1. Bring the water to a good boil in a stainless steel or enameled kettle and stir in the grits. Do not add salt yet. Bring them back to a boil, stirring.

2. Reduce the heat to a bare simmer, cover loosely, and cook, stirring occasionally, until the grits absorb all the moisture and are the consistency of a thick mush, about 1 hour.

3. When the grits are quite thick and tender, stir in a large pinch or so of salt. Let them simmer for a few minutes to absorb the salt, then taste and adjust the seasoning. Simmer a few minutes longer. They may be served as is, as a side dish, or fried in cakes as directed on the next page. Serves 4.

Fried Grits

This was a popular way of dispensing with leftover breakfast grits in those days when nothing was ever wasted or thrown out. Southerners traditionally serve fried grits both as a side dish for roasted or fried meat, poultry, or fish, or as a "carrier" under creamed chicken or seafood. It is especially nice with Mrs. Harriott Pinckney Horry's Stewed Crab (page 130).

Older recipes usually don't mention coating the grits with crumbs, but it does help hold them together, and that is how I usually make them at home, so I've included the crumbs here.

The fat used depends on what is served with the grits. Bacon fat is traditional, but can be a bit strong if the grits are to accompany delicate dishes like Mrs. Horry's Crabs. I like the crispness and flavor lent by lard, but if pig fat terrifies you, you may use peanut or vegetable oil.

4 cups hot cooked grits Basic Boiled Grits (page 285)

2 cups lard, or rendered bacon fat and lard or peanut oil mixed, or, if you must, all oil

2 large eggs, well-beaten

2 cups fine cracker crumbs (or matzo meal)

1. Rinse out a 9-inch-square glass baking dish or tall glass tumblers with water. Fill them with warm grits and let it sit until cold, about 2 hours. They will set into a solid cake.

2. Unmold the grits and cut them with a damp knife into slices about 3/4 inch thick. Tumblers will produce nice round cakes. Some chefs set the grits on a rimmed baking sheet and cut them with a biscuit cutter for the same effect.

3. Put the fat or oil in a large, well-seasoned iron or non-stick skillet over medium high heat. When the fat is melted and hot, but not smoking, quickly dip each grits cake in egg, roll it in the crumbs, and slip them into the fat until the pan is full without crowding. Fry quickly, turning once, until uniformly golden brown, about 2 minutes per side. Slow cooking will cause the gelatinous starch to soften and the cakes will fall apart before they have a hard crust to hold them together. Drain briefly on absorbent paper and serve hot. Serves 4.

THE GREAT RICE DISHES OF SOUTH CAROLINA

The Carolina Lowcountry differs from other cultures of the South mainly because it is the only part of the South in whose cash crop was food: rice. The development of Carolina rice culture has provided the world with one of its most interesting and unique cuisines, one that is unparalleled in American cookery. Its influence spreads all across the Deep South, reaching as far west as Louisiana and Texas. The full history is beyond both my knowledge and the scope of this book. For those who would like to know more, Karen Hess has written a lovely, reverent, and impeccable tribute to this cuisine and culture in *The Carolina Rice Kitchen: The African Connection (1992).*

The story begins in ancient India, where long-grain rice has been cultivated for thousands of years. Long-grain rice gradually found its way into China, Persia, and the African West Coast (where a different variety of native rice was already being cultivated), and by way of the Turkish Empire, throughout the entire Mediterranean basin. When rice was introduced to the Carolina coast, the English settlers knew next to nothing about it, either in the field or the kitchen, but they were quick to realize that certain slaves from West Africa had skills and knowledge that they lacked. Thus, the West Coast had a direct and early influence. In their skilled hands, Carolina Gold, as the rice was eventually named because its ripe grain looked like waves of molten gold in the field, became so prized that its name became generic for the best rice one could get.

A similar synthesis happened in the kitchen. French Huguenot settlers, fleeing religious persecution in France and, later, the slave revolts in Haiti, probably brought some knowledge of the rice cookery of Provence, enhanced, no doubt, by further connection with West African slave cooks on the islands. In the skilled hands of slave cooks throughout the Lowcountry, these factors came together, and gradually melded into a unique cookery that was once celebrated throughout the country.

The Carolina rice culture flourished so long as there were slaves who understood rice cultivation and could be made to do the dangerous and backbreaking hand-cultivation required by the Lowcountry's rich but boggy marshes—ideal ground for growing rice with the flooded field method. But the slavery and boggy fields that nourished the rice culture were also to cause its demise. When slavery was abolished, former slaves who had a choice began gradually to leave the fields. Carolina's rice farming faltered, then collapsed altogether when machines took over the labor-intensive work. The marshes were too boggy for machines and commercial cultivation migrated westward to firmer, artificially irrigated land. It lingered in Carolina, but barely. In the early part of this century, a hurricane flooded the rice fields and an entire year's crop was lost. The industry collapsed, and, in 1927, according to John Martin Taylor, the last commercial crop was planted.

Since 1988, Carolina Gold has once again been cultivated on an old rice plantation just north of Savannah. Dr. Richard Schulze and his wife Patricia persuaded the government to propagate seeds from a small store in the National Archives. Now joined in the effort by their son, the work of the Schulzes is more of a love offering than anything else, and their production is naturally limited. It can hardly be called a renaissance of Carolina rice culture, but at least Carolina Gold grows once more as it first did more than three hundred years ago. This rice is available from a handful of cooking specialty shops, or by mail from Turnbridge Plantation, P.O. Box 165, Route 1, Hardeeville, South Carolina, 29927. Its price is rather dear, but the proceeds go to charity.

Since the first edition of this book, the Schulzes' efforts have also sparked a movement to re-introduce rice culture to South Carolina, and others have joined the Schulzes in the cultivation of Carolina Gold and other aromatic long-grain rice, such as a strain of Jasmine rice grown by The Carolina Rice Plantation in Orangeburg. But such farms cannot sustain the region's rice demand, and so the Carolina rice kitchen ironically remains one of the few in the world that isn't fed by rice from its own region. As outsiders flood the coastal plain with new development and locals succumb to an increasingly homogenized American diet, that rice kitchen is in danger of vanishing. But as long as markets in Charleston and Savannah sell rice in 50- and 100-pound sacks, though the rice they contain comes from Texas, Louisiana, or Arizona, the legacy of the old culture lingers.

The Types of Rice To Use

Carolina Gold is considered "long grain" but is actually not as long as most modern long-grain rice. Obviously, it's ideal for this cuisine, but its cultivation remains limited, and its price is prohibitive for everyday cooking. My own preference is a Southeast Asian long grain rice such as basmati, which has a pleasant, nutty flavor and the long, slender grains Carolinians prize. Domestic varieties such as Texmati are an acceptable alternative. A distant third choice is commercial long grain, which, though its shape is closer to Carolina Gold, has much less flavor and character. Medium-grain rice, available in many markets, is also acceptable, and some are more flavorful than commercial long grains. Short, round-grained rice such as those used by Italians for risotto and Japanese for sushi, are not appropriate for this cuisine. The qualities that make these varieties ideal for those dishes are contrary to what one wants in pilau.

Basic Boiled Rice

There are a few basic rules that you should always remember when cooking rice in the Carolina method:

* Carolina rice is never stirred while it is cooking. When it is done (and in those dishes that require it during the cooking) it is fluffed by picking it with a fork. The fork to use is one with wide, narrow prongs such as a real formal dinner-sized or carving fork. Nowadays I use a pastry-blending fork.

* Carolina rice is always washed before it goes into the pot, even when the packaging says it is pre-washed. Put it in a large bowl filled with water. Gently pick it up and rub and stir it with your hands until the water is milky. Drain and repeat until the water is clear.

* In some old recipes, the rice was both washed and soaked. Besides washing away excess starch, this also helps restore moisture to the grains.

* Use salt sparingly, but do use it.

> 1 cup raw long-grain rice, preferably basmati Salt
> 2 cups water

1. Wash the rice as directed above. Cover it with water and let it soak a few minutes, then pour off the water through a wire sieve. Drain the rice and put it into a heavy-bottomed pot.

2. Add the water and a healthy pinch of salt, and turn on the heat to medium-high. Bring it to a boil. Stir it to make sure that the rice isn't sticking, then put the spoon away.

3. Reduce the heat to low and set the lid askew on the top (when I'm cooking basmati, I leave the lid off altogether). Let it simmer for 12 to 14 minutes. There should be clear, dry steam holes formed on the surface, and most, if not all, of the water should be absorbed. Gently fold the top rice under with a fork, "fluffing" but not stirring it.

4. Put the lid on tight and leave it over the heat for a minute more to rebuild the steam, then turn off the heat. Move the pot to a warm part of the stove (if you have an electric stove, this is it's only advantage; leave it where it is; the residual heat in the burner should be just right.) If you don't have a warm spot, put the pan in a larger pan of hot water.

5. Let it steam 12 minutes longer. You can hold it like this for up to an hour without harm, but 12 minutes is the minimum. When you are ready to serve the rice, fluff it by picking it with a fork, turn it out into a serving bowl, and serve at once. Serves 4.

NOTES: *Remember—if the grains burst and split at the ends, they are overcooked, though you should never have that problem if you have followed this method.*

A Carolina Pilau

In this dish is the very essence of Carolina rice cookery. It's a kissing cousin to the paellas of Spain and the pilaus of Provence, since all have their roots in the ancient pilaus of Persia. West Coast African cooks pressed into service in Lowcountry kitchens naturally understood the pilau technique, as it had long been a part of their own cuisine. As a descendent of Persian cookery, one would expect this dish to be perfumed with onions, garlic, herbs, saffron, and spices. Yet, if we take the old recipes verbatim, a Carolina pilau had none of them, not even a lonely sprig of parsley. I cannot believe that they weren't there. Native Charlestonian Elizabeth Hamilton, in introducing the 1976 reprint of *Two Hundred Years of Charleston Cooking*, explains that the use of herbs, onions, and other aromatics was assumed, that the recipe was only an outline of method. However, that doesn't entirely explain things. Sarah Rutledge was most of the time quite specific about herbs and spices in recipes, and was not shy about onions and garlic, either. And yet her recipe for Carolina Pilau makes no mention of any. Possibly the exact herbs varied in each household, and Miss Rutledge was indeed providing a skeletal recipe, knowing that, otherwise, she would be attacked by what Margaret Mitchell called "a bunch of old pea hens" for having gotten them wrong. Moreover, the African cooks who made these dishes were well known for guarding their kitchen secrets. I have added optional suggestions for seasoning based on common modern practice; not in an attempt to be coy, but so you will know where Miss Rutledge leaves off and my guessing takes over.

1/2 pound dry salt-cured pork (do not use smoked bacon, but Italian pancetta is an excellent substitute)

1 medium-sized onion, chopped fine (optional)

3 cups water

1 young chicken, weighing not more than 2 pounds

Salt and whole black pepper in a peppermill

1 Bouquet Garni (page 34) (optional)

1 tablespoon chopped fresh parsley (optional)

1 whole pod cayenne pepper (optional)

1 cup raw rice, washed as directed on page 289

1. Put the pork, optional onion, and water in a kettle that will later hold all the ingredients and turn on the heat to medium-high. Let it come slowly to a boil, skim off the scum that rises, and lower the heat to a bare simmer. Loosely cover the pot and simmer it for half an hour. Meanwhile, wash the chicken, season it inside and out with salt and pepper, tuck the wings under the back and tie the legs together.

2. When the pork has completed its preliminary simmer, add the chicken and the optional herbs and whole pod of cayenne. Raise the heat to medium-high and bring it back to a boil, then reduce it to a bare simmer. Cover the pot tightly and simmer until the chicken

is tender, about 45 minutes. Miss Rutledge added the rice to the pot with the chicken, but I find it easier to control if they cook separately, as given here.

3. Carefully lift the chicken out of the pot, remove the pork and cayenne, if used, and add the rice. Let it come back to a simmer, then cover and simmer gently 12 minutes. If there is any liquid left after this time, drain it off, but reserve it. Gently fluff the rice with a fork.

4. Put the meat and chicken back—on top of the rice—cover the pot as tightly as possible, and let it steam for another 12 minutes. When the rice is tender, take up the chicken and pork.

5. Fluff the rice with a fork. If it seems dry, moisten it with some of the reserved broth, remembering that it should not be soupy. Arrange the chicken on a serving platter, and turn the rice out around it. Thinly slice the pork and arrange it on top of the rice. Serve at once. Serves 4.

NOTES: *Miss Rutledge was not specific about the kind of bird: her words were "put in the fowls (one or two, according to size)." If you have access to game birds, guinea hens, or some nice, fat domestic quail or squab, they would make a fine pilau. You can also cut the chicken up, as for frying, if you like, in which case the cooking time would be reduced to about 30 minutes. Or, as is commonly done nowadays, you may skin the chicken, pick the meat off the bones, and toss it with the rice at the end.*

A final note on the aromatics: I have felt bound as a historian to stay strictly within known traditions of Lowcountry kitchens in suggesting flavorings for this recipe. You needn't feel such constraints. Today, no Gullah cook would make this dish without green bell peppers and garlic in the pot. Allow 1 medium pepper, stemmed, cored, seeded, and diced small, added with the onion. When they've softened, add 2 large cloves garlic, crushed, peeled, and minced. Many regional cooks also add tomatoes; allow 1-1/2 cups of peeled, seeded, and diced tomatoes, with their juices, and cut back the liquid by 1/2 cup. I often vary the herbs, adding mint, basil, marjoram, or sage, whichever comes to mind at the moment. A large piece of lemon zest put in along with the bouquet garni makes this dish positively sing.

Hoppin' John

The origins of the name of this old Lowcountry dish of peas and rice are lost in legend. Many legends. Almost everyone is ready with a pop-culture story about who John was and why he was hopping (as if the supremely satisfying combination of peas and rice were not as good a reason as any), but few of them are really plausible and many are downright insulting. The dish itself is much older than the Charleston rice culture where it flourished and where most of the stories originate. Karen Hess has devoted an entire chapter to the complexities of the history of Hoppin' John in *The Carolina Rice Kitchen*, and elaborating on it here would be out of place. Mrs. Hess points to Middle-Eastern bean pilaus as reinterpreted in West Africa, where bean pilau had long been a part of the cuisine and may even have been indigenous. There can be little doubt that Hoppin' John did at least come to South Carolina by way of West Africa. Mrs. Hess further hypothesized that the name is probably a corruption of an Arabic-Hindi construct such as bahatta kachang (the b is pronounced like a "p" and the ch sounds as "j"— phonetically very close to the sounds "hoppin' John"). Other historians favor the theory that it derives from French West Indian Creole patois, *pois de pigeon* or *pois pigeon*, again just a short drive to "hoppin' John." At any rate, it is almost certainly a case of a language breakdown where familiar English words have been substituted for unfamiliar words with similar sounds.

Today, Carolinians eat Hoppin' John on New Year's Day for luck, supposedly because it's humble fare, but seldom has humility been so lusciously rewarding. I already knew that the South was in trouble, but just how much trouble hit me the day I mentioned at the office that there was a bowl of Hoppin' John waiting for me at home, and was met with a chorus of *"Hoppin' John?!* What's *that?"* Here. In Savannah. The shame of it; I went home so depressed I could hardly eat—and for me, that's depressed.

2 cups cowpeas, fresh, frozen, or dried, see notes below	1/2 teaspoon dried thyme
1/2 pound lean salt-cured pork	1 bay leaf
1 large onion, finely chopped	Whole black pepper in a peppermill
2 cloves garlic, minced (optional)	Salt
1 pod dried hot red pepper (preferably cayenne)	1 cup raw rice, washed and rinsed as directed on (page 289)
	8 to 10 fresh mint leaves

1. Wash and drain the peas. If you are using dried peas, soak them for 4 hours (or overnight) in water to cover. If you are fortunate enough to have fresh ones, they will need no preliminary soaking. Wash and drain them and proceed with step 3.

2. Put the peas into a large pot with about 3 pints of water and bring them to a boil over

a medium heat. Do not add salt. Carefully skim off the scum, reduce the heat to a slow simmer, cover the pot, and simmer for half an hour. Add the salt pork, onion, optional garlic, whole pepper pod, thyme, bay leaf, and a grinding or so of black pepper. Cover the pot again and let the peas simmer until tender—about half an hour longer. Skip to step 4.

3. To cook fresh or frozen peas, bring the water to a boil in a large, heavy-bottomed pot. Add the salt pork, onion, garlic if using, whole hot pepper, thyme, and bay leaf. Reduce the heat to low and simmer at least 30 minutes. Raise the heat, add the peas, and let it come back to a boil. Skim off the scum and add a liberal grinding of pepper. Cover, lower the heat to a simmer, and cook until the peas are tender, about 30 minutes more.

4. Taste and correct for salt (if the pork is very salty, it may not need any), keeping in mind that the broth must be highly seasoned to flavor the rice. Remove and discard the hot pepper.

5. Drain, reserving the liquids, and add 2 cups back to the pot. Add the rice and let it come back to a boil. Reduce the heat, cover the pot, and let it simmer 12 minutes. Turn off the heat and remove the pot to a warm spot (such as a pot of hot water) for another 12 to 15 minutes.

6. When it is ready, fluff the rice and peas with a fork, tossing rather than stirring. If the Hoppin' John is too dry, add a little reserved broth, but remember that this is a pilau; it shouldn't be soupy. Traditionally, the pork is served in one piece on top of the peas and rice, but you can chop it and mix it in or leave it out altogether. Just before serving, cut the mint into fine slivers and sprinkle over the Hoppin' John (otherwise, the residual heat will turn them brown). Serves 4 to 6.

NOTES: *The ingredients are straightforward, but there has been so much confusion about them that they deserve a few comments:*

Peas: *I used to think that the kind of peas didn't much matter—old recipes exist with cowpeas, black-eyes, crowders, and red peas—but that was before I became the food writer for the* Savannah Morning News. *Red peas were the original and most authentic pea, but were eventually supplanted by the more ubiquitous black-eyed pea. When I said as much in the newspaper, it set off a firestorm, and I was relieved to know that red-pea Hoppin' John survives. African-American chef Nita Dixon serves up an authentic and delicious red-pea Hoppin' John at her Savannah restaurant, Nita's Place. "Cowpea" is a generic name that is sometimes applied to all of them, as is their other common name, "field" pea, but there are places in the Carolinas where cowpea means black-eyes and other places where it means red peas. What can I say?—it's the*

South. I have eaten Hoppin' John both from my own and other people's kitchens made from a number of peas, and all have been authentic tasting and satisfying, so feel free to experiment. I would only caution against two types. Black beans were suggested in Two Hundred Years of Carolina Cooking *(1930), whether by the original cooks or by Lettie Gay, the New York dietitian who tested and rewrote the recipes, is not clear. I suspect Mrs. Gay was the culprit. Black beans will not produce a Hoppin' John that any Carolinian would recognize. In Mrs. Hill's New Cook Book, Mrs. Hill suggested making the dish with chicken and green peas, and it does sound lovely, but it's not Hoppin' John.*

Pork: *Smoked bacon is usual in modern recipes, possibly because the old recipes have been misunderstood, and not because of any long-standing tradition. Miss Rutledge's recipe calls for bacon, it's true, but in 1847, "bacon" was not smoked but pickled (brine-cured) pork. Smoked bacon began creeping into the pot shortly thereafter, when cookbook authors Mrs. Hill in Georgia and Miss Brown in South Carolina vigorously preached against it. I am very fond of smoked bacon, but find it wearying in peas; salt pork or old ham are by far more satisfying for this recipe, and by far and away, more authentic. The meat should be lean, but must have some fat, which is critical to a proper pilau. Indeed, many recipes call for bacon fat and no meat. If you are worried about animal fat, whether for health reasons or because you are just paranoid, either cut the amount of pork by half or use well-trimmed country ham, but don't cut it out altogether. If you are a vegetarian or can't eat pork, use a few spoonfuls of olive oil and add a minced onion for flavor.*

Herbs and Aromatics: *The history of the use of aromatics as seasoning in Lowcountry rice dishes is problematic. Certainly, their Middle-Eastern and West African antecedents contained herbs, pepper, onions, and garlic. However, the early Carolina recipes make no mention of them. Miss Rutledge didn't include cayenne pepper, but it is almost universal in the rest of the older sources. Her suggested mint, which has disappeared from Carolina, is the only lingering trace of Middle-eastern aromatics, and it strikes a lovely note in the composition.*

Red Rice, or Tomato Pilau

In modern cookbooks, this is often called "Savannah Red Rice," a name so imbedded in the Southern lexicon that many think it is a long-standing tradition—but it isn't. Savannah has only been associated with red rice in living memory, when a local restaurant appealing to tourists appended Savannah to its name on the menu. Old Savannahians knew it as "mulatto rice," a name used as late as Harriet Ross Colquitt's *The Savannah Cookbook* (1933)—neither an ethnic slur nor a reference to its origins, but a reference to color. The rice resembles the lovely, ruddy skin tones of people of mixed African and Native American blood that mulatto originally described. Some local cooks insist that mulatto rice is a different dish altogether—but that does seem like hair splitting. Either way, the earliest recipes were called Tomato Pilau, and usually contained chicken.

Though this is a simple dish and still commonplace in the region, I seldom see modern recipes that are quite right. This is a pilau, and to be done well, it must follow that technique. The best utensil is a cast-iron Dutch oven or skillet, as nothing else holds and distributes the heat quite as well. A good second choice is a flameproof earthenware casserole.

1/4 pound salt pork, fat old ham, or thick-sliced bacon, cubed

1 medium white or yellow onion, trimmed, split lengthwise, peeled, and chopped

1 cup raw rice, washed and soaked (page 289)

1 pound tomatoes, peeled, and chopped as directed on (page 262), or Italian canned plum tomatoes, with their juice

Salt, cayenne pepper, and whole black pepper in a peppermill

1/2 cup Chicken Broth (page 82)

1. Put the bacon or salt pork in a cast-iron skillet or kettle and turn on the heat to medium. Fry until it is crisp and its fat is rendered. Add the onion and sauté until translucent, about 5 minutes.

2. Add the rice and stir it until its grains are coated and heated through, about 3 minutes. Add the tomatoes with their juice, a healthy pinch of salt, cayenne to taste, and a liberal grinding of pepper. Bring it to a boil, stirring frequently. Gently stir in the broth and put the spoon away.

3. Loosely cover the pan, reduce the heat as low as possible and let it simmer 12 to 14 minutes. Uncover and, using a large dinner or meat fork, very gently fold the top grains of rice under. Cover and cook at the lowest possible temperature for 12 minutes more, or until the rice is just tender. Each rice grain must be distinct and separate. Remove it from the heat and let it steam for 5 minutes, fluff it with a fork, and serve at once. Serves 4.

NOTES: *Most modern cooks include sweet green (bell) peppers and celery; neither appear in the older recipes, but they are very good additions. Allow a medium pepper and large rib of celery, both chopped fine, and put them in with the onion in step 1. Many Savannah cooks nowadays add hot pepper sauce or a teaspoon of Worcestershire sauce with the tomatoes in step 2. This is recent practice, but you may add them if you like. Oh, and forget sugar, no matter whose recipe called for it. It has no place here.*

Annabella Hill's Sausage Pilau

This is down-home Georgia cooking, but the technique is, once again, the basic pilau. Modern Georgia cooks use smoked sausages, but historically it was not smoked. As Mrs. Hill pointed out, the taste of smoke is too harsh for most rice dishes. If you don't make your own, choose a mild fresh sausage such as an Italian luganega. Little breakfast link sausages will also work, though they tend to be on the bland side, so choose a brand that is spicy. Balls of Bulk Sausage (page 195) will also work, though they don't hold together as nicely.

1-1/2 pounds pork link sausage, or bulk sausage formed into 1-inch balls	Salt, whole black pepper in a peppermill, and cayenne pepper
1 medium onion, chopped	1 cup raw rice, washed and soaked (page 289)

1. Cut the sausages crosswise into 1-inch-thick pieces. Put in a deep skillet or flameproof casserole over medium heat. Brown well on all sides, being careful not to let them scorch.

2. Drain off all but 2 tablespoons of the fat and add the chopped onion. Sauté until it is softened, but not browned, about 5 minutes. Add the water and let it come to a boil. Lower the heat to a bare simmer, cover the skillet tightly with a lid, and simmer for half an hour.

3. Taste the broth and season it with salt, a few grindings of black pepper and a pinch of cayenne—how much will depend on the amount of seasoning in your sausage. If the sausage is very bland, add half a teaspoon of dried thyme or sage and a bay leaf.

4. Bring the liquid back to a boil and add the rice, stir once, and let it come back to a boil. Reduce the heat to low, cover the pan and simmer 12 minutes. Turn off the heat and let it steam for another 15 minutes. Fluff the rice with a fork and serve warm. Serves 4.

NOTES: *Most modern Georgia cooks add tomatoes to their Sausage Pilau. Allow 1 cup of peeled, seeded, and finely chopped fresh (or canned Italian) tomatoes, reduce the water to 1-1/2 cups, and add the tomatoes with the water in step 2. If the sausages you are using are short on herbs, you may also want to add half a teaspoon of thyme and a bay leaf in step 3.*

Shrimp Pilau

There are as many versions of this pilau as there are coastal towns, but everywhere there is a seacoast, the happy union of shrimp and rice is celebrated with some form of this dish. I have made one minor change from the old recipes. Instead of water, I do as many modern cooks do and use a stock from the shrimp heads and shells, which makes a distinctive difference. Though this is mentioned in a few old recipes, it was rare. If you have trouble finding shrimp with their heads still attached, see if you can persuade a fishmonger to get them for you. Much of the flavor and fat of the shrimp is in the head, and any shrimp dish is the better for it when they can be left on, or, in this case, used to flavor the liquid. If you are not able to get them, frozen whole crawfish make acceptable shellfish stock and can be substituted for the heads.

2 pounds whole (head-on) shrimp, or 1-1/4 pounds headless weight

4 thin slices salt pork or thick-cut bacon (about 1/4 pound)

1/2 cup minced white onion

1/2 cup minced green bell pepper

1/2 cup minced celery

1 cup raw rice, washed and soaked (page 289)

3 large, ripe tomatoes, blanched, peeled, seeded, and chopped, or 4 canned ones, seeded and chopped, with their juices

Salt and whole black pepper in a peppermill

1. Snap off the tails of the shrimp at the base of the head. Peel the tails, cover the meat and (refrigerate until needed). Put the heads and shells in a pot with 2 cups water and turn on the heat to medium. Let it slowly come to a boil, then reduce the heat to a simmer, loosely cover, and simmer until the liquid is reduced to 1 cup, at least 1 hour. Strain, discard the shells, and put the stock back in the pan. Cover and keep warm.

2. Put the pork in a deep cast-iron skillet or casserole, and turn on the heat to medium. Fry until its fat is rendered, remove it, and spoon off all but 2 tablespoons of fat. Add the onion, pepper, and celery and sauté them until the onions are translucent, but not browned, about 5 minutes.

3. Add the rice and toss until the grains are evenly coated with fat. Add the tomatoes, the strained stock, a healthy pinch of salt and a few grindings of pepper. Stir once and bring it back to a boil. Cover loosely, reduce the heat to low, and simmer for 12 minutes.

4. Remove the lid and, using a fork, carefully fold the top grains of the rice under to the bottom. Spread the shrimp over the top of the rice, cover tightly, and let the steam build for 2 minutes. Turn off the heat and, without removing the lid, steam 15 minutes more, just until the rice is tender and the shrimp are pink. Remove the pilau from the heat as soon as it is done, fluff it with a fork, tossing to mix in the shrimp, and serve at once. Serves 4.

NOODLES AND DUMPLINGS

Ask a Southerner for traditional Southern "pasta" dishes and most likely they will laugh you into next week. The Italian name for noodles and dumplings has only recently been used here, but that doesn't mean that Southerners have not long enjoyed them. It is true that pasta has not held a prominent place in the Southern diet, but imported Italian factory pasta such as vermicelli and macaroni (the long tubes) has long been used here, and Southern egg noodles are identical to the homemade egg pasta of Emiglia-Romagna (both are made with low-gluten, soft wheat flour). Nearly every Southerner was raised on dumplings, though these owe more to English and German antecedents than Italian ones.

For most modern Southerners, "dumpling" brings to mind soft pillows of baking powder–raised flour dumplings, simmered in chicken broth. But once there was a wide variety of sweet and savory dumplings in Southern cookery. Most followed English and German traditions and were made with suet or lard pastry. But there were also delicate gnocchi-like potato dumplings. Modern cooks like North Carolina chef and food writer Bill Neal have treated us to marvelously savory herb dumplings, but these have no historical precedent, at least, not that I can find.

Potato Dumplings

These delicate dumplings are essentially the same as Ligurian potato gnocchi. Though eggs help hold potato dumplings together, their absence here makes the texture lighter and more delicate. They date back in central Georgia at least a hundred and forty years, but have virtually disappeared, both from Georgians' living memories and from their culinary repertory. Why is a mystery; when properly made they are absolutely alluring.

2 pounds mealy potatoes, cooked as for Boiled Potatoes (page 241)

About 2 cups flour

1. Let the potatoes cool just enough to handle, then peel and put them through a ricer. The pulp should be mealy and quite dry. Spread it to air dry for a few minutes if it isn't.

2. Mound the potatoes on a clean, dry work surface. Sprinkle a cup of flour over them, and knead it in. It will be slightly sticky. Gradually knead in more flour until the dough is holding together and no longer sticky, but still quite soft. Gather it into a ball.

3. Clean the work surface of any bits of dough that are sticking to it and lightly dust it with flour, using only as much as it takes to keep the dough from sticking. Lightly and quickly roll it out to a thickness of about 1/2 inch. Flour it and cut it into 1-inch squares. Or, you can take handfuls of the dough and roll them with your hands into a 1-inch diameter sausage shape and cut them into 1-inch lengths.

4. Lightly dust a baking sheet with flour and lay the dumplings on it. Let them dry for at least 10 minutes before cooking them. They can be cooked plain, in salted water, and sauced with melted butter, or, though unorthodox, in any of the following recipes. They're especially nice made in the broth of stewed game, beef, or ham. Serves 4 to 6.

Raised Dumplings

This is really a light biscuit dough, and is handled in much the same way. Soda and baking powder make the dumplings swell as they cook into fluffy, delicate pillows. As is true for biscuits, they should be made only from soft winter wheat flour.

10 ounces (about 2 cups) unbleached, all-purpose flour

1/2 teaspoon baking soda

2 teaspoons Single-Acting Baking Powder (page 318), or 1 teaspoon commercial double-acting powder

1 teaspoon salt

4 tablespoons unsalted butter or lard

1 cup whole milk buttermilk or plain, all-natural whole milk yogurt thinned to buttermilk consistency with water or milk

1. Sift together the flour, soda, baking powder, and salt into a mixing bowl. Cut in the butter or lard with a pastry blender (or two knives) until the flour resembles coarse corn meal.

2. Make a well in the center of the flour and pour in the buttermilk or yogurt. Using a wooden spoon and as few strokes as possible, quickly stir the ingredients together.

3. Shaping the dumplings: There are two types of dumpling that can be made with this dough. Their differing shape affects both their texture and the way that they absorb the broth. Both are still used in Southern cooking, and each has its distinct charms. To make flat, noodle-like dumplings, skip to step 4. To make drop dumplings, take the dough out onto a floured surface, flour it lightly, and fold it in half. Pat it flat and repeat this 4 or 5 times. Pinch off 1-inch round pieces of dough and cook quickly in any of the following recipes.

4. To make flat dumplings (sometimes called "slipperies"), lightly flour a smooth wood or plastic laminate work surface and turn the dough out onto it. Flour your hands and gently push the dough away from you to flatten it. Fold it in half, gently press flat with the heel of your hand, and give it a quarter turn. Repeat this until the dough is just smooth, about 12 to 15 folds. (This is Bill Neal's technique; it isn't kneading, so use a very light hand.) Dust the work surface and the dough with more flour and roll it out to a thickness of 1/8 inch. Quickly cut into 1-inch strips, and then cut each into 2-inch lengths. Cook immediately in any of the following recipes. Serves 6.

Southern Chicken and Dumplings

A die-hard Southerner's eyes will light up at the mere mention of this dish, despite all the horrible things that have been done to it over the years. It is a frequent item on cafeteria menus, but seldom an edible one. More often than not, the chicken is indifferently boiled and the dumplings are made with anything from canned biscuits (they are as awful as they sound) to store-bought lasagna noodles. Yet their popularity endures, for when properly made, there is nothing that is more satisfying to eat: meltingly tender little pillows of raised pastry simmered in a rich, flavorful broth.

2 quarts Chicken Broth (page 82), made with a whole 5-pound stewing hen

The whole hen from the broth

1 Bouquet Garni (page 34), made with the optional marjoram

1 tablespoon chicken fat (from the broth), or unsalted butter

1 large white onion, trimmed, split lengthwise, skinned, and chopped

Salt and whole white pepper in a peppermill

1 recipe Raised Dumplings (page 299)

1/4 cup parsley, plus 2 tablespoons more for garnish

1 tablespoon each fresh, chopped sage and thyme or 1/2 teaspoon each dried

1. After making the broth, remove the chicken from it, allow both to cool, and degrease the broth. Add the bouquet garni to the broth and turn on the heat to medium. Bring it to a boil and simmer, uncovered, until it is reduced by one-fourth. Meanwhile, skin and bone the chicken and cut it into 1/2-inch cubes. Cover and set aside.

2. Put the fat and onion in a skillet over medium-high heat. Sauté until the onion is translucent and just beginning to color, about 4 minutes. Turn off the heat, and add the onion to the broth. Season with a healthy pinch of salt and a few grindings of white pepper to taste.

3. Make the dumplings according to the recipe. You may either do drop dumplings, which will be puffy and round, or rolled, flat dumplings—whichever you prefer. Add the herbs to the broth and drop in the dumplings a few at a time. Simmer them for about 5 minutes. Add the chicken and simmer it for about 2 minutes more, or until the dumplings are tender. Ladle the chicken and dumplings onto a deep platter or individual soup plates, sprinkle with parsley, and serve at once. Serves 6.

NOTES: *Many modern Southern cooks make yellow dumplings: add a pinch each of saffron and turmeric to the broth with the onions in step 3. Though it is seldom mentioned in old recipes, nowadays I add a couple of minced garlic cloves as well. And while unorthodox by Southern standards, you can also substitute Potato Dumplings.*

MaMa's Ham Dumplings

Every year until I had finished college, the end of the Christmas holidays was marked by my grandmother's delectable ham dumplings. It was her way of using up what was left of the Christmas ham, but I think we looked forward to having those dumplings more than the ham.

The first choice of ham for this dish is a dry-cured old or country ham, but it is even respectable made with a brine-cured baked ham—just so long as it hasn't been impregnated with artificial "smoke flavoring."

The bone from a country ham or 3 pounds ham hock or knuckle

3 quarts cold water

1 large white onion, peeled and halved

1 large carrot, peeled and cut in large chunks

1 Bouquet Garni (page 34) (optional)

6 whole peppercorns

1 recipe Raised Dumplings (page 299)

1 cup leftover boiled (or raw) country ham, cut into julienne

1/4 cup chopped parsley, plus 2 tablespoons more for garnish

1. Put the bone into a large stockpot and pour the water over them. Turn on the heat as low as you can get it and bring the water slowly to the boiling point, carefully skimming off the scum as it pops to the surface. It will take about 45 minutes.

2. Add the onion, carrot, the bouquet garni, if liked (my grandmother didn't use herbs), and the peppercorns. Simmer slowly for at least 1 hour; 2 is better. Strain, discarding the solids, return the broth to the pot, bring it back to a boil, and reduce it to 1-1/2 quarts (about half).

3. Make the dumplings according to the recipe, folding and rolling them into a flat pastry as directed in step 4. Drop the dumplings a few at a time into the simmering broth and let them simmer for 5 minutes. Stir in the ham and parsley and simmer for 2 to 3 minutes more. Ladle the ham and dumplings onto a serving platter or individual soup plates, sprinkle them with more parsley, and serve at once. Serves 6.

Squirrel or Rabbit Dumplings: MaMa made a variation of these dumplings with squirrels, freshly killed in the fall when they were full of the flavor of summer nuts and berries. If you hunt, or are blessed with a friend or relative who does, cook squirrels or rabbits as for Rabbit Stew (page 164), using 2 quarts of water for the broth, and make the dumplings as directed above.

Macaroni Pie or Pudding

An elaborate version of this pudding was often credited to Dr. William Kitchiner's *The Cook's Oracle*, a book widely used in the Deep South. But actually, macaroni puddings long predate Dr. Kitchiner. They were true puddings, steamed in a mold, and rich with real Parmesan cheese, cold roast fowl, and ham. Annabella Hill and Theresa Brown both offered this simplified version bound together with an egg custard and baked. It became a standard in upstate kitchens; I was raised on my grandfather's macaroni pie, made from this same recipe, passed to him from his own mother, and differing from Mrs. Hill and Miss Brown only in detail.

On the ingredients: Soda crackers were not always salted, so salt was included in the older recipes; if you are using saltines with salted tops, be judicious with the salt. Try to find well-aged cheddar cheese that doesn't have orange dye in it, and remember: This is not Italian food by any stretch of the imagination, so don't worry about "al dente" and enjoy it.

1 pound macaroni (see notes)	2 cups grated sharp cheddar or Parmigiano-Reggiano cheese, or a mixture
Salt	
2 tablespoons unsalted butter	Whole black pepper in a peppermill
1 cup crushed saltine crackers	2 large eggs
	1-1/2 cups milk or half-and-half

1. Position a rack in the center of the oven and preheat it to 400 degrees F. Meanwhile, bring 4 quarts of water to boil in a large pot, add some salt, and stir in the macaroni. Cook for about 4 minutes, or until the macaroni is softened, but not quite done. Drain the macaroni thoroughly and add the butter, tossing until the butter is melted and all the pasta is well-coated.

2. Choose a casserole large enough to hold all the ingredients, butter it, and spoon a layer of macaroni into the bottom. Spread over the pasta about one-fourth of the cracker crumbs and one-fourth of the cheese. Repeat this with a layer of macaroni, crumbs, and cheese until all are used up, finishing it with cheese. Sprinkle the top with a few grindings of pepper.

3. In a bowl, beat the eggs until smooth and light. Stir in the milk gradually. Pour this over the casserole, place it in the center of the oven, and bake until it is set and the top is golden, about half an hour. Don't overcook it or the eggs will separate and make the pie watery. Serves 6.

NOTES: *Macaroni, in Italy, is a long tube that resembles fat, hollow spaghetti. This is the kind of pasta that would have been familiar to nineteenth-century cooks, as elbows were a product of this century. If you find real macaroni, by all means use it in this dish, but break it up into short pieces, because that is the way the old cooks did it. If you aren't able to find long macaroni, the short, straight tubes such as penne are preferable to the elbow type, but even the latter will work in a pinch.*

The Southern Baker's Art

THE STORY OF SOUTHERN BAKING IS CENTERED on the home hearth. Based on an agrarian economy, the nineteenth-century South was a largely rural culture. Except in its port cities and a few inland urban centers, commercial bakeries were not a viable undertaking, and even where they existed, many families continued to prefer the bread from their own ovens. Consequently, baking in our region continued to be a home-based occupation much longer than it did elsewhere in America. In fact, a Southern cook's reputation was judged more by her baking than any other culinary endeavor. Even women who had an accomplished cook in the kitchen took particular care with the baking, often to the point of doing it themselves.

Baking and cooking are two different, divergent occupations. There are many excellent cooks who are terrible bakers, and lackluster cooks whose breads and pastries shine. That many Southern cooks of the old school excelled at both is a tribute both to their versatility and dexterity in the kitchen.

Until recently, Americans who traveled to Europe came back in awe of the wide variety of fine regional breads that each country had to offer. Their usual refrain was a lament that America had no such variety. Yet, once we had many regional breads, as diverse as the many cultures from which our ancestors had come. Fortunately, there has been a revival of fine bread making in America. But in the South, where home baking had deep roots, professional bakeries have been slower to get established except in our largest cities, and those that do exist tend to specialize in breads from other countries, largely ignoring the hundreds of traditional regional specialties that originated on home hearths. To have paid just tribute to the entire repertory would have doubled the size of this book and still left many avenues unexplored. The recipes of this chapter are few, and merely representative, but I hope evocative of that fine heritage.

AN INTRODUCTION TO YEAST COOKERY

Before we go on to the recipes, it is appropriate to begin with a few words on the baker's art. If you are a novice to baking yeast-leavened bread, it is helpful to know a little about the basics. Yeast bread making is some of the world's oldest cookery; it has been deftly practiced by millions of simple people for a very long time and is not complicated. But there are certain basics that one needs to know.

The Ingredients

ON YEAST

"Know ye not that a little leaven leaveneth the whole lump?"

—St. Paul, I Corinthians 5:6 (KJV)

"It is axiomatic among serious bakers that the tiniest possible proportion of yeast to flour produces the finest bread."

—Karen Hess, Introduction to the American edition of
Elizabeth David's English Breads and Yeast Cookery

In order to make bread rise and give it the characteristic texture, it must be aerated, that is, filled with little pockets of trapped air. This can be accomplished using a chemical reaction between an acid and alkali (baking powder), or by taking advantage of a methane-producing fungus that we know as yeast. This fungus is a living organism that is all around us. Early bakers and brewers, in fact, depended almost entirely on natural airborne fungi. Yeast works by feeding on the starches and natural sugars in the flour. As it eats and multiplies, the gas it produces are trapped by the gluten strands in the dough, making pockets of air that cause the dough to expand.

As a general rule, the trouble with American yeast cookery is that we tend to use too much. The reasons we have come to this are several, not the least of them our impatient insistence on instant gratification. That is, the more yeast one uses, the faster the rising will be. But there is a price to be paid: The bread will inevitably have a sour, over-yeasted taste.

The most obvious possible explanation for overdoing the yeast, as Mrs. Hess pointed out to me, may have to do with a misunderstanding of old recipes because of the kind of yeast once used by home bakers. One of the most common forms throughout the nineteenth century was homemade "patent" yeast. Recipes for it are plentiful in early printed and manuscript cookery books—a mixture of water, hops, flour, cornmeal, and brewer's yeast. This was allowed to ferment, then spread out in a shady spot to dry. The dried yeast was finally cut into small, even cakes. For all its excellent keeping qualities, it was not nearly as strong as today's yeast, and larger doses were needed. Misinterpretations of old recipes may be one reason most American ones today call for so much dry yeast.

The most commonly available type of yeast today is active dry yeast, the little packets of granules one finds in the supermarket. It is much stronger than we imagine. A quarter of a teaspoon of dry yeast is an ample equivalent for the amount of patent yeast usually given for a quart (4 cups, or 20 ounces) of flour. The first rising will be slower, but the resulting bread will be stronger, finer in texture, and better tasting. Always keep in mind that, while the initial rising may be slow, it occurs on its own time; many doughs can be left unattended overnight or even while you are at work. Once the dough has been through its first rise, the yeast will have multiplied on its own, and final rise after the shaping will go quickly.

The kind of yeast to use: Superior to active dry yeast, and, unfortunately, difficult to find, is compressed fresh yeast pressed into a cake. If you can't find it in the market, sometimes a baker can be persuaded to sell you a little, and it can be mail-ordered from specialty baker's shops. Buy only what you can use within 2 weeks, since it is more perishable than dry yeast and won't last much longer than that, and store it in the refrigerator. Look for an even light tan color and a clean yeasty smell. Avoid any that is dry, crumbly, and gray.

The yeast that most of us have to be content with, is active dry yeast. Many of them are now preservative-free, which is preferable, and will usually be labeled as such. Like all living things, yeast is perishable, but it can live in a dormant state for long periods of time, and does not need preservatives to keep it alive. By using preservative-free yeast, you can be relatively certain that the yeast you get will be fresher. If the brand in your supermarket isn't preservative-free, try your local health food store. Be sure you are buying baker's yeast and not "dietary" (labeled brewer's or nutritional) yeast, which health stores often sell as a nutritional supplement. Some markets now sell "rapid-rise" yeast, genetically engineered to grow like mad and cause the dough to rise in much less time (they claim half). I am old-fashioned and find that a slow-rise from slow yeast growth makes better bread in the long run, so I've never used it.

Some bakers store their dry yeast in the refrigerator after the packet is opened, and in a warm climate, that's not a bad idea, but a cool, dry cupboard will suffice for most climates.

Measuring by Weight

Just about everything that I know about good bread making I learned from possibly the best home baker in America—my friend and mentor, Karen Hess. It was from her that I learned a baker's most important lesson: The capriciousness of volume measuring flour. I used to make scrupulous use of the measuring cup, sometimes succeeding, more often failing, always wondering vaguely what went wrong. Enter Mrs. Hess. She quickly convinced me that the biggest problem with volume measures is consistency. There are too many variables; the same weight of flour can be doubled in volume by sifting, or compacted to half its volume by tamping. Moisture content also affects volume. Old bakers who used volume measures understood this and called for "enough water to make a good dough" or, conversely, a specific volume of liquid and "enough flour worked in to make a soft dough." My great-grandmother made her bread in an oblong wooden bread bowl. She put in the flour at one end, poured liquid into the other, and gradually worked in the flour until it had the right feel. In short, she measured by touch.

All the recipes here were worked out using weight measures. It is by far the most dependable method, but it is not foolproof: The final test must lie in the feel of the dough, as my great-grandmother knew. The absorbency of flour can vary substantially; you may find that one batch of dough will need slightly less water, while the next one from the same bag of flour may need more. This is one reason that I recommend a brief hand kneading when the bread is mixed in a food processor. The machine cannot tell you when the dough is too slack or too stiff, but your hands, once they know how the dough is supposed to feel, can do it unerringly.

Within the text, I have given volume measures only where they will not do critical damage to the structure of the recipe. I estimated them by dipping the cup into the flour, lightly tapping the side of the cup two or three times to eliminate air pockets, and smoothed off the excess with the flat side of a knife. I then weighed the results.

Flour and Meal

Approximating early-nineteenth-century water-stone ground wheat flour, of course, is impossible. For one thing, modern soil conditions, water and seeds are different; we literally cannot produce the same grain. But the real difficulty lies in the reality that we can never really know what that early grain and its resulting flour were really like—either in flavor or appearance. There is lively disagreement even among historians.

The biggest blow sustained by our flour was the invention of the steel roller mill in the middle of the nineteenth century. Not only does roll-milling ruin the texture of the flour and squeeze out virtually all the bran, it makes it possible to mill the tough grains of high-protein hard summer red wheat. Most of the flour grown in colonial and early Republican America was soft winter wheat, which was easily milled by stone. Hard wheat was too rough on the old mill-stones, but was ideal for steel roller mills. Hard wheat flour has a high protein content, and is therefore higher in glutens than soft wheat flour. But this does not necessarily mean that it makes better bread, popular wisdom notwithstanding. The amount of gluten is not nearly as critical as the quality of that gluten. But hard wheat flour will stand up to the abuse that commercial baking equipment metes out, and its high gluten content does insure a better rise, so it has come to be accepted as the preferred bread flour.

All-purpose flours are a blend of both soft and hard wheat. In the South, they tend to have a higher proportion of soft than hard wheat. Elsewhere, it may be the other way around. This regional difference makes it difficult to use. My editor, who is an experienced baker, related a disaster she had using a Southern all-purpose flour in a recipe that had been designed for hard-wheat flour. Conversely, Mrs. Randolph's wheat bread was formulated by that lady using soft wheat flour. I can't promise happy results with a hard wheat flour. All the same, I have had success with these recipes using unbleached all-purpose flour from all over the country.

Flour whitens naturally as it ages; in the old days the process was quickened by spreading it in the sun. Commercially milled unbleached flour is whitened by storing. It is still not stark snow-white, but a very light beige. Commercially milled flour that is labeled "bleached" has been whitened chemically. The process removes not only color, but many nutrients, so bleached flour is always enriched with vitamin additives. I have just one thing to say about chemically bleached flour: don't use it. Not only is it devoid of flavor, color, and nutrients, the chemicals used to bleach it are of questionable safety and are largely unregulated. The "improvements" are even more questionable and manufacturers are not required by law to list them. The only thing I can say in favor of bleached flour is that it makes pretty good white glue. Think about that.

What to use: All that said, I do not mean to suggest that you can't make very good bread from commercially milled flour. The best one to use for these recipes is that made from soft winter wheat. However, unbleached all-purpose flour should work fine for all the yeast breads and even biscuits. Even after the western hard summer wheat fields were opened, the South still preferred soft wheat, and in many areas, the flour continued to be milled on water-powered stones. Southern bakers used soft-wheat flour even for yeast bread, and their recipes are designed for it. Finding such glories as stone-ground soft-winter wheat flour today is difficult. I have a friend who actually mills her own from organically grown Pennsylvania grain. As you can imagine, her whole meal bread is indescribable. Short of my friend's drastic measures, reasonably good water-stone ground flour can be found, in limited quantities, from small millers still using the old water-powered stone mills of the last century. You can order them by mail, and some health food stores carry them. Commercially milled soft-wheat flour is also available by mail from White Lily Foods and from the King Arthur flour company (ask for their unbleached pastry flour—it's made from soft wheat). Sources for mail ordering these flours are on page 50.

I use only unbleached soft-wheat or all-purpose flour. To imitate the flour of our ancestors, before weighing it, I take up as much whole wheat pastry flour as I can hold in my hand for every pound of flour in the recipe and put it into the bottom of the scale's bowl, then add the white flour until I've reached the weight needed. The bread is still "white"—actually a nice, golden beige—but it has a lovely crumb and rich, wheaty flavor. While I won't pretend that it reproduces anything like the bread our ancestors knew, it makes an awfully good loaf.

Water

The chemicals that are used to purify municipal water will sometimes purify—that's to say, kill—yeast. If your city water is heavily treated, you will do well to use filtered or bottled spring or distilled water to dissolve the yeast and make up the dough.

Many American recipes specify heated water, or worse, warm tap water. Warmed water is an artificial stimulant for yeast. While it does need warmth in order to grow, it doesn't require nearly as much as has been popularly supposed and does not actually need warm water to activate it. Yeast seems to be healthiest when dissolved in water that is at room temperature (for most of us that's between 70 and 75 degrees F). The artificial boost that warm water gives the initial growth acts on it like a runner who begins the race with everything he's got in the first few laps, only to find that he does not have enough energy left to finish. Warm tap water can do even more damage, since hot tap water is unsuitable for drinking. Needless to say, it won't do your yeast any good, either. If you are making bread in the winter and the water is actually cold, let it sit until it has come to room temperature, or warm it briefly and let it cool to less than 90 degrees F.

Milk

Milk is often used in Southern breads, an enrichment that makes for a lighter, softer crumb and improved keeping qualities. All the old recipes called for the milk to be scalded because it contained enzymes and other organisms that inhibit yeast growth. Pasteurization has taken care of that, but I still warm milk used in bread, as I'm seldom organized enough to take the milk out of the refrigerator early enough to let it warm to room temperature; warming it saves the wait. Also, the warm milk is often used to melt butter or other fat that is to be added to the dough. Always let the milk cool to less than 90 degrees F before adding the yeast, and in no case add hot milk (more than 130 degrees F) to yeast, because it will certainly kill it.

Sugar and Other Sweeteners

I don't consider sugar either a necessary or desirable ingredient for serious bread making. Contrary to popular wisdom, yeast doesn't need sugar to grow properly, and I find it gives the yeast an artificial stimulation that does it no good in the long run. The only thing sugar and other sweeteners properly lend to dough is sweetness. Unless the bread is meant to be sweet, sugar is superfluous.

THE PROCESS

The Sponge

In classic old French and English bread making, the yeast is activated in a thin batter called a "sponge." In this moist, relatively warm environment, the yeast thrives and multiplies naturally, and the fermentation process is enhanced. I find that a sponge makes it possible to use far less processed yeast. You can make acceptable bread by omitting the sponge process, but the dough should still go through a double rise for the best development both of aeration and flavor.

Burying the sponge: In the bread recipe that follows, Mrs. Randolph used the old French practice of burying the sponge in the rest of the flour, to prevent it from crusting and drying out. I often mix the sponge in the food processor and put the flour on top of it, but I also have had good results by burying the sponge in the bowl of flour (that is, a layer of flour in the bottom of the bowl, the sponge, then a layer on top).

On Mixing and Kneading

I have made several references here to the food processor and electric mixer. I am not a gadget-oriented cook, but am not opposed to laborsaving devices when they actually do the job. While machines will not, perhaps, ever equal bread made by practiced hands, both the food processor fitted with a plastic blade, and the mixer fitted with a dough hook make fine bread. I like to mix the starter and sticky doughs such as Sally Lunn with the machines, but do find that care must be taken, especially with the food processor. The machine can overheat the dough and damage the glutens if it's allowed to overwork it. When using the food processor, always use the plastic blade; the metal one is too hard on the glutens. Pulse the machine just until the dough is cohesive (there may be a few stray bits that never stick to the ball, but they should look soft and moist, not dry and crumbly). Let the machine knead it for 1 minute. Turn it out of the bowl to finish the kneading by hand, about 5 minutes more. The mixer's dough hook does a better job all round than the food processor and can do all the kneading. Traditionalist that I am, however, I prefer to knead the dough by hand. A machine cannot tell you that the dough is getting too warm or overworked, but your hands can. When I mix a dough in one of the machines, I still like having it in my hands for a few minutes, just to be sure.

I used to tell my cooking students that kneading bread was a great way to take out their aggressions, but now I know better. In *Hoppin' John's Lowcountry Cooking*, John Martin Taylor wrote, "You will get out of a loaf of bread only what you put into it . . . get into a good mood while you knead the loaf. If you try instead to take out your anger on the dough, you will end up with a knotty, uneven bread." John is an excellent baker who knows his business. It never does to be in a bad mood in the kitchen; I have the scars to prove it. Of all the failures in bread making, most can be traced back to inadequate kneading. Except for quick breads, where the dough must be handled as little as possible, most dough depends on a thorough, persistent working. Over-kneading is possible, but this is seldom the problem unless you have used a machine to do it.

The secret to good kneading is to find a movement and rhythm that is comfortable for you and your hands. The one that has given me the best and most consistent results is as follows. Put the ball of dough on a lightly floured surface. Take the heels of your hands and push the dough away from you to stretch and flatten the ball. Double the end that is farthest from you back over the dough, like folding a sheet of paper in half. Press it down with the heel of your hand and give it a quarter turn. Push it out again, fold it back, and press down. Keep doing this until the dough is elastic, smooth, and springs back into shape when lightly press it with a finger.

The Oven

Until the iron range became commonplace, bread was baked either in a wood-fired brick oven or in a Dutch oven—a deep iron pot with legs and a deep-rimmed lid. This kettle was set over hot coals and the rimmed lid was piled with more coals, creating an even heat throughout. It was the oven most often used for cakes and quick breads such as Soda Biscuits (page 319).

In upper-class households, most yeast breads were baked in the dome-shaped brick oven set in the side of the kitchen fireplace. The oven was heated with a wood fire and swept clean. The bread was then "cast" on the floor of the oven; that is, it was slid into the oven on a long-handled paddle and deposited on the oven floor with a quick, clean jerk of the paddle. The method had been used for millennia. Pan-baked bread was, of course, known, but did not become commonplace until the iron range replaced the old brick ovens.

But even the iron range was better for making bread than the oven of our modern ranges. The steel walls of our ovens will in no way approximate the heat-retaining properties of a brick, or even an iron, oven, because steel cannot evenly hold and radiate heat as iron and clay do. To imitate the brick oven, I've settled on a compromise that uses a pizza baking stone (or unglazed terra cotta tiles) and a little supplemental steam.

You will need a ceramic baking stone, which are widely available at any kitchenware store and in most department store cookware departments. If you can't find one, unglazed terra cotta tiles make a good substitute. Scrub them with detergent and let them dry completely before using them. Line a rimmed baking sheet with the tiles and use them as you would the stone. You will also need a wood baker's peel (available at any kitchenware store, and often sold as a kit with the stone), rimless cookie sheet, or other flat, sturdy tool for sliding the bread into the oven.

Position a rack in the lowest position of a cold oven and place the baking stone on it (or see below for using tiles.) Put a rimmed baking sheet or metal pie plate on the floor of the oven. Turn on the oven and preheat it to 450 degrees F for least 30 minutes so that the stone is thoroughly and evenly heated. Don't ever put the stone into an oven that is already hot; this will cause it to break. Have about 1/4 cup of water handy. Put the bread dough on a well-floured peel (some cooks use cornmeal) and extend the peel to the far end of the stone, then, using a quick, sharp jerk, pull back the peel, leaving the loaf on the stone. Throw the water into the pan on the oven's floor, being careful not to hit the heating element if your oven is electric, or to extinguish the pilot (as I have) if it is gas-fired. And be especially careful not to throw any cold water directly on the stone, or it could crack.

My experience is that all baked goods are the better for having baked on the stone, and mine almost never comes out of my oven except when I am doing high-temperature roasting. But, in the event that you do take it out, always make sure it has cooled completely before doing so.

Wheat Bread

This is essentially manchets, the daily bread of the English upper classes from at least the fourteenth century through to the early days of American colonization. Until the mid-nineteenth century, it was the daily bread of America as well, at least of the upper classes, but as the open hearth and its brick oven gradually gave way to the cast-iron stove, the old bread also began to be displaced by lighter, sweeter, puffier pan-molded loaves that are usual today. Everyone who tastes this bread is amazed that it is an old "American" recipe. It deserves to have its place in the repertory of American home bakers restored.

Before you begin, please review the preceding notes on ingredients and processes.

1/4 teaspoon active dry yeast, or 1/2 ounce compressed fresh yeast

1-1/2 cups water, at room temperature

20 ounces (1-1/4 pounds—about 4 to 4-1/2 cups) unbleached all-purpose flour, including a handful (about 1 ounce) whole-wheat pastry flour

2 teaspoons salt

1. Dissolve the yeast in the water and let it proof 10 minutes. Make the starter, or sponge, in a large mixing bowl by stirring the proofed yeast into 1-1/2 cups of the flour with a wooden spoon, beating until it is smooth.

2. Cover the starter with all but 1 scant cup of the flour. Sprinkle the salt over the top and cover the bowl with a damp, double-folded linen towel or sheet of plastic wrap. Let it rise until doubled, about 2 to 4 hours, depending on the warmth of the day and of your room.

3. When the sponge has doubled and long fissures form in the flour on top, work in the flour and salt, then turn it out onto a lightly floured work surface and knead, gradually working in the reserved flour, until it is elastic and smooth, at least 8 minutes. The dough should spring back into shape when you press into it with your finger. These steps can be done in a food processor fitted with a plastic dough blade or with a mixer. Refer to the notes at the end of the recipe.

4. Gather the dough into a ball, pinching it together on the bottom, and lightly flour it. Wipe out the mixing bowl and return the dough to it. Cover with a damp, double-folded linen towel or sheet of plastic wrap, and let it rise until doubled, from 4 to 6 hours, again, depending on the warmth of the room. If you set it in a fairly cool spot, it can be left to rise overnight.

5. Turn the dough out onto a lightly floured surface and knead lightly for a minute or two until it is just smooth again. Shape it into a large, single ball or pull off 12 equal handfuls and shape each into a roll. Place the loaf on a floured baker's peel, or, if you have made

rolls, a lightly greased baking sheet. Cover it with a damp linen towel and let it rise until nearly doubled.

6. Prepare the oven with a baking stone and pan (page 311) and preheat it at 450 degrees F while the bread does its final rise, but for no less than 30 minutes. Have 1/4 cup of water ready. If you are baking the bread in rolls, skip to step number 9.

7. If you are baking the bread in a single loaf, uncover and slash it in a tick-tack-toe pattern with a single-edged razor. Place the peel on the stone, and with a quick, sure jerk, quickly slide it out, depositing the loaf on the baking stone. Quickly, but carefully, throw 1/4 cup water into the pan on the floor of the oven and shut the door at once.

8. Bake for 15 minutes. Reduce the heat to 400 degrees and bake another 10 minutes, then check the bread. If it is browning unevenly, turn it carefully, wearing a pair of oven mitts. If it is browning too quickly, reduce the temperature to 350 degrees F. Bake until it gives off a hollow thump when tapped on the bottom, about 10¬ to 12 minutes more. Cool it on a wire rack.

9. You can approximate Mrs. Randolph's rolls baked on the floor of the brick oven by depositing all the rolls at once with a peel, but it's tricky. It's easier to bake them on a baking sheet. Place it directly on the stone, throw in the water, and immediately close the oven door. Bake for about 18 to 20 minutes. If they're browning too quickly after 10 minutes, turn the heat down to 400 degrees F. They are done when they produce the same hollow thump as the large loaf. Makes 1 round loaf, or 12 rolls.

NOTES: *The mixing and initial kneading can be done in a mixer or food processor. The dough does not, perhaps, have as nice a texture because hand mixing offers more control, but it does the job well enough. Fit the food processor bowl with the plastic blade and put in the yeast and water. Pulse to mix and let it proof 10 minutes. Add 1-1/2 cups of the flour and turn on the machine for about half a minute or until the starter is smooth. Add all but a cup of the remaining flour, top with the salt, and cover the bowl. Let it stand until the starter is doubled, about 2 to 4 hours (depending on the warmth of the room). Turn on the machine and process until the dough forms into a ball. Let it knead for a minute in the machine, then turn it out onto a floured surface and finish the kneading by hand, working in the remaining flour. This affords better control than using the machine to do all the kneading, and it does produce a better texture in the end.*

To use a mixer, fit the machine with the paddle and mix the starter as directed above. Remove the bowl from the mixer and cover the sponge with all but a cup of the remaining flour and salt. Cover the bowl and let the sponge rise. Using the paddle and a shield on the mixing bowl, work the flour and salt into the sponge. Remove the paddle from the mixer and change to the dough hook. Knead with the hook until it is elastic and smooth, gradually adding the remaining flour, about 8 minutes. When using the mixer, I still like to knead by hand for a minute or two so I can feel the dough and know that all is as it should be.

This bread can also be baked in a pan for a more regular, rectangular loaf. Lightly grease two 9-inch loaf pans and divide the dough between them for the final rising. Make a long, single slash down the center of each loaf just before putting the pans in the oven. The pan loaves tend not to rise as much once they go into the oven, so be sure they have doubled before baking them.

Secession Biscuits

In early American cookery books, "biscuits" continued to be much as they had been in Europe, that is, what we now know as crackers. But the yeast-leavened biscuits of this recipe, from patriotic kitchens of Confederate North Georgia, are the kind Americans have come to know— light, leavened bread rolled or cut into small cakes. As is often the case with patriotically named recipes, the recipe itself is much older than its name would suggest. Actually, it is only a renamed variation of old-fashioned "French" rolls common in antebellum books. Except for its shaping, it differs from those earlier rolls only in detail. "French," incidentally, was a common name in England and America for breads enriched with eggs and milk; bread so named seldom had little to do with actual French baking practice.

I wouldn't have had a clue about shaping these biscuits were it not for my grandmother. The recipe made it clear that the bread was shaped by hand, "as for common soda biscuits," but said nothing as to how. Then, one afternoon MaMa and I were talking about bread. She had not made biscuits in more than thirty years, and could only halfway talk her way through, but as she talked I noticed her hands. They were still going through the motions that her conscious mind had forgotten, the shaping that her mother and grandmother had taught her. It was a rare glimpse through a rapidly closing window on the mid-nineteenth century. My grandmother's recollection, burned into her mind by rote practice, is hardly conclusive, but the shape survives as "cat's head" biscuits, and I am convinced that it is how they were done.

For the sponge:

1/2 cup water

1/2 cup milk, scalded and cooled to less than 90 degrees F

1/4 teaspoon active dry yeast, or 1/2 ounce compressed yeast

5 ounces unbleached all-purpose flour (about 1 cup)

For the dough:

1 large egg

3/4 cup milk, scalded and cooled to 90 degrees F

20 ounces (1-1/4 pounds, about 4 cups) unbleached all-purpose flour, including a handful (about 1 ounce) whole-wheat pastry flour (optional)

2 teaspoons salt

2 tablespoons lard or unsalted butter

1. To make the sponge, mix together the water and milk and dissolve the yeast in it. Let it proof 10 minutes, then beat in the flour and beat until it's smooth.

2. Sprinkle the sponge with about a cup of the flour for the dough, but don't mix it in. Cover with a double-folded damp linen towel or plastic wrap, and set aside to rise until doubled and deep fissures form in the flour, from 3 to 4 hours, depending on the warmth of the room.

3. To make the dough, break the egg into a separate bowl and beat until light and smooth. Gradually stir in the milk, then pour it into the sponge and work it in until it's smooth.

4. Sift or whisk together the remaining flour and salt in a mixing bowl. Cut in the lard or butter until it resembles fine meal. Make a well in the center and pour in the sponge, scraping out any of it that may be clinging to the bowl. Gradually work it into the flour. The dough can be mixed through this step in a food processor; refer to the notes at the end of the recipe.

5. Turn the dough out onto a lightly floured work surface and start kneading. It should be a fairly soft dough, so don't be afraid to add a little water if it seems too stiff. Knead the dough for another 8 minutes, until it is elastic and smooth. Put it into a bowl and cover it with a damp, double-folded linen towel or plastic wrap. Let it rise until doubled, about 4 hours.

6. Lightly butter a baking sheet. Dust your hands with flour and pinch off a small handful of the dough. Roll it quickly into a 2-inch ball. Lay the ball onto the sheet and press it gently with the backs of your knuckles to flatten it. Repeat until all the dough has been shaped. Lay a clean linen towel over the biscuits and set them in a warm place to rise while the oven preheats.

7. Prepare the oven with a baking stone and pan (page 311), and preheat it to 450 degrees F for at least 30 minutes. When the biscuits have doubled, you may slash their tops in a star pattern if you like, but Mrs. Hill probably did not do this. Bake directly on the baking stone until nicely browned, about 18 to 20 minutes. Makes about 20 biscuits.

NOTES: *This is, as mentioned in the headnotes, a very old enriched dough. It was often shaped in other ways than the round one given here. You may roll it out to a 1/2-inch thickness and cut it into conventional biscuits, or roll it slightly thinner, cut it into rounds, crease them in the center with a knife, and fold them in half for "pocketbook" rolls, another popular shape. Most modern Southern cooks brush the tops of their yeast rolls with melted butter just before baking them.*

Food processor notes: The sponge and dough (steps 1–4) can be mixed in the food processor. Fit it with the plastic blade and put in the yeast and liquid. Pulse to mix and proof 10 minutes. Add 5 ounces of flour and pulse until smooth. Omit the topping of flour on the sponge, cover the bowl and let it double. When it has doubled, put the egg and additional liquid in the bowl with the starter and process until smooth. Sift or whisk together the remaining flour and salt and cut in the fat by hand. Add it to the sponge and process until it forms a smooth ball. Let it knead in the machine for 1 minute, then turn it out and finish the kneading by hand.

Sally Lunn

This light, rich tea bread is a classic English variation of brioche. Virginia has made Sally Lunn its own, complete with a popular legend that the bread was first made in America by the early settlers of Jamestown as a reminder of home, a story almost as picturesque as the English legends about the name, and equally as unlikely. Virginia's earliest author, Mary Randolph, gave no recipe for it. One of the earliest Southern recipes (though certainly not the first American one) that I've found is Annabella Hill's (*Mrs. Hill's New Cook Book*), and while she did have Virginia roots, they were a generation and three states removed. Sarah Rutledge included a recipe in *The Carolina Housewife* (1847). But sweetened and leavened with baking powder, it bore no resemblance to the original, which was not sweetened at all. Yeast-leavened Sally Lunn survives in the South, but is almost invariably sweetened.

Of the many stories about the origins of the name, the most plausible is that it is a corruption of an older French name, *soleil-lune*, or sun and moon, which the molded buns were supposed to have resembled.

1/4 teaspoon active dry yeast or 1/2 teaspoon compressed fresh yeast

1 cup milk, scalded and cooled to 90 degrees F

3 eggs

20 ounces (about 4 cups), unbleached all-purpose flour

1 teaspoon salt

2 ounces (4 tablespoons) butter, at room temperature

1 bundt or tube cake pan

1. Stir the yeast into the milk and let it proof 10 minutes. Break the eggs into a bowl, beat them lightly, and then stir the milk and yeast.

2. Put the flour and salt in a large mixing bowl and work the butter into it until it resembles coarse meal. Make a well in its center. Pour the milk and egg into it and gradually work it in until smooth. Turn the dough out onto a lightly floured surface and give it a light kneading, about 5 minutes. Gather it into a smooth ball. Wipe out the bowl and return the

dough to it. Cover with a damp, double-folded linen kitchen towel or plastic wrap, and set it aside to rise in a warm spot, about 4 to 6 hours, or in a not very warm one overnight or while you are at work.

3. When the dough has doubled, lightly punch it down and knead lightly for 1 to 2 minutes. Lightly butter and flour a bundt or tube cake pan as you would for a cake (page 333), or prepare large muffin tins in the same manner. Dust the dough with flour and roll it into a long sausage shape, or divide it into 12 equal balls. Place the single piece in the pan and gently press the ends together, or place the small balls into the muffin tins. Cover the pan with a damp towel and set it aside until it has doubled once again.

4. Prepare the oven with a baking stone and pan (page 311) and preheat it to 400 degrees F for at least 30 minutes, or position a rack in the lower third of the oven without the stone and preheat to 400 degrees F. Bake directly on the stone or in the lower third of the oven until the top is a light gold and the crumb is cooked through, about 30 minutes for the ring loaf, 20 minutes for buns. Makes 1 ring-shaped loaf or 12 buns.

NOTES: *Almost all modern Sally Lunn recipes today contain sugar, but the oldest American recipes do not. It began to appear, in very small doses, before mid-century and, thereafter, the proportion of sugar and liquid increased. Today, the sugar may be increased to as much as half a cup. This recipe remains faithful to the early versions. If you can get good cream, try Elizabeth David's recipe: omit the butter and substitute heavy cream (minimum 36% milk fat) for the milk, increasing the liquid to 1-1/2 cups.*

SOUTHERN BISCUITS AND QUICKBREADS

Ah, fluffy, light, Southern biscuits. Our most famous bread, served up in countless Southern fast-food diners and still the pride of many of our best cooks. As old as the hills. Well, no. Chemically leavened breads were known to Southern cooks by the end of the eighteenth century, but what most Southerners today recognize as biscuits date from no earlier than the second quarter of the nineteenth century. Originally, they were only served at breakfast—their quick mixing and rising a boon to the sleepy cook who had to be up before the sun.

Before the recipes, here are some notes to remember on the leaven and other ingredients for quick bread:

On the leavening: After some of the sharp things that I have said about baking powder elsewhere, I have braced myself for an avalanche of complaints. Actually, I have nothing against baking powder properly and discreetly used in its place. However, I do have an old-fashioned and somewhat cranky preference for single-acting baking powder. It was the leaven originally used in these recipes and is what they were formulated with. Single-acting powder is a simple combination of acid and alkali, usually cream of tartar and bicarbonate of soda. It is no longer commercially made, but is easy to make at home, and a recipe follows. Double-acting powder contains both the acid and alkali leaven, which goes to work the moment the bread is mixed, and a second, heat-activated chemical that begins working only after the bread is exposed to heat.

If you prefer using double-acting baking powder, look for an aluminum-free brand such as Rumford. The most common mistake people make using commercial double-acting baking powder is that they use far too much. When the same quantity is used as is called for with single-acting powder, the rising is spectacular, but there is a price paid for it. The bread is less substantial and invariably has a sour, chemical aftertaste.

Single-Acting Baking Powder

It is best to make this in small quantities and to store it in a tightly sealed, airtight container. Cream of tartar is available in the baking section of many markets and at drug stores.

3 level tablespoons cream of tartar

2 level tablespoons bicarbonate of soda (baking soda)

3 level tablespoons rice flour or plain wheat flour

1. Combine all the ingredients in an airtight container and shake until they are well mixed.

2. Store tightly covered and away from moisture. It won't keep well, so try to use it up within a month. Makes 1/2 cup.

On the type of flour to use: Flour made from soft winter wheat is used in all Southern baking, but its low-gluten content makes it especially critical for biscuits and pastry. If you can't get it locally, it can be ordered from selected mills, or use a local brand of unbleached pastry flour (not cake flour), which is exactly the same thing. For ordering information and more on soft-wheat flours, refer to the notes on ingredients, (pages 307 to 308), at the beginning of this chapter.

On working the dough: Probably the most common mistake in biscuit making lies in overworking the dough. Overworking melts the fat and excites the glutens into action, resulting in heavy, greasy, tough bread. However, biscuit dough does need to be worked a little or the bread will be uneven and crumbly. The secret is a light, judicious, and preferably cool, hand. The exception is Beaten Biscuits (page 320), which, as their name suggests, are worked a great deal.

Soda Biscuits

These are the classic original Southern raised biscuits. The leavening is achieved by the reaction between soda and the acid in buttermilk. If you can't get buttermilk where you live, you can substitute a good-quality, all-natural whole milk yogurt, thinning it to buttermilk consistency with a little milk if necessary.

The sour milk does more than activate the leaven, however. It lends a pleasant sweetness and tenderness to the crumb and makes an especially tender biscuit.

10 ounces (about 2 cups) unbleached all-purpose flour

1 teaspoon Single-Acting Baking Powder (page 318), or 1/2 teaspoon commercial double-acting powder

1 teaspoon baking soda

1/2 teaspoon salt

2 tablespoons lard or unsalted butter (see notes)

1 cup whole milk buttermilk or plain, whole-milk yogurt thinned to buttermilk consistency with milk or water

1. Position a rack in the upper third of the oven and preheat it to 450 degrees F. Lightly grease a 9 x 14-inch baking sheet.

2. Sift or whisk together the flour, baking powder, soda, and salt into a mixing bowl. Cut in the lard with a pastry blender, pastry fork, or two knives until it resembles coarse meal (raw grits or polenta) with lumps no larger than small peas.

3. Make a well in the center and pour in the buttermilk. Using a wooden spoon and as few strokes as possible, quickly stir the ingredients together.

4. Lightly flour a smooth work surface (wood or plastic laminate is best, but marble will work) and turn the dough out onto it. Flour your hands and gently push the dough away from you to flatten it. Fold it in half, gently press it flat with the heels of your hands, and give it a quarter turn. Repeat this until the dough is just smooth, about 8 to 12 folds. Don't knead—but fold, so that the dough just holds together without activating the glutens, thereby making them tough.

5. Lightly dust the work surface and dough with flour and roll or pat it out 1/2 to 3/4 inch thick. Dip a biscuit cutter in flour and quickly cut the dough into biscuits, going straight into it without twisting the cutter, which would seal part of the side and cause uneven rising. Scraps can be gently reworked with care: gather and use the folding technique 2 to 3 times, then cut as before. Lay the biscuits on the baking sheet about 1 inch apart. (Some cooks put the biscuits close together so that they rise against one another and form a cluster that is torn apart after baking.) Many traditional cooks let the biscuits rise for a few minutes before baking them.

6. Bake in the upper third of the oven until golden brown on the top, about 10 to 12 minutes. Immediately remove them from the pan, pile them into a napkin-lined basket, and serve at once. Makes 1 dozen biscuits.

NOTES: *Lard makes by far and away the best biscuit dough and is the most traditional flavor. But there is more than flavor at work here; lard actually helps to tenderize the crumb. If you aren't able to use it, unsalted butter makes acceptable biscuits and is preferable to vegetable shortening.*

Beaten Biscuits

"People . . . who enjoy a physical relationship with their doughs should be in heaven here. There is no getting around the activity. Fifteen minutes of heavy, consistent abuse is the minimum."
—Bill Neal, *Biscuits, Spoon Bread, and Sweet Potato Pie* (1990)

These are true biscuits in the European sense: crisp and short, though not quite as thin as English biscuits (what we would call cookies or crackers). As Mr. Neal suggested, their name is literal; you mix the dough and then beat the hell out of it with a mallet or rolling pin until it blisters and makes a distinct cracking sound. Many Southern households had a box contraption with ribbed twin rollers for this job, like an oversized pasta machine. The dough was put through it over and over until the blistering and cracking began. I know this sounds like a lot of work, but they aren't nearly as difficult as they sound, and beating the dough is a fine way to take out your frustrations. It's the one time that being in a bad mood can be a good thing; as Mr. Neal put it, you can't be too vigorous or too physical. The advantage of these biscuits lies in the fact that they can be made in quantity and stored for weeks in a sealed tin box.

As the African cooks who so patiently beat this dough exited Southern kitchens, the biscuits began to disappear as well, and probably would be totally archaic now were it not for the advent of food processors. The food processor sees plenty of work in my kitchen, especially when I am baking, and beating biscuits is one task that it does fairly well, with far less trouble and noise, as long as you give them a finishing beating by hand to develop the flaky layers that are the hallmark of a true beaten biscuit.

As a reminder, use only soft winter wheat flour for these biscuits. Even if you are mixing the dough in the food processor, be sure to read all of the recipe before starting. You will still need to be familiar with the hand-beating method. For the hand method, you'll need a heavy, *unbreakable* weapon for beating the dough such as a wooden rolling pin or mallet. I have even known of people who used a sledgehammer or the flat side of an ax. It doesn't matter, as long as it's heavy and unbreakable. Also, the work surface must be sturdy enough to withstand all the pounding. If you have a marble or tile countertop in your kitchen, *DO NOT* use it. It's a good idea to put away anything fragile or made of glass or the vibrations could cause them to shatter. The fat and water should be cold to keep the dough from overheating while it is being beaten.

20 ounces (about 4 cups) unbleached soft-wheat flour	4 ounces (1/2 cup) chilled lard (preferred) or unsalted butter
Salt	About 1-1/2 cups ice water

1. Position a rack in the upper third of the oven and preheat it to 400 degrees F. Sift or whisk the flour together with a healthy pinch of salt into a large mixing bowl. Cut the shortening into 1/2-inch bits, handling it as little as possible (if it starts getting oily, chill it again). Add it to the flour and, with a pastry blender or two knives, cut it in until it resembles coarse meal.

2. Stir in enough ice water, a little at a time (start with 3/4 cup; you may need as little as that to as much as 1-1/2 cups in all), until a smooth, but stiff dough is formed.

3. Put the dough onto a lightly floured, sturdy work surface. Using a flat mallet or wood rolling pin, beat it flat and fold it in half, then beat it flat again. Keep this up until it blisters, about 20 minutes. Those who adhere to counting the strokes give anywhere from 300 to 1,001, but the real test is the appearance and feel of the dough. It should be blistering distinctly, and be smooth and slick, but not sticky.

4. Lightly grease a large baking sheet and have it close at hand. Dust the work surface again with a little flour, roll out the dough 1/2 inch thick, and cut it with a small biscuit cutter, no more than 1-1/4 inches in diameter. Lay the biscuits on the prepared baking sheet with about 1/2 inch between them. They won't swell as much as regular biscuits, and needn't be spaced too far apart. Prick through them with a large dinner fork that has widely spaced, preferably round, tines, making two or three rows of pricks in the center. There used to be a special cutter available in the South that had sharp prongs built into it, like some kind of miniature medieval torturing device. If you come across one, it will make short work of the cutting and pricking.

5. Put the pan on the upper rack and bake the biscuits until they are very lightly colored, about 25 or 30 minutes. The outside should be crisp and the inside slightly soft, but quite dry. Cool them on a rack and store them in airtight tins. Makes 4 dozen biscuits.

NOTES: *To mix and beat the dough in the food processor, it is especially important that the fat and water be cold, as the machine will otherwise overheat the dough. It also helps to chill the processor blade before using it. Put the flour and salt into the bowl of the processor fitted with a steel blade and pulse to sift. Cut the fat into 1/2-inch pieces, add it, and pulse until it resembles coarse meal. With the motor running, immediately begin pouring in the ice water through the feed tube. When the dough is smooth and stiff, stop adding water; you may not need the entire amount. Let the machine run for about 2 minutes, then turn it off and finish the beating by hand (see step 3), folding and beating no less than 8 times, and preferably twice that many, for about 5 minutes longer, to introduce the characteristic flaky layering within the biscuits.*

If you have an old biscuit break and want to use it, omit the beating and roll it through the machine, folding the dough in half each time as you would when kneading pasta dough through the rollers of the pasta machine. It will take just as long as the hand hammering method, but doesn't require quite as much elbow grease.

CORNBREADS

Wheat bread continued to be the staple of city dwellers and planter aristocracy in the South, but even in wealthier households, Indian bread—that is, bread made from cornmeal—was known and relished. For slaves and poor small farmers, it was the daily bread, and the Southern staff of life came to be distinguished by the crisp grit of meal. At first it was basic, primitive, bread: a thick paste of meal, water, and salt baked either in the hot ash of the fire, directly on the heated hearth, before it on a board, or over it on the blade of a hoe. But, by the middle of the nineteenth century, it had evolved into the bread that we recognize today: cornmeal mixed with salt, rendered pork fat, and sour milk, then baked in a heavy, preheated iron pan. It changed little until well into the twentieth century, and is still one of the most satisfying breads in the world.

It is popular nowadays to attribute cornbread entirely to Native Americans. We do know that American Indians made simple bread from maize long before Europeans arrive here—there were what amounted to tortillas in Central America and corn pone (ash cakes) in the north, to name just two, and probably others—Pre-Colombian cookery is poorly documented. However, coarse meal mixed with water and baked on a heated stone or wrapped in leaves and hot ashes was the first bread that anyone knew, and was pretty nearly universal. The name "pone," at least, is Native American, and natives certainly taught the Europeans to cultivate maize, so their contribution can't be discounted, but it must be pointed out that the basic concept of these breads was already known to the colonists. Virtually the same techniques had been used in Europe for centuries before colonization began. There are the oatcakes of England and Scotland, to name just two. For the colonists, it would have been simpler to keep on making the griddle and ash cakes they had known at home, merely substituting cornmeal for oat, barley, or rye meal. It is also significant to note that the colonists used plain corn meal ground from whole corn, whereas the native breads were probably made with *masa*—meal made from *nixtamal*, or lye-soaked hominy—a very different thing.

On enrichments: As soon as European and African cooks began using pans to make cornbread, they began adding various enrichments to the basic paste of meal and water. The most telling is the addition of more liquid. Slack dough makes softer bread, as a rule. Scalding the meal in the heated liquid also softened the bread. Later came eggs, milk, and melted fat, all conspiring for a more tender, richer crumb.

On the use of iron pans: Though some Southern cooks use tin cake pans for their cornbread, the best bread is made in cast iron. Traditionally, it was a Dutch oven or a spider (a lidded iron skillet raised on legs so that it could sit over hot coals). Still used by hunters and fishermen who camp out, this old method is rediscovered on many coastal hearths whenever a hurricane knocks out the electricity. At home, in a conventional range oven, modern cooks simply use a well-seasoned regular iron skillet.

The secret to the crackling crisp crust that Southerners prize is to thoroughly preheat the iron pan so that the batter actually sizzles when you pour it in. This practice first begins to appear in Southern cookery books as early as Lettice Bryan's *Kentucky Housewife* (1839). It is seldom actually mentioned, I suspect because it was taken for granted. Of course, an equally convincing argument can be made in the other direction—that it was seldom mentioned because it was not at all widespread. Moreover, there are old recipes that specify tin pans, which do nothing to benefit the bread when preheated. I believe the preheated pan was universal in part because it is common in modern kitchens, and, historically most other Indian meal breads—johnnycakes, hoe cakes, lacy cakes, and the like—were cooked on a preheated griddle (or hoe blade), which produces a crisp crust and often a lacy edge, a texture that must surely have been preferred.

Soda Cornbread

The old combination of soda and buttermilk in this recipe makes a sweet, light-tasting cornbread. It was not, however, the earliest form of leavened cornbread on Southern tables. The old formula for "Indian" bread, that is, bread that was made by Europeans from corn (Indian) meal, as set down by Mary Randolph, was actually leavened with real yeast; chemical leaven was not mentioned. We do know that some Indians did use a form of chemical leavening in their bread—potassium carbonate from wood ash—but just how widespread this was is a matter of debate. Chemical leavenings were already known and used by European Americans even before the Revolution. However, Mrs. Randolph made spare use of them. Later, cooks learned to combine potassium carbonate or bicarbonate of soda with sour milk to boost it's leavening action, and eventually the bread we know today evolved, replacing the old yeast bread altogether, which did not survive the nineteenth-century.

2 cups stone-ground cornmeal

2 teaspoons baking soda

1 teaspoon salt

2 eggs

1-1/2 cups whole milk buttermilk, or plain, whole-milk yogurt thinned to buttermilk consistency with milk or water

4 tablespoons rendered bacon fat, or melted butter or lard

A well-seasoned cast-iron 9-inch round, stick, or muffin pan

1. Position a rack in the upper third of the oven and preheat it to 450 degrees F. When it has reached that temperature, lightly, but thoroughly grease a 9-inch iron skillet, two 7-well iron cornstick pans, or a 12-well muffin pan and heat in the oven for at least 10 minutes. Meanwhile, stir together the meal, soda, and salt in a large mixing bowl. In a separate bowl, beat the eggs until smooth and beat in the buttermilk and 2 tablespoons of the melted fat.

2. When the pan is well heated, make a well in the center of the meal and pour in the milk and eggs. Using as few strokes as possible, quickly stir it together until there are no dry lumps.

3. Take the pan out of the oven and add to it the remaining fat. It should just cover the bottom. If you are using a cornstick or muffin pan, rub the fat equally into each well with a thick cloth. If using butter, use a cold stick still wrapped in its paper and rub a little into each well. It will sizzle if the pan is hot enough. (If it doesn't, put the pan back into the oven for about 5 minutes more.) Immediately pour the batter into the pan. It must sizzle when it touches the pan or the pan is not hot enough. If you are using a cornstick or muffin pan, fill each well about 2/3 full.

4. Bake in the upper third of the oven until golden brown and the center is springy, but firm, about 25 minutes for cornsticks or muffins and 35 minutes for a skillet cake. Immediately invert the pan over a plate (for the skillet) or a linen towel (for sticks or muffins). The bread should come right out of the pan. Serve piping hot with plenty of good butter. Makes one 9-inch cake or 12 to 14 corn sticks or muffins.

Crackling Bread: Cracklings are the solids left from rendering pork fat into lard (page 44). They've been used to enrich regional breads in Europe for thousands of years, and have been traditional in Southern cornbread for at least two centuries. To make crackling bread, substitute 1 cup of broken up or roughly chopped cracklings for the 2 tablespoons of fat called for in the batter. Mix them into the meal with the soda and salt in step 1. Bake in a preheated 9-inch iron skillet that is greased with 1 tablespoon of lard or bacon drippings.

Mary Lizzie's Lacy Cakes

My dear friend Mary Lizzie Kitchengs wanted it made clear, up front, that she was nowhere near old enough to be included in an anthology of nineteenth-century food. But her Georgia lacy cakes are. The batter is dropped from a spoon onto a lightly greased, hot iron pan, causing fine air holes to form all around the sizzling edges, hence, "lacy" cakes. Her recipe is classic, very much like the one set down by Mrs. Hill a hundred and forty years ago. Mrs. Kitchengs offered this advice: "Your fat had better be hot, I mean *hot*, but for goodness sake, don't let it catch fire! And be ready to stay right there with it; don't turn your back even for a second."

1 cup stone-ground corn meal	Bacon drippings or lard, for greasing the pan
1/2 teaspoon salt	Artery-clogging butter and sorghum syrup
1-1/2 cups water	(optional), for serving

1. Sift the meal and salt into a mixing bowl. Make a well in the center and pour in the water. Mix the batter together with a few swift strokes of the spoon, working it as little as possible. Set the batter aside for a few minutes.

2. Heat an iron griddle or skillet over medium-high heat. Lightly grease it with fat and let it heat until the fat is almost smoking.

3. Quickly stir the batter again. It should be a little thinner than pancake batter; if it seems too thick to pour easily from the spoon, stir in a little more water. With a large spoon with a pointed tip that will hold at least 2 tablespoons of the batter, dip the batter and pour it from the end of the spoon onto the griddle. It should make a lively sizzle when it hits the fat, or the pan is not quite hot enough. Cook for about 1 minute, until the bottom is nicely browned and the edges are lacy. Turn and brown the other side. The outer crust should be crisp but the cake should not be hard, so be careful not to overcook it. Remove it with a slotted spatula and keep it warm.

4. Add more fat to the pan and repeat until all the batter is cooked. Serve the cakes with lots of artery-clogging butter and, if liked, sorghum syrup. Makes about a dozen cakes.

NOTES: *All kidding aside, if you are unable to cook with animal fat, substitute olive oil (not extra virgin, which has too low a smoking point). It makes delicious lacy cakes. A good second choice is corn oil, which allows the taste of the meal to remain pristine. No matter which fat you use, go easy—these are meant to be griddlecakes, not fried bread. Too much fat will make them heavy, not enough will prevent the lace from forming on the edges. I've found that the least amount of fat you can manage, the better.*

This is unorthodox treatment, but lacy cakes make a spectacular dessert when rolled around a spoonful of Fresh Peach Sauce (page 379) or your favorite fruit preserves. Dust with powdered sugar and serve with a dollop of Lettice Bryan's Cold Cream Sauce (page 378) or whipped cream or Crème Fraîche (page 48). The lacy cakes get brittle as they cool, so roll them while still piping hot.

Spoon Bread

This lovely, soft soufflé-like bread has become such a hallmark of Southern baking, that Bill Neal named his fine book on baking *Biscuits, Spoon Bread and Sweet Potato Pie.* "Spoon bread," however, is a name that has only been associated with the bread since the end of the nineteenth century, having evolved from the way it is served—literally, with a spoon. The bread is much older than the name, appearing in cookbooks under older names like "mush bread" or "batter bread." Rarely were the eggs separated in older recipes, and the texture was naturally less like a soufflé than most modern versions, which usually call for separately beaten whites.

The utensil in which batter bread was baked varies from region to region and cook to cook. Mary Randolph and many early Virginians baked the batter in small individual pans, like popovers. Others have used square tin cake pans, still others, pottery pudding dishes. Some recipes even suggest china teacups. My own preference is a standard round soufflé dish.

Baking powder has an important place in Southern baking, but late in the nineteenth century, it began to appear in places where it did not belong. Spoon bread was one of those places. Though the dose was minimal and did help the novice insure that her bread would not fall, it is omitted here. It is superfluous when the eggs are well beaten and carefully incorporated.

3 cups half-and-half	1 teaspoon salt
1 cup fine cornmeal	3 large eggs, separated
3 tablespoons butter	

1. Position a rack in the center of the oven and preheat it to 350 degrees F. Prepare the bottom of a double boiler with water. Bring it to a boil and reduce the heat to medium-low. Scald the half-and-half in the top part of the double boiler over direct heat and then set it over the simmering water.

2. Stirring constantly with a whisk or wooden spoon, gradually add the meal, adding it in a thin, but steady, stream, either from between your fingers or from a pitcher with a good pouring spout. When all the meal is incorporated, cook, stirring constantly, until it forms a thick mush, about 5 minutes. Take it from the heat, beat in the butter and salt, and set it aside to cool slightly.

3. Lightly butter an 8-inch soufflé dish or round casserole (or 8-inch square one that is at least 2 inches deep). Separate the eggs, putting the whites in a clean metal or glass bowl. Beat the yolks until light and smooth, and stir them into the mush. With a clean wire whisk or mixer, beat the egg whites to stiff but not dry peaks. Fold them gently but thoroughly into the mush. Pour the batter into the prepared baking dish and bake it in the center of the oven until it's puffed and golden brown, about 45 minutes. It should be set, but still soft, like a soufflé. Serve at once directly from the baking dish with a large spoon. Serves 4.

TWO CLASSIC SOUTHERN FRIED BREADS
Cornbread Fritters

Hush Puppies

These morsels of fried cornmeal batter are something of an enigma. They're so commonplace in Southern cookery today that it seems as if they have always been around. There's even a popular legend, supported by early recipes titled "fried pone," crediting them to Native Americans. However, the earliest recipes I have found that are recognizably like modern hush puppies date no earlier than turn-of-the-century New Orleans. They were called *beignets de mais*, and were lightly sweetened puffs of cornmeal, egg, and milk, deep-fat-fried and dusted with sugar. Only in the second decade of the twentieth-century did unsweetened recipes for fried pone and cornmeal fritters begin to appear, and I have been unable to date them back any further.

As to the name "hush puppy," it, at least, can definitely be said to be modern; it appears to go back no further than World War I, if that far. The earliest that I have found so named are in the 1941 edition of Mrs. Dull's *Southern Cooking* (with three recipes), closely followed by Marjorie Kinnan Rawlings' *Cross Creek Cookery* (1942). Both ladies talk of them as if the name were commonplace by their day. As to the name's origins, I'll leave that to the folk etymologists. The claim that it originated in Georgia is not supported by any of the Georgia books (Mrs. Dull's original recipe in the 1928 edition of *Southern Cooking*, is called Fried Pone, and Harriet Ross Colquitt (*The Savannah Cook Book*, 1933) titled hers corn bread fritters. Yet all these women were from Georgia, so it is possible. Mrs. Rawlings' story—that the name evolved when hunters used fried bits of cornbread batter to placate their whining dogs—is the one most often repeated and is as good as any.

Modern hush puppies know no in between. Like the little girl with the curl: when they are good, they are very, very good, and when not good, well, nothing is worse.

2 cups whole milk buttermilk or plain, whole milk yogurt thinned to buttermilk consistency with milk or water	1/2 teaspoon salt
	1/2 cup finely minced green or regular yellow onion (optional)
2 cups stone-ground cornmeal	2 large eggs
1 tablespoon butter	Lard or oil, for frying
1 teaspoon baking soda	

1. Bring the milk almost to a boil over low heat. Gradually stir in the meal in a thin stream until it is incorporated. Turn off the heat and stir in the butter, baking soda, and salt. If you want to make modern hush puppies, stir in the minced onion. Let it cool slightly.

2. Separate the eggs into separate bowls and beat the yolks until smooth. Add them to the batter. Separately beat the egg whites to stiff but not dry peaks and fold them into the batter.

3. Put enough lard or oil into a deep skillet or deep-fat fryer to cover the bottom by at least an inch, but no more than halfway up the sides. Heat it over medium-high heat until the fat is very hot, but not smoking, about 375 degrees F.

4. Drop the batter by spoonfuls into the fat until the pan is full but not crowded. Fry until they are a rich brown, about 3 or 4 minutes, turning once if necessary. Take them up with a wire frying skimmer, drain well, and blot briefly on absorbent paper. Pile them into a napkin-lined basket or platter and serve at once. Makes about 2 dozen, serving about 8.

Maum Peggy's Breakfast Fry Breads

Breakfast Rice Fritters or Croquettes

"Maum" and "Da" are two Gullah names for the African-American nurses and cooks who were the pillars of so many of Charleston's white households. Their contribution to Southern culture and gastronomy is as enormously important as it is undocumented. Maum Peggy, for example, was one of only five African cooks whose contributions to the *Carolina Rice Cook Book* (1901) were directly credited. Her "breakfast fry breads" are, of course, rice fritters, similar to the *beignets de riz* of Southern France and rice calas of the Creole West Indies and New Orleans. They are to be found virtually everywhere where there are African cooks.

Maum Peggy's fritter batter is thin, more like griddle cake batter than the stiffer dough used for calas. You may vary this basic recipe by doubling the amount of rice, adding a little sugar and nutmeg, or onions and herbs, alone, or with a cup of grated ham or cooked chicken.

In the Carolina and Georgia Lowcountry "fritter" is used to describe other fried dumplings, but those made with rice are invariably known as croquettes. They were a versatile workhorse in the Lowcountry kitchen, pressed into service not only as a plain or sweet breakfast fritter, but as a side dish, dessert, or, when mixed with cooked meat, even the main course.

1 cup Basic Boiled Rice (page 289)	Salt
1/2 cup unbleached all-purpose wheat flour	Lard or oil for frying
1 large egg	Powdered sugar (optional)
1 cup plain, whole milk yogurt, or a scant cup of whole milk buttermilk	

1. Put the rice and flour into a large mixing bowl and work them together until they are well mixed. The rice should still hold its shape, so don't overwork it.

2. Break the egg into a separate bowl, beat it lightly, and then beat in the yogurt or buttermilk. If the rice has already been salted, it shouldn't need more salt. If not, add a healthy pinch of salt and beat until it dissolves.

3. Make a well in the rice and flour and pour in the egg and milk. Stir lightly, but thoroughly, until it is a smooth batter.

4. Put in enough lard or vegetable oil to cover the bottom of a deep skillet by 1/4 inch. Heat it over medium-high heat until it is hot, but not smoking, about 375 degrees F. Drop in the batter by large spoonfuls (about 2 tablespoons per croquette). Fry, turning once, until they are a uniform, light golden brown. Lift them out with tongs or a wire frying skimmer, drain well, and blot briefly on absorbent paper. If you like, dust them lightly with powdered sugar, but serve them piping hot. Makes about 2 dozen, serving 8 to 10.

NOTES: *Though not traditional, yogurt produces finer fritters than commercial buttermilk, and I prefer it in this recipe. The fritter batter can be deep-fat-fried, but the fat should not be more than an inch deep. Otherwise, the thin batter will separate when it is dropped into the fat. For sturdier croquettes, double the amount of rice. These fritters needn't be confined to breakfast; they are a fine accompaniment for any meal.*

RICE BREAD

Though breads made with rice and rice flour are not unique to the rice-growing regions of the Carolina and Georgia Lowcountry, these types of bread have a long tradition in our part of the South. Rice was cheap and plentiful; however, it was more than just an economical filler in expensive wheat bread. It often helped improve the shelf life of the bread and lent a rich moistness to the crumb. In *The Carolina Housewife*, as one would expect, Sarah Rutledge recorded dozens of rice breads that were common in Charleston households. But Georgia native Annabella Hill, who never lived in the rice-growing region of the coast, also included an impressive collection of rice breads in *Mrs. Hill's New Cook Book*, showing us that these breads were once common throughout the region.

Spider Rice Bread

Cooking bread in a spider (a cast-iron skillet on legs) is as Southern as it gets. In this venerable recipe from the Carolina Lowcountry, leftover boiled rice is pressed into service as a quick breakfast bread by mixing it with wheat flour and enriching egg. Though I here cross-reference Basic Boiled Rice for preparing the rice for the bread, you can naturally make it ahead or use 2 cups of leftover rice.

You needn't have a spider, unless you are trying to cook the bread over an open hearth; a regular 9-inch diameter cast-iron skillet will suffice.

2 cups Basic Boiled Rice (page 289), made with 2 teaspoons salt
2 cups unbleached flour
3 large eggs, well beaten
1 tablespoon unsalted butter

1. Position a rack in the center of the oven and preheat it to 400 degrees F. Put the rice in a large mixing bowl and, if it has just been cooked, let it cool completely.

2. Sift the flour into the rice and work it in with a wooden spoon, but not until the rice grains are disintegrated. They should still have their shape. It will be lumpy, loose, and yet slightly sticky.

3. Add the eggs and stir lightly until the dough is smooth and almost like a thick batter.

4. Put the butter into the skillet and heat it in the oven for about 10 minutes. When it is smoking hot and beginning to brown, carefully swirl the pan to coat it and pour in the dough. Smooth the top with the back of a wooden spoon or spatula. Bake in the center of the oven for about 35 or 40 minutes, until golden brown and firm at the center. The inside of the bread should be very moist, but not pasty. Makes one 9-inch round cake.

NOTES: *This bread can also be used as a side dish, instead of the more usual rice, pasta, or potato dishes. You can also bake the bread in individual muffins. A cast-iron muffin pan is preferable, but if you don't have one, a conventional muffin tin will suffice. Preheat the pan and, using a thick cloth, rub each well with the butter just before adding the batter. Completely fill each well with the batter and bake until the muffins are golden brown and firm, about 25 minutes.*

CAKES

"The process of compounding and baking of cakes being a delicate operation, it should not be left to careless hands, but should be carried on under the close supervision of the housewife."

—Annabella Hill, *Mrs. Hill's New Cook Book*, 1867

"Do not attempt to make cake without fresh eggs. Cream of tartar, soda, and yeast powders are poor substitutes for these."

—Marion Cabell Tyree, *Housekeeping in Old Virginia*, 1879

"Soda is used largely in modern cookery, entering into almost all bread, cakes, etc. It does certainly abridge the watchfulness, labor, and dexterity of the cook. As to its healthfulness, we leave that to the scientific investigators of physiology and hygiene."

—Theresa Clementine Brown, *Theresa C. Brown's Modern Domestic Cookery*, 1871

All cakes were originally leavened with yeast or beaten eggs. We would do well today to heed Mrs. Tyree's pointed remarks about fresh eggs. As Miss Brown noted, baking powder covers all manner of deficiencies in the cook's ability, but can in no way compete with the delicacy and character of one leavened with well-beaten fresh eggs. Yet that isn't to say that baking powder cakes are not and cannot be quite good; they can be. They occupy an important place in the repertory of the Southern baker. But they are not a substitute for an egg-leavened cake (or for one that is correctly leavened with aerated fat) and should not be treated as such. Nor should baking powder be used as a crutch in recipes where it does not rightly belong.

Cakes are the soul of a celebration, and any celebration worth a cake is worth a good one. Why people use boxed mixes is completely beyond me. The only thing a mix does, so far as I can see, is save the time it takes to measure the dry ingredients. If you want a cake that's edible, it still needs butter and eggs. And you still do the mixing, which is the hard part. Oh, well, we live in a time when speed is regarded above any other virtue. But if most of us took a trip to the average retirement community and saw how people fill the time they've "saved," we might well wonder if it was worth it.

Types of Pans

For all the air-leavened cakes that follow, the best pan is an angel food, or tube cake pan—a large round cake pan with a hollow, funnel-like tube in the center, but the cakes can also be baked in a bundt (ring-cake) pan or regular bread 9-inch loaf pan, unless noted otherwise.

Preparing the pans. Except for angel-food cake, which must adhere to the sides of the pan in order to rise properly, the bottom and sides of the pan are buttered and floured to prevent the cake from sticking. Lightly rub the pan with butter until the entire surface is thinly, but thoroughly coated. Add 2 to 3 tablespoons of flour and gently shake and tilt the pan until it is completely coated with a thin film of flour, then shake out the excess.

Pound Cake

(Master Recipe)

This ancient classic of the English baker's art has been an integral part of Southern baking for so long that there are Southerners who believe we invented it. The name derives, of course, from the quantity of the principal ingredients: A pound each of flour, butter, sugar, and (ideally) eggs. Ten eggs is the usual quantity, and some old recipes were fastidious enough to direct: "weigh twelve eggs; take their weight of butter, sugar, and flour." It's still the best insurance: as John Martin Taylor sternly reminded me, the weight (and moisture content) of eggs can vary substantially, depending on their freshness. I offer no volume measures for this cake; the proportions must be equal weights to assure success. There are good bakers who don't weigh anything, but they have an experienced hand and keen eye. Weighing helps insure consistent success and prevent a lot of heartache, especially for novices.

This cake was originally leavened only with the air that was trapped by beating it into the butter, or, occasionally, with separately beaten egg whites. The density of the crumb depended on whether the eggs were added whole or separately. When the whites are beaten stiff and folded in separately, the cake will rise more because of the additional trapped air. (It will also settle a bit as it cools, like a soufflé.) Either way, the cake certainly doesn't need the artificial boost of baking powder, but it gradually came to be added as insurance against sad streaks. By the third quarter of the nineteenth century, a small dose of it was usual. Most of the best bakers that I know today use a little; but with care, you will find that the cake doesn't really need it.

You will need a round tube cake (angel food cake), or bundt cake, or two 9-inch loaf pans.

1 pound (4 sticks) unsalted butter at room temperature

1 pound granulated sugar

10 large eggs, or 8, if very fresh (see headnotes), at room temperature

1 pound plain, unbleached Southern soft-wheat flour, pastry flour, or all-purpose flour

1/2 cup heavy cream or 1/4 cup each of bourbon (or brandy) and sherry (or 1/2 cup of either)

1 tablespoon Homemade Vanilla Extract (page 40), rosewater, or 1 teaspoon commercial extract

1. Position a rack in the center of the oven and preheat it to 325 degrees F. Butter and flour a tube (angel food) cake or bundt pan, or two 9-inch loaf pans as directed on page 333. With a wooden spoon or a mixer fitted with a paddle or rotary beaters, cream the butter well, and gradually beat in the sugar until it is very light and fluffy.

2. Break the eggs one at a time into a separate bowl. You may also separate the yolks and whites in separate metal or glass bowls if you want to try separately beating the whites.

3. Have the flour ready near the mixing bowl. Mix in the egg yolks or whole eggs and flour a little at a time, alternating one yolk or egg and a little of the flour, until both are incorporated. Beat in the liquid and seasonings until the batter is smooth.

4. If you're adding the whites separately, beat them with a whisk or a mixer fitted with a whisk until they form firm, but not dry peaks. Fold them gently, but thoroughly into the batter.

5. Spoon the batter into the prepared pans. Run a table knife through it in a back and forth S motion to take out any large air bubbles. Bake in the center of the oven for about 1-1/2 hours, depending on the shape of the pan. If egg whites have been beaten and added separately, the cake will rise a good deal more and the top will split. Make sure the cake is completely done before taking it from the oven; if you take it out before the center is completely done, it will collapse and have what Southerners call a "sad streak." A clean straw or cake tester inserted into the center should come out clean. Cool the cake completely before taking it out of the pan. If you've added separately beaten whites, the cake will settle some as it cools. Makes 1 tube or 2 loaf cakes.

NOTES: *Bonnie Carter and John Martin Taylor, both experienced bakers, suggest this cooling method as good insurance against sad streaks: Bake the cake until a straw comes out clean, about 1-1/2 hours, turn off the oven, crack the door, and leave the cake in the oven until cold.*

Variations: This batter is a classic base for a number of old-style cakes. Once you master it, a number of old classics are at your disposal merely by varying the flavoring and icing. For an orange or lemon cake, omit the vanilla or rose water and add the grated zest of an orange or lemon in step 5. Substitute the fruit's juice for part or all of the liquids (the cream or alcohol). For a chocolate pound cake, substitute 1/2 cup of cocoa for that amount of flour.

A Rich Fruitcake

Fruitcakes have long been the perfect centerpiece for all kinds of celebrations, including weddings, and have not always been banished to Christmas. A really good one, rich with spices and delicate dried fruit, is the best possible cake, and cause enough in itself for celebration. But given what mostly passes for fruitcake these days—dull, dry crumb tarted up with unnaturally colored, syrupy candied fruit, it's no wonder they've fallen from favor and become the brunt of so many jokes.

Sometimes called plum cake in England, fruit cake also went by that name in a few early Southern books, though, like plum pudding, there weren't actually any plums in it. Neither were there lurid, indigestible red and green cherries, syrupy slices of candied pineapple, or hard, tasteless chunks of candied fruit peelings.

I know a lot of people who claim to hate fruitcake, but no one who hates this one. If you really want to up the ante, add another pound of dried fruit such as figs, dates, or even pitted prunes cut in small pieces. The citron in those days was a preserved melon, and not the candied peel used today. John Martin Taylor, following the lead of old Carolina and Georgia cooks, substitutes watermelon rind preserves and it makes a spectacular difference. If the amount seems daunting, you may halve or even quarter the recipe, as long as the weights are kept to the same proportions.

1 pound currants

1 pound seeded raisins

1 pound candied citron and/or 1 pound Candied Citrus Peel (page 387)

1 recipe Pound Cake batter (page 333), using 1/4 cup each brandy or bourbon and sherry instead of cream

1/4 pound almonds, blanched and sliced

1/4 cup rose or orange flower water

1 whole nutmeg, grated

1 teaspoon powdered mace

1 teaspoon powdered cinnamon

Grated zest of 1 lemon

1/4 cup all-purpose flour

2 recipes Almond Icing (page 346) (optional)

1. Put the currants, raisins, and citron in a metal or heatproof glass bowl and cover with boiling water. Let soak for 10 minutes and then drain off and discard the water. Pat the fruit dry. Some old recipes call for the fruits to be soaked in brandy or sherry. If you like, return them to the bowl and use the liquor called for in the base recipe. Leave them to soak for at least an hour, or up to 8 hours, then drain off any liquor that remains to make the cake batter. Spread them on a large linen towel and pat dry.

2. Position a rack in the center of the oven and preheat it to 325 degrees F. Butter and flour the cake pans as directed on page 333. Make the batter through step 5 of the master recipe, using whole eggs instead of separately beating the whites. Stir the rose or orange flower water, the spices, and the zest into the cake batter and beat it until they are thoroughly incorporated.

3. Put the fruit into a bowl. Dust them with the flour and toss until lightly coated. Gently fold the fruit and nuts into the batter, mixing until they're equally distributed, and spoon it into the prepared pans. Run a table knife through each to get out any large air bubbles. Bake in the center of the oven, not touching one another, until a straw or cake tester inserted into the middle comes out clean, about 2 hours. Allow the cakes to cool completely in their pans.

4. Nowadays, few people put icing on fruitcakes, and truth to tell, this one doesn't need it, but all the old recipes called for icing. If it appeals to you, ice them with Almond Icing and decorate with whole almonds, citron cut into leaf shapes, and homemade cherry preserves or good-quality glacéed cherries. Makes 2 tube or 4 loaf cakes.

Confederate Fruitcake, or Peach Pound Cake: This comes from Annabella Hill's *Mrs. Hill's New Cook Book,* and is one of a number of patriotically re-named recipes. Make it following the recipe for Rich Fruit Cake, above, substituting 2 pounds of dried peaches, coarsely chopped, for the citron, currants, raisins and candied peel. Mrs. Hill omitted the almonds, but you could substitute 1/4 pound of shelled, chopped Georgia pecans for a real down-home Georgia cake.

BAKING POWDER CAKES

After some of the unkind things that I have said about baking powder in pound cake, perhaps you are surprised to find cakes leavened with it here. There's nothing wrong with baking powder in its place; I do use it in my baking, especially in the two recipes that follow.

There are very early recipes for chemically leavened cakes such as gingerbread, but the classic Southern baking powder cakes came from the second half of the nineteenth century. Most evolved from old cake recipes whose only leaven had been egg whites. At first, the cakes contained both, and the combination made them puff spectacularly and gave an exceptionally tender crumb. Recipes containing both survive, but most had dropped the separately beaten egg whites by the turn of the century.

Southern baking powder cakes are always baked in layers. This was a fact I simply took for granted without wondering why, until Nathalie Dupree pointed out to me what should have been obvious: Chemically leavened breads and cakes are baked in smaller portions because it would take tremendous quantities of baking powder to leaven a large cake or loaf, lending a harsh chemical aftertaste that would be overwhelming. Layers make it possible to use the smallest possible dose of leaven.

Plain, or 1-2-3-4 Cake

My grandmother used this recipe for her basic layer cakes. Its name changed with the filling. The egg yolks and good butter provide its trademark golden color, the simple flavoring its fine balance with more complex fillings. Its understated flavor is why it is often called "plain," but it is almost never served that way. It is also sometimes called "1-2-3-4," because of the volume measures of the four main ingredients.

4 large eggs, at room temperature

8 ounces (1 cup or 2 sticks) unsalted butter, at room temperature

2 cups granulated sugar

14 ounces (3 light cups) all-purpose flour

3 teaspoons Single-Acting Baking Powder (page 318) or 2 teaspoons double-acting powder

1 teaspoon salt

1 cup whole milk

2 teaspoons Homemade Vanilla Extract (page 40) or 1-1/2 teaspoons of vanilla extract

1. Position a rack in the center of the oven and preheat it to 350 degrees F. If the rack isn't wide enough to hold all the pans at once without touching, arrange two racks in the center. Butter and flour the cake pans as directed on page 333. Separate the eggs, placing the whites in a glass or metal bowl. In a large mixing bowl cream the butter until fluffy and gradually beat in the sugar until the mixture is light, lemon-colored, and fluffy. Beat in the yolks of the eggs, one at a time.

2. Sift or whisk together the flour, baking powder, and salt. Alternately beat in the flour and milk in about four additions, beating only until it is smooth. Stir in the vanilla.

3. In their separate bowl, beat the egg whites with a clean whisk or electric mixer until they form firm, but not dry, peaks. Temper the whites by folding a little batter into them, then

add them to the batter and gently fold them in until no large lumps of egg white remain.

4. Divide the batter equally between the pans, then tap them sharply on the counter several times to make any large air bubbles rise to the top of the batter. Bake in the center of the oven, with the pans not touching and, if they are on more than one rack, staggered so that one pan is not directly over another, for 25 to 30 minutes, until the tops are lightly colored and a straw or tester inserted in the center comes out clean. Cool the cakes on a wire rack before taking them out of the pan and icing them in one of the following recipes or with your favorite frosting. Makes three 9-inch round or two 9-inch square layers.

Chocolate Layer Cake

This is not actually a chocolate cake, but yellow layers iced with a rich chocolate icing. As best I can determine, it is the original "chocolate" cake, turning up in the South just after the War Between the States. By the third quarter of the nineteenth century, true chocolate cake batters began to appear, but this one remained a favorite of most Southern cooks.

Often today the cake layers are split horizontally, as is directed here, so that there are multiple thin layers of cake and frosting. For a less rich cake, leave the layers whole. Fudge frosting appeared early in the twentieth century and had soon replaced the tricky egg white–based Chocolate For Cakes used in the older version of the cake. Since it is more traditional today, I have included it here as an option.

1 Plain, or 1-2-3-4 Cake (page 337), baked in three 9-inch-round layers

1 recipe of Chocolate For Cakes (page 348), or Dark Fudge Frosting (page 349), not made ahead but where indicated in the recipe below

1. When the cake layers have cooled completely, put each one on a flat work surface and cut it in half with a long bread knife or with floss or thread as follows. Take a 2-foot-long length of thread or unflavored floss and wrap each end securely around the forefingers of each hand. Hold your knuckles flat to the work surface as a guide and slice the layer in half by pulling the thread quickly through it. Put one layer onto the cake plate, cut side down.

2. Make the frosting according to the recipe and be prepared to work quickly, especially if you're using fudge frosting. As soon as it is ready, spread a large spoonful thickly over the bottom layer. Put another layer over this, again cut side down, and cover it with frosting. Continue until all the layers are stacked and frosted, then cover the sides with the remaining frosting. Makes one 6-layer cake.

MaMa's Coconut Cake

This is one of the most extraordinarily moist cakes you will ever encounter. MaMa's great secret for the moistness is also the reason her cake tastes more intensely of coconut than any other one I know. Lightly sweetened fresh coconut juice bathes every layer before it is frosted and topped with freshly grated coconut. Except for briefly heating the juice to melt the sugar, no part of the coconut is cooked, so the flavor isn't diluted or blunted by heat. Don't even consider writing to ask me if you can use a package or can of coconut instead of a fresh nut. Even my grandmother, the queen of packaged gelatin salad, would never use anything but a fresh coconut.

Coconut cake is a traditional Christmas cake in the part of Carolina where I grew up, and MaMa always made ours because nobody could manage to get it quite like hers. She made it every Christmas but one. That was the year she decided we would never know the difference and bought one from a local bakery. Granddaddy told her we wouldn't like it, but MaMa, with her typical modesty, didn't think there was anything special about her cooking. The one from the bakery looked like hers, so they conspired to say nothing of its origins. When it was cut and passed around, my older brother quietly, thoughtfully, ate his portion and then announced: "Well, it was alright, I guess, but it wasn't MaMa's." He, who loved coconut cake best of all, refused to eat any more of the impostor. She never tried to fool us again.

Where the recipe came from, MaMa no longer remembered, though from my research it appears to have been a regional practice centered in North Georgia, East Tennessee, and the western Carolinas. My paternal grandmother made pretty much the same cake, though, God rest her, not with the same finesse. Well, whether it was a family recipe or one that spanned the region is moot: what matters is that it's the best coconut cake you'll ever eat.

Choose a coconut that sloshes happily when you shake it. There must be juice and plenty of it.

1 Plain, or 1-2-3-4 Cake (page 337), baked in three layers, or 1 Silver or Lady cake (page 341)

1 medium fresh coconut, with juice

2 to 3 tablespoons granulated sugar

1 recipe of Seven-Minute, or Boiled Icing (page 347), made at the stage indicated below, not ahead of time

1. Make the cake according to the recipe, and while it is baking, pierce the holes that make a little face on one end of the coconut with an ice pick or other pointed object such as a screwdriver, tapping with a hammer (sit down and hold the nut between your knees). Drain the nut through a wire sieve into a bowl, shaking it gently to get out all the juice.

2. This step must be done on a concrete floor or brick-paved patio or door stoop. It will crack

tile that is laid over wood and permanently damage countertops. Lay the coconut on its side, steadily and firmly tap its equator with a hammer, rolling the nut, until it cracks and splits in half.

3. Take up one half and, armed with a wide, sturdy blade such as an oyster knife, pry loose the meat from the shell. It will pop off in pieces. Try to keep the pieces large, especially if you are using a hand grater to grate it.

4. Remove the brown skin with a vegetable peeler or paring knife, and grate the nutmeat into a large bowl. I use a rotary cheese grater, but a regular grater will work fine. You may also use a food processor fitted with a fine grating blade, following the manufacturer's instructions.

5. Measure the reserved coconut juice. If there's less than a cup, add enough water to make up the difference. Put it in a heavy-bottomed saucepan with 2 or 3 tablespoons of sugar, more or less, to taste. Heat it over medium-low heat, stirring occasionally, until the sugar has just dissolved. Don't let it boil. Set it aside to cool while you make the frosting.

6. Invert a cake layer over a cake plate to carefully remove the pan. Slowly spoon 1/4 cup of the coconut juice over it. Gently spread it with a thin layer of frosting, being careful; the cake surface tears easily when the frosting is worked too much. Sprinkle one-fourth of the coconut evenly over it and invert the second layer over it. Spoon another 1/4 cup plus a tablespoon of juice over this layer (since the liquid seeps to the bottom, adding a little more to each layer will evenly baste the cake). Spread this layer with icing and another fourth of the coconut, then add the final layer and spoon all but 3 tablespoons of the juice over it.

7. Frost the top and sides of the cake, turning the plate so that the unfrosted areas face you as you go, and pat the rest of the coconut evenly over the frosting. Spoon the remaining juice over the top of the cake a spoonful at a time, letting it soak in before adding more. Restrain yourself and let the cake sit for at least 24 hours before cutting it. Once it is cut, keep it well covered and, if the cake should last more than 3 days (I wouldn't know; mine never has), keep it refrigerated. Makes one 9-inch round, 3-layer cake.

Silver, or Lady Cake

There is no silver, and you needn't be a lady. Both names for this cake derive from the characteristically pale, delicate color. Only the whites of the eggs are used, so the cake remains light. This is basically a sponge cake, originally leavened only with egg whites, that today has become the foundation for a number of classic Southern cakes distinguished from one another by only the filling that goes between each layer. It is the traditional base for all variations of Lane Cake, and is often used for coconut cake (see MaMa's Coconut Cake, page 339). It can also be spread thickly with lemon curd between each layer and frosted with Boiled, or Seven-Minute Frosting (page 347), for an old-fashioned Victorian Jelly Cake.

8 ounces (1 cup or 2 sticks) unsalted butter	1/2 teaspoon salt
2 cups granulated sugar	1 cup milk or water
12 ounces (about 2 2/3 cups) all-purpose flour	1 teaspoon rosewater or orange-flower water (better for color), or 2 teaspoons Homemade Vanilla Extract (page 40) or
2 teaspoons Single-Acting Baking Powder (page 318), or 1-1/2 teaspoons double-acting baking powder	1 teaspoon vanilla extract, or 1 lemon
	7 large egg whites

1. Position a rack in the center of the oven and preheat it to 375 degrees F. If the rack isn't wide enough to hold all the pans without touching, position two racks at the center. Butter and flour the pans as directed on page 333. Cream the butter until fluffy and then gradually beat in the sugar until it is very fluffy, light, and lemon-colored.

2. Sift or whisk together the flour, baking powder, and salt and gradually beat it into the batter, alternating with the milk in about four additions and beating well after each addition. Beat in the flavoring. If you are using lemon, grate in the rind and then squeeze the juice into the batter through a strainer.

3. With a wire whisk or mixer fitted with clean beaters or the whisk attachment, beat the egg whites into soft peaks. Fold in a bit of batter to temper them, then carefully, but thoroughly, fold them into the batter. Divide the batter equally among the pans, smooth the tops, and bake in the center of the oven (staggering them on two racks so that no pan is over another, if necessary), for 25 to 30 minutes, or until a straw or tester inserted into the center comes out clean. Makes 2 thick or 3 thin 9-inch-round layers.

Emma Lane's Prize Cake

Lane Cake

In 1898, an Alabama matron named Emma Rylander Lane published a slender little cookbook simply titled *Some Good Things to Eat*. Among those good things was a recipe that she called her "prize cake." In the late-nineteenth century, cakes that were layered with a filling of fruits and/or nuts were very popular and Mrs. Lane's cake was an immediate success. Though her book has slipped into obscurity, the cake has become a Christmas institution, not only in Alabama, but all over the South.

Mrs. Lane's filling contained only raisins. Modern recipes seldom adhere to her original formula, and usually include both coconut and pecans. Occasionally, candied cherries, which I find positively ghastly, make an appearance as well. The recipe that follows is not taken directly from Mrs. Lane, but was given to me by my friend Lillie King of Talladega, Alabama. Miss Lillie got the recipe from her mother-in-law when she was a young bride, and it has been the family's traditional Christmas cake ever since. Her recipe deviates from Mrs. Lane's in only two respects: the filling includes coconut and pecans, and the frosting is omitted.

1 recipe Silver, or Lady Cake (page 341) baked in two 9 x 9-inch square layers and flavored with vanilla

4 ounces (1/2 cup or 1 stick) unsalted butter

7 egg yolks (use those leftover from making the cake base)

1 cup sugar

1 cup chopped raisins

1 cup freshly-grated coconut

1 cup chopped pecans

1/2 cup bourbon

2 teaspoons Homemade Vanilla Extract (page 40) or 1 teaspoon vanilla extract

Salt

1. Let the cake cool completely in its pans. Prepare the bottom of a double boiler with simmering water. In the top pan, melt the butter over low direct heat. Beat the yolks and sugar together in a separate bowl. Beat in the melted butter and then pour it back into the top of the double boiler.

2. Place it over the simmering water and cook, stirring constantly, until the custard thickens enough to coat the back of the spoon. Remove it from the heat and let it cool slightly. Mix in the raisins, coconut, pecans, bourbon, vanilla, and a small pinch of salt, stirring until evenly mixed.

3. Invert the first layer onto a cake plate and remove the pan. Spread it evenly with one-third of the filling. Let it stand for a few minutes to allow the liquids to soak into the cake, then put on the top layer and cover the top and sides with the remaining filling. Cover and let it soak for at least 24 hours before cutting it. If it lasts longer than 3 days, keep it refrigerated. Makes one 9-inch cake.

NOTES: *Some recipes suggest that wine may be substituted for the bourbon, but Mrs. Lane specified "whiskey or brandy." Don't be tempted to douse the cake with more booze than is called for on the presumption that if a little is good, a lot will be even better; too much will impart a harsh, sharp bite.*

To achieve Mrs. Lane's cake as authored, omit the coconut and pecans from the filling, and spread all of it between the layers. Cover the cake with Boiled, or Seven Minute Frosting (page 347).

Stack Cake

This is really a simple torte filled with stewed fruit, most often apples. Once a regional standard in the hills of Carolina, Georgia, Alabama, and Tennessee, an Upcountry cook's reputation rose and fell with her stack cake, but this confection had all but disappeared from Southern tables until the last decade of the twentieth century, when professional pastry cooks and cookbook authors began to rediscover and revisit regional classics. Fortunately most of them have not found a way to be too clever with stack cake, and have sensibly left it alone.

For the filling:
1 pound dried apples (see notes)
1 teaspoon ground cinnamon
1 teaspoon ground allspice
1 teaspoon freshly grated nutmeg
1/2 teaspoon salt
1 cup demerara or turbinado ("raw" sugar), or light brown sugar

For the cake layers:
12 ounces (about 2 2/3 light cups) all-purpose flour
1-1/2 teaspoons Single-Acting Baking Powder (page 318) or 1 teaspoon double-acting baking powder
1 teaspoon baking soda
1/2 teaspoon salt
1 teaspoon dried, powdered ginger
1/3 cup molasses
1 cup demerara, turbinado, or light brown sugar
1/2 cup (1/4 pound, or 1 stick) unsalted butter
2 large eggs

1. The night (or 8 hours) before making the cake, wash the apples and put them in a glass bowl. Cover them with cold water by 1 inch, cover, and set in a cool place for at least 8 hours.

2. Put the apples, remaining soaking liquid, spices, salt, and sugar in a stainless steel or enameled saucepan. If they're a bit dry, add half a cup or so of water. Bring to a simmer over medium-low heat and cook until the apples are tender and the liquid is evaporated, about 20 minutes. Let cool.

3. Meanwhile, sift or whisk together the flour, baking powder, soda, salt, and ginger. In a large mixing bowl, using a mixer or eggbeater, blend together the molasses, sugar, butter, and eggs until they are smooth. Gradually stir in the dry ingredients, mixing until it is completely smooth. It will be very stiff, like a cookie dough. Cover and chill the dough for at least half an hour.

4. Position a rack in the center of the oven and preheat it to 350 degrees F. Butter and flour six 9-inch round cake pans as on page 333. (If you only have two or three, bake the layers in batches). Divide the dough into six equal lumps. Lightly flour a work surface and roll them out into rounds that will just fit the pans. They should be no more than 3/16 inch thick. Bake them, three at a time, until golden, about 15 to 18 minutes. Cool completely before removing them from the pans. They will be firm, like cookies.

5. Roughly mash the apples with a potato masher, leaving them rather chunky. Put one cake layer on the bottom of a cake plate. Cover with one-fifth of the apples. Add another layer, cover with another one-fifth of the filling, and continue until all the layers are stacked, leaving the top dry. Cover with a cake dome or foil and let sit for several hours before cutting it, so the filling can soak into the layers, softening them into more of a cake-like consistency. Makes one 9-inch round cake.

NOTES: *Though not traditional, the cake can be iced just before serving with lightly sweetened whipped cream, or simply dusted with powdered sugar.*

Sliced, dried fruits are widely available year-round in Southern markets, and should be available in most cities. Ask for unsulphured fruit. If your market doesn't carry them, check with your local natural food store. Most of them usually carry several varieties.

ICINGS AND TOPPINGS FOR CAKES AND COOKIES

Almond Paste

The essential ingredient for almond paste, bitter almonds, are not available that I know of anywhere in this country. Peach kernels (the nut inside the pit), which are distantly related to almonds, are an often suggested substitution. Failing that, the only other substitution I have found that works fairly well is oil of bitter almonds (available in some markets and health food stores) or, if the dough can stand the added moisture, a little amaretto. Commercial almond extract can be rather harsh, but you could substitute 1/4 teaspoon of it for the oil.

The paste was originally made with a mortar and pestle. Fortunately, the food processor does a good job, and makes short work of a once laborious process.

1 pound whole almonds	1/2 teaspoon oil of bitter almonds or
2 cups granulated sugar	1/4 teaspoon almond extract
1 tablespoon rose water	

1. Bring a large teakettle of water to a boil and prepare a large bowl of cold water. Put the almonds into a heatproof bowl and cover them with boiling water. Let stand for 5 minutes, drain, and immediately plunge them into the cold water. Let stand 1 to 2 minutes more, drain, and slip off the skins.

2. Let the almonds cool, then put them in the food processor with the sugar, rosewater, and oil of bitter almonds. Process until the paste is smooth, about 2 to 3 minutes.

3. If you aren't using the paste immediately, store it, well covered, in the refrigerator. Makes about 2 pounds of paste.

Almond Icing

This rich icing was basic for fruitcakes and pound cakes, and makes a spectacular alternative to white icing on wedding cakes.

Like most icings, this one should only be made when you are ready to use it. Be prepared to work quickly, or the icing will crust over and have hard lumps.

1 pound Almond Paste (see page 345) or commercial almond paste

1 cup granulated sugar
4 large egg whites

1. Break up the almond paste and mash it a little with a fork.

2. Put the sugar into either a heatproof glass or porcelain-lined or stainless steel pan and pour 1/2 cup of water over it. Bring it to a boil over medium heat. Cook the syrup until it falls from the spoon in short drops. Remove it from the heat and let it cool just slightly.

3. Lightly beat the egg whites to mix them and slowly add the hot syrup, beating constantly with a hand eggbeater or an electric mixer. Beat until it is light and white and forms soft peaks. Beat this into the almond paste, a little at a time, until it is thoroughly incorporated and the frosting is smooth. Immediately spread it over the cake, using a broad icing knife or spatula. Ices 1 pound cake.

Boiled, or Seven-Minute Frosting

(Master Recipe)

So called because it cooks, you guessed it, for seven minutes, it's other name, like "boiled" custard, is misleading: it should never actually boil or it will be ruined. A hand-held mixer makes the job of beating this frosting much easier, but a wire whisk or hand-cranked eggbeater will do.

This is my maternal grandmother's recipe for this universal frosting. It can be varied by changing the flavoring, or colored with a few drops of saffron, beet juice, or even spinach juice, but stay away from chemical food coloring if you want to be historically authentic. Modern recipes often contain cream of tartar or lemon juice (to help the eggs hold their volume) and sometimes corn syrup, but neither is included in the earliest versions, and they are omitted here.

Only make this icing when you are ready to frost the cake, or it will crust over.

4 large egg whites

2 cups granulated sugar

9 tablespoons water

1. Prepare the bottom pan of a large double boiler with water and bring it to a simmer over medium heat. Off the heat, combine the egg whites, sugar, and water in the top pan of a double boiler and beat until the sugar is dissolved and the mixture is smooth.
2. Put the top pan over the simmering water, making sure that the water doesn't touch the upper pan at any point. Beat for 7 minutes, or until the frosting holds soft peaks.
3. Remove it immediately from the heat and beat in the desired flavoring. Continue beating until the frosting is thick enough to spread, and ice the cake at once. Makes enough for three 9-inch round layers.

NOTES: *This frosting can also be used to make delicate decorations for cakes by coloring it and piping it into shapes with a pastry bag onto sheets of buttered parchment or wax paper. Let them harden completely before trying to remove them, using a thin, wide-bladed knife or spatula.*

Seven-Minute Lemon Frosting: Grate the zest of 1 lemon and substitute the juice for part of the water. Beat the zest into the icing as directed in step 3.

Seven-Minute Orange Frosting: Follow the same procedure as for lemon, using the grated zest of half an orange and substituting its juice for all the water. (If you can get bitter oranges, their tart juice and bright rinds make an even better icing than regular juice oranges.) Beat the zest into the icing as directed in step 3.

Chocolate For Cakes

As best as I can determine, this frosting is what made the original "chocolate" cake. The layers are made with golden Plain, or 1-2-3-4 Cake (page 337), and layered with this frosting. It became popular in the South in the 1870's, and continued to be a favorite well into the twentieth century, when it was eventually displaced by the richer fudge frosting common today.

It is every cookbook author's worst nightmare. The first edition of this book was about to go to press and I was still fiddling with this recipe. Finally, triumphantly, I got it right and sent off the corrections just under the deadline, sure it was being corrected in the final copy. Then my first copy arrived and my proud heart sank: the corrections had been garbled, making the recipe hopelessly wrong. I called Julia Child in a panic, and in her generous way she calmed me as best she could: "My dear, it's happened to all of us. Probably no one will notice, but if they do, just say it's being corrected in the next edition." Who knew that edition would be a decade late?

1/4 pound unsweetened dark chocolate	2 cups granulated sugar
4 large egg whites	9 tablespoons water

1. Have the bottom pan of a large double boiler ready with boiling water. Finely grate the chocolate onto a sheet of wax paper and set it aside. Off the heat, combine the egg whites, sugar, and water in the top pan of the double boiler and beat until smooth with a whisk or hand mixer.

2. Put the top pan over the boiling water in the lower half of the double boiler, making sure that the water does not touch the upper pan at any point. Beat for 7 minutes. Remove it from the heat and continue beating until the frosting is thick enough to spread.

3. Fold in the chocolate until the icing has a smooth, even color, and immediately spread it on the cake. Ices three 9-inch layers.

NOTES: *Adding any kind of fat to an egg-white-based icing is tricky—whether it is citrus oil, nuts, or in this case, chocolate. Fold the article in and don't stir any more than necessary to make the icing uniform. Never beat the mixture after the chocolate is added or you'll end up with a gooey, runny mess flying all over the place.*

Old-Fashioned Dark Fudge Frosting

This is the "new" chocolate frosting found in Southern kitchens today. New, of course, is relative, because it has been around for at least a century. It's richer and less temperamental than the preceding recipe, but, like fudge candy, should not be made on a humid day.

3 cups granulated sugar

1 cup cocoa, preferably Dutch process

1 teaspoon salt

1-1/2 cups heavy cream (minimum 36% milk fat)

4 ounces (8 tablespoons or 1 stick) unsalted butter

4 ounces (about 1 cup) bittersweet chocolate, roughly chopped, or bittersweet chocolate chips

1 tablespoon Homemade Vanilla (page 40) or 2 teaspoons vanilla extract

1. Combine the sugar, cocoa, and salt in a heavy-bottomed saucepan and whisk to mix. Slowly whisk in the cream and turn on the heat to medium. Bring it to a boil, stirring occasionally, and add the butter and chocolate, stirring until they are melted and smooth. Let it come back to boil and cook, stirring occasionally, until it reaches the soft-ball stage (234 degrees F on a candy thermometer), about 2 to 3 minutes.

2. Remove from the heat and stir in the vanilla. Let it cool, undisturbed, until it is just warm (no more than 110 degrees F). Beat the frosting with a mixer or wooden spoon until it is thick enough to spread, and spread it immediately onto the cake. Ices three 9-inch layers.

TEA CAKES AND COOKIES

Tea Cakes

This simple, versatile sugar cookie dough can be made into dozens of different cookies by changing the flavorings or toppings. At Christmas, I make at least half a dozen batches, giving each a different flavoring, and cut or roll them into varying shapes. The favorite around here is flavored with the orange zest and flower water, rolled extra thin and made into sandwiches with a filling of melted bittersweet chocolate. You could add spices, chopped nuts, or a few crushed pralines, or roll them while still hot in powdered sugar flavored with citrus zest or spices, or spread them with Almond Icing (page 346), or—well, you get the idea.

1 pound (2 cups, or 4 sticks) butter, or 1 cup
    butter plus 1 cup lard

2 cups granulated sugar

3 large eggs, lightly beaten

Zest of 2 lemons or 1 orange (optional)

20 ounces (4 cups) all-purpose flour

2 teaspoons Single Acting Baking powder
    (page 318) or 1-1/2 teaspoons commer-
    cial double-acting powder

1 tablespoon rose or orange flower water,
    Homemade Vanilla Extract (page 40), or
    1 teaspoon commercial vanilla extract

1. In a mixing bowl that will hold all the dough, cream the butter well and gradually beat in the sugar until it is very light and fluffy. Beat in the eggs, one at a time. If you are flavoring the cookies with citrus zest, stir it in. Sift or whisk together the flour and baking powder.

2. Gradually work the flour into the batter. Finally, mix in the flower water or extract (use either rose or orange water with the lemon zest, orange flower with the orange, or any of them if using neither). Continue mixing until it is smooth. Cover and chill at least a half an hour.

3. Position a rack in the center of the oven and preheat to 375 degrees F. Lightly grease a baking sheet. Flour a work surface and roll out the dough fairly thin—no more than 3/16 inch—thinner, if you can manage it. Quickly cut, using a round- or fancy-shaped cutter, and transfer the cookies to the baking sheet. Bake, in batches if necessary, until lightly browned, about 15 minutes. Cool them on the pan. Store them in an airtight container. Makes about 6 dozen.

NOTES: *For a sweeter sugar cookie, brush the tops with beaten egg white and dust with granulated or demerara sugar before baking. For almond or pecan tea cakes, mix in a cup of lightly toasted, finely chopped nuts and a teaspoon of cinnamon, then press a single nut into the top of each cut cookie before baking it. This is also an excellent dough for gingersnaps. Substitute finely crushed demerara or brown sugar for the regular sugar and mix in 1/2 cup finely chopped crystallized ginger or 2 teaspoons powdered dried ginger. Omit the flavoring extract, or use orange flower water.*

Lettice Bryan's Almond Cones

These are lovely cookies, as pretty on the plate as they are on the tongue. They are actually macaroons, crisp, airy almond cookies that in Italy are known as amaretti. In that country, a similar almond paste dough is mixed with glacéed fruit and whole nuts, pinched into rough pyramids and called, not without reason, "*brutti ma buoni*"—ugly but good. Mrs. Bryan's neatly rolled cones take care of the ugly part, making them a lovely thing to have on a formal tea or reception table.

Nut paste cookies are ancient confections, popular at least since the early Middle Ages. They contain no flour, depending, for body, entirely on the nut paste. Though popular in America throughout the nineteenth century, they have lately fallen out of favor in the Deep South. When I first began teaching, my students were amazed at the prospect of cookies that did not contain any flour. They deserve a revival.

21 ounces Almond Paste (page 345), or 3 (7-ounce) packages commercial paste

3 large egg whites, more or less (see step 2, below)

1 lemon

Flour, for dusting

Superfine sugar, for dusting

1. Position a rack in the center of the oven and preheat it to 325 degrees F. Break up the almond paste with a mixer or food processor fitted with a steel blade until it is fluffy.

2. In a separate bowl, beat the egg whites until frothy. Juice the lemon and beat the juice into the egg whites, then beat until they hold stiff but not dry peaks. Gradually work the egg white into the almond paste. The dough should be very stiff, but still workable, so hold back some of the egg if you feel it will make the dough too soft.

3. Line a baking sheet with parchment paper. Carefully clean, dry, and lightly dust your hands with flour. Take up a small bit of the dough no larger than a nutmeg. Quickly and lightly roll it into a cone. The less it is handled, the better. Put it point up on the parchment. Repeat, dusting your hands with flour as needed, until all the dough is shaped, spacing them an inch apart.

4. Dust the tops generously with sugar and bake until barely colored, about 10 minutes. Reduce the heat to 150 degrees F. Crack the oven door open for a minute to dissipate some of the intense heat, then close it and let the macaroons dry, about 30 minutes. Take them up (loosening with a spatula if necessary) and transfer them to a wire rack to cool. Store in an airtight container. Makes about 30 cookies.

NOTES: *You can skip the shaping of the cookies and merely drop them onto the parchment from a small teaspoon. It is a lot less trouble, and the cookies certainly won't suffer any from the lack of handling. The process for drying the macaroons is borrowed from Karen Hess, suggested in her notes on* Martha Washington's Booke of Cookery. *Mrs. Bryan didn't mention it.*

Annabella Hill's Coconut Tea Cakes

Once again, nuts provide the only body for these delicious cookies. Because they contain whole eggs and butter, they are softer and richer than the usual coconut macaroons. Though wholly unorthodox by Mrs. Hill's standards, they are incredible coated with melted dark chocolate.

1 medium fresh coconut, or 12 ounces (4 cups) unsulphured, unsweetened frozen grated coconut

For every 4 cups of coconut:

1 cup granulated sugar

4 ounces (1 stick, or 1/2 cup) unsalted butter, softened

3 large eggs

All-purpose flour

1. Position a rack in the center of the oven and preheat it to 325 degrees F. Drain, open and peel the coconut as directed on (page 339). Grate the meat and measure it; adjust the amount of sugar, butter, and eggs accordingly.

2. In a large bowl that will hold all the ingredients, cream together the sugar and butter until it is fluffy. Break the eggs into a separate bowl and then beat them in, one at a time, until mixture is light and smooth. Mix in the coconut and gradually add just enough flour to make the dough fairly stiff.

3. Line a baking sheet with buttered parchment. Lightly flour the work surface and turn out the dough onto it. Pat or roll it out about 1/4 inch thick, and cut into rounds with a sharp biscuit cutter, or, using a sharp knife, into 1-1/2-inch squares. Transfer them to the baking sheet with a spatula, spaced about 1/2 inch apart.

5. Bake in the center of the oven until lightly browned, about 20 minutes. Cool the cookies on the pan. Store them in an airtight container.

NOTES: *The flavor of freshly grated coconut is, naturally, preferred for these cookies, but good-quality unsulphured, grated coconut (available in natural food stores) is a real time-saver and works well in the recipe. Be certain that it is unsweetened. Parchment lessens the tendency for the cookies to stick but you can also bake them on a well-greased baking sheet. They may stick a little, but are easily scraped loose with a thin metal spatula.*

PASTRIES

Basic Pastry for Pies and Tarts

Many historical pastry recipes differed somewhat from modern ones. Often the object was not so much to produce an edible pastry (and sometimes, it wasn't) as a hard casing that would help to seal meats and pies for baking and provide a protective coating for them when they were stored in the pantry for cold breakfasts, teas, and suppers. But for the purposes of the pastries included in this book, and for most modern pie recipes, this is a good all-purpose pastry. It may not look as spectacular as puff pastry, but it is flaky and tender and lacks absolutely nothing. The secret to it is lard, which helps to make any pastry tender. A little of it will make even puff pastry more delicate, though the old recipes never mention it. However, if you are not able to cook with lard, you may omit it and use an extra 2 tablespoons of butter instead.

10 ounces (about 2 cups) all-purpose soft-wheat flour

1/2 teaspoon salt

4 ounces (8 tablespoons, 1 stick) chilled unsalted butter, cut into bits

1 ounce (2 tablespoons) chilled lard, cut into bits

About 1/3 to 1/2 cup ice water

1. Sift or whisk together the flour and salt in a mixing bowl. Add the butter and lard, toss to coat each bit, and work the fat into the flour with a pastry blender or two knives (not your hands), until it has the texture of coarse meal.

2. Add the ice water, starting with 1/3 cup, and lightly stir it in until the pastry is moistened and beginning to clump. Stir in additional water by tablespoonfuls until the dough is soft and smooth, but not sticky. Lightly dust it and your hands with flour and gather it into a ball. Wrap it well with plastic wrap and let it rest in the refrigerator for half an hour.

3. To roll out the pastry, lightly flour a cool work surface (marble is ideal, but wood or plastic laminate is fine) and roll out the pastry from the center of the lump outward, giving it regular quarter-turns as you go, until it is evenly rolled to the thickness required in the recipe. For most of the pastries in this book, it should be 1/8 inch thick unless noted otherwise. Makes two 9-inch pie shells or one 9-inch pie with top crust.

NOTES: *The pastry can be put together in the food processor. In fact, it does a superior job of it if you are careful not to over-process it. The blade's speed causes it to heat up quickly, which can make the fat oily. To prevent this, chill the blade before using it.*

Fit the processor with the steel blade and put in the flour and salt. Pulse it a few times to sift it, then add the bits of butter and lard. Pulse the machine until the flour resembles coarse meal. Add 1/4 cup of water and pulse again until it is mixed and beginning to clump together. Add water by tablespoonfuls, pulsing the machine, until it clumps together but is not sticky or wet looking. If you aren't used to using the machine, turn it out into a mixing bowl after the first 1/4 cup of water and, by hand, work in the remaining water in tablespoonfuls.

Puff Pastry

Light, delicate, and airy, this pastry was once the standard for the best company piecrust. It is not difficult to make, if you keep everything as cold as possible and weigh all the ingredients carefully. The old instructions were to make up the pastry in a cool place, preferably early in the morning. It's still sound advice, even in our days of artificially-cooled houses.

The recipe here is the usual one, for a pound of butter and 20 ounces of flour. If it's more than you need for the recipe you are making, it will keep, well-wrapped, in the refrigerator for up to a week. It also freezes well, and can be stored frozen for several months. If neither of these options is feasible, you can cut the recipe in half with care—just keep the weights in proportion.

For an elegant garnish for soups, old cooks frequently cut the pastry in squares and baked them plain. It also makes an impressive first course when cut into individual portions, baked, split, and filled with Creamed Oysters (page 134) or Mushrooms in Cream (page 229).

20 ounces (about 4 cups) soft wheat pastry or all-purpose flour

1 pound (2 cups, 4 sticks) chilled unsalted butter

1 teaspoon salt

About 3/4 cup ice water

1. Weigh the flour and set aside 2/3 cup of it.

2. Divide the butter into quarters. Cut three of the quarters in half (into 1/8 pound, or 4-tablespoon chunks), cover, and refrigerate them. Working quickly, cut the remaining quarter into bits, handling it as little as possible. Put it in a bowl and chill it briefly until it is firm again.

3. Sift or whisk together the remaining flour and the salt in a mixing bowl. Add the cut up butter, toss to coat it with flour, and cut it in using a pastry blender or two knives until it is the texture of raw grits or polenta. Don't use your fingers unless you have virtually no circulation and they're always cold: otherwise, the heat from your hands will make the butter oily and toughen the pastry.

4. Make a well in the center and add 1/4 cup of ice water. Stir it in lightly, then keep adding water by the tablespoon until the pastry is smooth, but not sticky. Lightly dust your hands and the pastry with some of the reserved flour and gather the dough into a ball. Wrap it well in plastic wrap, and refrigerate for half an hour. These steps can be done in the food processor fitted with a chilled steel blade (see notes on Basic Pastry, page 352), but be careful not to over process it.

5. Roll the dough out into a rectangle 1/2 inch thick. Thinly slice 1 of the 1/8-pound chunks of butter and scatter the slices evenly over two-thirds of the pastry, gently smooth it with a palette knife or pastry scraper, dust it lightly with a little of the reserved flour, and fold the blank, unbuttered third over the center, then fold the other side over it, like a letter. Dust the top with a little flour and roll it out until it is again 1/2 inch thick. Repeat this step with each of the 1/8-pound chunks of butter until all the butter and flour are incorporated into the pastry. This introduces the flaky, puffed-up layers that are the hallmark of puff pastry.

6. Finally, roll the pastry out to 1/2 inch thick, fold it, and roll it out again. Fold the pastry once more, wrap it well, and let it rest, refrigerated, for at least 1 hour before using. Makes 2 pounds of dough, enough for 4 open-faced or 2 closed (top crust) 9-inch pies.

NOTES: *If at any time the dough starts to soften or get too warm, wrap it well and refrigerate it until its firm again. This may seem overly cautious, but why go to all this trouble with your pastry and have it end up tough and oily? When rolling out puff pastry, or any pie dough, use only as much flour as it takes to keep the pastry from sticking, and use as light a hand as possible. Ideally, this pastry should stay cold right up to the moment it goes into the oven.*

A Pre-Baked Puff-Pastry Lid

This was once a common covering for company pies, and it makes a gorgeous presentation. The pastry is cut to fit and decorated, then cooked separately. It is placed on top of the pie just before serving, so that it remains light and crisp.

1/2 recipe of Puff Pastry (page 354)	1 egg white beaten with a tablespoon of water (optional)

1. Position a rack in the center of the oven (if you have a baking stone, put it on the rack—it makes a real difference with pastry), and preheat it to 400 degrees F.

2. Roll out the pastry just under 1/4 inch thick. Cut it into a shape the size of your pie. Lightly butter a baking sheet at least 12-inches wide and lay the pastry on it. Cut the remaining scraps of pastry into decorative shapes (leaves, hearts, flowers—whatever excites you). Brush their backs with a few drops of water and arrange them on the top of the pastry. To glaze the top, brush with the beaten egg white. Prick the pastry through in several places with a fork.

3. Bake until puffed and golden, about 20 minutes. Let it cool on a rack before topping the pie. Covers a standard 9-inch pie.

Pre- and Partially Baking A Pastry Blind (Without Filling)

In many cases, a pastry is completely or partially baked before it is filled. Usually this is when the filling is already cooked, but there are also times when a short pre-cooking helps insure a light, delicate crust that won't get soggy even when the filling bakes with the pastry.

1/2 recipe Basic Pastry for Pies and Tarts (page 353) or Puff Pastry (page 354)

1-1/2 to 2 cups pie weights, dried beans, or raw rice

1. Position a rack in the center of the oven and preheat it to 400 degrees F. Roll the pastry out to about 1/8 inch thick (or to the thickness indicated in the recipe). Line a pie plate with it, crimp the edges, and prick the bottom well with a fork. Butter a piece of foil and put it over the pastry, buttered side down. Gently press it into the corners, being careful not to mash the edges of the pastry or tear it. Pour in the weights and gently shake it to level them. Bake 20 minutes.

2. Take the pastry from the oven and carefully remove the foil and weights. Bake for another 10 minutes, or until the pastry is beginning to color. If you are partially baking the shell, remove and cool it on a rack before filling it.

3. If you are completely baking the shell, cover the edges with strips of foil to keep them from over-browning and bake the pastry until it is uniformly browned, about 10 minutes more. Makes 1 pie shell.

A Raised Pastry

For Meat Pies and Cobblers

The leavening in this pastry produces a light, soft pastry that is traditionally used for cobbler (page 363) and meat potpies. It also makes nice dumplings when rolled thin, cut into strips, and dropped into a simmering, well-seasoned broth. Lard is the preferable fat in this pastry, as it contributes both lightness and tenderness, but butter will also work fine.

10 ounces (about 2 cups) all-purpose soft wheat pastry flour

1/2 teaspoon salt

1 teaspoon baking powder

1/2 teaspoon baking soda

6 ounces (3/4 cup) chilled lard (or butter)

About 1/3 to 1/2 cup cold buttermilk or plain, whole milk yogurt thinned to buttermilk consistency with milk or water

1. Sift the flour, salt, baking powder, and soda together into a metal or ceramic bowl. Cut the lard into bits and add it to the bowl, handling it as little as possible. Work the fat into the flour, using a pastry blender or two knives, until it is the texture of coarse meal (grits or polenta).

2. Add 1/3 cup buttermilk and lightly stir it into the dough, adding more by spoonfuls until is it soft and smooth, but not sticky. This pastry will be softer—more like biscuit dough than pie pastry—but too much liquid will make it unmanageable. Lightly dust with flour and gather it into a ball.

3. This pastry must be used immediately. Lightly flour a work surface and roll it out at once for use as directed in the individual recipe. Makes 1 deep-dish cobbler.

Almond Cheesecake

This "cheesecake" is really a butter and egg custard that actually contains no cheese at all. Such custards are quite old, dating back to medieval English cooking. An integral part of American baking from the beginning, they are the foundation for many famous Southern pastries, most notably chess (chess being an old spelling for cheese or "curd"), coconut custard, and pecan pie. While observant Southern cooks will recognize the basic structure of these standards in our baking repertory, English cooks will recognize one of theirs: Bakewell pudding.

1 recipe Puff Pastry (page 354) or Basic Pastry (page 352)

8 ounces Almond Paste (page 345) or commercial almond paste

1 teaspoon rosewater

1/4 cup granulated sugar

1/4 pound butter, softened

4 large eggs

1. Position a rack in the center of the oven and preheat it to 450 degrees F. Line a 9-inch pie plate with pastry and partially bake it as directed on page 355. Let it cool on a rack. Reduce the temperature to 400 degrees F.

2. Break up the almond paste in a large mixing bowl. Beat in the rosewater, sugar, and butter, beating until it is fluffy and light.

3. Break the eggs into a separate bowl and beat them until they are light and smooth. Beat a little bit of them into the almond paste to loosen it, then slowly beat in the remaining eggs. It should be frothy and very light.

4. Pour it into the prepared pastry shell and bake in the center of the oven until set (a toothpick inserted into the center should come out clean), and lightly browned, about 45 minutes. Makes one 9-inch pie.

Variation: Groundnut (Peanut) Cheesecake: In *The Carolina Housewife*, Sarah Rutledge offered this variation on almond cheesecake. It is made in exactly the same way, except the nut paste is made with 4 ounces shelled, blanched raw (not toasted) peanuts, 4 ounces (1/2 cup) sugar, and 1 tablespoon brandy or bourbon. Grind all the ingredients to a paste in a mortar or the food processor. Make the cheesecake according to the previous recipe, substituting the peanut paste for the almond paste, and brandy or bourbon for the rosewater.

Victoria's Pudding

Whether or not Queen Victoria had anything to do with this pastry is anybody's guess; but if she really liked everything that was named for her, it's no wonder the dear woman was as round as a house. The recipe is from *The Carolina Housewife*, and is another variation on the old English custard cheesecakes. Miss Rutledge is the only source that used this name; other versions turned up, divided into tartlets as "maids of honor," or, without almonds, as "bride's maids." Some merely called it jam pie, but variations have long been popular in the South.

If you serve the pie on a thin pool of chocolate sauce, you will be completely out of line, as far as Miss Rutledge is concerned, but your company will flat roll over and bark.

1/2 recipe Basic Pastry (page 353)
1 whole egg and 3 large egg yolks
2/3 cup granulated sugar
1/4 cup blanched almonds

4 ounces (1/2 cup, 1 stick) butter, melted and cooled
About 1/3 cup seedless raspberry jam (or strained if not seedless)

1. Have everything except the pastry at room temperature. Line a 9-inch pie plate with the pastry, prick it well with a fork, and chill it in the refrigerator for at least half an hour.

2. Position a rack in the center of the oven and preheat it to 325 degrees F. Beat the egg and egg yolks together in a large mixing bowl until they are well blended and smooth, then stir in the sugar.

3. Grind the almonds to a paste in a blender or food processor, or, if you want to be strictly authentic, with a mortar and pestle. Add a little of the custard to the almonds to loosen them and then gradually mix them into the rest of the custard. Stir in the melted butter.

4. Stir the jam until it is smooth. Spread it evenly over the prepared pastry, making a layer a little more than 1/8 inch thick. Stir the custard again to blend it and pour it over the jam.

5. Bake for about 45 minutes, or until the filling is set (a toothpick inserted in the center should come out clean) and a nice golden brown crust forms. Cool on a rack before cutting. Refrigerate it if you have made it more than 4 hours ahead. Fortunately, it is as good cold as it is warm, and holds up handsomely without getting watery as some custards are prone to do. Makes one 9-inch pie.

NOTES: *Good raspberry jam is widely available in most of the country, but it's not universally popular in the South. For Southern cooks who have trouble finding it, either blackberry or dewberry preserves make a good substitute. In fact, they would be far better than using an artificially flavored commercial raspberry jelly. Force the seeds out by straining the jam through a wire mesh sieve. As with the previous recipes, you can substitute almond paste for the ground almonds, but cut the sugar to 1/2 cup.*

Damson Custard Pie

Damsons are oval, purple-blue plums with a distinctive, tart flavor that once made them very popular not only for pies, but also for jams and preserves. I don't know what has happened to them, but they have almost completely vanished. There are a couple of pretty good imported French Damson preserves available, and occasionally our cousin Dorothy Merritt shares the fruit from her tree with my mother, but I have unfortunately not been able to get any fresh plums to make my own preserves as my mother used to when I was small, and those lovely homemade preserves made the best pies.

This custard was a favorite dessert at home in those days. Maybe it's only nostalgia, but commercial preserves lack something that my mother's had. Still, they make a pretty good pie.

1/2 recipe Basic Pastry (page 353)

4 large eggs

1 cup granulated sugar

4 ounces (1/2 cup, or 1 stick) butter, melted and cooled

Salt

1 teaspoon Homemade Vanilla Extract (page 40) or 1/2 teaspoon commercial extract

1 cup damson plum preserves

1. Position a rack in the center of the oven and preheat it to 450 degrees F. Line a 9-inch pie plate with the pastry, prick the bottom well with a fork, and partially bake it as directed on page 355. Let the pastry cool on a rack. Reduce the heat to 350 degrees F.

2. Break the eggs into a large mixing bowl, lightly beat them until smooth, and add the sugar, beating steadily, until the mixture is light and lemon-colored. Slowly beat in the melted butter, and stir in a stingy pinch of salt and the vanilla.

3. Stir a little of the custard into the preserves to soften them and then beat them into the custard. Pour it into the prepared crust and bake in the center of the oven until the custard is set, about 35 to 40 minutes. A toothpick inserted in the center should come out clean and the top will be a lovely, rich brown. Let the pie cool on a rack before serving. Makes one 9-inch pie.

Sweet Potato Custard

Sweet potato custard is a traditional Thanksgiving and Christmas dessert in Georgia. Already commonplace in the Carolinas, Georgia, and Alabama when Annabella Hill set it down in *Mrs. Hill's New Cook Book* (1867), it survives in north Georgia little altered from her formula. While similar to pumpkin pie, the spices are few (Mrs. Hill's version had none at all) and by comparison, it's rather plain. But in this instance, discretion is the better part of valor; the rich, but delicate flavor of good sweet potatoes does not need to be tarted up.

Though desserts are not really my thing, this has long been one of my favorites. I've been known to make supper of it with a cold glass of milk or sherry.

1 recipe Basic Pastry (page 353)	Salt
1-1/2 pounds (about 3 medium) hot	Whole nutmeg in a grater
Oven-Roasted Sweet Potatoes (page 246)	Grated zest of 1 lemon
8 ounces (2 sticks) unsalted butter	About 1 tablespoon bourbon or brandy, or
1-1/2 cups granulated sugar	Homemade Vanilla Extract (page 40), or
6 large eggs	1 teaspoon commercial vanilla extract

1. Position a rack in the center of the oven and preheat it to 375 degrees F. Line two 9-inch pie plates with the pastry and prick well with a fork. Chill them in the refrigerator while you make the filling.

2. Peel the sweet potatoes while still hot and put them through a ricer, or cut them in chunks, put them in a bowl, and mash well with a fork or potato masher.

3. In a large mixing bowl, cream the butter and sugar until fluffy and light. Beat in the sweet potatoes and then the eggs, one at a time. Stir in a pinch of salt, a generous grating of nutmeg, the lemon zest, and, if you like, a tablespoon or so of bourbon or brandy, or the vanilla.

4. Pour the filling into the prepared pastry and bake in the center of the oven, not touching, until they are set and the pastry is nicely browned, about 40 to 45 minutes.

5. Serve cold with a healthy dollop of lightly sweetened whipped cream flavored with a little bourbon or sherry, or wait until everybody has gone to bed, sneak down to the kitchen, cut a wedge, pour a glass of milk and dig in. Makes two 9-inch pies.

Great Grandmother Alice's Apple Meringue Pie

Fruit tarts topped with meringues were once popular as an elegant company dessert, but today they are virtually unknown. When my grandmother was very young, her mother used to make these pies whenever she had company that she wanted to impress. MaMa remembers them quite vividly, standing in an impressive row on the sideboard, their delicately browned meringues glistening with crystal droplets of moisture.

Still rarer, and more difficult to accomplish, was a pie in which the stewed fruit was folded into the meringues for an airy, fragile filling. The version given here, however, is the one my grandmother remembers, and was the most usual.

1/2 recipe Basic Pastry (page 353)	Whole nutmeg in a grater
6 medium-sized tart apples	4 large eggs
Granulated sugar	2 tablespoons butter, softened
1 lemon, zest grated and reserved, halved	

1. Prepare and partially bake the pastry as directed on page 355. Set it aside on a rack to cool.

2. Peel, core, and slice the apples and put them into a stainless steel or enamel-lined pan with enough water to half cover them. Bring them to a boil over medium heat, reduce the heat to low and simmer gently, uncovered, until the apples are tender, about 10 to 15 minutes.

3. Position a rack in the center of the oven and preheat it to 375 degrees F. Put the apples through a potato ricer (or food mill fitted with a disk with large holes) into a mixing bowl. Sweeten to taste with sugar and add the lemon zest, a little juice from the lemon if needed for tartness, and a generous grating of nutmeg.

4. Break the eggs and separate the whites from the yolks, placing the whites in a clean metal or glass bowl. Cover the whites and set them aside.

5. Beat the yolks into the apples and then beat in the butter. Pour the filling into the prepared pastry and bake in the center of the oven until the filling is set, about 30 to 40 minutes. Remove the pie and set it on a rack to cool slightly. Raise the oven temperature to 400 degrees F.

6. Beat the egg whites until frothy. Beat in a teaspoon or so of juice from the lemon and continue beating them to soft peaks. Lightly sweeten the meringue with about 1 tablespoon or so of sugar and continue beating until it forms stiff peaks. Spread the meringue thickly over the pie and bake until it is set and lightly browned on top, about 10 minutes. Cool completely before serving. Makes one 9-inch pie.

Cobbler Pie

I have been unable to date the translation of the word cobbler from shoemaker to drink to pie. In culinary terms, it originally described a cool drink of sweetened wine, rum, or whiskey and fruit (see Sherry Cobbler, page 66). By the mid-nineteenth century, however, the drink was pretty much archaic. The first printed Southern use as the name of a deep-dish pie that I have been able to uncover is *The Kentucky Housewife*, 1839. Mrs. Hill records that in Georgia the same pie was popularly called "cut and come again," but uses "cobbler" in the old-fashioned way, to name the drink. After the mid-1860s, cobbler was understood to mean this deep-dish pie, and recipes for it became commonplace.

By all accounts, cobblers were homey family desserts, not fancy enough for company, much as they are today. The crust is meant to be thick, and is often layered with the fruit for an effect not unlike dumplings. The results may not be elegant, but that does not, of course, stop it from being deeply satisfying, as Mrs. Bryan aptly noted.

1 recipe Raised Pastry (page 357), or 2 recipes Basic Pastry (page 353)

Sugar

5 cups fresh prepared fruit or berries

Whole nutmeg in a grater and ground cinnamon (optional)

2 tablespoons bourbon (optional)

4 tablespoons unsalted butter

Heavy cream, Boiled Custard (page 377) or Vanilla Custard Ice Cream (page 375)

1. Position a rack in the center of the oven and preheat it to 375 degrees F. Roll out the pastry about 1/8 inch thick and line the sides of a deep glass or pottery casserole that is at least 9-inches round by 2-1/2-inches deep. Sprinkle it lightly with sugar.

2. Sprinkle the fruit with sugar (how much will depend on how sweet the fruit is already—taste it first and don't overdo it) and add spices to taste. Spread half of it over the bottom of the dish, sprinkle with a tablespoon of bourbon, if using. Dot with a tablespoon of butter.

3. Cut half the remaining pastry in strips and lay them over the fruit, sprinkle lightly with sugar, and add the remaining fruit. Season with more spices and the remaining bourbon, if you are using them. Dot the top with another tablespoon of butter.

4. Lay on the top crust, so that it overlaps the edges. Trim the excess and crimp the edges of the pastry side and top together. Make several gashes on the top. If there is any pastry left, you may cut decorative shapes, brush the backs of them with water, and decorate the top with them.

5. Bake in the center of the oven for about 20 minutes. Meanwhile, melt the remaining butter. When the crust is beginning to color, brush it with the melted butter, sprinkle it with sugar, and continue baking until nicely browned and bubbly at the center, about 20 to 25 minutes more. Serve hot, warm, or cold with plain heavy cream, whipped cream, Boiled Custard or Vanilla Custard Ice Cream. Makes one deep 9- or 10-inch pie.

NOTES: *You can make cobblers from virtually any fruit. Here are a few of the more commonly used fruits and berries with notes on how to prepare them.*

Apples: *Allow 4 to 5 apples. Wash, peel, core, and slice them lengthwise into thick slices.*

Peaches: *Allow 5 to 6 small, ripe peaches. Wash and peel them over a bowl to catch all their juice. Cut them in half and remove the pit, then slice thickly and add them to their juice.*

Blackberries, blueberries, strawberries, or raspberries: *Wash them gently and remove any stems that are still attached. Cut large strawberries into halves, but otherwise leave them whole.*

Sweet potatoes (yes, sweet potatoes): *Allow 2 to 3 medium-sized sweet potatoes. Peel and cut them into 1/4-inch-thick slices. If the potatoes are especially large, cut each slice into halves or quarters. Put them in a tight-fitting pan with just enough water to cover them. Bring the liquid to a rolling boil over high heat, then reduce the heat to medium-low and simmer until they begin to soften, but are still quite underdone, about 4 to 5 minutes. Drain, reserving their cooking liquid, and let them cool. Layer them in the pie as directed for the fruit in steps 2 and 3, adding to each layer enough of the reserved cooking water to cover the potatoes. Many cooks also substitute light brown sugar for the sugar in the main recipe and 1/2 cup of bourbon for some of the cooking liquid.*

Desserts

FOUR BASIC KINDS OF DESSERT once dominated Southern cookbooks and household notebooks. If the frequency with which they appeared is any indication, steamed puddings, charlottes, molded jellies, and ices also dominated our dessert boards. Such recipes filled the community cookbooks and household notebooks—*Housekeeping in Old Virginia* devoted an entire chapter to puddings, and a separate one to charlottes. But the problem in using such books as guides, as has been noted elsewhere, is that they record recipes that were used infrequently and that hadn't been committed by rote use to memory. Still, their universality suggests that such desserts, while not a part of everyday cooking, were, nonetheless, well liked. In spite of this popularity, or because of it, they have all but vanished from Southern tables.

With few exceptions, most early American baked goods and desserts remained solidly English: steamed, boiled or baked puddings; sweet dumplings; trifles; great cakes; cheesecakes; tea cakes; jumbles; and molded jellies. Nowhere else is the common link of English cookery more apparent than on the dessert board. Household notebooks from New England are full of the same recipes that dominated Southern ones. Part of the reason for this uniformity is that, while other aspects of Southern cooking deviated into its own territory with spices and produce that were foreign to English cooking, baking remained little changed from its English roots, in part because dessert-making in general remained the province of the mistress of the household.

Of those four common sweets, boiled, steamed, and baked puddings, arguably the most English of them all, have become the most rare today. Except for an occasional Christmas Plum Pudding, they're practically extinct. One classic baked pudding (Queen of Puddings, next page) is included here, but it barely scratches the surface of the dozens upon dozens of archaic crumb, batter, and dough puddings that were commonplace throughout the nineteenth century.

A fruit charlotte is a simple, homey confection of stewed fruit encased in a crust of toasted leftover bread. Its uptown cousin, charlotte russe, while richer and more sophisticated, was still the same idea made with sponge cake and a filling of rich Bavarian cream. It became very popular in the South, and eventually replaced those plain fruit charlottes of earlier days. Frequently, the cream appeared without even a casing of cake, and occasionally was even frozen.

Another popular sweet was molded jelly. Once the mark of a truly special occasion, these delicacies were almost wholly eclipsed at the beginning of the twentieth century by the advent of flavored packaged gelatins. Not only were these products coarse, they made molded gelatin so ordinary that it now seems plebeian, institutional, and, at least to serious cooks, not quite nice. The ghost of this type of dessert lingers on modern Southern tables in the form of a dismal and wholly inedible mess loosely (and irresponsibly) called congealed salad. These horrific concoctions, spawned by the advent of reliable home refrigerators, reached peak popularity in the 1950s and early 60s. They would be completely unrecognizable to nineteenth century cooks who justifiably revered the molded jellies of their day.

The last of these sweets are ices: frozen creams, custards, and fruit juice. Thomas Jefferson is often credited with having brought ices back from France, and they were certainly a favorite sweet at Monticello. His cousin, Mary Randolph, gives us the first extensive collection of ices to appear in an American book, including ones for chocolate, coffee, and Roman punch (a slushy, alcoholic sherbet that was also very popular). However, ices were enjoyed by America's gentry for at least a generation before Jefferson. As commercial ice manufacture made these once rare treats more accessible, they displaced old-fashioned custard creams and syllabub, that luscious, creamy froth that had been popular in colonial America. Today, ice cream has become so commonplace that it is difficult for us to appreciate that it was once a rare and expensive treat.

The recipes that follow are few and merely representative of the vast repertory of fine old desserts that were once a part of every Southern celebration. I hope that they will awaken you, as they did me, with their startling delicacy and finesse.

Queen of Puddings

This simple baked pudding, which Jane Garmey (*Great British Cooking*) says originated in English nursery cooking, was once popular with Southern adults; *Housekeeping in Old Virginia* provided as many as five different recipes. After the War Between the States, this pudding often appeared, with only minor variations, under patriotic Confederate names like "Secession," "Jeff Davis," or "Dixie." The crown of meringue lends a showy presentation that makes the reason for its name pretty obvious.

The antecedents of this version are the classic English steamed and boiled puddings. As the iron range became standard equipment, those methods of cooking puddings began to be replaced by baking. Another variation on Queen of Puddings was actually a meringue-topped trifle. Such "puddings" became very popular in the South; one of the most famous and popular of them is banana pudding, the recipe for which follows this one.

2 cups fine, soft breadcrumbs	4 large eggs, whites and yolks separated
2 cups (1 pint) half-and-half, at room temperature	1 lemon
1 cup plus 3 tablespoons sugar	1 cup raspberry or blackberry jam
4 tablespoons unsalted butter	1 recipe Hard (Brandy or Wine) Sauce (page 380)

1. Position a rack in the center of the oven and preheat it to 350 degrees F. Bring a large teakettle full of water to a boil. Meanwhile, put the crumbs in a bowl and pour the half-and-half over them. Let it stand until the crumbs are saturated, about 30 minutes.

2. In a large mixing bowl, cream together 1 cup of the sugar and the butter until fluffy and lemon-colored. Beat in the egg yolks, one at a time, and then beat in the saturated crumbs. Grate in the zest from the lemon, then juice the lemon into it through a strainer. Beat until smooth.

3. Butter a 1-1/2- to 2-quart baking dish (a soufflé dish is ideal) and pour in the batter. Put the dish in a large, deep pan and set it on the center rack of the oven. Pour boiling water into the pan halfway up the sides of the dish and bake until the pudding is set and browned, about 40 minutes. Lift it from its water bath and let it cool slightly on a rack. Raise the oven temperature to 400 degrees F.

4. Put the egg whites into a metal or glass bowl. Beat until they are frothy, and gradually beat in 3 tablespoons of sugar. Continue beating until they form stiff, but not dry, peaks. Spread a thin layer of jam over the pudding, cover it with the meringue, and bake it in the center of the oven until the meringue is lightly browned and set, about 10 minutes. Serve warm with Hard Sauce. Serves 6 to 8.

A Banana Pudding

This is a really a trifle, composed of layers of fruit, cake and custard, but it is what most Southerners today would recognize as "pudding." Many people were surprised that I intended to include the recipe in this book, believing, as I once did, that it was modern. But it is older than any of us would have believed, and can be dated back at least to the turn of the twentieth century.

This was a popular dessert when I was growing up, and when well made, it is excellent. Unfortunately, it so seldom is: all too often, the crumb layers are made of artificially flavored vanilla wafers; a packaged pudding and non-dairy topping replace the custard and meringue. The only real thing is a banana. My great-grandmother would be ill just having it described to her.

This is the old recipe, and it's a nice one. If you prefer, you may leave out the bourbon or rum, though it does round out the flavor. If you prefer cookie layers in this pudding, omit the cake and substitute about 2-dozen Tea Cakes (page 349), or your favorite shortbread.

Pound Cake (page 333) or sponge cake,
  cut into 1/2-inch thick fingers

Bourbon or rum

4 bananas, peeled and sliced 1/4-inch thick

1 recipe Boiled Custard (page 377), made with
  6 egg yolks and 1/4 cup flour

4 egg whites

3 tablespoons sugar

1. Position a rack in the center of the oven and preheat it 425 degrees F. Cut the cake into 1/2-inch thick fingers. Cover the bottom and sides of a deep, 2-quart ovenproof dish with the fingers of cake and sprinkle it with a tablespoon of bourbon or rum.

2. Cover the cake layer with a layer of sliced bananas, pour a third of the custard over them, and put in another layer of cake. Sprinkle with another spoonful of whiskey and cover it with bananas and another third of the custard. Repeat with another layer, finishing with the remaining custard.

3. Put the egg whites in a metal or glass bowl and beat them until they are frothy. Gradually beat in the sugar and continue beating until they form stiff, but not dry, peaks.

4. Top the pudding with the meringue, swirling it decoratively as it suits you. Place it in the center of the oven and bake until the meringue is lightly browned, about 10 minutes. Don't overcook it, as longer baking could cause the custard to break and the bananas to throw off liquid, making the custard watery. Allow the pudding to cool completely before serving. Serves 6 to 8.

NOTES: *Though modern banana pudding recipes all brown the meringue in the oven, the problem presented by subjecting the delicate custard and raw fruit to a hot oven is that it can easily be ruined by overheating. It is much easier to control if you omit the baking and brown the meringue with a salamander (the iron disk used for caramelizing sugar in a crème brûlée set), or, as I do nowadays, with a blowtorch.*

Mary Randolph's Charlotte

This is the old-fashioned charlotte, a simple, homespun French tart of stewed fruit that put the old stale bread to good use. It was popular in eighteenth-century England and America, and remained so in the South through the early part of the nineteenth-century, then all but disappeared, eclipsed by its showy, frothy descendent, Charlotte Russe. Fruit charlottes became rare on Southern tables in the twentieth century, but such a lovely and easy dessert deserves to be popular again. They're so delicious with the first, crisp apples of autumn, or with crisp seasonal pears, peaches, and mangoes. It's encouraging to see them making something of a comeback, and to find their classic double-handled French mold in local kitchenware stores.

Mrs. Randolph's advice as to spices was to "season it in any way you like best." If the fruit is really good and sweet, what I like best is none at all, but there are a few suggestions for spices at the end of the recipe.

4 to 6 tart stewing apples, such as Winesaps or Granny Smiths, or other ripe fruit	3/8-inch-thick slices homemade bread (about half of a 1-pound loaf, see step 3, below)
Sugar for stewing the fruit, plus 2 tablespoons	6 tablespoons butter
Spices to taste, see notes below (optional)	1 recipe Boiled Custard (page 377)

1. Wash peel, core, and slice the fruit as you would for a fruit pie. If it has a lot of natural juice, as peaches or mangoes are prone to, do this over a strainer fitted in a bowl to catch those juices.

2. Put the fruit in a stainless steel or enameled stewing pan with their collected juices or 1/2 cup of water. Add sugar to taste (how much will depend on the natural sweetness of the fruit) and bring it to a boil over medium heat. Reduce the heat to a simmer and stew until the fruit is tender, but still firm, and its juices are thick and nearly evaporated. Turn off the heat.

3. Meanwhile, trim the crust from enough sliced bread to line the bottom and sides of a 9-inch pie plate or 4-cup charlotte mold and also to cover the top. Melt the butter in a frying pan over medium-high heat and pour it into a cup. In batches, brush the bread with melted butter on all sides and fry it in the hot pan until it's golden-brown, but still slightly soft in the center. Don't let them get too brown and crisp or absorb too much butter or the crust will be tough and greasy.

4. Position a rack in the center of the oven and preheat it to 450 degrees F. Line the pie plate or charlotte mold with the bread, overlapping it slightly, completely covering the bottom and sides. Pour in the stewed fruit and completely cover it with the remaining bread, overlapping slightly.

5. Bake until the top is nicely browned and slightly set, about 15 to 30 minutes. Invert a flame-proof plate over the charlotte and carefully flip it over. Let it stand for 15 minutes if using a pie dish, 30 minutes if you're using a charlotte mold. Carefully remove the dish or mold.

6. Position a rack so that the top of the charlotte will be about 4 inches below the heating element, and preheat the broiler for 15 minutes. Dust the charlotte with 2 tablespoons of sugar, and broil until the sugar melts and the top glazes. Watch it carefully so that it doesn't get too brown on the top. If you prefer, you can glaze it using a salamander or blowtorch instead (see Banana Pudding, page 368). Serve warm or at room temperature with custard passed separately.

NOTES: *If you really wanted to gild the lily, use Sally Lunn (page 316) for the toast. It's heavenly. If you want to spice it up, a little grated nutmeg is good with peaches and mangoes, crushed cardamom is good with anything; a stick of cinnamon is lovely with apples; and a bay leaf or two lends a nice flavor to pears. A splash of bourbon, sherry, Madeira, or claret added to the fruit as it stews wouldn't hurt anything either. If the charlotte is served cold, that is, at room temperature, whipped cream can be a nice substitute for the custard.*

Charlotte Russe

The basic idea of a charlotte remains here, but instead of bread and fruit, slices of sponge cake encase a rich filling of Bavarian cream. Most modern recipes use ladyfingers instead of sliced cake for a more regular and elegant finish, but if they are store-bought, even rough cut homemade pound cake is an improvement over them. Modern Charlottes are often filled with Bavarian cream made with egg custard, which dates back to middle of the nineteenth century, but the original Bavarian was a light, sumptuous whipped cream set with isinglass (a gelatin made from sturgeon bladders).

Charlotte Russe is credited to the French chef Antonin Carême, whose hey-day was the first quarter of the nineteenth century. However, by the second quarter of the same century, it was already a popular standard in English and American cookery.

1 tablespoon unflavored gelatin	1/2 Pound Cake (page 333) or sponge cake
1/4 cup milk, at room temperature	2 tablespoons medium dry (amontillado) sherry
3 cups heavy (36% milk fat) cream	1/2 cup fruit preserves (optional)
1-1/4 cups sugar	7 large egg whites
1 tablespoon Homemade Vanilla Extract (page 40) or 1 teaspoon commercial extract	Fresh berries or cut fruit

1. Soften the gelatin in 2 tablespoons of cold water, then dissolve it in the milk and set it aside to cool, stirring occasionally to keep the gelatin from settling.

2. Put 2 cups of cream into a large mixing bowl. Whisk until it's frothy, then whisk in a cup of sugar. Beat until it holds stiff peaks. Fold in the vanilla. Stir the gelatin and milk and gently fold it into the whipped cream.

3. Choose a 3-quart mold or bowl and cut the cake into 1/2 x 1-inch fingers as long as the mold is deep. Line the mold with cake, leaving no gaps, but hold back enough to cover the top. Sprinkle the cake with sherry. If you like, spread on a thin layer of jam or preserves.

4. Beat the egg whites to stiff, but not dry, peaks and fold into the whipped cream. Spoon this into the mold, making sure there are no gaps or air pockets. Cover with the remaining cake.

5. Chill until the cream is set, about 4 to 6 hours. Gently run a knife under the edges of the mold to make sure that the charlotte hasn't stuck. Invert a plate over the charlotte, then carefully flip it upside down. Carefully lift off the mold.

6. Lightly sweeten the remaining cream and beat it until stiff. If you like, you can put it into a pastry bag and pipe it onto the charlotte, or simply spoon it on in decorative dollops, using it to cover any gaps in the outer layer of cake. Garnish with fresh fruit. Serves 6 to 8.

Wine Jelly

This is a very light and elegant summer dessert that has managed to survive in this century in spite of the onslaught of flavored commercial gelatins. Along the coasts of the Carolinas, Georgia, and Virginia, it was very popular, and Thomas Jefferson himself copied out a recipe for use at Monticello. It can occasionally be found in Southern Junior League and community cookbooks. Originally made with calves' foot jelly, later, modern granulated gelatin replaced the long process of extracting and clarifying jelly from calves' feet.

Though commercial gelatin is not nearly as delicate and a mere ghost of the original, it can still be quite good as long as you don't overuse it. If you are using a sweet wine, you may want to cut back the sugar, so taste it before adding all the sugar called for. Since the sugar's main job here is to add sweetness, the exact amount is not critical.

1-1/2 cups water	1 cup sugar
2 tablespoons (about 2 envelopes) unflavored gelatin	2 cups medium-dry (Amontillado) sherry or medium-dry (Sercial) Madeira
2 lemons	1 cup heavy cream (minimum 36% milk fat)
1 orange	

1. In a bowl that will hold all the ingredients, stir 1/2 cup of cold (room temperature) water into the gelatin and let it soak 10 minutes.

2. Bring the remaining cup of water to a boil. Meanwhile, juice the lemons and orange through a strainer into a bowl or measuring cup, discarding the rinds.

3. Slowly stir the boiling water into the dissolved gelatin. Add the sugar, wine, and citrus juices, stirring until the sugar dissolves. Pour the jelly into a mold or, to be authentic, stemmed jelly glasses, cover and chill until the jelly is set, at least 4 hours.

4. Just before serving, unmold the jelly by dipping the mold briefly in hot water, invert it over a plate and lift the mold carefully away. Lightly sweeten the cream and whip it until it is thick but pourable or until it holds firm peaks. Pass it separately in a pitcher or bowl if you have molded the jelly, or top each glass with a generous spoonful just before taking them in to the table. Serves 6.

NOTES: *Often, I get really lazy and set the jelly in one big bowl, then break it up and spoon it into individual champagne glasses, then float a thin layer of the heavy cream on top without bothering to whip it. The texture of the unsweetened, liquid cream against the jelly is a delightful and interesting contrast. In Virginia, it is traditionally served with Boiled Custard (page 377).*

ICE CREAM

"For making ice-cream, genuine cream is, of course, preferable."

—Annabella Hill, *Mrs. Hill's New Cook Book*, 1867

Well, of course. Though custard-based ice cream has become a specialty of Southern cooks, the old cooks understood it as an inferior substitute. For flavor, for feel on the tongue, for it's pure, silken richness, they knew that there is no substitute for cream. But cream was (and still is) expensive, and custard-based ice cream can be powerfully good compensation.

The amount of sugar given in these recipes, 1/2 pound, is Mrs. Hill's. It is less than is usual (actually, about half), but I tend to like ice cream that is not quite so sweet and have stuck to her proportions. Freezing blunts the sweetness, so if you find that the cream is not sweet enough to suit, you can add up to another cup of sugar for every quart of cream.

Genuine Iced Cream

(Master Recipe)

This is the original true iced cream. When it has not been flavored with any spice, it becomes a blank canvas over which many flavors can be layered successfully. Its subtlety is wonderful as a foil for many fruits and toppings. For the most delicate and authentic flavor, use only a vanilla bean to flavor this ice cream; extract, even the homemade variety, is too harsh. For another delicious and unusual old flavor, substitute a cinnamon stick for the vanilla.

1 quart heavy cream	1/2 pound (1 cup) sugar
1 whole vanilla bean or 3-inch stick cinnamon (optional) (see headnote)	Salt

1. Put the cream and vanilla or cinnamon, if using, in a heavy-bottomed saucepan and let it come almost to a boil over medium-low heat, stirring frequently to prevent scorching. Remove it from the heat. If you are not flavoring the cream with either spice, heat it until it is just warm. Stir in the sugar and a tiny pinch of salt. Let it cool completely, remove the vanilla bean or cinnamon (they can be rinsed, dried, and re-used), cover and chill, refrigerated, for at least 4 hours or overnight.

2. Prepare an ice cream freezer according to the manufacturer's directions. Pour the cream into the freezing chamber, and freeze it until it is almost set—a little stiffer than soft-serve ice cream.

3. Pack the ice cream into a mold or deep container and freeze until it is completely solidified. To unmold it, dip the mold in a basin of hot water or wrap it with a towel heated in a clothes dryer for a few minutes. Invert it over a serving plate and lift off the mold. If it won't come off, dip the mold again or rewarm the towel and wrap it for a minute or two more. Makes about 1-1/2 quarts (about 6 servings).

Georgia Peach Ice Cream

The secret of this ice cream's intense fruity flavor is that the fruit should be dead ripe and never see the inside of a pan.

Not all old recipes flavored peach ice cream with nutmeg, so I give it as optional. You might also try it with the base flavored with cinnamon instead of vanilla. Many Southern cooks make this with Vanilla Custard Ice Cream (next page) as the base, but this is one instance where I think there should be no substitutes for real cream. If you live where you can get good mangoes, substituting them for the peaches will turn this ice cream into a religious experience.

1 recipe Genuine Iced Cream (page 374), omitting the vanilla and made through step 2, but not yet chilled	4 to 6 ripe, juicy peaches
	1/4 cup sugar
	2 teaspoons lemon juice
1/2 teaspoon freshly grated nutmeg (optional)	

1. Make the iced cream base up through step 1. Stir in the optional nutmeg and let it cool slightly. Meanwhile, peel the peaches over a large bowl to catch all their juices. Halve and pit them, and roughly chop them or force them through a colander into the bowl. I like a mix of puree and roughly chopped peaches for extra texture. Sprinkle them with the sugar and lemon juice (to help prevent discoloring). Let them macerate for half an hour or so.

2. Pour the cream over the peaches, mix thoroughly, and finish the ice cream as directed in steps 2 and 3 of the Genuine Iced Cream master recipe. Makes about 2 quarts (about 6 servings).

Vanilla Custard Ice Cream

(Master Recipe)

Vanilla is so commonplace today that it's hard to realize that it was once a rare luxury. The expression "you're so vanilla," popular a few years back as a description of someone who is predictable and boring, would have confused our ancestors, for whom this spice was expensive and exotic. But, no matter how commonplace, good vanilla custard ice cream is hard to beat, especially when it is slowly melting into a dish of hot blackberry or peach cobbler.

The amount of eggs in these recipes varied. Mrs. Randolph used eight, and was definite about using whole eggs; Mrs. Hill used as few as four. Whole egg custard is a little tricky and not as delicate as one made only with yolks, so I've settled somewhere between these two ladies.

2 cups whole milk	1 cup sugar
2 cups heavy cream (minimum 36% milk fat)	Salt
1 whole vanilla bean (see notes on other flavors below)	6 large egg yolks

1. Prepare the bottom of a double boiler with simmering water. In the top half of the pot, over direct heat, bring the milk, cream, and vanilla bean almost to a boil, stirring constantly. Add the sugar and a tiny pinch of salt, stirring until it dissolves, and put it over the simmering water.

2. Beat together the egg yolks in a separate bowl. Beat in a cup of the hot liquid to temper them and then stir them into the pot. Cook, stirring constantly, until it is lightly thickened (it should coat the back of the spoon. Remove it from the heat and stir it until slightly cooled, about 5 minutes. Remove the vanilla bean (it can be rinsed, dried, and reused). Let the custard cool completely, cover, and chill for at least 4 hours or overnight.

3. Prepare an ice cream freezer according to the manufacturer's directions. Pour the cream into the freezing chamber, and freeze it until it is almost set—a little stiffer than soft-serve ice cream.

4. Pack the ice cream into a mold or deep container and freeze until it is completely solidified. To unmold it, dip the mold in a basin of hot water or wrap it with a towel heated in a clothes dryer for a few minutes. Invert it over a serving plate and lift off the mold. If it won't come off, dip the mold again or re-warm the towel and wrap it for a minute or so more. Makes about 1-1/2 quarts, (about 6 servings).

NOTES: *This custard is an excellent base for other ice cream flavors. You may add a cup of Toasted Pecans (page 76) or slivered toasted almonds and 1/2 teaspoon of almond extract. If you experiment with other flavors, you can omit the vanilla, since it isn't always compatible with all flavors and fruits. It's an important agent in chocolate, but I find it incongruous with many fruits, almonds, or mint. Use your best judgment and don't let my prejudice strap you. If you like it, well, you like it. If you choose to use it, go to the trouble of using whole beans; the subtlety of it is a revelation. If you use extract, I don't want to know about it.*

Variation—Mary Randolph's Chocolate Custard Ice Cream: This one may be the oldest chocolate ice cream recipe in America and is still one of the best. For 1 recipe of Vanilla Custard Ice cream, grate 1/4 pound (4 1-ounce squares) unsweetened chocolate onto a sheet of wax paper. Make the Vanilla Custard Ice Cream up through step 1. Before adding the eggs in step 2, take up the wax paper in one hand, folding two edges together to make a funnel, and pour the chocolate gradually into the hot milk, stirring constantly, and keep stirring until it has completely melted. Finish the ice cream following steps 2 through 4.

SWEET SAUCES
Boiled Custard

Crème Anglaise

No anthology of Southern cookery is complete without this custard. Not only is it the foundation of many Southern desserts, it can also appear both as a sauce and a traditional holiday beverage. Boiled custard is a fine master dessert sauce to have in your repertory. Its character, body, and texture are altered merely by changing the flavorings, the temperature at which it is served, or by mixing it with wine, whiskey, or cream. This recipe produces a fairly thin, mildly sweet custard; if you need it to be thicker, use 6 large egg yolks. You can also add sugar if the amount given isn't enough to suit your taste.

When the custard will be used in a fresh fruit trifle such as Banana Pudding (page 368), beat 1/4 cup of flour into the yolks and sugar before beating in the milk. It makes a cruder custard, but the added starch is necessary to help the custard hold its body with the uncooked fruit.

2 cups half-and-half	4 large egg yolks
1 whole vanilla bean (optional)	Flavorings (see notes)
1/2 cup sugar	

1. Prepare the bottom of a double boiler with simmering water. Over direct medium heat, scald the half-and-half and, for vanilla custard, the optional vanilla bean in the top of a double boiler, bringing it just under the boiling point. When it is almost boiling, put it over the simmering water.

2. In a heatproof bowl, beat together the sugar and egg yolks until it is light and smooth and ribbons off the spoon. Slowly beat in 1 cup of the hot half-and-half to temper the eggs, then slowly beat the eggs into the remainder of the hot half-and-half.

3. Cook, stirring constantly until the custard is thick enough to coat the back of a spoon, about 5 minutes. Take the top pot from the heat and continue stirring until it has cooled slightly, about 4 minutes more. Remove the vanilla bean, if used, stir in any additional flavorings, and let it cool completely before serving. Makes about 2-1/2 cups.

Variations:

Bourbon (or Brandy) Custard: Use the vanilla bean and stir in a teaspoon or so of bourbon or brandy or substitute 1 tablespoon Bourbon Vanilla for the bean. Add a grating of nutmeg if you are using brandy.

Lemon Custard Sauce: Omit the vanilla bean and, after the custard cools, add the grated zest of half a lemon and 2 teaspoons lemon juice.

Wine Custard Sauce: Stir in 1 tablespoon of dry sherry or Madeira, a few generous gratings of nutmeg and 1 teaspoon of grated lemon zest.

Coffee Custard: Yes, this is authentic; it's from Sarah Rutledge's *The Carolina Housewife* (1847). Scald the half-and-half with a vanilla bean and a heaping tablespoon of dark-roasted whole coffee beans (or 2 teaspoons ground coffee). Strain it before adding the eggs and sugar.

Lettice Bryan's Cold Cream Sauce

The consistency of this lovely sauce is not unlike clotted cream or crème fraîche, due to the reaction between the cream and acidic lemon juice. It is a beautiful sauce to serve with a fruit compote, pound cake and sliced ripe peaches, fresh blackberries or strawberries, or over a fresh fruit tart. Best of all, it is as simple to make as it is good.

If you can get tart bitter oranges, they make a delicious substitution for the lemon.

1/2 cup sugar	1 lemon
2 cups heavy cream (minimum 36% milk fat)	Whole nutmeg in a grater

1. In a glass or stainless steel bowl, stir the sugar into the cream until it completely dissolves.

2. Grate the zest from half of the lemon into it, cut the lemon in half, and then squeeze in the juice from the zested half through a strainer, setting aside the remaining half. Stir until the cream is thickened, and season it to taste with grated nutmeg.

3. Let the sauce stand until it is quite thick, then chill until it is cold and very thick. If it doesn't thicken enough, stir in a little more lemon juice. Serve cold. Makes 2-1/2 cups.

Fresh Peach Sauce

Peaches, when they are perfectly ripened, have a delectable flavor on their own that needs no embellishment. Here they are turned into a sauce simply by mashing them with a little sugar and the barest suggestion of nutmeg and lemon juice. Like Georgia Peach Ice Cream (page 374), the secret to its fresh taste is that the fruit never sees the inside of a pan.

Lettice Bryan noted that this sauce made a very fine dessert on its own, with a little cream, and so it does. It is also superb over Pound Cake (page 333) or Vanilla Custard Ice Cream (page 375).

4 or 5 fresh, ripe peaches	Sugar
1/2 lemon	Whole nutmeg in a grater

1. Wash and dry the peaches and, over a bowl that will hold all the fruit, peel, halve, and pit them. Cut the peaches into small pieces and drop them into their collected juice.

2. Squeeze a little of the lemon juice over the peaches—not enough to distinctly taste it, but just enough to slightly brighten their flavor and prevent discoloring. Mash them to a smooth pulp.

3. Taste the pulp and lightly sweeten it with a little sugar, stirring until it completely dissolves. Grate in a little of the nutmeg to taste and let stand for at least half an hour before serving. Makes about 2 cups.

Hard (Brandy or Wine) Sauce

This is the classic English sweetened butter that invariably accompanies the holiday plum pudding. In American books, it often appeared under the apt name Cold Sauce, and so it is, though it is always served slowly melting into something that is warm. It makes a fine spread for warm, toasted Pound Cake (page 333), or Sally Lunn (page 316).

English hard sauce is always made with brandy, but wine is frequently used in Southern recipes. Whenever a recipe calls for brandy, I use a well-aged bourbon instead. It isn't merely a substitution; the bourbon lends a mellower, more distinctive flavor.

1 cup turbinado or light brown sugar

1 teaspoon grated lemon zest

1/2 pound (2 sticks) softened unsalted butter

Nutmeg in a grater

1/4 cup brandy, bourbon, or medium-dry (Sercial) Madeira

1. Pulverize the sugar to a powder, either in a mortar or a food processor or blender fitted with a steel blade. Cream the butter and then beat in the sugar until it is fluffy and light.

2. Gradually beat in the brandy or other liquid a spoonful at a time, making sure it has been incorporated before adding more. The butter will still be fluffy and solid. Beat in the lemon zest, if using, and a grating of nutmeg to taste. Keep cool. For prolonged storage, refrigerate it, but let it come up to room temperature before serving, and whip it once more to fluff it. Makes 2 cups.

Conserves

IT WOULD BE DIFFICULT TO IMAGINE the landscape of a Southern dinner table without an array of preserves, pickles and sweet relishes rounding out its corners. Condiments and relishes are an important element of a Southern meal, even in these modern times when, more often than not, the pickles have come from a grocer's shelf instead of the family's root cellar.

Before the days of refrigeration and freezing, the pickling and preserving of vegetables, fruits, and meats were important jobs that the mistress of the household took seriously. Even into this century, many of these women took personal responsibility for the food supply of the servants and tenant farmers that shared their land, and were careful to insure that there was a ready supply of conserves in the event of a crop failure. We may not feel such urgency today, but there is still a lot of satisfaction to be had from a store of your own pickles, relishes, and jams.

Canning is not difficult, but if you have never done it, it is instrumental to be familiar with certain key fundamentals before trying the recipes.

ON EQUIPMENT

Jars: For all preserves, it is important to use heat-resistant jars that are designed for canning. Old commercial jelly and pickle jars, while suitable for commercial sealing operations, are not designed for home use. Put them in the recycling bin and buy jars specifically made for home canning. They are available in quart, pint, and half-pint (1 cup) sizes. No matter how clean the jars appear to be, they must be sterilized before using them (see the notes on sterilization, below).

Lids: Use only new metal lids and rings that are free of rust. The rings can be reused, but not old lids; the sealing compound may be damaged. New jars are usually packed with lids, and replacements are available wherever jars are sold. For modern canning, do not use the old-fashioned glass clamp jars with rubber rings. All lids must be sterilized (see the notes on sterilization, below).

The canner: There are two types of canning processors available, pressure canners and regular water-bath canners. The latter pot is more versatile and can be used for things other than canning, and is the type I prefer. It is a deep enameled kettle fitted with a rack that keeps the jars from bouncing on the bottom of the pot or bumping into each other during the processing. It must be deep enough for the jars to be submerged in water by at least an inch. Actually, you don't need a special pot, so long as the interior is non-reactive. I have successfully canned in a clean, stainless steel soup kettle with a linen towel folded on the bottom to keep the jars from bouncing. However, a canning pot that is specifically designed for this operation is preferable.

Miscellaneous tools: Aside from the proper jars, lids, and processor, it is helpful to have a large pair of tongs for handling the jars, a stainless wide-mouthed canning funnel for filling them, and plenty of clean cotton or linen kitchen towels.

ON THE PROCESS

Sterilization: Once the pickle or conserve has been cooked, everything that touches it must be sterile to prevent spoiling after the jar has been sealed. Sterilize jars covered in boiling water for at least 10 minutes; boil the lids for 1 minute in a stainless pan, then turn off the heat and let them remain in the water until you are ready to use them. Don't touch the inside of the jars or the lids with your hands after they are sterilized.

Filling the jars: A wide-mouthed funnel is helpful in making a neat job of this. Don't touch pickles or fruit with your hands; transfer them to the jar with stainless tongs, spoons, or forks. For whole pickles and fruit preserves, leave no less than 1/2 inch of head room at the top of the jar, and cover them with the pickling or preserving syrup by at least 1/4 inch, leaving an overall headroom of 1/4 inch (pack them tightly so they don't float, but not so tightly that they won't be surrounded by the pickling solution or preserving syrup). For jams, marmalades and so forth, leave 1/4 inch of headroom. Once the jars are filled, place the lids on them with the tongs. (Never touch the inside of the lid with your bare hands.) Screw on the rings until just lightly tightened. Don't tighten the rings too much, or the air will not be able to escape, preventing a proper seal.

Processing: In the water-bath canning method, the jars are submerged in boiling water for a period of time. It is important that the kettle be deep enough for the water to cover the jars by at least 1 inch. Don't worry about water leaking into the jar; the steam build-up prevents this from happening. During processing, steam builds in the top of the jar (which is why there must be headroom) and is forced out, creating a vacuum. The ring of sealing compound then seals the jar. Different preserves require varying lengths of time in the bath, so refer to the individual recipes for times.

Cooling the jars: When the jars first come out of the bath, they are very hot and fragile. They must not touch each other or any cool surface. Spread out clean, double-folded cotton or linen towels. Take the jars out of the bath with tongs and set them on the towels, never allowing them to touch one another or the bare counter or floor. Otherwise they could crack. As the jars cool, the vacuum inside pulls the dome of the lid inward, making a "popping" sound as it seals. Let the jars sit for 24 hours before storing them; any that don't seal should be refrigerated and used as soon as possible.

Storing Conserves: Unprocessed conserves must be refrigerated. They should keep for up to 2 months if packed in a sterile jar. Processed conserves should be stored in a cool, dark cupboard or pantry. I try to use canned goods within a year, though most will last a lot longer. Do not eat any conserve with a bulging lid. If you are ever in doubt about any conserve, don't eat it; throw it out. It is better to lose the little bit of work and material of a single jar of pickles than to end up poisoned.

Cranberry Preserves

English settlers who first came to America had long been accustomed to tart berry sauces for game and poultry, so they kept right on making them with the berries that they found here. Cranberry preserves are one such condiment. This one is a fine thing to have with all sorts of roast poultry—turkey, duck, goose, quail, or even chicken—and is also wonderful with venison, such as Pan-Fried Medallions of Venison with Cranberries and Madeira (page 169). But it need not be confined to the relish bowl. It is also an unexpectedly good filling for pre-baked tart shells, and an excellent sauce to spoon over a slice of pound cake or Vanilla Custard Ice Cream (page 375) or, for that matter, a little of both.

3 pounds fresh, ripe cranberries

1 pound demerara or light brown sugar

1/4 cup bourbon

1. Wash all the cranberries and drain them well in a colander.

2. Weigh out a pound of them and put them into a 4-quart stainless steel or enameled pot. Lightly crush them with a wooden spoon and add just enough water to barely cover them. Turn on the heat to medium and bring it gently to a boil, skimming it carefully. Reduce the heat to low and simmer, uncovered, until the juices are thick, about 45 minutes. Turn off the heat.

3. Pour the berries and juice into a cloth jelly bag (or clean piece of muslin set in a sieve) over a bowl. Force the juice through the cloth into the bowl and discard the pulp. Put the juice back into the pot and add the remaining whole berries and sugar.

4. Turn on the heat to medium and bring it back to a boil, again skimming carefully, then reduce the heat as low as you can get it and simmer until the berries are tender and transparent, about 45 minutes. Turn off the heat and stir in the bourbon.

5. Divide the berries among sterilized half-pint jars, seal them, and process in a water bath (see page 383). Make sure that all the jars are properly sealed before storing them. Refrigerate any that don't seal and use them up within the month. Store sealed jars in a cool, dark pantry or cabinet. Makes 3 pints.

NOTES: *I gave the whiskey as optional in the first edition of this book, for those who do not wish to cook with alcohol, since it was not universal, but I've never made these preserves without it. You can leave it out if you prefer, but it adds a subtle depth to the flavor that is inimitable. Also, though the source recipe did not mention it, I often add the julienned zest of an orange in step 3, a delicious twist and especially good when it will accompany the Thanksgiving turkey and game birds.*

A PAIR OF PEACH CONSERVES
Bourbonated Peaches

This classic preserve is traditionally called Brandied Peaches, even when whiskey is substituted for brandy. But the use of bourbon is more than a mere substitution; the smoothness of well-aged bourbon lends a whole new dimension to the fruit. This conserve is traditionally served as a relish for game or country ham, but when chilled and served with Lettice Bryan's Cold Cream Sauce (page 378), it also makes a very fine dessert.

Dean Owens, one of Savannah's great wits and host to some of its best parties, was particularly partial to bourbon. When anyone asked for bourbon and "a little water" he replied "We like it well enough to have it piped into the house." He never explained whether he meant the water or the bourbon, though I suspect it was both. Dean called anything that has a dose of good corn whiskey "bourbonated," and it's an apt name for these peaches.

1 pound (5 or 6) small ripe but firm peaches
1/2 pound demerara or turbinado (or light brown) sugar

Well-aged bourbon (see step 3)

1. Bring a large teakettle filled with water to a boil. Wash the peaches and place them in a close-fitting heatproof bowl or basin. Pour the boiling water over them and let them stand for 1 minute. Immediately drain and plunge the peaches into cold water.

2. Peel and put them in a close-fitting, stainless steel or enameled pot. Add the sugar and enough water to just cover. Turn on the heat to medium and bring it slowly to a boil, skimming the top carefully. Reduce the heat to low and simmer gently until the peaches are tender, but still firm. Lift them out with a slotted spoon and pack them in sterilized quart jars.

3. Raise the heat to medium and boil the syrup until it is reduced by a little more than half. Turn off the heat and let it cool slightly. Measure the syrup and mix in an equal portion of bourbon. Pour this over the peaches until they are completely covered.

4. Cover the jar with a well-fitting lid and let it steep for 48 hours before using. Refrigerate after 48 hours. They will keep for a couple of months. The peaches can also be sealed for prolonged storage using the water bath method (page 383). Makes about 1 quart.

NOTES: *The leftover syrup makes a very good cordial that is fantastic over Vanilla Custard Ice Cream (page 375). Filter it to be sure there are no lingering bits of fruit. Add another tablespoon of bourbon for every cup of liquid, and store it well-sealed in a sterilized bottle or jar.*

For an unorthodox, but spectacular dessert, try—Minted Bourbonated Peaches: *Halve and pit the number of peaches you'll need and put them in individual glass serving bowls. Spoon a bit of syrup over each, top with a heaping tablespoon of Lettice Bryan's Cold Cream Sauce (page 378) or with lightly sweetened whipped cream, and sprinkle chopped fresh mint leaves over all.*

Peach and Orange Marmalade

This is not a true marmalade, but more of a thick conserve like a fruit butter. Marmalade is, however, the name under which it generally appeared in nineteenth-century books. Often, the fruit was flavored with a little citrus juice and zest, usually of lemons, but my late aunt Alice Fisher Vermillion, whose culinary instincts I trusted without question, decided that oranges would do as well. As usual, she was right on. The combination is an old one, but had almost disappeared in recent years.

This conserve can also be made with good-quality, unsweetened frozen peaches. The initial macerating will not be necessary with frozen fruit.

Tastes in thickness vary, so don't take my cooking time as gospel, but let your own preferences guide you. You may find that the juices are not thick enough after an hour.

> 2 pounds ripe peaches   1 tart orange
> 1 pound sugar

1. Blanch and peel the peaches as directed in step 1 of Bourbonated Peaches (previous recipe). Over a bowl to catch all the juice, split the fruit in half, remove the pits, and slice into thin wedges.
2. Stir the fruit and sugar together in a glass or stainless steel bowl. Peel the zest from the orange, cut it into fine julienne, and add it to the peaches. Juice the orange through a strainer into the peaches and toss to mix well. Cover and macerate for 2 or 3 hours.

3. Pour it all into a large stainless steel or enameled pot. There should be plenty of juice, but if they seem a little dry, add just enough water to keep the fruit from scorching. Turn on the heat to medium and bring it to a boil, skimming the scum as it rises to the top. Reduce the heat to a low and simmer, uncovered, until the fruit is very tender and the liquid has mostly evaporated, about an hour. The mixture should be quite thick.

4. Gently crush the fruit with a potato masher into a coarse pulp —it should still be quite lumpy. Simmer 3 or 4 minutes longer and then transfer it to sterilized half-pint jars. Seal and process in a water bath (page 383). Makes about 4 half pints.

Candied Citrus Peel

Most people nowadays are astonished and unattractively skeptical when they find out that this delicious conserve is nothing more than the part of their grapefruit that they have always thrown away. European in origin, candied citrus peel was a favorite with cooks all over the South during the nineteenth century. It was considered both a conserve for use in other recipes such as fruitcake, and a candy on its own. Some Charlestonians believe that Sarah Rutledge invented this candy, so popular had it become since the recipe was first published in *The Carolina Housewife* in 1847, but history does not bear this claim out.

There are two simple secrets to making successful candied peel. First, the outer skin must be very thick and firm. Second, the skin must be well blanched in several changes of water to remove the sharp, bitter oils that fill the pores of the outer layer. Otherwise, if you follow the recipe carefully, there's virtually no way to mess it up.

To prepare the rinds, quarter the fruit and carefully scoop out all the meaty pulp and white connective tissues, but leave the thick, white part of the rind intact. The rind of two medium-sized grapefruits will yield about a pound of candy.

1 pound orange or grapefruit rind, cut into quarters	About 1 2/3 cups sugar

1. Bring a large pot of water to a boil and drop in the rinds. Let it come back to a good boil and simmer it for about 5 minutes. Drain off the water and pour cold water over the rinds until they are completely covered. Bring it back to a boil, simmer 5 minutes and drain again. Repeat this process twice more and then thoroughly drain the peelings. Rinse them with cold water and drain it off.

2. Thoroughly dry the peelings and cut them into large dice or thin strands (I like the former for grapefruit and the latter is better for orange or lemon). Put these pieces back into the kettle with 2/3 cup of sugar. Put the pot over low heat and stir until the sugar is completely dissolved. Cook until the rind has absorbed all the sugar and there is no syrup left. Be careful not to let it scorch—keep the heat very low and stir often. Remove the pot from the heat and let the peel cool slightly.

3. Take a large rimmed baking sheet and spread the remaining sugar over it. Turn out the peels onto the sugar and toss until the pieces are thoroughly coated with the sugar and are separated. Spread them out carefully and dust off any caked-up sugar. Dust them lightly with more sugar and leave them out to dry. If you make this candy on a humid day—which isn't a good idea, but assuming that you have no choice—then dry it out in a warm oven that has been preheated to 150 degrees F. Turn it off and let the candy dry without opening the door. Before storing it, be sure that the candy is dry—that is, about the consistency of a gumdrop—and not damp and sticky, or it will mold and spoil in no time. Stored in an airtight container, candied citrus peel will keep a couple of months. Makes 1-1/2 pounds.

NOTES: *You may make this candy with virtually any citrus fruit except limes, with which I have never had any luck. Not by any means traditional, candied grapefruit rind is spectacular dipped in melted chocolate. Use a good-quality chocolate specifically produced for candy-making, and be sure that the candy is completely coated. Let it set on wax paper.*

KETCHUPS (OR CATSUPS) AND STORE SAUCES

Let's get something out of the way at the start: both spellings for this condiment—ketchup or catsup—are correct; they're Anglicized versions of Malaysian kechap or Amoy (a southeastern Chinese dialect) ketsiap, both of which are variations of the brine-fermented fish or shellfish sauce of Southeast Asia. When these sauces were introduced to English and American palates by early trade with the Far East, they were nothing new—the ancient Romans enjoyed a similar sauce made from anchovies and the English had long been using anchovy and oyster sauces in their cooking. But the name ketchup was quickly assimilated into English, and thus, American Colonial, cookery, and soon came to describe condiments that were neither fermented nor made from fish.

The next time you're in the market, notice that the ketchup bottles are labeled "tomato ketchup," a lingering reminder of happier days, when tomato was not the only kind around.

Once there were ketchups made from such heady stuff as oysters, mushrooms, anchovies, lemons, peppers, and even green walnuts. Until the nineteenth century, "ketchup," in English and American recipes, was understood to be one of those sauces. This was, of course, to change.

Our ubiquitous tomato ketchup came into use sometime around the end of the eighteenth century. The earliest known printed recipe, according to Karen Hess in her notes on *The Virginia House-wife*, is from an 1814 American edition of Maria Eliza Rundell's *A New System of Domestic Cookery*. Though this was an English cookbook, its American editions (which, after 1823, were re-titled *The Experienced American Housekeeper*) included some undeniably American recipes. Tomato ketchup may have been one of those additions, so that sneering French nickname for tomato ketchup—*sauce americain*—may have more of an element of truth about it than the American gourmet crowd would like to admit. I hope I do not need to tell you that the ridiculous myth that tomato ketchup was originally devised as a medicinal tonic is as silly as it is false.

In America, tomato ketchup quickly began to dominate and replace the other varieties. As early as 1839, The Kentucky Housewife provided, in addition to eight kinds of ketchup, a tomato-based "kitchen catsup" similar to the ones that dominate the condiment shelf today, except it was enriched with red wine and was in all respects finer than its commercial descendants.

Two recipes follow for mushroom and tomato ketchups, since both are used elsewhere in this book. If you would like to try Oyster Ketchup, the recipe for Pickled Oysters (page 394) can be adapted following the notes at the end of the recipe. A few gourmet food purveyors sell mushroom ketchup, but in the main there are no commercial substitutes for these sauces. If you are caught, try substituting Asian oyster sauce or Worcestershire sauce cut in equal parts with wine vinegar and sherry—about a teaspoon of each for every tablespoon called for.

Mushroom Ketchup

This lovely condiment was once very popular in English and American kitchens, and actually predates recipes so titled by at least a century. Recipes for pickled mushrooms are frequent in old English books, differing from later recipes called ketchup only in detail. While no two recipes agreed on the spices and other aromatics, the method remained much the same. With the advent of commercial sauces during the nineteenth century, its apparent popularity had begun to wane. Though it was included in a few general cookbooks such as *The Joy of Cooking* until the last decade of the twentieth century, it is treated without exception as an anachronism. By the time of Mrs. Dull's 1928 *Southern Cooking*, it had disappeared from Southern books altogether, and was not seen again until Bill Neal's *Southern Cooking* (1986)—a beautiful recipe, heady with garlic, onions, and herbs—to which this one owes much.

The process sounds time consuming but, actually, takes less than an hour of the cook's active attention. The steeping, simmering, etc. are pretty much unattended.

3/4 ounce dried boletus edulis (porcini or cèpes) mushrooms

3 pounds brown (cremini or portobello) mushrooms

2 tablespoons sea, kosher, or pickling salt

2 large shallots, trimmed, split lengthwise, peeled, and minced

4 large or 6 small cloves garlic, lightly crushed and peeled

1 whole cayenne pepper or 1/4 teaspoon crushed flakes

1/2 teaspoon whole black peppercorns

1/2 teaspoon whole cloves

1/2 nutmeg, freshly grated

1 teaspoon grated fresh ginger

2 bay leaves

2 tablespoons red wine vinegar

2 tablespoons dry red wine

1. Put the dried mushrooms in a heatproof bowl. Bring a cup of water to a full boil, pour it over them, and let them steep for half an hour. Lift out the mushrooms, dipping them to loosen any grit that may be clinging to them, and put them in a pan that will later hold all the mushrooms. Filter their soaking water through a coffee filter or un-dyed paper towel into the pan. Bring it to a simmer over medium heat and cook until the liquid is evaporated and absorbed, stirring frequently to prevent scorching. Turn off the heat.

2. Wipe the fresh mushrooms with a dry towel and chop roughly or shred them with the large shredding disc in the food processor. Put them with the reconstituted mushrooms in a heavy-bottomed stainless steel or enameled pot. Stir in the salt, cover, and set it in a cool place until the mushrooms have shed most of their liquid and their volume has reduced by half, about 2 hours.

3. Put the pot over medium-low heat. Bring it to a simmer and cook until the mushrooms are very soft. Strain the liquid through a fine wire mesh sieve, pressing hard on the solids to extract all their juice. Discard the solids and return the mushroom juice to the pot.

4. Add the shallots, garlic, spices, and bay leaves. Bring it to a boil over medium heat, reduce the heat to low and simmer gently for about 45 minutes, until it is fragrant and reduced to 1 3/4 cups. Add the vinegar and wine and simmer 5 minutes longer.

5. Strain, discarding the shallots, garlic, spices, and bay leaves, and pour the ketchup into a sterilized pint jar or bottle. Seal, let cool and refrigerate. It will keep for several months. Makes 1 pint.

NOTES ON THE INGREDIENTS: *If you can't get brown mushrooms and must use white champignons, use double the amount of dried wild mushrooms, reconstituted in 2 cups of water. Don't try to cut back on the salt. Many English recipes specified white wine, which does make a distinct flavor difference. If you substitute it, also use white wine vinegar. Most recipes used allspice or cloves and ginger; most Southern recipes included cayenne, and either nutmeg or mace, and, occasionally, both. Less frequently used were black pepper, shallots, and garlic, though they were usual in eighteenth-century English recipes. You may omit them if you prefer a subtler condiment.*

Tomato Ketchup

The biggest objection I have to most commercial tomato ketchups is their cloying sweetness. Good tomatoes and onions have a lot of natural sugar on their own, and when they are slowly simmered, as in this recipe, these sugars are naturally concentrated. Adding sugar only upsets the balance. This version is rich and spicy, its natural mild sweetness pointed up with a little wine and counterpointed by the subtle bite of mustard and horseradish. It is best made with fresh tomatoes, but canned tomatoes can be substituted out of season. Be warned: Once you start making your own tomato ketchup, it is addictive, but it's a taste that few young palates, used to the sugary sweetness of commercial ketchup, will care for. My great-grandmother would have died rather than allow a bottle of commercial ketchup on her table. It was not difficult to make and she didn't think the store-bought kind was fit to feed to the pigs.

5 pounds fresh, ripe tomatoes or 16 cups canned plum tomatoes	6 cloves garlic, crushed, peeled, and minced
1 teaspoon whole mustard seeds	2 tablespoons prepared horseradish, preferably freshly grated
1 teaspoon celery seeds	1 tablespoon grated fresh ginger
1 teaspoon whole black peppercorns	Salt
1 teaspoon whole allspice	1-1/2 cups red wine vinegar
1 teaspoon freshly grated nutmeg	1 cup dry red wine
2 large yellow onions, trimmed, split lengthwise, peeled, and minced fine	

1. If you are using canned tomatoes, skip to step 3. Blanch and peel the tomatoes as directed on page 262. Quarter and scoop out the seeds over a sieve fitted in a bowl. Discard the seeds, and put the tomatoes and their collected juices in a large, heavy-bottomed stainless steel or enameled pot.

2. Turn on the heat to medium and bring slowly to a boil. Reduce the heat to medium-low and stew, uncovered, until the tomatoes are tender, about an hour.

3. Purée the tomatoes through a food mill or in the food processor in batches and put them back into the kettle. Using a mortar and pestle or spice mill, powder the mustard, celery seeds, peppercorns, and allspice. Add them to the tomatoes with the nutmeg, onions, garlic, horseradish, ginger, a couple of healthy pinches of salt, and the vinegar. Bring slowly to a boil over medium heat, reduce to the slowest simmer you can manage and cook, uncovered, until reduced by a third and very thick; it will take at least 1 or as many as 3 hours. Stir it often to make sure it doesn't scorch. If it does begin scorching, don't scrape at it; pour the ketchup into a clean pot and discard the scorched bit.

4. Stir in the wine and taste for salt. Correct the seasonings, adding salt and spices to suit, and let it simmer 5 minutes more. Turn off the heat and divide the ketchup among sterilized pint canning jars, leaving 1/4 inch of headroom. Seal them and process in a water bath (page 383). Makes about 4 pints.

NOTES: *Following Sarah Rutledge's lead, John Martin Taylor added port to his ketchup in* Hoppin' John's Lowcountry Cooking. *It makes a wonderful difference. Feel free to experiment with other spices. Cinnamon and cloves are two that are frequently mentioned in old recipes. A bouquet garni of fresh herbs also makes a nice difference. If you use canned tomatoes, don't add salt until the end, then taste and adjust accordingly.*

Georgia Apple and Tomato Chutney

Chutney, a spicy Indian conserve of mangoes, has captivated Southerners for generations. But until mangoes were introduced to the Caribbean and Florida, they weren't available to most Southerners. Over the years, we've invented dozens of chutney spin-offs of peaches, pears, and apples. This one is adapted from Annabella Hill, whose chutney was the by-product of a recipe called "Imitation Chetney Sauce." Tart apples, tomatoes, onions, garlic, and raisins were macerated in a spicy vinegar and brown sugar bath, the liquor from which was used as a ketchup. The solids, she noted, were excellent for "devils, grills, and barbeques." They still are. I've incorporated the usual cooking from later chutney recipes, and added green pepper and a few spices that Mrs. Hill doesn't mention. The bay leaf and coriander are my own suggestion—they are completely out of line as far as Mrs. Hill is concerned, but today are usual, and very good.

1 large lemon (or 2 small ones)

1 orange

1 pound tart, hard apples

1/2 pound ripe tomatoes, cored, cut in half, seeded, and diced

1/2 pound green peppers, stemmed, cored, seeded, and diced

1/2 pound onions, trimmed, split lengthwise, peeled, and diced

1/2 pound raisins

1 tablespoon minced fresh ginger

1 tablespoon minced garlic

2 bay leaves (optional)

1 teaspoon celery seeds

1 tablespoon mustard seeds

1 teaspoon freshly grated cinnamon

1 teaspoon freshly ground allspice

1 teaspoon coriander seeds (optional)

Whole white pepper in a peppermill

Ground cayenne pepper

1/2 pound (1 cup) demerara, turbinado, or light brown sugar

1 teaspoon salt

1 cup cider vinegar

1. Peel the zest from the lemons and orange and cut it into fine julienne. Juice the lemon through a strainer into a large stainless steel or enameled pot. Set the orange aside for another use.

2. Peel, core, and dice the apples. Add them to the pot and toss until well-coated with the juice. Add the citrus zest, tomatoes, peppers, onions, raisins, ginger, garlic, bay leaves, and whole and ground spices. Season with white pepper and cayenne to taste, and toss until well-mixed.

3. In a separate bowl, dissolve the sugar and salt in the vinegar. Stir it into the pot, loosely cover, and slowly bring it to a boil over medium heat. Reduce the heat to low and simmer gently, stirring occasionally, until the apples and vegetables are tender and the juices are thick, about 1 hour.

4. Ladle into hot, sterilized half-pint jars, seal, and process in a water bath (page 383). Refrigerate any jars that don't seal and use them within a month. Store the rest in a cool, dark pantry or cabinet. Makes about 5 half pints.

NOTES: *You can substitute peaches, pears, or mangoes for the apples in this recipe, and feel free to experiment with the spices until you find a combination that suits you.*

Chutney is an indispensable accompaniment for Country Ham in Champagne (page 200), Roast Turkey (page 147), and any venison or pork dishes that don't have a sweet sauce.

TWO PICKLED SHELLFISH RECIPES

Pickled Oysters

Pickled oysters and their liquor were once widely used in English cooking as a seasoning. They're also delicious on their own as an hors d'oeuvres or as a first course salad, and will keep for several weeks in the refrigerator if you store them in a sterilized jar and use only a clean spoon or fork to take out what you need. The pickling brine itself will keep even longer, and can be used as a seasoning condiment or ketchup. Refer to the variation notes at the end of the recipe.

One recipe recommended serving the oysters with raw cranberries, probably as a substitute for lemon—an interesting, if mouth-puckering, idea.

2 pints shucked oysters with their liquor	8 whole cloves
Salt	1 teaspoon whole white peppercorns
White wine vinegar	2 teaspoons whole allspice
2 to 3 blades mace or a pinch or so of powdered mace	Cayenne pepper
	The zest from 1 lemon (optional)

1. Pick over the oysters and remove any lingering bits of shell. Put them with their liquor in a stainless steel or enameled pan with a healthy pinch of salt and bring them to a simmer over medium heat. Poach until they are just plump and their gills begin to curl. Turn off the heat and immediately remove the oysters with a slotted spoon to a glass bowl.

2. Strain and measure the liquor and put it back in the pan. For every 3 parts liquor, add 4 parts vinegar (1-1/3 cups vinegar for each cup). Add the mace, cloves, peppercorns, allspice, a good pinch of cayenne, and bring to a boil over medium heat. Reduce the heat to low and simmer 5 minutes. Turn off the heat and let it cool.

3. Divide the oysters among 3 sterilized pint jars, add a piece of lemon zest to each jar, and pour the spiced liquids over them until they are completely covered. Seal and marinate, refrigerated, for at least 24 hours before using. It will keep, well-sealed and refrigerated, for several weeks.

4. To serve the oysters as an hors d'oeuvre, put them in a glass bowl nestled in crushed ice, or as a first course over lettuce leaves with sliced lemons, chopped parsley, and minced onions. Makes about 3 pints.

Variation: To make Oyster Ketchup, boil the leftover liquid for 5 minutes, add a tablespoon of white wine vinegar to every cup of liquid. Strain it through a clean wire sieve into a sterilized bottle or jar, seal and cool it, then store it in the refrigerator.

Pickled Shrimp

Along the eastern seaboard in the South, Pickled Shrimp have a long tradition. Once, nearly every fish market sold them, and a few still do, but they are at their best made at home. They make a fine hors d'oeuvre to serve with drinks and one of the most refreshing shrimp salads you'll ever taste. To make it, mix the quantity given below mixed with a thinly sliced Vidalia sweet onion, a thinly sliced lemon, 1 roasted and peeled red bell pepper cut in strips, and 1/2 cup of good olive oil. Serve it over crisp romaine lettuce.

2 teaspoons whole cloves	4 bay leaves, crumbled
4 teaspoons allspice	2 pounds (headless weight) small shrimp
4 teaspoons whole mustard seeds	6 cloves garlic, lightly crushed and peeled
2 teaspoons celery seeds	Salt
4 teaspoons whole coriander	2 cups white wine vinegar
1 whole pod cayenne, or a healthy pinch of ground cayenne	Zest from 1 lemon, cut into fine julienne (optional)
2 teaspoons whole white peppercorns	1/4 cup minced shallots (optional)

1. Bring a large kettle of water to a boil. Meanwhile, mix the cloves, allspice, mustard and celery seeds, coriander, cayenne, peppercorns, and bay leaves together in a small bowl.

2. Put the shrimp in a stainless steel or enameled pot with half the spice mixture, the crushed garlic, and a healthy pinch of salt. Toss until well mixed. When the water is boiling, pour it over the shrimp until they are just covered. Cover and let stand 5 minutes. Strain off, but reserve, the liquid.

3. Peel the shrimp and put them in a glass or glazed pottery crock. Wipe out the pot and pour the liquid back into it. Bring it back to a boil over medium heat, skimming carefully, and boil until it's reduced to 1 cup. Add the vinegar and remaining spice mixture. Let it come back to a full boil, lower the heat, and simmer 5 minutes. Turn off the heat.

4. Mix the zest and shallots with the shrimp, if using, and completely cover them with the hot liquid. Let it stand 2 minutes, then toss until it is cool enough to arrest any further cooking, and let it cool completely. Cover and marinate, refrigerated, at least 24 hours.

5. For prolonged storage, divide the shrimp among sterilized pint jars and cover them with the liquid. Float a couple of tablespoons of olive oil on top of each jar and cover tightly. They will keep, covered and refrigerated, for up to 3 weeks.

6. To serve the shrimp as a salad, lift them out of the liquid and, for each cup, mix in a tablespoon each of olive oil and freshly squeezed lemon juice. Heap them onto fresh lettuce leaves and garnish with lemon wedges and chopped parsley. Makes 3 pints.

NOTES: *Don't be alarmed that the liquid is milky; it's supposed to be. Though bay leaves are not mentioned in the old recipes, bay laurel grows practically wild in the Georgia and Carolina Lowcountry, and today is a common herb for pickled shrimp and many other seafood dishes.*

Bibliography

WHERE ALL THIS CAME FROM: SOME NOTES ON THE SOURCES

Well into this book, a friend of mine asked if it was "real." Eying a stack of tattered manuscript that was rapidly approaching the ceiling, I said, "Honey, if it isn't real, one of us is a lot crazier than even a Southerner ought to be." But, of course, what she really meant was obvious: How much of this was from genuine, historical documentation and how much was just plain made up? Perhaps it's hard to believe, because none of this reads like a textbook, but everything on these pages has been thoroughly researched, documented, cross-referenced, and tested. Although history and fact share pages with some outlandish tales, all the recipes are from genuine nineteenth-century Southern sources, and I have cooked my way through every one of them. In that sense, they are just as "real" as they can be. My only contribution has been to translate this fine old cooking into the language of modern kitchens, and, in some cases, to spell out ways to get around the fact that a modern kitchen is where you have to cook them. I have "updated" nothing, and offered no packaged substitutes, even though that is the present trend.

The following is a list of books and manuscripts from which the recipes have come. Many of these are still available, either in facsimile reprints or through continuous publications, and I have noted these where I am aware of them. All of these books are a treasury of Southern culture, still lively with the personalities of Mary Randolph, Sally Rutledge, Lettice Bryan, Henrietta Dull, Annabella Hill, and Theresa Brown, to name a few.

The most precious records, though, are the manuscript books and collected loose recipes, the treasures of countless Southern families. Such collections were once fairly common among middle and upper class housewives, each of them filled with traditional family recipes, new things from friends and relatives (often, letters were pinned to pages with dressmaker's pins and old needles), and common home remedies for routine ailments. In using such books, it is important to keep in mind that the housewife recorded recipes in inverse proportion to the frequency that she actually used them. Some historians are misled by these books into supposing that vegetables were an infrequent part of Southern diets, because they are hardly mentioned, and that desserts were disproportionately important. Actually the opposite was true. Who could remember how to make, from one season to the next, a plum pudding that was made only once or twice a year? And conversely, who needed to write down a process that was routinely performed on a daily basis?

Many of these manuscript books were fragile, their bindings gone from years of use, their faded pages stained by years of splatters, their notes littered with penciled changes as family recipes evolved from one generation to another. That I was allowed to see them at all, much less take them home and keep them for months at a time, is still a wonder that is met with my deepest gratitude.

But whether published, unpublished, or by word of mouth, these are the vital link to the cooking that I have tried to bring to life in this book. And so to the sources.

Acton, Eliza. *Modern Cookery for Private Families.* London: Longman, Brown, Green and Longmans, 1845 and 1855.

Miss Acton was a perceptive and excellent food writer, one of England's best until Elizabeth David. *Modern Cookery* was edited for American audiences by Mrs. Sarah J. Hale and published in Philadelphia in 1845. According to Karen Hess, it enjoyed nine editions in America.

Beeton, Isabella. *Beeton's Book of Household Management.* London, 1861.

Mrs. Beeton compiled her book for her husband's publishing enterprises when she was twenty-five. She died only three years later. It seems impossible that she could have tested and authored so many recipes (the original book had over 1000 recipes). Indeed, much of the work, especially the bread section, is borrowed from Eliza Acton. Early editions of Mrs. Beeton were used in the United States, and her recipes turn up from time to time in period community cookbook collections. Mrs. Beeton is today a household institution in Britain, but almost nothing of the original remains in the book on most British kitchen shelves.

Bingham, Lillie, and Leana Bingham Castleberry. Collected recipes. (Unpublished, private collection): Binghamwood, Talladega, Alabama.

Binghamwood was the plantation homestead of a Pennsylvania family who settled in Talladega in the 1840s. No household notebook survives from the estate, even though the household remained essentially intact until 1979, but Mrs. Castleberry's daughters have preserved a number of loose recipes used by their mother, aunt, and grandmother during happier days at Binghamwood. Most are typical of those used throughout the South. By the way, the family kitchen handbook was *Mrs. Hill's New Cook Book.*

Bremer, Mary Moore. *New Orleans Recipes.* New Orleans: General Printing Company, 1932. Referenced: 8th printing, 1942.

The earliest recipe I have ever found for pecan pie. Mrs. Bremer remains true to some early recipes, but the deterioration that plagues later books had already begun.

Brown, Theresa Clement(ine). *Theresa C. Brown's Modern Domestic Cookery.* Charleston, SC: Edward Perry, Printer, 1871. Reprinted in facsimile by The Pendleton District Historical And Recreational Commission, (printed by The Journal, Inc., Williamston, S.C.), 1985.

An educated spinster from a prominent Anderson, South Carolina family, Miss Brown in many ways continued old-fashioned practice. Though she used chemical leavening in a number of recipes, she protested vigorously against their over-use. Her yeast breads are classic and excellent. She stood on the cusp of the technological revolution that so drastically changed American cookery during the latter part of the century. Like Annabella Hill, she was much influenced by William Kitchiner.

Bryan, Lettice. *The Kentucky Housewife.* Cincinnati: Shepard and Sterns, 1839. Facsimile with introduction by Bill Neal, Columbia: University of South Carolina Press, 1991.

This excellent book is encyclopedic in its scope, and provides a telling record of early nineteenth-century cookery. Mrs. Bryan was a professional class housewife with Virginia connections and wrote her book while still in her thirties. Unfortunately, the USC Press edition is no longer in print.

Bullock, Helen, editor. *The Williamsburg Art of Cookery.* Williamsburg, VA: Colonial Williamsburg, 1938.

Mostly a collection of recipes taken from *The Compleat Housewife* (see Smith) and *The Virginia House-wife* (see Randolph), there are also a number of recipes from old household notebooks. But it is of limited use to scholars, since all the recipes are transcribed and some are altered.

Carswell, Sarah Anne Devine (Mrs. John W.), manuscript notebook, Bellevue Plantation, Burke County, GA, c. 1861. (Private collection.)

Mrs. Carswell was born in New Haven, CT, the daughter of staunch Congregationalists, who disowned her when she accepted an inheritance including a Georgia plantation and several slaves in 1828. The family connection is unclear and the Burke County Courthouse has burned.

She married John W. Carswell in Georgia in December of 1830. The notebook begins in reverse in a remembrance album given to Mrs. Carswell by her friends when she left Connecticut and is dated March 27, 1861, late in Mrs. Carswell's life as a housekeeper. If there was an earlier manuscript book, it has not survived. Most of the recipes are modern—that is, contemporary with the date. There is baking powder and gelatin and such modern names as "Confederate Pudding." And despite Mrs. Carswell's roots, they are markedly Southern.

Colquitt, Harriett Ross. *The Savannah Cook Book.* Charleston: Walker Evans, & Cogswell Co., 1933.

Subtitled "A Collection of Old Fashioned Receipts From Colonial Kitchens." Old-fashioned, they certainly are, but one could hardly call them colonial. Most of Mrs. Colquitt's sources are mid-nineteenth century and later. However, she does transcribe a number of the recipes verbatim. Reprinted by Colonial Publishers, Charleston, SC.

Confederate Receipt Book. Richmond: West & Johnson, 1863. Transcription, Athens: University of Georgia Press, 1960.

More interesting as a document of social rather than of culinary history, this book is primarily a collection of recipes for medicine, candles, beer, yeast, imitation coffee, and other goods in short supply during the War Between the States.

The Congressional Cook Book. Washington, DC: The Congressional Club, 1927, revised edition, 1933.

A collection from the Congressional Club (wives of members of Congress), this book contains many Southern recipes. The deterioration of the cooking is alarming. It is important, however, because the preface contains a transcription of several recipes recorded in Thomas Jefferson's handwriting in a copy of *The Virginia House-wife* that Mary Randolph had given to Jefferson's daughter, Martha Randolph. The book is inscribed by the author "For Mrs. Randolph, Monticello, From her affectionate friend and sister." Mary Randolph was Thomas Jefferson's cousin and his daughter Martha's sister-in-law. In short, a typical Southern family. The book was still in the White House Archives as of 1933.

Couper, Frances. Collected Papers, c. 1800–1820. Georgia Historical Society Collection, Savannah, Georgia.

The Creole Cook Book. New Orleans: New Orleans Picayune, 1900. Transcription of 2nd edition (1901), with marginal notes by Marcelle Bienvenu as The Picayune's Creole Cook Book. New Orleans: The New Orleans Time Picayune, 1987. Also referenced: 5th (1928) edition.

Dull, Henrietta Stanley. *Southern Cooking.* Atlanta: Ruralist Press, 1928. Facsimile, Atlanta: Cherokee Press, 1989.

Mrs. Dull's book is a little late for the period covered by this book, but she was already in her sixties when her landmark opus was published, and many of the older recipes survive almost completely intact. Also referenced, 1942 edition.

Evelyn, John, Esq. *Acetaria: A Discourse on Sallets.* London: B. Tooke, 1699. Reprint, Brooklyn, NY: The Women's Auxiliary of the Brooklyn Botanic Gardens, 1937.

Anyone who thinks that early Englishmen, and, ergo, early Americans, were indifferent to vegetables should be tied to a chair and made to read this book.

Fox, Minnie C., editor. *The Blue Grass Cook Book.* Louisville, KY: 1904. Facsimile with commentary by Toni Tipton-Martin, Louisville, KY: University Press of Kentucky, 2005.

Glasgow, Kate McPheaters. Manuscript household notebook, Fincastle, VA, 1880-1911. Private collection.

Mrs. Glasgow's husband ran an inn at one of the South's many natural spring spas during the last quarter of the nineteenth century. Heavy on sweets, sauces, and preserves (both sweet and savory), this book was begun by Mr. Glasgow's first wife and continued, after her death, by Kate McPheaters, her successor. Mostly recipes for dressings, cakes, and preserves. There are several recipes for tomato ketchup that are close to the modern variety.

Gordon, Eleanor Kinzie (Mrs. William W.), household notebooks, c. 1858–1910, 2 volumes. Collection of the Juliette Gordon Low Birthplace (Girl Scouts of America, Savannah, GA).

Eleanor Kinzie Gordon, known affectionately in Savannah as "Miss Nellie," was born and raised in Chicago. She married William Washington Gordon II of Savannah in 1858 and is best known as the mother of Juliette Gordon (Daisy) Low, the founder of the Girl Scouts of America. Though not a Southerner, Mrs. Gordon recorded a number of her neighbors' and her black cook's recipes, and her book is one of the few surviving records of the cooking of

Leila (Mrs. Fred) Habersham, a noted Savannah matron who ran one of Georgia's first cooking schools.

Grierson, Alice Kirk. *An Army Wife's Cookbook.* Tucson: Southwest Parks and Monuments Association, 1972.

A manuscript cookbook, c. 1854–1888, kept by the wife of a Cavalry officer, published posthumously with commentary and recipe translations. Mrs. Grierson was from Ohio, but her book is interesting in showing the universality of many American recipes.

Hess, Karen. *Martha Washington's Booke of Cookery and Booke of Sweetmeats.* New York: Columbia University Press, 1981. Reprint in paperback, University of South Carolina Press.

A transcription of the Custis family manuscript cookery books, c. 1650–1690, by Karen Hess, with historical commentary and "copious notes." The manuscript was a Custis family heirloom which had belonged to Frances Parke Custis, mother of Daniel Custis, when it passed into Martha Washington's possession upon her marriage to that gentleman in 1749. Mrs. Washington gave it to her granddaughter, Eleanor Parke Custis Lewis, in 1799. The original author and transcription date are not known, but Mrs. Hess presents a persuasive argument for the theory that it predates Frances Parke Custis (who is popularly supposed to have written it) by two generations and may have been copied out in England.

Though by Martha Washington's day the book could hardly have been more than an heirloom, and was probably rarely, if ever, used at Mount Vernon, it nonetheless gives us an important look at the cookery of seventeenth-century England that was imported into the colony of Virginia in its early days. Mrs. Hess calls the period the golden age of English cooking, and a glance at the sumptuous cuisine of this manuscript certainly confirms it. Required reading for any student of culinary history.

Hill, Annabella P. *Mrs. Hill's New Cook Book.* New York: James O'Kane, Publishers, 1867. Some 1867 editions also list James A. Gresham, New Orleans, in conjunction with O'Kane. Facsimile reprint, 1872 edition, Damon Lee Fowler, ed., Columbia: University of South Carolina Press, 1995.

Mrs. Hill was the wife of Edward Y. Hill, a superior court justice in LaGrange, Georgia. She was an educated, well-read woman, and her remarkable book shows the influence of Kitchiner, Alexis Soyer, Mary Randolph, and Eliza Leslie, among others. But it also provides interesting insights into the cookery of western Georgia during the late antebellum period.

Hooker, Richard J. Horry, editor. *A Colonial Plantation Cookbook: The Receipt Book of Harriott Pinckney Horry, 1770.* Annotated transcription, Columbia: University of South Carolina Press, 1984.

Mrs. Horry was Sarah Rutledge's aunt, and the daughter of Eliza Lucas Pinckney, the celebrated lady planter who helped pioneer indigo farming in South Carolina. Her notebook, begun in 1770 and continued until near her death in 1819, is a wealth of information on Southern aristocratic cooking during the early days of the United States. Some of her recipes came from her mother and the cooking follows the Lucas/Pinckney English tradition, but it also is illuminating about farm life during the first century of English settlement.

Kitchiner, William, M.D. *The Cook's Oracle.* London: Printed for Robert Cadell, Edinburgh, by Whitaker, Treacher, and Co., 1831 edition. Also referenced, 1855(?) edition. Originally published in London, 1817.

There were a number of American editions of Dr. Kitchiner, beginning as early as 1822. The Cook's Oracle was widely used in the South, and was very influential.

The Ladies' Aid Society of the First Presbyterian Church of Fincastle. *The Housekeeper's Friend.* Fincastle, Virginia: private publisher, 1896.

A treasury of one-of-a-kind recipes (see "A Fine Oyster Pie" in the text), this book contains many classic Virginia dishes. Some things had slipped—the beef pot roast recipe is somewhere between ordinary and awful. But such recipes as spiced beef, pickled oysters, escalloped mushrooms and fine cakes more than make up for that shortcoming. Several of Kate Glascow's (see above) recipes appear verbatim. So far as I know, this book had only one edition and copies of it are rare.

Ladies of the Bishop Beckwith Society. *Favorite Recipes from Savannah Homes, Many Before Unpublished: A Collection of Well Tested and Practical Recipes.* Savannah: The Morning News, Printers, 1904.

A charity cookbook to benefit the Manual Training School. Like most such collections, it contains recipes ranging from kitsch to gorgeous.

Lane, Emma Rylander. *Some Good Things to Eat.* Clayton,

Alabama, 1898. Transcription reprint, Clayton, AL: Rebecca Parish Kelly, 1976.

Mrs. Lane's little book is the one that gave the South its famous bourbon-laced Lane Cake, and it is largely on the reputation of that cake that the book survives.

Leslie, Eliza. *Miss Leslie's New Cookery Book*. Philadelphia: T. B. Peterson and Brothers, 1857.

Miss Leslie was one of the best and most prolific food writers of her day in America. Her books, especially *Directions For Cookery*, 1837, were widely used and respected in the South, with good reason.

Manning, Mrs. Stephen C., manuscript receipt book, circa 1890–1910 (private collection).

Mrs. Manning was a part of the Anglo community in New Orleans, whose cooking is often overshadowed by the more famous Creole and Cajun cookery. Her notebook is copied out in good girls' school script, probably from her own mother's book for her hope chest (and maybe even by her mother; the handwriting in the book and the signature in the front are clearly not the same person, but that part is speculation). Anglo cooking is very different from what is usually associated with New Orleans; Mrs. Manning makes no use of hot pepper and garlic and is sparing with herbs. Her cooking was understated, perhaps in places even a little bland, but on the whole it has a simple elegance that more exuberant Louisiana cooking perhaps lacks.

McColloch-Williams, Martha. *Dishes and Beverages of the Old South*. New York: McBride, Nast & Co., 1913. Facsimile, Nashville: The University of Tennessee Press, with introduction by John Egerton, 1988.

This book is more of a highly romanticized memoir of childhood on a North Tennessee plantation in the "good old days" than a reliable record of old Southern cooking. McColloch-Williams mostly wrote short stories and poems for fashionable periodicals, and this was her only venture in food-writing. Nonetheless, she wrote with originality and charm.

Meldrim, Frances Casey (Mrs. Peter W.), and Sophie Meldrim Shonnard. Household notebook, Savannah, Georgia, 1890–1915 (private collection).

Mrs. Meldrim's book was transcribed in the early 1970s and the original manuscript was, unfortunately, lost. Much of this notebook was published within the text of *Georgia Entertains* in 1983 (see DeBolt below). The wife of a prominent magistrate, Mrs. Meldrim was, from 1892 until 1943, mistress of one of Savannah's most celebrated mansions (now St. John's Church Parish House). Her notebook, kept during her heyday as one of Savannah's premiere hostesses, is an interesting look into the condition of Savannah cookery at the turn of the century.

Newington, Thomas. Manuscript Receipt Book. Brighthelmstone (Brighton), England. Transcription, Philip James, ed., as *A Butler's Recipe Book*, 1719. Cambridge: Cambridge University Press, 1935.

Parloa, Maria. *Miss Parloa's New Cook Book*. Boston: Estes & Lauriat, 1885. (First edition: 1880)

Principal of the Boston Cooking School, Miss Parloa was a prolific and popular food writer from the nineteenth century. Though not a Southerner, her books, including *The Appledore Cook Book*, 1871, were widely used throughout America and were very influential in the second half of the nineteenth-century.

The Ladies of Westminster Presbyterian Church. *The Savannah Cook Book*. Savannah, GA.: The Morning News, 1909. Not to be confused with the Colquitt book of 1933.

Randolph, Mary. *The Virginia House wife*. Washington: Davis and Forth, 1824. Revised and enlarged facsimile, 1825 and 1828. Facsimile, with historical and editorial notes, Karen Hess, editor, Columbia: University of South Carolina Press, 1984.

The edition includes transcriptions of the recipes added by Mrs. Randolph in 1825 and 1828. The South's first and still best food writer.

Ravenel, Rose P. and Elizabeth Ravenel Harrigan, editor. *Charleston Recollections and Receipts: Rose P. Ravenel's Cookbook*. Columbia: University of South Carolina Press, 1983.

Miss Ravenel lived from the antebellum glory days of Charleston well into the twentieth century, and kept detailed diaries and receipt books. Unfortunately, Mrs. Harrigan did not transcribe Miss Ravenel's recipes verbatim and many are altered.

Rector's Aid Society of St. John's Episcopal Church. *The Ever Ready Cook Book*. Savannah: Privately published, n. d. (but before 1915).

A lot of cans of things, but there are surprises and many quality recipes.

Rhett, Blanche S., with Lettie Gay and Helen Woodward. *Two Hundred Years of Charleston Cooking.* Reprint of 1930 original publication: Columbia: University of South Carolina Press, 1976.

Though very late for the period, Mrs. Rhett and Mrs. Woodward were determined to collect traditional Charleston cooking. Unfortunately, the recipes were tested and transcribed by Lettie Gay, a dietician in New York, who sometimes misunderstood the original.

Rutledge, Sarah. *The Carolina Housewife,* or *House and Home.* Charleston: W. R. Babcock & Co., 1847. [Also referenced: second (1851) and third (1855) editions.] Facsimile with introduction and historical notes by Anna Welles Rutledge, Columbia: University of South Carolina Press, 1979.

This book was very influential throughout the southeast. Miss Rutledge was an excellent editor, and her eye for characteristic Lowcountry cookery made this book an invaluable record of antebellum Carolina cooking.

Simmons, Amelia. *American Cookery.* Hartford: Hudson and Goodwin, 1796. Facsimile, with foreword by Mary Tolford Wilson, by Oxford University Press, 1958; reprint as The First American Cookbook by Dover Publications, Inc., 1984.

Though other English cookery books had been published in America during the eighteenth century, Miss Simmons' book is widely believed to be the first penned by an American. It is especially valuable in demonstrating the common Englishness of most early American cooking.

Smith, E[liza ?]. *The Compleat Housewife: or, Accomplsh'd Gentlewoman's Companion.* London: R. Ware, et al, 1727. Referenced: fifteenth (1753) edition.

This book circulated in Colonial America and was eventually printed in Williamsburg by William Parks, 1742, becoming the first known printing of a cookbook in America (essentially a reprint of the fifth London edition). It was very influential.

Stoney, Louisa Cheves Smythe, editor. *Carolina Rice Cook Book.* Charleston: The Lucas-Richardson Co., 1901. Published in facsimile by The University of South Carolina Press as part of The Carolina Rice Kitchen, 1992 (see Hess, below).

Telfair, Sarah Gibbons, and Mary Telfair. Household notebook, (manuscript), c. 1820–1875. Georgia Historical Society collection, Savannah.

The Telfairs were one of Savannah's oldest and most influential families. They were well known for their philanthropic work, which included the Georgia Historical Society headquarters building, a hospital for women, and the bequest that established Savannah's Telfair Academy for the Arts and Sciences, which is housed in the old family mansion. The manuscripts are full of typical antebellum recipes, and Mary Telfair provided an interesting and exhaustive list of "Nostrums that are used at fashionable entertainments."

Texas Cook Book. Houston: The Ladies Association of First Presbyterian Church, 1883. Printed in Facsimile with introduction by David Wade and Mary Faulk Kooch as *The First Texas Cook Book.* Austin: Eakin Publications, Inc., 1986.

Reportedly the first cookbook published in Texas, there is very little of what most would recognize today as Texas cookery. There is a distinct eastern influence and recipes from Mrs. Randolph, Mrs. Hill, and others appear.

Thornton, Phineas. *The Southern Gardener and Receipt Book.* Columbia, SC: private publisher, 1840. Second Edition, Newark: A. L. Dennis, 1845. Facsimile, 2nd edition, Birmingham: Oxmoor House, Inc., 1984.

Tucker, Martha Goode. Household Notebook, Rose Hill, Milledgeville, Georgia, c. 1855–1868. Transcription, The Milledgeville Town Committee of the National Society of the Colonial Dames of America in the State of Georgia. *Housekeeping Diary of An Antebellum Lady.* Milledge-ville: Studio Designs Printing, 1990.

The manuscript is in a private collection.

Townsend, Abbie (Mrs. Charles B. Lansing). *Recipe Book.* In manuscript, signed Miss Abbie Townsend and dated July 28th, 1849, Albany, New York.

Townsend, Abigail Spencer (Mrs. John). *Receipts.* In manuscript, undated, but possibly as early as 1810. Mrs. Townsend died in 1849, the year her daughter dated her own book. If nothing else, the calligraphy is clearly an older style than her daughter's, and she uses the old-fashioned word "receipt."

These mother/daughter manuscripts are especially valuable in demonstrating how little American baking varied between Northern households and white households of the South. There is a hilarious recipe for "The Southern Mode of Curing Northerners" which involves a hunting rifle . . .

Tyree, Marion Cabell, editor. *Housekeeping in Old Virginia.*

Louisville, KY: John P. Morton and Company, 1877. Facsimile reprint of the1879 printing, Louisville, Ky.: Favorite Recipes Press, 1965.

This early recipe collection for charity was edited by a Virginia housewife in Washington. A few of Mrs. Randolph's and Mrs. Hill's recipes make an appearance, demonstrating that both books were in regular use in post-bellum Virginia.

Waring, Mary Joseph. *The Centennial Receipt Book.* Anonymously published as being authored "by a Southern Lady." Charleston, SC (?): privately published, 1876.

Copies are extremely rare. True roasting, properly done before a fire, lingers here. There are very nice recipes for rice breads, oysters, fish, and such local specialties as "atzjaar" pickle. Oddly enough, there are no pilaus.

Warren, Mrs. Jane. *"Sweet Home" Cook Book.* Buffalo: J. D. Larkin & Co., 1888.

Promotional cookbook for Larkin & Co.'s Sweet Home soap.

Webster, Mrs. A. L. *The Improved Housewife.* 20th Edition, Hartford: Ira Webster, 1854.

Dozens of Mary Randolph's recipes appear verbatim, but the really interesting aspect is that the baking chapters differ little from Southern ones. Mrs. Webster is one of the few writers to acknowledge that American cooking followed English practice.

Wilson, Mrs. Henry Lumpkin (editor). *Tested Recipe Cook Book.* Atlanta: The Foote and Davies Company, 1895. Facsimile, with introduction by Darlene Roth, as *The Atlanta Exposition Cookbook,* Athens, GA: Brown Thrasher Books (University of Georgia Press), 1984.

A souvenir book from the Cotton States and International Exposition of 1895 compiled by the Board of Women Managers. The deterioration of Georgia cooking from Mrs. Hill to this book is alarming.

Reading List

Nathalie Dupree remarked that recipes are not created in a vacuum, and it is perfectly true; few creative endeavors occur in absolute isolation, and so it has been with this book. Aside from the period historical works referenced above, the following materials were used in researching and writing this book. Some may seem to have little to do with Southern cooking, per se, but they have been a profound influence in shaping the ideas and precepts that I have tried to convey.

Referenced contemporary books on Southern Food:

Aunt Julia's Cook Book. No publisher or date, c. 1936. A promotional for Esso service stations and products. Just one of dozens of such "Auntie" cookbooks.

Bailey, Lee. *Lee Bailey's Southern Food and Plantation Houses.* New York: Clarkson-Potter, 1990.

———. *Lee Bailey's New Orleans.* New York: Clarkson-Potter, 1993.

Bronz, Ruth Adams. *Miss Ruby's American Cooking.* New York: Harper-Collins Publishers, 1989.

———. *Miss Ruby's Cornucopia.* New York: Harper & Row, 1991. Miss Ruby is fun to read and cook from, and approaches

cooking with a refreshing sensibility and raucous sense of humor.

Booth, Letha, editor. *The Colonial Williamsburg Cook Book.* Williamsburg: The Colonial Williamsburg Foundation, 1971.

Brown, Marion, *The Southern Cook Book,* University of North Carolina Press, Chapel Hill, 1951. Revised, as *Marion Brown's Southern Cook Book,* 1968.

Burn, Billie S., *Stirrin' The Pots on Daufuskie,* Daufuskie Island, SC: Burn Books, 1985.

Cox, Eugenia Barrs, editor. *Low Country Cooking: A Collection of Recipes from Liberty County and the Georgia Low Country.* Hinesville, GA: Liberty County Historical Society, 1988.

DeBolt, Margaret Wayt, Emma Rylander Law and Carter Olive. *Georgia Entertains*. Nashville: Rutledge Hill Press, 1988 (Originally published as *Georgia Sampler Cookbook*, 1983).

———, with Emma Rylander Law. *Savannah Sampler Cookbook*. West Chester, Pennsylvania: Whitford Press, 1978.

DeMers, John. *Arnaud's Creole Cook Book*. New York: Simon and Schuster, 1988.

Dupree, Nathalie. *Cooking of the South*. New York: Irena Chalmers Cookbooks, Inc., 1982.

———. New *Southern Cooking*. New York: Alfred A. Knopf, 1986.

———. *Nathalie Dupree's Southern Memories*. New York: Clarkson-Potter, 1993.
Nathalie always provides good food and easy to follow, thoroughly tested recipes.

Edminston, Mrs. Jack R., and Mrs. James W. Heacock, Jr., editors. *When Dinnerbells Ring*. Talladega, AL.: The Talladega Junior Welfare League, 1978.

Egerton, John. *Southern Food*. New York: Alfred A. Knopf, 1987.
The bibliography alone is priceless.

———. *Side Orders*, Atlanta: Peachtree Publishers, 1990.
John Egerton always makes good reading. Always.

Episcopal Church Women, St. John's Church. *Heritage Receipts from St. John's*. Savannah: Kennickell Printing Company, n. d., but c. 1978.

Flexnor, Marion W. *Dixie Dishes*. Boston: Hale, Cushman & Flint, 1941.

Fox-Genovese, Elizabeth. *Within A Plantation Household, Black and White Women in the Old South*. Chapel Hill: University of North Carolina Press, 1988.

Georgia Salzburger Society, Ebenezer, GA. Y*e Old Time Salzburger Cook Book*. Kansas City, MO.: Circulation Service, ND.

Glenn, Camille. *The Heritage of Southern Cooking*. New York: Workman Publishing, 1986.
Mrs. Glenn is the Grande Dame of modern Southern cookery. Her book is an elegant mix of old and new, based on her many decades of experience as a teacher, writer, and cook.

Gulf Fare: Favorite Seafood Recipes. Panacea, FL.: Iris Garden Club of Wakulla County (printed Shawnee Mission, Mo., by Circulation Service), ND.

Guste, Roy F., Jr. *Antoine's Restaurant Cookbook*. New York: W. W. Norton & Company, 1980.

Harper, Pat, editor, with Elaine Simmons. *Savannah Style*. Savannah: The Junior League of Savannah, Inc., (Kingsport Press), 1980.

Huguenin, Mary Vereen and Anne Montague Stoney, editors. *Charleston Receipts* (The Junior League of Charleston). Charleston: Walker, Evans & Cogswell Co., 1950.

Lewis, Edna. *In Pursuit of Flavor*. New York: Alfred A. Knopf, 1988.

———. *The Taste of Country Cooking*. New York: Alfred A. Knopf, 1978.
Edna Lewis ought to be made a national landmark.

Lustig, Lillie S., editor, with S. Claire Sondheim and Sarah Russel. *The Southern Cook Book Of Fine Old Recipes*. Asheville: The Three Mountaineers, Inc., 1938.

McCoin, Choice, editor. *300 Years of Carolina Cooking*. Greenville, SC: The Junior League of Greenville, 1970.

McRee, Patsy. *The Kitchen and the Cotton Patch*. Anniston, AL: Higginbotham, Inc., 1982 (tenth printing, originally published 1948).

Neal, William F. *Bill Neal's Southern Cooking*, (Revised Edition). Chapel Hill: The University of North Carolina, 1989.
A beautiful, heart-felt book, short on history, but long on good food.

———. *Biscuits, Spoonbread, and Sweet Potato Pie*. New York: Alfred A. Knopf, 1990.

Nesbit, Martha Giddens. *Savannah Collection*. Orlando: Noran Printing Company (for the author), 1986.

The Quaker Cook Book. High Point, NC: The Women's Auxiliary of High Point Friends Meeting, 1954.

Rawlings, Marjorie Kinnan. *Cross Creek Cookery*. New York: Macmillan Publishing Company, 1942 (also referenced, NY: Charles Scribner's Sons, 1970 edition).

Reid, Catha W., and Joseph T. Bruce, Jr. *The Sandlapper Cookbook*. Lexington, SC: The Sandlapper Press, 1973.

Rudisill, Marie. *Sook's Cookbook*. Atlanta: Longstreet Press, 1989.
Infused with personality and warmth, this is an excellent cookbook and memoir from a lovely lady with a typically eccentric Southern family. Mrs. Rudisill writes as well as her nephew, Truman Capote. It must run in the family.

The Shadows Service League. *The Shadows-on-The-Teche Cookbook*. Huntsville, AL: Southeastern Color Printing for, 1982.

Smart-Grosvenor, Vertamae. *Vibration Cooking, Or Travel Notes of A Geechee Girl*, 3rd Edition. New York: Ballantine Books, 1992.
Vertamae Grosvenor is a treasure. This book is even more fun than its title suggests.

Taylor, John Martin. *Hoppin' John's Lowcountry Cooking*. New York: Bantam, New York, 1993.
One of the best regional American cookbooks in years and THE best Lowcountry cookbook since Miss Rutledge.

Thompson, Lois and V. V. (Pete), editors. *Authentic Southern Recipes From The Colonial Inn*. Hillsborough, NC: The Colonial Inn, 1972.

Warren, Mildred Evans. *The Art of Southern Cooking*. Garden City, NY: Doubleday and Company, 1967.

Wilson, Justin. *The Justin Wilson Cook Book*. Gretna, LA: Pelican Publishing Company, 1976 (originally published 1965).

Other Referenced Works:

Aresty, Esther B. *The Delectable Past*. New York: Simon and Schuster, 1964.
Mrs. Aresty's "translations" of the recipes are often questionable, but her bibliography is instructive.

Beard, James. *James Beard's American Cookery*. Boston: Little, Brown, and Company, 1972. Mr. Beard was no historian and his historical notes are flawed, but he wrote from the heart.

Brilliat-Savarin, Jean Anthelme, *The Physiology of Taste* (translated by M.F.K. Fisher). New York: The Heritage Press, 1949.

Clark, Libby (editor), with Janet Cheatham Bell (food writer), and Jessica B. Harris (food consultant), *The Black Family Reunion Cook Book*. Tradey House, publishers, for The National Council of Negro Women, 1991.

Child, Julia. *From Julia Child's Kitchen*. New York: Alfred A. Knopf, 1982.

Crump, Nancy Carter. "Foodways of the Albemarle Region." *Journal of Early Southern Decorative Arts*, Volume XIX, Number 1, May 1993.

Darden, Norma Jean and Carole. *Spoonbread and Strawberry Wine*. New York: Fawcett Crest, 1978.

David, Elizabeth. *English Bread & Yeast Cookery, American Edition*, (Karen Hess, editor). New York: Penguin Books, 1982.
Worth having for Mrs. Hess's notes alone, this book is a lucid history of English baking.

———. *Spices, Salts and Aromatics in the English Kitchen: English Cooking Ancient and Modern, Volume 1*. New York: Penguin Books, 1970.
Mrs. David is probably the best food writer the twentieth century will see.

Del Conte, Anna. *The Gastronomy of Italy* (American Edition). New York: Prentice Hall Press, 1987.

Donovan, Mary, with Amy Hatrak, Frances Mills, and Elizabeth Shull. *The Thirteen Colonies Cookbook*. New York: Praeger Publishers, 1975.

Garmey, Jane. *Great British Cooking: A Well Kept Secret*, New York: Random House, 1981.

Hazan, Marcella. *The Classic Italian Cookbook*. New York: Alfred A. Knopf, 1976. Craig Claiborne put it best: "Marcella is a national treasure both in this country and in Italy." Karen Hess called this book "practically flawless." It is.

———. *More Classic Italian Cooking*. New York: Alfred A. Knopf, 1978.

———. *Marcella's Italian Kitchen*. New York: Alfred A. Knopf, 1986.

Hedrick, U. P., editor. *Sturtevant's Edible Plants of the World.* New York: Dover Publications, Inc., 1972. (Original publication: *Sturtevant's Notes on Edible Plants*, J.B. Lyon Company, Albany, 1919.)
What would any serious food historian do without this book?

Hess, John L., and Karen Hess, *The Taste of America.* Columbia: University of South Carolina Press, 1989 (Third Edition).
Required reading for anyone who is serious about food.

Hess, Karen. "The American Loaf: A Historical View," *The Journal of Gastronomy*, Volume 3, Number 4, Winter 1987/88.

———. *The Carolina Rice Kitchen.* Columbia: University of South Carolina Press, 1992, including in facsimile the *Carolina Rice Cook Book* (see Stoney in period works). A thorough, beautifully written study of one of America's most unique cuisines.

Krieger, Louis C. C. *The Mushroom Handbook.* New York: Dover Publications, Inc., 1967.

Massey, Mary Elizabeth. *Ersatz in the Confederacy: Shortages and Substitutes on the Southern Homefront.* Columbia: University of South Carolina Press, 1952. (Reprinted with introduction by Barbara L. Bellows, 1993.)

Montagne, Prosper. *The New Larousse Gastronomique.* New York: Crown Publishers, Inc., 1977.

Ortiz, Elisabeth Lambert. *The Complete Book of Caribbean Cooking.* New York: M. Evans and Company, Inc., 1973.
The parallels between Caribbean Creole cookery and Southern cooking are striking.

Peterson, Lee Allen. A *Field Guide to Edible Wild Plants: Eastern and Central North America.* Boston: Houghton Mifflin Company, 1977

Renwick, Ethel H. *Let's Try Real Food.* Grand Rapids, Michigan: Zondervan Publishing House, 1976.
A devastating indictment of America's "agri-business" and much-adulterated food industry.

Shapiro, Laura. *Perfection Salad.* New York: Farrar, Straus & Giroux, 1986.

Smith, Michael. *The Afternoon Tea Book.* New York: Athenaeum, 1986.

Toklas, Alice B. *The Alice B. Toklas Cook Book.* New York: Harper & Row, Publishers, 1954, (1984 edition referenced).
Mrs. Toklas was the real personage of the Stein-Toklas household. Her writing is a delicious as her cookery.

Williams, Susan. *Savory Suppers and Fashionable Feasts: Dining in Victorian America.* New York: Pantheon Books, 1985.

Index

Metric Conversion Chart

Liquid and Dry Measures

U.S.	Canadian	Australian
¼ teaspoon	1 mL	1 ml
½ teaspoon	2 mL	2 ml
1 teaspoon	5 mL	5 ml
1 tablespoon	15 mL	20 ml
¼ cup	50 mL	60 ml
⅓ cup	75 mL	80 ml
½ cup	125 mL	125 ml
⅔ cup	150 mL	170 ml
¾ cup	175 mL	190 ml
1 cup	250 mL	250 ml
1 quart	1 liter	1 litre

Temperature Conversion Chart

Fahrenheit	Celsius
250	120
275	140
300	150
325	160
350	180
375	190
400	200
425	220
450	230
475	240
500	260